# Applied Communication Research
## A Dramatistic Approach

**John F. Cragan**
Illinois State University

**Donald C. Shields**
University of Missouri—St. Louis

**Waveland Press, Inc.**
Prospect Heights, Illinois

For information about this book, write or call:

Waveland Press, Inc.
P.O. Box 400
Prospect Heights, Illinois 60070
(312) 634-0081

This book, *Applied Communication Research: A Dramatistic Approach,* is dedicated to Ernest G. Bormann, Professor of Speech Communication, University of Minnesota.

# Contents

v

# Preface

In *Applied Communication Research: A Dramatistic Approach* we have focused intentionally on only one communication theory and one basic research method in an effort to provide an in-depth understanding of our approach to applied communication research.

The book is organized into six parts. Part I contains three essays that introduce and explain Ernest Bormann's dramatistic communication theory and its application in communication research. Part II contains four examples of how the theory is used in critiquing contemporary American rhetoric. Part III includes three previously published studies of the presidential campaign of 1976 that, in a coordinated fashion, used Bormann's theory. The section also contains an original essay in which we sketch out the theoretical and methodological implications of Bormann's theory, and our methods for managing future political campaigns. In addition, the section contains the media critique of our computer generated political speech. Part IV encompasses three organizational communication studies we did that were rooted in dramatistic communication theory. Part V contains six essays that are designed to explain the application of Bormann's dramatistic communication theory to marketing research. Part VI provides several aids that are intended to assist communication researchers wishing to utilize this dramatistic approach to applied communication research including a critical standard for critiquing factor analysis studies.

We wish to thank the Speech Communication Association, the Central States Speech Communication Association, the United States Department of Commerce, Doane Agricultural Service, Inc., Shell Chemical Company, The St. Paul Fire Service and The Upjohn Company for allowing us to report much of the research that is presented in this book. In addition, we wish to thank the graduate faculty and our fellow "Turtle Racer" graduate students in the Department of Speech Communication at the University of Minnesota who provided us with the intellectual stimulus to conduct the line of research reported in this book. We especially wish to thank Professor Ernest G. Bormann in whose honor this book is dedicated.

John F. Cragan
Normal, Illinois
Donald C. Shields
St. Louis, Missouri
1980

# PART I:
## A Dramatistic Communication Theory

# I:  A Dramatistic Communication Theory

With more than a decade of experience in applied communication research, we have concluded that theories of communication are not right or wrong, they are just useful or not useful. While the humanities and the social sciences contain few predictive theories, the research reported in this book does appear to support a particular communication theory's ability to provide both a why explanation of reality and predict future events in the real world.

Ernest Bormann's dramatistic communication theory, proposed in 1972, spawned some fifty pieces of research during the 1970's. Using the concept of *message* as the starting point for building the theory and assuming that *meaning, emotion* and *motive* for action are in words as well as in people, Bormann broke fresh theoretical ground for speech communication scholars. Bormann conceived of a rhetorical world in which here-and-now phenomena and dramatistic symbols interact to create our social reality. As people seek to make sense out of their environment and events around them they chain-out *fantasies* that eventually swirl together to provide a credible interpretation of reality. This total dramatistic explanation of reality Bormann called a *rhetorical vision*. A rhetorical vision is a symbolic drama that contains a dramatic *scene*, dramatic *characters* (heroes, villains, supporting players), *plotline* (scenarios) and a *sanctioning agent*. Meaning, emotion and motive are contained in the rhetorical vision, and people caught up in the vision will act it out as their sense or understanding of social reality dictates.

If Bormann were to revisit his first theoretical piece, we suspect he would add many refinements to the theory and that it would show an increased theoretical parsimony given the findings of research conducted in the past eight years. Nevertheless, Bormann's original article presents the initial theoretical parameters for the research reported in *Applied Communication Research: A Dramatistic Approach.* The piece which follows provides an overview of our uses of the theory in conducting applied communication research. The piece which precedes Bormann's original article provides our explanation of the theory of rhetorical vision, describes the methods to be used in conjunction with it to do applied communication research, and sketches out possible areas of application.

3

# 1

# A Dramatistic Approach to Applied Communication Research:

## Theory, Methods, and Applications

DONALD C. SHIELDS

The rich and beautiful valleys of Wyoming are destined for the occupancy and sustenance of the Anglo-Saxon race. The wealth that for untold ages has lain hidden beneath the snow-capped summits of our mountains has been placed there by Providence to reward the brave spirits whose lot it is to compose the advance-guard of civilization. The Indians must stand aside or be overwhelmed by the ever advancing and ever increasing tide of emigration. The destiny of the aborigines is written in characters not to be mistaken. The same inscrutable Arbiter that decreed the downfall of Rome has pronounced the doom of extinction on the red men of America.

*Cheyenne Daily Leader,*
March 3, 1870 (as cited in
*Bury My Heart at Wounded Knee,* by Dee Brown)

The above editorial illustrates a prevalent rhetorical vision of the mid-1800's. In it appear characters, scenarios, scenes and sanctioning agents. The excerpt mirrors the kinds of communication content with which *Applied Communication Research: A Dramatistic Approach* is concerned. The materials in this text reflect how a dramatistic theory and communication based research procedures may be used in consort to study communication in the real world of applied research.

While the essays and research reports contained herein introduce the reader to an exciting new theory which has substantive utility for communication research, it would seem helpful to provide an overview to serve as a focus for the remainder of the text. With that goal in mind, this essay will: (1) define the theory's nomenclature; (2) discuss the methods necessary to do research with the theory; and (3) characterize in a general way the kinds of applied problems that the theory and methods described therein will help solve.

# The Theory's Nomenclature

Any good social science theory provides a *why explanation* of human events and actions. This why explanation is accomplished as the theory builders put together *concepts* with *relationship statements* that define the parameters of the theory. The key concepts of a Bormannean based dramatistic communication theory stem from the assumption that people construct a social reality that differs from the mere existence of phenomena. This rhetorical reality is created through the interchange of public symbols. The basic or smallest unit of communication is the *fantasy theme* which is a complete scenario or dramatistic statement.

Fantasy themes vary in intent based upon their use to depict major concepts within Bormann's theory of *rhetorical visions* (the composite dramas that catch up large groups of people into a common symbolic reality). The major concepts include the *dramatis personae,* the *plotline,* the *scene,* and the *sanctioning agent* for a given rhetorical vision.

The *dramatis personae* are in essence the *characters* that are given life within the drama. Thus, fantasy themes may depict *heroes, villains,* and *supporting players,* graphically describe their characteristics, assign motives to their actions, portray them doing certain things or manifesting certain behaviors, and place them in a given setting or scene. From this perspective it can be seen that a given fantasy theme may mirror the entire rhetorical vision, or it may simply embellish the character from one dramatistic perspective, i.e., character qualities, or plotline actions, or scenic placement.

In the vision excerpted from the *Cheyenne Daily Leader* the characters include both heroes and villains. Heroes are variously described as the Anglo-Saxon race, brave spirits, advance-guard of civilization, and tide of emigration. Villains are variously described as Indians, aborigines, and red men of America.

*Plotline* is a concept that refers to the action of the drama. Who is doing what to whom and how? Often called *scenarios,* plotlines can be identified as those fantasy themes which identify whether the rhetorical vision is passive or active, a comedy or tragedy, a quest or surreal, etc. As well, the scenario type fantasy themes indicate the time of the vision (past, present, or future orientation). Finally, they give insight into the *deep structure* of the vision, that is, at a meta-level is the drama a *righteous, social,* or *pragmatic* vision?

Plotlines evidenced in the introductory excerpt include valleys for occupancy and sustenance, wealth as reward, advancing and increasing settlement, and the doom of extinction. The deep structure reflected in such all or nothing scenarios is, of course, righteous.

*Scene* as a major concept of the theory serves much the same purpose as the word itself implies when thinking about a play. In essence, it is the setting, the place where the action takes place, the place where the characters act out their roles. Thus, some fantasy themes within a rhetorical vision will graphically describe the scene by telling its scope, describing its elements, identifying the vital props, etc.

The scenic elements in the opening quotation name Wyoming and characterize its rich and beautiful valleys, and hidden wealth beneath its snow-capped summits.

The *sanctioning agent* is the source which justifies the acceptance and promulgation of a rhetorical drama. Sometimes, the sanctioning agent is a higher power (God, justice, democracy, etc.). Other times, it is a particularly salient here-and-now phenomenon (the atomic bomb, a warring conflict, a crucifixion and resurrection, etc.). As well, the most salient *motives* for action are contained in the fantasy themes which describe the sanctioning agent of the drama.

For the writer of the *Daily Leader* editorial the Manifest Destiny Drama's sanctioning agents included destiny, Providence, and the inscrutable Arbiter's decree of the downfall of Rome.

*Relationship statements* tell how the concepts of the theory are tied together and provide the link as to how the theory can go beyond description and provide a why explanation of human events and actions. The *power* of the Bormannean dramatistic theory to explain and lead to prediction stems from three attributes. First, the ability of the four major dramatistic concepts to describe elegantly symbolically created rhetorical reality. Second, the theory's direct assumption that *meaning, emotion,* and *motive* are not in the skulls and viscera of people but are in their rhetoric thereby providing a direct link between communication phenomena and behavior. Finally, the identification of basic units of communication — *dramatistic fantasy themes* — that manifest meaning, emotion, and motive.

As indicated above, the most salient motives for action are contained in the fantasy themes which describe the sanctioning agent of the drama. As well, motives are reflected in attributes ascribed to the dramatis personae, actions accentuated in given scenarios, and descriptions of scenic elements. Similarly, the fantasy themes of rhetorical visions contain and describe the emotions of the people who participate in the drama, and they exhibit the meanings that people hold dear. How different might the plight of the American Indian have been had the deep structure of the dominant rhetorical vision been social (e.g., acculturation) or pragmatic (e.g., assimilation) rather than righteous (i.e., manifest destiny).

By knowing that meaning, emotion, and motive are in the drama, by using the dramatistic concepts to describe a given drama, and by identifying the deep structure of a drama, the speech communication researcher is in a position not only to provide a why explanation of people's behavior, but to predict future behavior, the goal — or sanctioning agent, if you will — of all social science research.

## The Methods

*Applied Communication Research: A Dramatistic Approach* illustrates the methods and procedures necessary to the successful identification, uncovery, and discovery and verification of a given rhetorical vision. Some methods are simple, others are more sophisticated and elaborate. Their selection for use in studying applied communication problems depends upon the nature of the problem and the level of scientific inquiry desired by the researcher. The reader will discover that some methods are humanistic in their approach while others bridge the chasm (for some schism) between humanistic and scientific inquiry as they describe newly invented techniques for conducting research with the theory. Many of the techniques' labels (rhetorical analysis, content analysis, focus group interviewing, Q-sorts, and graphics questionnaires) may make the methods appear old hat to the experienced researcher. However, it is their particular combination, make-up, and configuration when used with the dramatistic theory that provides the invention. Henry Ford did not invent the automobile. He did invent mass production. Similarly, our decade long application of Bormann's dramatistic communication theory to real world research questions led Dr. Cragan and me to design instruments and theory adaptations that should benefit the community of speech communication scholars wishing to conduct applied communication research. These methods are the focal point of the studies reported in *Applied Communications Research: A Dramatistic Approach.*

The several *methods, instruments, procedures,* and *analysis techniques* comprising our approach to applied communication research become manifest throughout the essays and studies appearing in *Applied Communication Research: A Dramatistic Approach.* They include several *humanistic techniques* (rhetorical analyses of communication messages gathered from literature searches, personal interviews, and focus group interviews) and several *quantitative techniques* (content analysis, factor analysis, and discriminant analysis). As well, the dramatistic approach to communication research necessitates the ability to build several *instruments:* structured dramatistic scenario based interview outlines, three dimensional matrices which structure dramatistic content at a meta-level by visions, issues, and graphics; dramatistic Q-sort decks that embody the content of rhetorical visions in competition across relevant issues, and graphics questionnaires that reflect demographic, sociographic, psychographic and product graphic characteristics.

The extent to which any particular method, procedure, instrument, or analytical technique is selected and used for studying an applied research problem will depend upon several issues: the nature of the problem being studied, the degree of validity imposed upon the research findings, time restraints, monetary restraints, logistical constraints, and the availability and access to rhetorical phenomena or communication messages. Thus, sometimes all of the above methods are used while at other times only selected ones are.

Explanations of the various methods appear throughout the text of *Applied Communication Research: A Dramatistic Approach.* However, specific methodological essays are also included. To study the qualitative fantasy theme analysis of printed messages see especially Bormann's essay on "Fantasy and Rhetorical Vision" in Part I. To study the qualitative analysis of dramatistic group communication see Shields' "Dramatistic Communication Based Focus Group Interviews" in Part V. For an in-depth understanding of factor analysis see Shields' "Critiquing Factor Analysis Studies" in the Appendices. For an explanation of Q-sorts and Quantitative Analysis see Cragan and Shields' "Uses of Bormann's Rhetorical Theory" in Part I and their "New Technologies for Market Research" in Part V. Of course, these methodological essays are brought to life by the various research reports appearing in the text. For now, suffice it to say that there is a beginning to approaching applied communication research dramatistically. There is also a step-by-step process.

The first thing a researcher must do when using a dramatistic approach to applied communication research is *learn to identify and capture the fantasy themes that comprise a rhetorical vision.* At the heart of this humanistic research procedure is the ability to do *dramatistic based rhetorical analyses.* Here, instead of looking for elements of ethos, pathos, or logos or styles of speaking, the researcher is looking for elements of the dramatic structure (characters, scenarios, scenes, santioning agent) of the rhetorical vision which the public rhetoric of a speech or speeches, speaker, or group or movement represents.

Once the researcher has mastered the technique of fantasy theme analysis, he or she will possess the basic skills necessary to adopt the *empirical designs* reported in the political, organizational, and marketing research essays of this book. The key is to be able *to take the content of the rhetorical analyses and build the given fantasy themes from competing rhetorical dramas into a research instrument called a Q-sort.* This instrument will allow the researcher to capture empirically the rhetorical dramas in which people participate. The best means of insuring that the rhetorical messages built into the Q-deck reflect the elements of the competing rhetorical visions is to utilize a *three dimensional matrice* where one axis represents the competing visions, another axis represents the key issues about which the dramas are in competition, and the third axis represents graphics questions that can later be used to describe the characteristics of the people who participate in specific rhetorical visions.

The Q-deck is administered. The data is retrieved and coded and analyzed via factor analysis. The factor analysis groups people who reacted to the messages in the Q-deck in a similar way. Then, depending upon the nature of the research problem, output may be analyzed either to find the dramas or fantasy themes to which most people resonate or to segment and differentiate people based upon their participation in different rhetorical dramas.

If sufficient rhetorical "stuff" is not available, as is often the case when conducting applied communication research, it is necessary to collect rhetorical material through *dramatistic communication based personal or focus group interviews.* Structured dramatistic scenarios may be used by the moderator or interviewer to elicit rhetorical comment from the interviewee(s). The goal is to capture the *universe of ideas* on a given subject and, once this material is available, to then subject it to a fantasy theme analysis.

## Typical Applications

The proof is in the pudding! So states the household test of utility for recipes and cooking. A similar test of utility exists for assessing the value of a social science theory — Is the theory useful or applicable to real world problems? Thus, with the Bormannean dramatistic theory the question becomes, "Is the why explanation of communication behavior useful in describing, interpreting, evaluating, and predicting behavior in real world settings and contexts?" As will be seen from the research reports appearing in this text, the answer is, "Yes." Whether critiquing American rhetoric, studying group communication, analyzing or managing political campaigns, determining intervention strategies for organizational communication, or developing, assessing, and guiding marketing activities, we have found the Bormannean dramatistic theory relevant and beneficial.

To assist you in your own research with the theory and methods it should be useful to sketch out in a general way the kinds of applied problems where the theory and methods have been applied. Many of these problems have stood the test of tasting; others are in various stages of cooking either by us or our students. Still others are suggested as potential recipes for research by you.

### Rhetorical Criticism

One of the initial applications of Bormann's theory concerned the study of rhetoric. Was the theory useful in describing, interpreting, and evaluating rhetorical material (persuasive postures, specific movements, speeches) that comprise the symbolic reality of groups of people? Some three dozen rhetorical studies have been completed by several independent scholars. Many have been published in our discipline's major journals. Such studies took two thrusts in studying rhetoric. First, the study of on-going contemporary rhetoric, and second, the study of past rhetoric.

The outcomes of these studies indicated that the theory is well suited for studying the symbolic realities of not only individual speakers, but of multiple speakers' contributions to a given rhetorical vision. Here, the researcher is seeking out recurrent fantasy themes that appear in the rhetoric in an attempt to describe the characters, scenarios, scenes, sanctioning agents and deep structure of the dramas. Specific dramas have been examined as well as competitive dramas about the same subject. The four essays in Part II enable you to see the theory applied to the rhetoric of an individual speaker (Malcolm X), the contemporary creation of a rhetorical drama (the Eagleton Affair), the failure of a movement to create a viable drama (Rhetorical Strategy), and multiple dramas about the same issues with the subsequent evolution of a complete rhetorical vision (Origins and Nature of the Cold War).

As a student, you could make similar applications by using the theory to critique the contemporary rhetoric around you. What is the rhetorical vision of speakers you hear regarding such issues as religion, selective service registration, abortion, energy, the value of a college education, interpersonal relationships, etc.? Similarly, what have some of the visions concerning these subjects been in the past? How have the visions evolved and developed over the years?

**Small Group Communication**

Another early application of the theory concerned the analysis of group communication. Indeed, the link between group communication and the chaining out of a symbolic reality filled with heroes, villains, scenarios, and scenes became the initial impetus for the creation of the dramatistic theory by Professor Bormann and his students at the University of Minnesota in the early 1970's. Observation of group communication indicated that groups tended to create a new symbolic reality as they interpreted here-and-now problems, built a group identity, created a common culture, and gained cohesiveness.

Several initial studies centered on describing such group created symbolic realities. For example, Chesebro, Cragan, and McCullough studied groups to identify the stagic development and capture the rhetorical vision of radical revolutionaries in consciousness-raising sessions. As well, with the development of a dramatistic based focus group procedure, group discussions became a fruitful means for eliciting contemporary rhetorical visions. Thus, Shields used group interaction to discover the private and projected character of the St. Paul Fire Fighters and the rhetorical vision of swine producers regarding the gestation litter condition XLP-30. Moreover, Cragan and Shields used group interaction to identify the elements of the competitive rhetorical visions regarding such diverse subjects as public fire education, farm management, and beef production.

As a student you could make similar applications by using the theory to study the rhetorical visions and dramatistic reality of groups around you. What is the symbolic reality of fraternity/sorority members versus independents, your group at work versus others, communication majors versus psychology or sociology? What meanings, emotions, and motives stem from individuals' commitments to black organizations, or women's organizations, or crisis center counseling? These and other groups all exhibit a symbolic reality awaiting your description, interpretation, and evaluation.

**Political Communication**

A continuing line of research using the dramatistic theory concerns the study of communication in American politics. The research reports in Part III illustrate this research line as they provide insight into how qualitative research techniques may be coupled with data gathering instruments and quantitative analysis techniques to capture a rhetorical vision empirically. In such an approach the researcher is attempting to insure that the discovered vision is a direct product of the collectivity being studied, rather than just an aberration within the mind of the rhetorical critic. In other words, the theory is being tested and validated as opposed to being merely reified through repeated use. The result is a bridging of the gap between humanistic and scientific inquiry.

As a student researcher, you could use either qualitative or qualitative-quantitative methods to study the rhetorical visions of particular politicians, parties, or public interest groups and pinpoint the issues about which the dramas are created. Also, you could study the visions created by the political discussion of such issues as right to work, Sunday blue laws, pornography legislation, government subsidies for transportation and private corporations, etc. Those of you interested in mass communication could study the visions created by the media or mediated by the media in the areas of energy, candidate image, equality for women, the "me" generation, etc.

**Organizational Communication**

The dramatistic theory and methods have also been used to study and recommend strategies for improving communication within the organization. Specific reports of such applications appear in Part IV. Here too, both qualitative and quantitative approaches are illustrated. By their use, the researcher is seeking to capture the dominant rhetorical vision within the organization, identify any competing rhetorical dramas, isolate both the positively and negatively charged fantasies within the organization, and determine which employees are caught up in which dramas.

The reports in Part IV describe the application of the theory and methods as a personnel evaluation tool (fire safety), as a public relations aid (fire fighters' dramatis personae), and as a management training and marketing aid (farm management). Other applications that we or our students have made in the area of organizational communication include: the identification of attitudinal communication barriers, discovering common ground getween work groups in conflict, assessing employee satisfaction, and guiding employee selection and orientation. In each of these areas, the dramatistic approach has worked well demonstrating both interpretative and predictive success.

**Marketing**

Perhaps our most thorough application of the dramatistic approach to applied communication research has ocurred in the area of marketing. Here the theory and methods illustrated in *Applied Communication Research* provide a direct link between a product's attributes, needs of the consumer, and advertising and promotional messages.

We have used the dramatistic approach to test marketing concepts both qualitatively and quantitatively, to identify potential users, to segment markets by both attitudes and graphics, to increase the diffusion curve concerning product knowledge, and to develop and test advertising and promotional material.

The essays in Part V illustrate concept testing qualitatively through dramatistic based focus group interviews (XLP-30), as well as how major markets may be segmented dramatistically. The student of applied communication research should recognize that an understanding of dramatistic theory and methods, coupled with a flair for designing research to solve marketing problems, will stand him or her in good stead as they enter the applied world of marketing research.

# 2

# Fantasy and Rhetorical Vision:
## The Rhetorical Criticism of Social Reality

## ERNEST G. BORMANN

Recent research in small group communication reveals a process that can interrelate important features of communication and rhetorical theory. Just as some psychologists and sociologists have studied the small group in order to discover features of larger social structures, so can investigations of small group communication provide insight into the nature of public address and mass communication.

For several years the small group communication seminar at Minnesota has studied the decision-making process in group discussion.[1] The seminar began with two major lines of inquiry: content analysis of group meetings and extended case studies of individual groups. Careful case studies over periods of several months provided an understanding of group process and communication which was often more complete and useful than much of the quantitative data generated by using various category systems. To develop a method for process analysis which captured the richness of case studies while allowing generalization, the seminar studied the transcripts of the small group meetings as a rhetorical critic might analyze the text of a public speech.

Most of the attempts to make a rhetorical criticism of small group communication proved relatively barren until Robert Bales published *Personality and Interpersonal Behavior* in 1970.[2] What Bales and his associates had been discovering while working with natural groups in the classroom was very like what we had been working on at Minnesota. But Bales provided the key part to the puzzle when he discovered *the dynamic process of group fantasizing*. Group fantasizing correlates with individual

*Quarterly Journal of Speech*, 58 (1972), 396-407. Reprinted with permission from The Speech Communication Association.

[1]For a description of the Minnesota Studies and a report of the major conclusions of the research see Ernest G. Bormann, *Discussion and Group Methods: Theory and Practice* (New York: Harper and Row, 1969).

[2](New York: Holt, Rinehart).

_Symbolic Convergence Theory,_ (handwritten)

dience fantasizing and to the
orical critics have long known
mmon yet, still, are different.
dramatistic terms. Now Bales
w dramatizing communication
: and with a way to examine
·e, motivation, emotional style,

:loped twelve content analysis
One original category, "shows
natizes." Continued work with
discovery of "group fantasy
iication coded as "dramatizes"
mpo of the conversation would
upt one another, blush, laugh,
forget their self-consciousness. The tone of the meeting, often quiet and
tense immediately prior to the dramatizing, would become lively, animated,
and boisterous, the chaining process, involving both verbal and nonverbal
communication, indicating participation in the drama.

What is the manifest content of a group fantasy chain? What do the
group members say? The content consists of characters, real or fictitious,
playing out a dramatic situation in a setting removed in time and space from
the here-and-now transactions of the group. (The "here-and-now," a
concept borrowed from sensitivity and encounter group practice, refers to
what is immediately happening in the group. Thus a recollection of
something that happened to the group in the _past_ or a dream of what the
group might do in the _future_ could be considered a fantasy theme.)

How can a fantasy chain be interpreted? Often the drama is a mirror of
the group's here-and-now situation and its relationship to the external
environment. The drama played out somewhere else or in some other time
often symbolizes a role collision or ambiguity, a leadership conflict, or a
problem related to the task-dimension of the group. Just as an individual's
repressed problems might surface in dream fantasies so those of a group
might surface in a fantasy chain and a critic might interpret the manifest
content with an eye to discovering the group's hidden agenda.

But the chaining can also be an expression in a given social field of the
individual psychodynamics of the participants. A dramatic theme might
relate to the repressed psychological problems of some or all of the
members and thus pull them into participation.[4]

Bales's most important discovery for the integration of communication
and rhetorical theory, however, was the process by which a zero-history

---

[3]The original categories and the method of independent coders making a content analysis are
presented in Robert F. Bales, _Interaction Process Analysis: A Method for the Study of Small
Groups_ (Cambridge, Mass.: Addison-Wesley, 1950). Changing the category from "show of
tension release" to "dramatizes" did not change the essential procedure of coding items.

[4]Bales, _Personality and Interpersonal Behavior,_ pp. 136-155.

group used fantasy chains to develop a common culture. The group tended to ignore comments coded as "dramatizes" which did not relate either to the group's here-and-now problems or to the individual psychodynamics of the participants. Those that did get the members of the group to empathize, to improvise on the same theme, or to respond emotionally not only reflected the members' common preoccupations but served to make those commonalities public.

When group members respond emotionally to the dramatic situation they publicly proclaim some commitment to an attitude. Indeed, improvising in a spontaneous group dramatization is a powerful force for attitude change. Dramas also imply motives and by chaining into the fantasy the members gain motivations. Since some of the characters in the fantasies are good people doing laudable things the group collectively identifies in symbolic terms proper codes of conduct and the characteristics which make people credible message sources. A comparison with more direct here-and-now methods for establishing group norms clarifies the nature of fantasy chains. For instance, one way to discover a common ground in a zero-history group with a job to do is to confront the question directly. A member may say, "I think we all want to do a good job and we should all go to the library and do a lot of research. I know that I'm willing to do that." If the others enthusiastically respond with comments like, "Yes, that is a good idea." "Good, let's go to work," the problem is dealt with directly. The fantasy chain discovers the same common ground symbolically:

"Last semester my roommate took this course and he never worked so hard in his life."

"Really?"

"Yeah, it was really great though. He took field trips to hospital labs and everything."

"Yeah, I know this girl who took the course and she said the same thing. She said you wouldn't believe how hard they worked. But she said she really got something out of it."

Values and attitudes of many kinds are tested and legitimatized as common to the group by the process of fantasy chains. Religious and political dramas are tested. For example, if someone dramatizes a situation in which a leading political figure is a laughingstock and it falls flat that particular political attitude and value has been exhibited and not legitimatized. However, should the group chain out on that drama improvising on other laughable situations in which the politician has participated the group will have created a common character which they can allude to in subsequent meetings and elicit a smiling or laughing emotional response. (They have created an inside joke but they have also created an attitude towards a given political position.) As Bales described it:

> The culture of the interacting group stimulates in each of its members
> a feeling that he has entered a new realm of reality — a world of heroes,

villains, saints, and enemies—a drama, a work of art. The culture of a group is a fantasy established from the past, which is acted upon in the present. In such moments, which occur not only in groups, but also in individual responses to works of art, one is "transported" to a world which seems somehow even more real than the everyday world. One may feel exalted, fascinated, perhaps horrified or threatened, or powerfully impelled to action, but in any case, involved. One's feelings fuse with the symbols and images which carry the feeling in communication and sustain it over time. One is psychologically taken into a psycho-dramatic fantasy world, in which others in the group are also involved. Then one is attached also to those other members.[5]

My argument is that these moments happen not only in individual re-actions to works of art, or in a small group's chaining out a fantasy theme, but also in larger groups hearing a public speech. The dramatizations which catch on and chain out in small groups are worked into public speeches and into the mass media and, in turn, spread out across larger publics, serve to sustain the members' sense of communitity, to impel them strongly to action (which raises the question of motivation), and to provide them with a social reality filled with heroes, villains, emotions, and attitudes.

The composite dramas which catch up large groups of people in a symbolic reality, I call a "Rhetorical vision." Just as fantasy themes chain out in the group to create a unique group culture so do the fantasy dramas of a successful persuasive campaign chain out in public audiences to form a rhetorical vision.

A rhetorical vision is constructed from fantasy themes that chain out in face-to-face interacting groups, in speaker-audience transactions, in viewers of television broadcasts, in listeners to radio programs, and in all the diverse settings for public and intimate communication in a given society. Once such a rhetorical vision emerges it contains dramatis personas and typical plot lines that can be alluded to in all communication contexts and spark a response reminiscent of the original emotional chain. The same dramas can be developed in detail when the occasion demands to generate emotional response.

The relationship between a rhetorical vision and a specific fantasy theme within a message explains why so much "persuasive" communication simply repeats what the audience already knows. Balance theories explain attitude and behavior change on the basis of dissonance or imbalance, and yet many strikingly successful speakers have not created dissonances but have rather given voice to what the listener already knows or feels and accepts.[7] One perceptive commentator on Hitler noted, for instance, that:

[5]*Ibid.*, p. 152

[6]See for example A.J.M. Sykes, "Myth in Communication," *The Journal of Communication,* 20 (Mar., 1970), 17-31 and A.J.M. Sykes, "Myth and Attitude Change," *Human Relations,* 18 (Nov., 1965), 323-337.

[7]Exposition of typical balance theories can be found in Theodore M. Newcomb, *The Acquaintance Process* (New York: Holt, Rinehart, 1961) and Fritz Heider, *The Psychology of Interpersonal Relations* (New York: Wiley, 1958).

One scarcely need ask with what arts he (Hitler) conquered the masses; he did not conquer them, he portrayed and represented them. His speeches are day-dreams of this mass soul; they are chaotic, full of contradictions, if their words are taken literally, often senseless, as dreams are, and yet charged with deeper meaning... The speeches begin always with deep pessimism and end in overjoyed redemption, a triumphant happy ending; often they can be refuted by reason, but they follow the far mightier logic of the subconscious, which no refutation can touch. Hitler has given speech to the speechless terror of the modern mass, and to the nameless fear he has given a name. That makes him the greatest mass orator of the mass age.[8]

The explanatory power of the fantasy chain analysis lies in its ability to account for the development, evolution, and decay of dramas that catch up groups of people and change their behavior. A rhetorical movement contains small group fantasy chains, public fantasy events, and a rhetorical vision in a complex and reciprocal set of relationships. The subsystems fit into a larger communication system as follows: A small group of people with similar individual psychodynamics meet to discuss a common preoccupation or problem. A member dramatizes a theme that catches the group and causes it to chain out because it hits a common psychodynamic chord or a hidden agenda item or their common difficulties vis-a-vis the natural environment, the socio-political systems, or the economic structures. The group grows excited, involved, more dramas chain out to create a common symbolic reality filled with heroes and villains. If the group's fantasy themes contain motives to "go public" and gain converts to their position they often begin artistically to create messages for the mass media for public speeches and so forth. When they need to develop a message for a specific context they often find themselves shaping the drama that excited them in their original discussions into suitable form for a different public.

Some of the dramas of their public rhetoric now catch members of the audience in the situation which Bales called, "individual responses to works of art, when one is 'transported' to a world which seems somehow even more real than the everyday world." Those so transported take up the dramas in small groups of acquaintances, and some of these derivative dramas again chain out as fantasy themes in the new groups; thus the rhetorical vision is propagated to a larger public until a rhetorical movement emerges.[9]

[8]Konrad Heiden, *Der Fuehrer: Hitler's Rise to Power*, trans. Ralph Manheim (Boston: Houghton Mifflin, 1944), p. 106.

[9]A study that traces the conscious attempts of some participants to chain out group fantasies that individuate a rhetorical vision to radicalize the uncommitted is James W. Chesebro, John F. Cragan, and Patricia McCullough, "The Small Group Techniques of the Radical-Revolutionary: A Synthetic Study of Consciousness Raising," *Speech Monographs*, in press. The investigators discovered that in the opening phases of the consciousness raising sessions members dramatized events and characters prominent in the national rhetorical vision of Gay Liberation. After the dramatization of the national vision had formed a common bond the participants turned to dramatizing personal experience narratives.

Individuals in rhetorical transactions create subjective worlds of common expectations and meanings. Against the panorama of large events and seemingly unchangeable forces of society at large or of nature the individual often feels lost and hopeless. One coping mechanism is to dream an individual fantasy which provides a sense of meaning and significance for the individual and helps protect him from the pressures of natural calamity and social disaster. The rhetorical vision serves much the same coping function for those who participate in the drama and often with much more force because of the supportive warmth of like-minded companions.

In most instances a viable rhetorical vision accounts plausibly for the evidence of the senses so those who pick up the dramatic action and find it personally satisfying are not troubled by contradictory evidence from common-sense experience. On occasion, however, small, highly dedicated groups of people generate and sustain rhetorical visions so out of joint with the common-sense and everyday experience of the majority of a community that their appeal is very limited. The analogy of the more bizarre rhetorical visions with pathological states in individuals caused one observer, Richard Hofstadter, to refer to the former as paranoid.[10]

What answer can be given, then, to the question of the relation between public fantasies and "reality" or action or substance? Writers in General Semantics often argue that the word is not the thing.[11] Scholars in many disciplines often go on to assume that since the word is not the thing any discrepancy between words and things must necessarily be resolved by assigning the greater importance to things and the words are, therefore, to be discounted as misleading or unimportant.

One line of historical analysis, for example, suggests that although the abolitionists often argued from theological grounds that slavery was a sin and that to saver their eternal souls all persons must work for its elimination, the "real" reason the abolitionists fought with zeal to free the slaves was because they were members of a displaced social elite caught in a status crisis. The words of the abolitionists are discounted as being unimportant to the historical reality of the situation.[12]

Sociological analysis often starts from the premise that the words are generated out of the social context rather than that the words *are the social context*. Duncan laments the common view, "American sociologists simply do not believe that how we communicate determines how we relate as social beings. Most sociologists really think of symbols as photographs of some kind of reality that is 'behind' symbols . . . Class *exists* and *then* is

---

[10]Richard Hofstadter, *The Paranoid Style in American Politics and Other Essays* (New York: Knopf, 1965).

[11]See Wendell Johnson, *People in Quandaries: The Semantics of Personal Adjustment* (New York: Harper and Row, 1946) and S.I. Hayakawa, *Language in Thought and Action* (New York: Harcourt, Brace and World, 1964).

[12]For a quick survey of some representative historical accounts of the Abolitionists see "Introduction" in Richard O. Curry, ed., *The Abolitionists: Reformers or Fanatics?* (New York: Holt, Rinehart, 1965), pp. 1-9. See also David Donald, "Abolition Leadership: A Displaced Social Elite," *ibid.*, pp. 42-48.

expressed, it does not arise *in* the expression."[13]

When a critic makes a rhetorical analysis he or she should start from the assumption that when there is a discrepancy between the word and the thing the most important cultural artifact for understanding the events may not be the things or "reality" but the words or the symbols. Indeed, in many vital instances the words, that is, the rhetoric, are the social reality and to try to distinguish one symbolic reality from another is a fallacy widespread in historical and sociological scholarship which the rhetorical critic can do much to dispel.[14]

A critic can take the social reality contained in a rhetocial vision which he has constructed from the concrete dramas developed in a body of discourse and examine the social relationships, the motives, the qualitative impact of that symbolic world as though it were the substance of social reality for those people who participated in the vision. If the critic can illuminate how people who participated in the rhetorical vision related to one another, how they arranged themselves into social hierarchies, how they acted to achieve the goals embedded in their dreams, and how they were aroused by the dramatic action and the dramatis personas within the manifest content of their rhetoric, his insights will make a useful contribution to understanding the movement and its adherents.

How might the critic making a fantasy theme analysis proceed? There is not space to describe the technique in detail, but I shall raise some of the more general questions that a critic might choose to investigate. The critic begins by collecting evidence related to the manifest content of the communication, using video or audio tapes, manuscripts, recollections of participants, or his own direct observations. He discovers and describes the narrative and dramatic materials that have chained out for those who participate in the rhetorical vision. When a critic has gathered a number of dramatic incidents he can look for patterns of characterizations (do the same people keep cropping up as villains?) of dramatic situations and actions (are the same stories repeated?) and of setting (where is the sacred ground and where the profane?). The critic must then creatively reconstruct the rhetorical vision from the representative fantasy chains much as a scholar would delineate a school of drama on the basis of a number of different plays.

---

[13]"The Search for a Social Theory of Communication in American Sociology," Frank E. X. Dance, ed., *Human Communication Theory: Original Essays* (New York: Holt, Rinehart, 1967), p. 237.

[14]Not all social scientists start from the assumption that rhetoric differs from social reality. Hugh Dalziel Duncan's work is illustrative of one who viewed symbolic forms as social reality. A group of sociologists exploring what they often referred to as the sociology of knowledge also assumed that social reality was symbolic. See, for example, Peter L. Burger and Thomas Luckmann, *The Social Construction of Reality: A Treatise in the Sociology of Knowledge* (1966: rpt. Garden City, N.Y.: Doubleday Anchor Books, 1967). See also Wallace J. Thies, "Public Address and the Sociology of Knowledge," *Journal of the Wisconsin Speech Communication Association*, 1 (1971), 28-41.

Once the critic has constructed the manifest content of the rhetorical vision he can ask more specific questions relating to elements of the dramas. Who are the dramatis personas? Does some abstraction personified as a character provide the ultimate legitimatization of the drama? God? The People? The Young? (What are young people trying to tell us?) Who are the heroes and the villains? How concrete and detailed are the characterizations? Motives attributed? How are the members of the rhetorical community characterized? For what are the insiders praised, the outsiders or enemies castigated? What values are inherent in the praiseworthy characters?

Where are the dramas set? In the wilderness? In the countryside? In the urban ghetto? Is the setting given supernatural sanction?

What are the typical scenarios? What acts are performed by the ultimate legitimatizer? The neutral people? The enemy? Which are sanctioned and praised; which censored? What lifestyles are exemplified as praiseworthy?

What meanings are inherent in the dramas? Where does the insider fit into the great chain of being? How does the movement fit into the scheme of history? What emotional evocations dominate the dramas? Does hate dominate? Pity? Love? Indignation? Resignation? What motives are embedded in the vision? Would the committed work for or resist legal action? Violence? Would they resign this life to get ready for an after-life?

How does the fantasy theme work to attract the unconverted? How does it generate a sense of community and cohesion from the insider?

How artistic is the development of the fantasy theme? How skillful the characterization? How artistic the use of language? How rich the total panorama of the vision? How capable is the drama to arouse and interpret emotions?

A critic need not, or course, raise all of such questions for a given piece of criticism but for some in-depth critiques of a single message the critic might ask more questions and search for more details. A brief analysis of one important rhetorical vision from American history illustrates the way a critic might proceed.

The point relating to the way fantasy themes help people transcend the everyday and provide meaning for an audience is made graphically by the rhetorical vision embedded in the preaching of Puritan ministers to their small congregations huddled in unheated, crude, and undecorated meeting houses in the wilderness in the early years of the Massachusetts Bay Colony. The daily routine of the people was one of backbreaking drudgery. The niceties of life were almost nonexistent; music, the arts, decoration of home or clothing, largely unavailable. A discursive description of the emigration and the daily externals of life would be very grim. But the Puritans of Colonial New England led an internal fantasy life of mighty grandeur and complexity. They participated in a rhetorical vision that saw the migration to the new world as a holy exodus of God's chosen people. The Biblical drama that supported their vision was that of the journey of the Jews from Egypt into Canaan. John Cotton's sermon delivered when Winthrop's company was leaving for Massachusetts was on the text, ''Moreover I will appoint a place for my People Israell, (sic) and I will plant them, that they may dwell in a place of their own and move no more."[15]

The Puritan rhetorical vision saw them as conquering new territories for God, saving the souls of the natives, and, most importantly, as setting up in the wilderness a model religious community, a new Israel, patterned after the true meaning of the scriptures to light the way for the reformation still to be accomplished in old England and in all of Europe.

Such a vision gave to every social and political action a sense of importance. Every intrusion of nature or of other communities upon their inner reality also was given added significance. A time of troubles such as a drought or an Indian raid became evidence of God's displeasure and served as a motive to drive the Puritans to higher effort and greater striving to please God.

The Puritan vision also gave meaning to each individual within the movement. The scenario places each member of the audience firmly in the role of protagonist. Cotton Mather wrote to students preparing to be ministers that, "the *Gaining* of one Soul to GOD by your Ministry, will be of more Account with you than any *Gain* of this World; than all the *Wealth* in the World."[16]

In creating fantasy themes for specific sermons the minister would use all his art of assertion, imperatives, and descriptive language to search out the hiding places and bring each member of the congregation center stage to play out the drama of salvation or damnation. Turn and dodge as the listener might, the skillful minister kept driving the auditors to the recognition of their personal spiritual dramas. The odds against success were enormous, the fruits of victory unbelievably sweet, the results of defeat incredibly awesome and terrifying. Thomas Hooker, a first generation minister, does an excellent job of presenting the Puritan rhetorical vision in the following fantasy theme:

> Imagine thou sawest the Lord Jesus coming in the clouds, and heardest the last trump blow, *Arise ye dead, and come to judgment*: Imagine thou sawest the Judg (sic) of all the World sitting upon the Throne, thousands of Angels before him, and ten thousand ministring unto him, the Sheep standing on his right hand, and the Goats at the left: Suppose thou heardest that dreadful Sentence, and final Doom pass from the Lord of Life (whose Word made Heaven and Earth, and will shake both) *Depart from me ye cursed*; How would thy heart shake and sink, and die within thee in the thought thereof, wert thou really perswaded it was thy portion? Know, that by thy dayly continuance in sin, thou dost to the utmost of thy power execute that Sentence upon thy soul: It's thy life, thy labor, the desire of thy heart, and thy dayly practice

[15] John Cotton, "God's Promise to His Plantations," *Old South Leaflets,* Vol. 3, No. 53.

[16] Cotton Mather, *Manductuo Ad Ministerium: Directions for a Candidate of the Ministry* (1726; rpt. New York: Published for the Facsimile Text Society by Columbia Univ. Press, 1938), p. 114.

to depart away from the God of all Grace and Peace, and turn the
Tombstone of everlasting destruction upon thine own soul.[17]

For the members of the community who participated in the Puritan
rhetorical vision the events in the meeting house were significant far beyond
the crude externals of their living conditions. In their private prayers and in
public worship they participated in a social reality resonant with high drama
and rich symbolism.

An audience observing the drama from the outside might find it lacking
in suspense, find it inartistic because the basic assumption upon which it
rested was the *deus ex machina*. Man was completely dependent upon God
for election to sainthood. The plot was similar to the pattern of the classical
Greek plays. Reading the sermons today, we find the action static, the
protagonist an insect squirming helplessly in the hands of an all-powerful
Deity. But for the listener who chained out on the fantasy and imaginative-
ly took the central role, the suspense might well become unbearable. Each
hour might bring eternal salvation or eternal death. In his famous revival
sermon Jonathan Edwards said, "And it would be no wonder if some
persons, that now sit here, in some seats of this meetinghouse, in health,
quiet and secure, should be there (in hell) before tomorrow morning."[18]

The predominant emotion which the Puritan vision evoked was that of
awe. The focus is upon an afterlife with high potential for ecstasy or terror,
almost beyond the powers of the ministers to fantasize. The rhetoric
contained powerful pragmatic motivations. The preoccupation with time,
the fear of death before God's call to election, impelled the participant in
the fantasy to do as much as soon as possible to put herself or himself in the
proper posture for election to sainthood. The minutes wasted might be
those very ones when his time had come.

One basic action line contained the motive power for much of the
Puritan's tough and unrelenting effort to do good and to make good in the
material world, namely that a time of troubles was God's punishment for
the evil ways of an individual or a community, but that out of punishment
would arise an understanding of guilt and a rebirth and regeneration so that
the punishment would really serve as a means to salvation. By a zealous
striving in the new direction, the guilt of their sins revealed by God's
punishment would be propitiated. Insofar as they were cleansed by the
experience in the sight of God, the new venture would increase and prosper.
When they began again to fall from God's grace they could anticipate more
hardships. To some extent, therefore, since in their view nothing happened
by chance, the prospering of worldly affairs was evidence of their ability to
please God. (Without this dramatic line one might well expect that a vision
that emphasized the afterlife would result in contemplative inaction in this
life.)

[17]Perry Miller and Thomas H. Johnson, eds., *The Puritans*, I (1938; rpt. New York: Harper
Torchbooks, 1963), p. 298.
[18]Wayland Maxfield Parrish and Marie Hochmuth, eds., *American Speeches* (New York:
Longmans, Green, 1954), p. 88.

The fantasy themes in which good Puritans took each setback and difficulty as a sign from God and made good use of them to become better persons contained strong motives for action and retained strong motives for action and reform.[19] Contemplation, inactivity, impracticality, and apathy were undesirable in the context of the scenario. Working, striving, acting in a hardheaded way, involvement, were all positive values. The drama began with a rite of self-abasement which loaded the participant with a high charge of guilt and turned to a plan of action which was providentially the path to salvation furnished by God. By working hard and doing the right thing they released the charge of guilt, and success became the final evidence that their conscience need no longer be troubled. The rhetoric used failure as evidence that they had not tried hard enough, or been good enough and must therefore work even harder and be even better.

Two common fantasy themes expressed the Puritan rhetorical vision. The first was the pilgrim making his slow, painful, and holy way, beset by many troubles and temptations. The second was the Christian soldier fighting God's battles and overcoming all adversaries in order to establish the true church. The first emphasized their militancy. Those who participated in the rhetorical vision exhibited an active and if need be, violent, bloody temper. When they could not convert the Indians they fought them and they fought, as well, their fellow Englishmen in the old country for the true faith.

The motivations embedded in the Puritan rhetorical vision, therefore, required great energy and overt activity. Morison, writing a history of Harvard, noted that Emmanuel College, Cambridge was a Puritan stronghold and produced many of the early leaders who emigrated to Massachusetts. Emmanuel College also had an active group of Cambridge neo-Platonists. Morison regrets that "the tolerant and generous philosophy of these men...could not have set the tone of Harvard College." But even as he regrets it, he recognized that "Harvard must have been puritan, or not have existed. A neo-Platonist could not be a man of action, a pioneer, an emigrant, any more than a Hindu. The kingdom of God was within him, not in Massachusetts Bay."[20]

Of course to do justice to a fantasy theme analysis of the rhetorical vision of the Puritans would require a monograph. However, even this sketch can point to some of the insights that a fantasy theme analysis could provide. If we view the Puritans as organisms gribbing away in the wilderness to keep alive or create material wealth or to achieve status or to reach self-actualization we find the enterprise relatively mean and trivial. However, if we examine the internal fantasy of the community as revealed in the

---

[19]Cotton Mather's advice to stammerers is typical of the Puritan vision which saw each affliction as an opportunity to improve in God's eyes. The stutterer should "fetch Good out of Evil...and make a very pious Improvement of your very humbling Chastisement which a sovereign GOD has laid upon you," quoted in Ernest G. Bormann, "Ephphatha, or, Some Advice to Stammerers," *Journal of Speech and Hearing Research,* 12 (Sept. 1969), 457.

[20]Samuel Eliot Morison, *The Founding of Harvard College* (Cambridge: Harvard Univ. Press, 1935), pp. 99-100.

sermons of their ministers, we discover the characters of the drama, their emotional values, their actions, and their relationship to an over-reaching supernatural power. We come to a new understanding of the grubbing in the wilderness and we have an opportunity to be in possession of much more of the Puritan experience.

Of course, nature does intrude upon our fantasies. Factual descriptions of our common-sense perceptions of the world are also part of the manifest content of rhetorical discourse. A total rhetoric consists of both discursive material and fantasy themes. Cassirer provides the rhetorical critic with an approach to the relationship between discursive material and fantasy themes when he writes, "...myth, art, language and science appear as symbols; not in the sense of mere figures which refer to some given reality by means of suggestions and allegorical renderings, but in the sense of forces each of which produces and posits a world of its own."[21]. In Langer's words Cassirer was helped, "by a stroke of insight: the realization that language, man's prime instrument of reason, reflects his mythmaking tendency more than his rationalizing tendency. Language, the symbolization of thought, exhibits two entirely different modes of thought. Yet in both modes the mind is powerful and creative. It expresses itself in different forms, *one of which is discursive logic, the other creative imagination.*"[22]

When the authentic record of events is clear and widely understood the competing visions must take it into account. If two teams play a game and team A beats team B by 5 to 4, the two teams may chain out different fantasies about the game. Team A may participate in a drama to the effect that justice has been done and the best team has won by superior play. Team B may fantasize that they did not really lose and that the game was stolen from them by an inept official or by dirty play on the part of their opponents. However, the outcome of the game as represented in the authentic record by a score of 5 to 4 is accounted for and incorporated into the explanatory system of both fantasies.

Whenever occasions are so chaotic and indiscriminate that the community has no clear observational impression of the facts, people are given free rein to fantasize within the assumptions of their rhetorical vision without inhibition. On such occasions fantasy themes become the main explanatory systems for the events. Rumors are illustrations of the principle in action.[23]

The conventional wisdom of communication theorists that "meanings are in people not messages" is much too simple for the critic who wishes to study the rhetorical vision of a movement, an organization, or a

[21]Ernest Cassirer, *Language and Myth*, trans. Susanne K. Langer (New York: Harper, 1946), p. 8.

[22]Cassirer, pp. viii-ix.

[23]See, for example, Tamotsu Shibutani, *Improvised News: A Sociological Study of Rumor* (Indianapolis: Bobbs-Merrill, 1966).

community.[24] In a very important way meanings *are* in messages. When the members of a group chain out a fantasy they emerge from the meeting with new meanings, that may not have existed before, else how can we account for novelty and innovation? The new meanings are embedded in the messages created during the meeting. The members have appropriated them by sharing in their creation through public dramatization. (One might as well say the meanings associated with *Hamlet* are in the people who know the play rather than in the productions or the manuscripts. The trouble with that view, of course, is that until the first production of *Hamlet* very few people had the meanings. Unless the meanings relating to *Hamlet* are to some extent in the communication transactions associated with a performance of the play, the new meanings could never have been created.)

The emotions associated with the meanings are, also, partly in the message as well as in the people participating in a fantasy chain. The rhetorical vision provides its participants with an emotional evocation. Thus, the critical analysis of emotional appeals is illuminated by the process of fantasy theme analysis. Physiological studies of emotions reveal that changes in blood chemistry, heart rate, endocrine secretion, palm sweat, and so forth vary little from emotion to emotion.[25] Whether an individual's aroused physiological state is interpreted as hate, fear, anger, joy, or love is partly determined by the drama that accompanies the emotional state.

Finally, and most importantly, motives are in the messages. The rhetorical vision of a group of people contains their drives to action. People who generate, legitimatize and participate in a public fantasy are, in Bale's words, "powerfully impelled to action" by that process. Motives do not exist to be expressed in communication but rather arise in the expression itself and come to be embedded in the drama of the fantasy themes that generated and serve to sustain them. Motives are thus available for direct interpretation by a community of scholars engaged in rhetorical criticism.[26]

When an actor assumes a role in a drama he gains with the part constraining forces (the dramatic action of the unfolding plot) which impel him to do and to say certain things. When a person appropriates a rhetorical vision he gains with the supporting dramas constraining forces which impel him to

[24]A seminar in organizational communication at the University of Minnesota taught by Professor David Smith in 1972 analyzed organizational myths (rhetorical visions) of all or part of four organizations in the Metropolitan Twin Cities area. Included in the study was a religious organization, a division of a major computer facility, a small family-owned business supply company, and a station of the University of Minnesota hospitals. The investigators used interviews to elicit narratives about the organizations and then submitted the resulting dramas to fantasy theme analysis.

[25]For a representative analysis of emotions by a psychologists see Normal L. Munn, *Psychology: The Fundamentals of Human Adjustment*, 5th ed. (Boston: Houghton Mifflin, 1966), pp. 189-221.

[26]My notion is not the same as Kenneth Burke's concept as interpreted by Richard E. Crable and John J. Makay, "Kenneth Burke's Concept of Motives in Rhetorical Theory," *Today's Speech*, 20 (Win. 1972), 11-18. Crable and Makay present a survey of various commentaries of Burke's view of motives in rhetorical theory and provide an interpretation of their own.

adopt a life style and to take certain action. The born-again Christian is baptized and adopts a life style and behavior modeled after the heroes of the dramas that sustain that vision. The devout Puritan in Massachusetts was driven by his vision. Likewise the convert to one of the counterculture in the 1960's would let his hair and beard grow, change his style of dress, and his method of work, and so forth. Concurrently a person might participate in a number of narrower visions related to such issues as foreign policy, taxation, civil rights, and women's rights.

One widespread explanation of human motivation posits a fixed schedule of motives that most people have within them. When one uses a schedule of motives as a check-list in preparing persuasive discourse or in critically analyzing it, several shortcomings become apparent. While the schedule is fixed, human behavior is not, thus, accounting for action by attributing a motive to the actor tends to work only after the fact. For instance, when a person chooses a martyr's death the notion that the most fundamental of human motives is self-preservation does not predict the behavior. After the fact the critic can select some other motive from the schedule and argue that it has clearly become more compelling for the martyr than self-preservation.

When a critic begins instead with the approach that each rhetorical vision contains as part of its substance the motive that will impel the people caught up in it, then he can anticipate the behavior of the converts. If the critic discovers that a person faced with the choice of martyrdom participates in a rhetorical vision that includes the fantasy of persons assuring themselves eternal salvation by dying for God's purposes, he can anticipate the act itself.

The notion that motives are hidden within individuals makes them difficult to study in a critical way, and that same inaccessibility makes it possible for people involved in argument and conflict to attribute motives to their friends and enemies. Indeed, a person who tries to get a fantasy to chain out often uses the technique of attributing motives to characters in a dream. A speaker can characterize a hero by attributing praiseworthy motivation, or create a bad image by suggesting unsavory motives. Almost every major evangelist in American history has become a central character in several rhetorical visions, which alternately portray him as a villain seeking money, power, and notoriety, or as a selfless hero trying to better the human condition and do God's will. Those whose rhetorical vision in the 1960's contained the draft resister as hero saw him motivated by a high moral commitment to do good for humanity and those whose fantasy saw

Much closer to my view of motivation is that developed by Karlyn Kohrs Campbell, "The Ontological Foundations of Rhetorical Theory," *Philosophy and Rhetoric*, 3 (Spr. 1970), 97-108. She writes, for instance, of theorists who "contend that human motivation is distinct from that of other beings because the nature and structure of language are themselves motivating forces and because the interaction between man and his language profoundly transforms his physical, biological, and animal needs, drives and desires.... In addition, the interaction between man and language is viewed as a process which destroys all purely 'animal' or 'biological' motives." (p. 104).

him as a villain often attributed to him a cowardly motive to save his own skin.

For the scholar, at any rate, to view motives as embedded in the rhetorical vision rather than hidden in the skulls and viscera of people makes it possible to check the critic's insights by going directly to the rhetoric rather than relying on inferences about psychological entitites available for analysis.

Not only does the fantasy analysis of rhetorical visions provide at least as great if not greater power of prediction than the fixed schedule of motives approach but, more importantly, once we participate in the rhetorical vision of a community or movement, even if we keep an aesthetic distance, we have come vicariously to experience a way of life that would otherwise be less accessible to us, we have enlarged our awareness, we have become more fully human. Certainly the discovery and appreciation of rhetorical visions should be one possible function of criticism.

# 3

# Uses of Bormann's Rhetorical Theory in Applied Communication Research

## JOHN F. CRAGAN and DONALD C. SHIELDS

In 1972, Bormann posited a theory of communication that would be useful for analyzing the rhetoric of collectivities of people. The fruits of utilizing the theory to critique contemporary rhetoric are manifested by the selection appearing in Part II of this text. This essay illustrates the change in theoretical focus necessary to conceptualize the use of the theory in applied communication research.

It is our belief that Bormann's theory is best considered not as a method for doing fantasy theme analysis but as a metatheory for constructing rhetorical visions. Viewing Bormann's theory at the meta level has wide application to applied communication research. Just as general systems theory has served as a metatheory for building systemic theories in a number of disciplines, so Bormann's metatheory can be used to build rhetorical theories that provide why explanations of communication phenomena. His theory is more limited than general systems theory, as it only provides a metaexplanation of human communication events, while general systems theory is not only used to build theories of human events but also is used to build natural science theories.[1] This essay then deals with the utility of using Bormann's rhetorical theory (which conceives of a symbolic reality in which meaning, emotion, and motive are present in the rhetoric and which focuses on the message as opposed to the situation or the speaker.)[2] Cragan's study of cold war rhetoric from 1946-1972 and the American Indian movement of the early 1970's, has convinced us of the

---

[1]For examples of applications of general systems theory in speech communication, see F. Aubrey Fisher and Leonard C. Hawes, "An Interact System Model: Generating a Grounded Theory of Small Groups," *Quarterly Journal of Speech,* 57 (1971), 444-453; and Bernard L. Brock, James W. Chesebro, John F. Cragan and James F. Klumpp, *Public Policy Decision-Making: Systems Analysis and Comparative Advantages Debate* (New York: Harper and Row, 1963).

[2]See Ernest G. Bormann, "Fantasy and Rhetorical Vision: The Rhetorical Criticism of Social Reality," *Quarterly Journal of Speech*, 58 (1972), 396-407.

value of Bormann's metatheory in constructing dramatistic rhetorical realities that provide both a useful nominal explanation of American public address and a basis for insight in the form of rhetorical criticism.[3] However, in 1976, we discovered some research procedures and ultimate applications of Bormann's theory that have led us into new directions in the application of Bormann's theory. Shields laid the groundwork in 1974 when he demonstrated how to validate one of the theory's concepts (heroic personae) using William Stephenson's Q-Methodology.[4]

In 1976 we discovered that we could build competing rhetorical visions systematically into a structured Q-sort.[5] Our research on how American foreign policy played in Peoria demonstrated to us that it was possible to do essentially a fantasy theme analysis of the dramatistic rhetoric on foreign policy that existed in popular media, build systematically three rhetorical visions (Cold War, Isolation, Power Politics) and then have Peorians choose the symbolic reality in which they participated. This procedure had the advantage of producing an analysis of a potential audience using an instrument that retrieved rhetorical data. This is an advantage in that most of the instruments that we have been using in the past for analyzing audiences in a quantitative fashion have been instruments borrowed from sociology, political science, psychology, and the data tended to be retrieved on the basis of attitude scales, semantic differential scales, and the results of the data then had to be converted into rhetorical form. Our procedure has the advantage of a direct application from the empirical data to the act of speech writing. In fact, one of the outputs of our previous research was to generate a political speech that was directly based upon the rhetorical dramas in which Peorians participated. The fact that this speech was "manufactured" inside of a computer with some empirical base for predicting its success, produced a wildly chaining fantasy in the national media that essentially characterized us as unethical sophists who could potentially manipulate the American political mind.[6]

The major weakness of our Peoria research was not so much its unethical overtones, in our judgment, but it was our inability to tie the dramatistic rhetorical space that we had discovered to real flesh and blood people. This

[3]See John F. Cragan, "The Cold War Rhetorical Vision, 1946-1972," unpublished diss., University of Minnesota, 1972; and John F. Cragan, "Rhetorical Strategy: A Dramatistic Interpretation and Application" (Selection 5, p. 67).

[4]William Stephenson, *The Study of Behavior: Q-Technique and Its Methodology* (Chicago: University of Chicago Press, 1953.)

[5]See John F. Cragan and Donald C. Shields, "Foreign Policy Communication Dramas: How Mediated Rhetoric Played in Peoria in Campaign '76," *Quarterly Journal of Speech,* 63 (1977), 274-289.

[6]For some of the sources that "chained out" fantasies on our computer written speech, see Mark Starr, "Politics by Computer," *Chicago Tribune,* April 13, 1977, 1; Bob Greene, "Computer Creates Peoplespeak," *Chicago Sun Times,* January 17, 1977, 6; Harper Barnes, "Political Speech Would Play Well in Peoria," *St Louis Post Dispatch,* October 28, 1976, 1F; Reuter News Service, "Computer Can Write a Political Speech," *Christian Science Monitor,* May 11, 1977; and Jaan Kangitaski, "Perfect Political Speech," *The Bulletin of the American College of Physicians,* 18, 11 (1977), 13-14.

was due to the fact that we had used a small sample procedure developed by William Stephenson which allowed us to discover the universe of dramatistic rhetorical space of people but had the disadvantage of not having a sufficiently large sample to generate predictions with regard to their demographic or sociographic or politicographic backgrounds.[7] In other words, we could not say for sure whether the people who participated in the Cold War were a mostly white, mostly uneducated, mostly World War II veterans, living mostly on the southside of Peoria. Without such demographic and sociographic data, our procedure would have limited utilitarian value in a real political campaign.

During the last three years we have devised ways to bridge the gap between small sample and large sample research design and develop a more elaborate method for applying Bormann's theory to everyday problems, one of them being political campaigns.[8] We believe that the pivotal, methodological activity in gathering dramatistic rhetorical data for doing any sort of applied communication research, whether it's political campaigns or whether it's market research, is in the building of a three-dimensional matrix. "In single variable research, we are used to plotting the relationship of one variable by means of two coordinates (X and Y). Here we are talking about adding a third coordinate (Z) and conceptualizing the axes and occurring perpendicular to each other within one cube. One axis will represent visions, one axis will represent the dramatistic structure, salient themes and issues, and the third axis will represent the demographic, sociographic and psychographic variables."[9]

The three procedures necessary to build a matrix are a rhetorical criticism of previously captured statements, rhetorical criticism of personal interview data, and a rhetorical criticism of focus group interviews. These three rhetorical criticisms are then used to build the three dimensional matrix. The rhetorical visions form the top of the matrix and the left side of the matrix is essentially the dramatistic structure, hero-villains, etc., and the key issues that produce differences in the visions. The back side of the cube would then be demographics, the psychographics, and sociographics of the population being studied.

We have applied this research method to three research questions that are essentially outside the field of speech communication with some interesting results.[10] In addition to studying the dramatistic foreign policy visions that

---

[7]For an explanation of Stephenson's method, see William Stephenson, *The Study of Behavior: Q-Technique and Its Methodology* (Chicago: University of Chicago Press, 1953).

[8]See Donald C. Shields and John F. Cragan, "A Communication Based Political Campaign: A Theoretical and Methodological Perspective."

[9]Ibid, pp. 4-5.

[10]See John F. Cragan and Donald C. Shields, "The Identifying Characteristics of Public Fire Educators," National Fire Protection and Control Administration, Department of Commerce, United States Government, 1977, (mimeo); John F. Cragan, Donald C. Shields and N.E. Nichols, "Marketing Farm Management Services: An Internal Study, Phase I," Doane Agricultural Services, St. Louis, Missouri, 1978, (mimeo); and Donald C. Shields and John F. Cragan, "A Market Segmentation Study for Lutalyse," Marketing Research Division, Upjohn Corporation, Kalamazoo, Michigan, 1978, (mimeo).

**Table 1**

**Dramatistic Communication Theory
Three Dimensional Matrix**

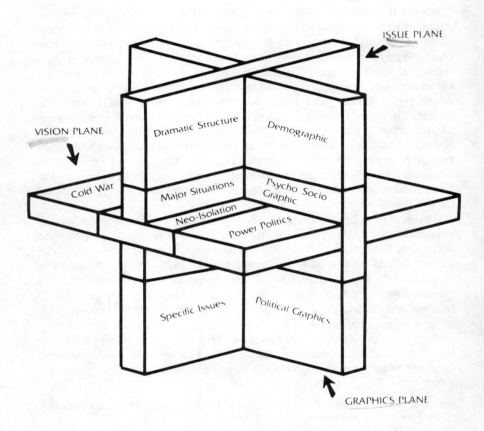

Peorians participated in, we have examined the rhetorical visions of fire-fighters with respect to fire education, farm managers with respect to their organization and the service they perform, and cattle producers in terms of their fantasies towards reproduction of cattle. Each research project had a different question that needed to be answered, but our approach to each problem was essentially the same in that we used Bormann's dramatistic rhetorical theory as a metatheory to construct the rhetorical dramas that people participated in that were relevant to the question we were studying.

In the fire research, the Department of Commerce asked us to determine what characteristics would identify a fire fighter who was participating in essentially a public fire education drama of the fire service. They wanted to know an answer to this question so that they could provide support monies to encourage the development of more public fire education fire fighters. Doane Agricultural Service wanted us to determine the different conceptualizations that their farm managers have about the service they are performing for absentee landlords. In other words, Doane wanted us to assess what farm managers were participating in what dramas so that they would devise training programs to move their organization in a predetermined direction. The Upjohn Company had an even more complex problem. They essentially wanted a market segmentation study for a product that was not yet on the market. Upjohn was introducing their product in a year and wanted to know who would be the first people to buy it, and so forth, and they wanted to know who these people were in terms of the dramas they participated in with respect to reproduction of cattle, and they also wanted to be able to know these people in terms of where they lived, how many cows they had, and in terms of their demographic and sociographic backgrounds.

We answered these three different research questions by following essentially the same procedure. The first step was to go out and find what kind of rhetorical reality these people were participating in. So in the case of the fire fighters we conducted personal interviews and focus group interviews in which we encouraged fire fighters to fantasize about their profession as fire fighters. Through this procedure and subsequent analysis we discovered that they participated in basically three dramas which we labeled the Suppressionist View, the Inspection View, and the Public Education View. The focus group interviews also revealed which issues tended to call forth these three different dramas in competition or antagonism with each other.

In the case of the farm managers, we also did both individual and focus group interviews with the farm managers. In addition, we surveyed and did a rhetorical thematic analysis of the printed literature on farm management and of that particular company's published material. This organizational study revealed three dominant dramas that we called the Traditional Company, the Family Company, and the Profit-Oriented Company.

Once the audio tapes of these focus group interviews and the audio tapes of the personal interviews are gathered, it is a laborious and artistic effort to build a structured Q that will form two sides of the cube: the top side being the visions and the left side being the dramatic structure and the "here-and-now" issues that call forth the dramas. The following tables display the two sides of the matrix of applications we have made of Bormann's theory in applied communication.

## Table 2

### Peoria Study

| Dramatic Structure | Cold War | Neo-Isolationism | Power Politics |
|---|---|---|---|
| 1. Dramatic Scene | X | X | X |
| 2. Hero Persona | X | X | X |
| 3. Villain Persona | X | X | X |
| Main Actors | | | |
| 4. U.S. Self-Image | X | X | X |
| 5. Russia | X | X | X |
| Supporting Players | | | |
| 6. Kissinger | X | X | X |
| 7. CIA | X | X | X |
| Situations (turf) | | | |
| 8. Africa | X | X | X |
| 9. Angola | X | X | X |
| 10. China | X | X | X |
| 11. Latin America | X | X | X |
| 12. Mid-East | X | X | X |
| 13. Panama | X | X | X |
| 14. Lesson of Vietnam | X | X | X |
| Issues (non-turf) | | | |
| 15. Arms Control | X | X | X |
| 16. Detente | X | X | X |
| 17. Grain | X | X | X |
| 18. Intervention | X | X | X |
| 19. NATO Troops | X | X | X |
| 20. Terrorists | X | X | X |

The second table displays foreign policy dramas from the Peoria study, the third is the firefighter study, and the fourth is the farm management study.

In addition to the sixty to sixty-three card deck of dramatistic statements that these matrices represent, we also built a questionnaire that every subject filled out. In the case of the fire study, 400 subjects sorted

**Table 3**

**Fire Study**

|  | Suppression | Inspection | Public Education |
|---|---|---|---|
| **Dramatic Structure** | | | |
| 1. Plot Line | X | X | X |
| 2. Hero | X | X | X |
| 3. Villain | X | X | X |
| 4. Scene | X | X | X |
| 5. Cause (reality link) | X | X | X |
| **Attributes of Fire Educator** | | | |
| 6. Can educator be non fire fighter | X | X | X |
| 7. Responsibility to fire education | X | X | X |
| 8. Role mix of fire fighter/educator | X | X | X |
| 9. Time commitment in fire education | X | X | X |
| 10. Skills/knowledge level | X | X | X |
| 11. Motive | X | X | X |
| **Persona of Fire Education Program** | | | |
| 12. Education. Does it make a difference? | X | X | X |
| 13. Fire education contributes to fire service image | X | X | X |
| 14. Priority Choice; fire education vs. equipment | X | X | X |
| 15. What is public fire education? | X | X | X |
| 16. How do you measure program's effectiveness? | X | X | X |
| **Support for Fire Education Program** | | | |
| 17. City administrator | X | X | X |
| 18. Chief's view | X | X | X |
| 19. Public's view | X | X | X |
| 20. View of federal campaign on fire education | X | X | X |

the deck and filled out a questionnaire. In the farm management study, the 45 members of the divisions sorted the deck and filled out the questionnaire. So in two cases we had a stratified sample sufficiently large to generate to the population and in the latter case, we literally had a census.

The questionnaire contained the demographic, psychographic and sociographic questions that we needed in order to attach rhetoric to people. It is difficult to demonstrate that Bormann's metatheory is operating behind the building of the three-dimensional cubes, so allow us to select rhetorical statements from each one of the studies in an attempt to demonstrate how Bormann's theory operates in the building of these decks.

## Table 4
## Doane Study

|  | Tradition | Family | Profit-Oriented |
|---|---|---|---|
| **Dramatic Structure** | | | |
| 1. Sanctioning philosophy | X | X | X |
| 2. Doane Image | X | X | X |
| 3. Hero | X | X | X |
| 4. Villain | X | X | X |
| 5. Client | X | X | X |
| 6. Scene | X | X | X |
| **Division** | | | |
| 7. Division model | X | X | X |
| 8. Regional manager | X | X | X |
| 9. Training | X | X | X |
| 10. Job, work standard | X | X | X |
| 11. Motivation | X | X | X |
| 12. Satisfaction | X | X | X |
| 13. Job appraisal | X | X | X |
| **Product** | | | |
| 14. Product services | X | X | X |
| 15. Consultation | X | X | X |
| 16. Support services | X | X | X |
| **Marketing Strategy** | | | |
| 17. Doane competitive edge | X | X | X |
| 18. Marketing strategy | X | X | X |
| 19. Advertising | X | X | X |
| 20. Limits to new business | X | X | X |

In the political study, we discovered that any foreign policy rhetorical vision that had a chance of acceptance by the American people had to account for the "here-and-now" phenomena of Russia. So in that deck we built in a dramatization from the three rhetorical visions. They read respectively: (Cold War) "Despite all the claims to the contrary, Russia is still a Communist state. Its leaders still subscribe to the policy of world domination and they seek to enslave the free people of the world." (Isolationist) "Russia is becoming a more mixed state. It has moved from pure Socialism to a gradual introduction of capitalistic incentives. As trade increases with the West, it will become a technological state much like the United States." (Power Politics) "Russia today is more like the Romanoff Empire than the Stalin Regime. It is a super-power that will seek to expand its sphere of influence. It will interact with other major powers in rational ways that are in its self interest." Bormann's theory points to a need for the hero to be visible in a dramatic scene. In the fire study the scene cards read: (Suppressionist) "When I think of actually saving lives and property, I visualize a fire ground full of fire fighters and apparatus and equipment battling a raging fire." (Inspection) "When I think of saving lives and property, I visualize fire fighters vigorously inspecting buildings for code violations and seeing that buildings are brought up to code." (Fire Education) "When I think of saving lives and property, I visualize a room full of wide-eyed children listening to a talk on how to make their homes safe from fire and what to do in case of fire."

Bormann also talks about the necessity of a sanctioning agent that justifies the drama. In our study of the Doane Farm Management Division we found that the sanctioning agent was a necessary element that had to be built into the three visions. Thus, the sanctioning philosophy for the three visions in this deck are as follows: (Traditional) "The governing philosophy of the Doane Company is to bring modern scientific agricultural practices to farming communities in order to save the land and maintain continuous profit for the absentee landowner through professional management supervision." (Family Company) "The governing philosophy of the Doane Company is to maximize profit. Each employee has an obligation to maximize profitability of their job function for both their own and the company's good.

We have discovered that it is not necessary to systematically replicate all the dramatic elements of the three different visions in order to determine who is participating in that vision. The same is true with respect to "here-and-now" events. Not all "here-and-now" events need to be listed, but only those that produce essential differences between the three visions, if in fact the purpose of your research is to attach different rhetorics to different people.

An initial observation that we have made in the course of building rhetorical visions into a deck is that we find that three visions tend to exhaust most of the potential fantasizing on a subject. By that we mean that we find it difficult in our research to systematically structure in a fourth vision.

Obviously, in theory there could be as many different rhetorical visions as there are people, but for purposes of research we find that the three major or most widely "chained-out" visions are sufficient for most research projects in that most people will be attached to one of the three major dramas.

However, time and some half-dozen studies have tempered this observation. We now have the data to indicate the existence of deep structure to Bormann's meta-theory. In essence, just as Freud described the id, ego and super ego as warring factions, so, too, are there warring rhetorical dramas and there are three. One is pragmatic, one is social, and one is righteous. These deep structure dramas are akin to William James' three types of self: the social, the spiritual and the material.[11] This discovery was made possible by viewing Bormann's theory as a meta-theory.

Once we have had a sufficiently large sample of subjects sort the deck, we then factor-analyze their sorting behavior and the resultant factors are essentially separate visions. We then attach the people to the vision and merely do first a frequency count on their answers to the questionnaire and then a discriminant analysis that determines which questions on the questionnaire discriminate people from one vision to another. This particular procedure has allowed us to produce useful answers to the questions that were asked of us. For example, in the fire study, we were able to discover that there were basically four characteristics which predicted in seven out of ten cases that a given fire fighter would be participating in the public fire education drama. The four variables were: years of formal education, the existence of photography and art as a hobby, and high scores on two separate artistic creativity tests. Furthermore, we discovered that the fire fighters that opposed public fire education, while quite vocal in the fire service, were in the distinct minority when we summed up how many people were participating in what visions.

In the Doane organizational study, we were able to discover that all their regional managers were divided into two other rhetorical dramas. By looking at each issue, we were able to isolate specifically what "here-and-now" events were being dramatized differently, and thus set the groundwork for a retraining in the organization. The cattle research essentially revealed that the cattle industry is divided, for purposes of Upjohn's product, into six market segments. Four of those segments are potential buyers and two are non-buyers. Furthermore, we were able to specify exactly what characteristics cattle people possess that were most likely to buy the product, and also what specific fantasy themes they responded to with respect to grouping their calves and producing uniform calf weights at 205 days. The cattle research was subsequently used to design advertising, promotional and educational materials that hopefully will be effective in inducing cattle people to buy the new product, and use it correctly.

Our use of Bormann's dramatistic rhetorical theory as a metatheory for constructing rhetorical visions, combined with the methodology we have

[11]William James, *The Principles of Psychology* (New York: Henry Holt, 1890).

developed has been quite successful. The people who are using the results of this dramatistic research are quite pleased with what we have found. We are pleased that a rhetorical theory is governing this research and certainly if one is going to design persuasive communication to induce cooperation of some population of people, there ought to be a theory that governs the generation of those messages, and if there is such a theory, then that theory should be used in analyzing the audience before the messages are designed. Thus, we feel that our application of Bormann's theory is quite traditional in terms of the way in which we use it. That is to say that we have taken a rhetorical theory, used it as a means for analyzing an audience, and then have taken the results of that analysis and designed rhetorical messages that should be persuasive.

The problem that is currently troubling us relates not to the effectiveness of Bormann's theory or the procedures we have adapted it to, but really to the larger ethical question that was raised in the mass media when we first applied this procedure to politics. The theory is utilitarian. The questions is, is it ethical to use this theory in the way that we have done? Some of our students who have helped us build these decks insist that we should put on the front of each Q-deck a warning which would indicate that they should sort this deck at their own risk, for once they have revealed themselves through the sorting behavior and answering the questionnaires, we will know significant things about them. We suspect that it is the same sort of problem that Freudian psychoanalysts experienced when Freud's theory was not widely known. By that we mean, if a naive subject, decades ago, was asked to lie on the counselor's couch and describe his/her dreams, they might do so with great honesty and detail, and of course, those dreams were used as a means for analysis of the person's psyche. However, once subjects became aware of the assumptions behind Freud's theory and how Freud constructed reality, they then began to claim that they didn't dream. To counter this, psychoanalysts used sodium pentothal in an effort to induce them to describe their dreams and then they discovered that even in their subconscious, subjects doctored their dreams. So we suspect that as Bormann's theory gets more widely dispersed people will learn to conceal their fantasies and ultimately the rhetorical visions they participate in. However, the ethical question we wish to address is that once we have analyzed an audience in terms of their rhetorical visions, and we construct messages that we hope will be effective based on that research, what is an ethically designed message using Bormann's theory?

We have some benchmarks for ethics with respect to other rhetorical theories. For example, with Aristotelian theory, we have some notion of a well-made logical argument. Typically our argumentation books will discuss correct use of logic and the correct use of evidence. Furthermore, we have developed some general ground rules for the use of fear appeals and the balance between pathos and logos. However, with respect to Bormann's theory, we have no such guidelines. For example, what is regarded as too much use of heroic persona? Or, what is an unethical application of villain description? In other words, we simply do not have any guidelines for what would be the "ought" construction of an ethically sound persuasive speech based upon Bormann's dramatistic rhetorical theory. Frankly, given the results that we have obtained in our applied communication research, we think that ethics is a major issue.

In summation, then, we are convinced that Bormann's theory can function as a metatheory to build rhetorical visions of any "here-and-now" phenomena of any given population, and that this metatheory, combined with the procedures that we have developed, can prove to be highly utilitarian in such fields as political campaigns and market research. However, we are currently struggling with the ethical criteria we should be applying to ourselves in doing such research.

# PART II:

## Using the Theory to Critique
## Contemporary American Rhetoric

# II: Using the Theory to Critique Contemporary American Rhetoric

Neo-Aristotelian scholarship dominated the study of American Public Address from the 1930's to the mid-1960's. Such scholarship emphasized in traditional Aristotelian fashion the resources of the speaker. This school of criticism is reflected in the Speech Association of America's three-volume series, *A History and Criticism of American Public Address*.

The neo-Aristotelian approach contains a rich set of terms for describing, interpreting and evaluating a speaker's speech or set of speeches. Nevertheless, Aristotelian-based theory does not function well as a means for describing, interpreting and evaluating large slices of American Public Address, nor does it work well in keeping a common record of what is American public rhetoric. Instead, we find that scholars relying on Aristotelian-based theory have explained American Public Address by stringing together "great speakers" and "great speeches."

The neo-Aristotelian method as it was applied at its height in the 1940's and 1950's provided for the most part a rational explanation of public rhetoric, with a clear disdain for what it labeled irrational, emotional appeals. Thus for us, Aristotelian-based theoretical explanations of speaking phenomena did not provide a very satisfying explanation of why tens of thousands of people would cheer hysterically when Alabama Governor George Wallace said, "By God, if one of those long-haired hippies laid down in front of my car, it would be the last time"; or why many thousands of people still get teary eyed when they hear a recording of John F. Kennedy saying, "Ask not what your country can do for you, but ask what you can do for your country"; or Martin Luther King relating, "I had a dream last night."

The four essays included in this section illustrate the kind of description, interpretation and evaluation of American rhetoric that Bormann's theoretical lens allows. The first piece sketches out the formation of a large American rhetorical vision that we commonly refer to as "The Cold War." The piece shows that rhetorical dramas compete with each other as contradictory explanations of the same phenomena—in this case American foreign policy. This discovery of the competitive nature of rhetorical dramas becomes important in later essays where the theory is applied to organizational and marketing research.

The second essay provides a new interpretation of the traditional meaning of rhetorical strategy. It then illustrates the utility of using Bormann's theory as a means for critiquing social movements.

The third essay demonstrates that the ostensibly objective reporting of Malcom X's black unity addresses might be seriously questioned if Bormann's dramatistic theory is used to examine the speeches themselves and the media's reaction. The piece documents that the press dramatized Malcolm X and his views in a villainous social reality that was contrary to the drama present in the messages as well as the drama in which Malcolm X was participating.

In the final essay, Bormann focuses on one media fantasy, the Eagleton Affair, and traces it from its inception through its full development. In so doing, he explains how fantasies are created and how they might be controlled. This discovery proved valuable in creating a schemata for a communication-based political campaign that is presented in the next section.

The four essays together illustrate the ability of Bormann's theory to provide useful applied communication insights about American public address.

# 4

# The Origins and Nature of the Cold War Rhetorical Vision 1946-1972:

## A Partial History

### JOHN F. CRAGAN

The Cold War rhetorical vision that so many Americans participated in during the 1940's and the 1950's had lost much of its saliency by the 1970's. A few of the dramatic lines crop up now and then, however. Small clusters of Americans still are moved by various scenes from the original drama but there is the distinct feeling of an empty theater and the smell of musty chairs. The original film has been spliced and re-spliced so often that it has lost much of its wholesomeness. The show is over.

However, before we turn out the lights it may be useful to rerun the film one more time, stopping for comments on what seem to be the crucial points. Obviously, in this manuscript I cannot record the entire rhetorical history of the Cold War or in much detail, sketch its origins. However, I do believe there is space for an overview of the origins and nature of the Cold War.[1]

The method of criticism used in this paper was developed by Ernest B. Bormann.[2]

The Cold War, like World Wars I and II, was staged on a grand scale. In the first and second World Wars, America emerged victorious. The evil forces out to dominate and enslave the world had been defeated. The dramatic setting for the Cold War followed an established pattern. What was new about the dramatization of this war was the antithetical coldness of the conflict taking place in the shadow of the atomic mushroom cloud with

---

[1]For a more complete treatment of Cold War rhetoric see John F. Cragan, "The Cold War Rhetorical Vision: 1946-1972, Diss. University of Minnesota, 1972; also see John F. Cragan and Donald C. Shields, "Foreign Policy Communication Drama: How Mediated Rhetoric Played in Peoria in Campaign '76," *Quarterly Journal of Speech,* 63 (1977); and Wayne Brockriede and Robert L. Scott, *Moments in the Rhetoric of the Cold War* (New York: Random House, 1970).

[2]See "Fantasy and Rhetorical Vision: The Rhetorical Criticism of Social Reality," *Quarterly Journal of Speech,* 58 (1972), 396-407; "The Eagleton Affair: A Fantasy Theme Analysis," *Quarterly Journal of Speech,* 59 (1973), 143-159; and "Fetching Good Out of Evil: A Rhetorical Use of Calamity," *Quarterly Journal of Speech*, 63 (1977), 130-139.

its promise of fearful heat. In the new war for the hearts and minds of men, the battle was frozen between appeasement and the bomb. The rhetorical vision of the Cold War chained out and was firmly established in the minds of most Americans by 1948. Between 1945 and 1948, a struggle took place between three transitory rhetorical visions as they sought to explain the rapidly changing events on the international scene.

The rhetorical visions of One World of Wendell Willkie, Power Politics of Walter Lippmann, and Red Fascism of Karl Mundt constitute the immediate rhetorical origins of the Cold War vision.

## Origins of the Cold War Rhetorical Vision

As World War II commenced, the American people began participating in a war mobilization rhetoric that drew battle lines between the "peace-loving" and "aggressor" nations. In this rhetoric, America fantasized a future world in which the peace loving would form a world government based on democratic laws and not force. The last days of the second World War not only marked the end of the hot war rhetoric but the chaining out of a new rhetorical vision that was labelled, One World. The One World vision drew its persuasive power from the new world experience. The basic vision of pre-war American isolationism was enlarged to encompass the world of nation states. Just as America had learned to reject the "old world" of Power Politics, so now the world had finally learned from the destruction of World War II that military alliances and secret diplomacy must be rejected or the atomic bomb would annihilate us all. The One Worlders saw the past history of man as a series of unending wars with each new war more destructive than the last. The cause of these wars was Power Politics. The two important events for the participants of this vision were World War II and the atomic bomb. The One World vision dramatized the horrors of World War II and the power of the bomb as new experiences that altered the world situation. Messages reflecting this rhetorical vision presented a social reality of these two events that would clearly lead peace-loving nations away from the world of power and war and into the One World of reason and peace.

The One World speakers tended to ignore the dramatization of appeasement of totalitarianism leading to war and stressed instead the drama of millions of people who had just died in the cause of peace and if we did not stay away from Power Politics, then they would have died in vain. The One World drama was set in the future so the One World speakers dramatized the nature of the utopia that would accompany the world government. In an effort to provide a precise description of what the ideal world government would look like, the One Worlders dramatized historical examples of a smaller scale. Arthur Vandenburg repeatedly referred to the General Assembly of the United Nations as: "The town meeting of the world."[3]

---

[3]Arthur H. Vandenburg, "What Is Russia Up To," *Vital Speeches,* March 15, 1946, p. 323.

Colina asserted: "The tradonal view of sovereignty is an obsolete concept. It runs counter to reality, to the evident contradiction of the planet in terms of time and space. It belongs to the bygone era of slow communication and leisurely living."[4]

The hero of the One World drama was the idealistic American who envisioned a world government by democratic laws. In the One World vision, Woodrow Wilson emerged as the martyred hero of the past. As one speaker put it: "After the first World War, the great idealist, Woodrow Wilson, thought he saw a way to avoid that sort of thing, (wars) and his child, the League of Nations was born with which his nation would not affiliate."[5]

The hero of the One World vision was aware that the non-believers regarded him as a dreamer, an isolationist who had replaced Woodrow Wilson's fourteen points in the League of Nations with Roosevelt's four freedoms in the UNO. The hero did not reject the label, idealist, but instead referred to himself as a "practical idealist."[6] He believed he was an idealist in the Wilson tradition in that he believed that peace could only be achieved through a world government that replaced raw force with democratic laws. He believed he was a pragmatist and that the experience of World War II and the advent of the atomic age left the world with only two choices: government by law or the destruction of civilization. As Mr. Hoyt said: "It must be now the one world of Wendell Willkie or no world of the evil one."[7]

The villain of the One World drama was the pessimist who believed that the old practice of Power Politics was the only way to maintain world order. From the time of George Washington, the villain had engaged in the evil, selfish, unethical practice of Power Politics. The villainous activity of nation states playing Power Politics had led Europe into one brawl after another and if not stopped, it would lead to the destruction of mankind.

Owen Roberts, former Justice to the United States Supreme Court, argued that before World War I, "Nations wrangled what they wanted by the threat of force, by diplomacy as it was called."[8] James Byrnes reasoned that: "After World War I, there was a tendency to regard the League of Nations as something outside the ordinary range of foreign policy. Governments continued on old binds, pursuing individual aims, and following the path of power politics."[9]

Americans had always taken pride in the fact that the United States did not engage in the selfish practice of Power Politics. We were the pure,

[4]Rafael de la Colina, "The Americas and the World." *Vital Speeches,* February 15, 1946, p. 263.

[5]Owen J. Roberts, "Real World Parliament to Keep Peace." *Vital Speeches,* May 1, 1946, p. 426.

[6]James F. Byrnes, "Common Interests Far Outweigh Conflicting Interests," *Vital Speeches,* February 1, 1946, p. 240.

[7]Palmer Hoyt, "Last Chance," *Vital Speeches,* November 1, 1945, p. 60.

[8]Roberts, p. 426.

[9]Byrnes, p. 242.

moral nation that had avoided entangling alliances. The One World rhetorical visions retained the power of the old American Isolationist vision and intended to present the villain as internal to America, by describing the selfish power plays of domestic politics. For example, it was the political wrangling on the domestic scene that had caused the United States to reject the League of Nations. Wendell Willkie stated:

> I am satisfied that the American people never deliberately and intentionally turned their backs on the program for international cooperation. Possibly they would have preferred changes in the precise Versailles covenant, but not complete aloofness from the efforts of other nations. They were betrayed by leaders without conviction who were thinking in terms of group vote-catching and partisan advantage.[10]

In the One World vision of history, the people of the world had been victims of Power Politics. The hero and villain of the One World vision were known not by their race, nationality, religion, dress, or even their past behavior. The bomb and past war experience had taught all people that a new international behavior was needed. From now on, governments and their leaders would be judged by their new actions. If they engaged in open discussion and made public their agreements, then peace would be obtained within the framework of world government.

Whether the UNO was a town-house meeting, a world parliament, or a congress, the critical element that was out of focus was the nature of Russia. Russia had been a wartime ally but she was a communist nation and Joseph Stalin was the dictator. All three post-war visions had to deal with the meaning of Russia and her intentions. The One World vision could not plausibly account for the behavior of Russia after the war. The here-and-now events that were occurring in Eastern Europe in 1946 and 1947, combined with the unsuccessful negotiations that were taking place in the UNO, could not be explained by Willkie's characterization of Russia. As Russia lost the label of "peace-loving," she acquired its opposite, "aggressor." Thus, in 1946, Arthur Vandenburg argued before the United States Senate that: "Let us remember that the General Assembly pledged itself to encourage a world wide free press through the instrumentation to be created at its next session in September. Black-outs and iron curtains are not the insignia of liberty nor the trademark of peace."[11]

The ultimate sanction of the rhetoric of One World was the horror of atomic war. For the people who participated in the vision, the final, ultimate question was always, How can we avoid an atomic holocaust? The atomic bomb meant that world government was the only hope for mankind. They argued that Power Politics was the cause of past wars and would lead to the last one. They further believed that America's experience with democracy had provided a model that the world could adopt. Their ultimate frustration was that their vision was not seen by everybody. When the vision of

[10]Wendell L. Willkie, *One World* (New York: Simon and Schuster, 1943), pp. 199-200.
[11]Vandenburg, p. 323.

atomic destruction proved to be an insufficient justification for persuading nations to adopt a world government, the rhetoric contained no other rationale for why nations should surrender their sovereignty. The first two meetings of the UNO did not produce a world government and when international events indicated a return of power diplomacy, some speakers began to argue that the world government was the eventual goal but that Power Politics was the means to that end.

The rhetoric of Power Politics took the same here-and-now phenomena that the One Worlders and the Red Fascism dramas worked with but weaved a different symbolic reality. The Power Politics drama was sanctioned by the superior knowledge and intellect of the foreign policy specialists of the "informed" elite cadres in the American society. The drama was one of a world of competing nation states—an international struggle between Russia and the United States, the obstacle in the drama was not Russia but an uninformed and emotional citizenry that was participating in unrealistic fantasies (One World and Red Fascism). Thus, the historical dramas featured an American policy which was fluctuating between war and peace with no place for diplomacy. The way to avoid war was not world government or another ideological crusade but wise mature diplomacy. As Walter Lippmann stated: "If only our people would abjure their illusions about the nature of the world in which they have so recently become a leading power and would permit and assist those who wanted to form a policy, we can survive."[12] Regardless of how Power Politics was viewed by the One Worlders, its advocates believed it to be the only alternative the United States had. "If we will not use the classic procedures of diplomacy, which is always a combination of power and compromise—then the best we can look forward to is an era of disintegration in the civilized world followed by a war which once it begins will be savage and universal and indecisive."[13] The rhetoricians of the Power Politics vision presented the international scene as one dominated by two major powers—the Soviet Union and Russia. It was motivated not because one nation was peace-loving and the other was aggressive nor because of basic differences between communism and capitalism, but rather because England, France, Germany and Japanese power had declined and a new power would have to fill the vacuum.

The advocates of Power Politics dramatize themselves as realists. They rejected the competing visions as too simple. The One World vision was naive and the Red Fascism vision was simplistic and evangelistic. The Power Politics vision had the hero projected as a rational, cool-thinking political analyst who carefully assessed each critical variable while the villain was not Russia but by and large a personification of the American people—a sort of naive, emotional, uninformed John Q. Public. As professor of political science, Raymond McKelvey stated in 1945: "The American public is

[12]Walter Lippmann, "Philosophy and United States Foreign Policy, *Vital Speeches,* January 15, 1948, p. 244.
[13]*Ibid.*

likened to an innocent maiden plucking petals from a daisy murmuring, 'He loves me, he loves me not;' she is tossed into ecstasy or thrown into despair depending on the outcome of her petal count."[14] According to Spanier, the American people were characterized as believing that: "Peace is a state of harmony among nations while our wars become idealized crusades to make the world safe for democracy."[15] Walter Lippmann stated that it was the hero's task to find some middle ground between the two emotional states of the American people.[16]

The Power Politics vision did not long walk the tightrope between the twin villains of isolationism on one hand and evangelistic crusade to eradicate communism on the other, for it was very easy to dramatize the power expansion of the Soviet Union as spreading international communism which fit the Red Fascism drama. In fact, George Kennan, in his memoirs, laments the fact that his famous "x" article, which was written from the perspective of the Power Politics vision, was responsible for stimulating the chaining of fantasy themes that supported the Red Fascism view of American foreign policy. Kennan reports the term "containment" was "picked up and elevated by the press to the status of 'doctrine'—in this way it was established before our eyes, so to speak, one of those indestructible myths that were the bane of the historian." Kennan felt as though he had inadvertently loosened a large boulder from the top of a cliff and now helplessly witnessed its path of destruction to the valley below."[17] Kennan was indeed accurate in that it was in part the combination of Power Politics policies wrapped up in a Red Fascism rhetoric that best characterized the initial formation of the Cold War rhetoric.

The rhetorical vision of Red Fascism essentially portrays the struggle between good and evil. The evil was characterized as communistic slavery and the good was democratic freedom. Just as Hitler had conspired to enslave free men, so now Joseph Stalin was attempting the same thing using the same tactics. Communism and fascism had been linked together as expressions of totalitarianism for many Americans since the early 1930's.[18] The Hitler-Stalin pact during World War II simply strengthened the symbolic identification for many Americans. The Red Fascism vision took the same dramatic form as the wartime fantasy themes related to Nazi Germany. Speakers who participated in the Red Fascism vision provided a detailed

---

[14]Raymond G. McKelvey, "Daisies and Foreign Policy," *Vital Speeches*, December 1, 1945, p. 112.

[15]John Spanier, *American Foreign Policy Since World War II* (2d ed. rev: New York: Frederick A. Praeger, 1965), p. 14. The original edition was published in 1960.

[16]Lippmann, *Philosophy and United States Foreign Policy*, p. 244.

[17]George F. Kennan, *Memoirs 1925-1950* (Boston: Little, Brown and Co., p. 356; also see "x" (George F. Kennan), "The Sources of Soviet Conduct," *Foreign Affairs*, July, 1947, pp. 566-582; and Walter Lippmann, *The Cold War: A Study in the U.S. Foreign Policy (New York: Harper and Row, 1947)*.

[18]Les K. Adler and Thomas G. Paterson, "Red Fascism: The Merger of Nazi Germany and Soviet Russia in the American Image of Totalitarianism, 1930's-1950's," *American Historical Review* LXXV (April, 1970), 1046-1064.

comparison of the internal activities of nazi Germany and communist Russia. Senator Mundt observed that Russia has: "A policy exactly as Hitler's Gestapo called the NKVD."[19] General John R. Deane, in his book, *Strange Alliance*, commented that the marching of Russian soldiers "closely resembled the goosestep with arms rigid and legs kicked so stiffly to the front."[20] The Red Fascism drama saw an international conspiracy which was a replay of the Nazi conspiracy of the 1930's. The hero of the Red Fascism drama was the hero of World War II, namely the defender of freedom, the American patriot. By 1946, Red Fascism speakers were calling for the American hero to go forth again in the defense of world freedom. John Foster Dulles stated: "We Americans have played a leading part in the struggle for freedom...we must demonstrate in the present what our forebears have demonstrated in the past—that individual human freedoms can gloriously serve mankind."[21] Senator Dirksen echoed Dulles when he stated: "Lift your eyes like the prophets of old and look at the world horizon. Freedom is in jeopardy and hundreds of millions of people are looking to this country for a ray of hope."[22]

The Red Fascism hero was a loyal patriotic American who was "willing to stand up and be counted."[23] The villain was a Red Fascist out to subjugate the world. Although the rhetoricians of Red Fascism painted an international scene in which communists were on the march, fantasies usually focused on the internal communists who were boring from within. "The greatest danger to our American heritage of liberty comes not from without but from within. It comes not from open frontal assault but from a process of sapping and undermining"[24] And as J. Edgar Hoover often asserted: "The divide and conquer tactics did not die with Hitler. They are being employed with great skill today by American communists with their 'boring from within strategy'"[25] Attorney General Tom Clark, in a speech before the American Bar Association in 1945, pointed out that: "We know that there is a national and international conspiracy to divide our people, to discredit our institutions, and to bring about disrespect for our government."[26]

The Red Fascism fantasies portrayed the communists as a small but effective group. They were effective because they duped many liberal

[19]Karl E. Mundt, "Can We Get Along With Russia?" *Vital Speeches*, June 15, 1947, p. 518.

[20]John R. Deane, *Strange Alliance* (New York, 1947), p. 216, quoted in Adler and Paterson, p. 1053.

[21]John Foster Dulles, "State Control Versus Self-Control," *Vital Speeches*, July 15, 1946., p. 594.

[22]Everett McK. Dirksen, "Red Fascism," *Vital Speeches*, April 1, 1947, p. 359.

[23]J. Edgar Hoover, "Our Achilles' Heel," *Vital Speeches*, October 15, 1946, p. 11. Also see J. Edgar Hoover, "Red Fascism in the United States Today," *American Magazine*, February, 1947, p. 24.

[24]William Harry Chamberlain, "Liberty Pays Off," *Vital Speeches*, January 1, 1947, p. 174.

[25]Hoover, p. 10.

[26]Tom C. Clark, September 18, 1948, Stephen Spingarn Papers, White House Assignment, Harry S. Truman Library, quoted in Adler and Paterson, p. 1055.

elements of our society into doing their work. The people that associated with them and conspired with the communists, were referred to as "communist sympathizers," "fellow travelers," "phony liberals," or "progressives." And, in fact, by as early as 1948, Karl Mundt made an accusation in a speech in Chicago on June 4, 1948, which was typical of the Red Fascism rhetoric. He stated: It was not a pleasant thing when the FBI said 'you have over 200 communists in the State Department, Mr. President, who got in under the authority of your predecessor in office.'"[27]

In 1946 and 1947, the Red Fascism vision participants felt that a fight was on to save freedom for "the time will come and it may be close at hand when it will be essential to our national safety to break up the communist conspiracy."[28] The believers in the vision felt that the war with Russia was inevitable but that it would not occur for ten or fifteen years. In the meantime, America had to stop appeasing communists on the international scene and we had to stop communist infiltration and refurbish American freedoms at home.

As the American people listened to the fruitless debates in the UN, and as they read fantasy themes dramatizing the disturbing events in Europe, the Red Fascism vision became more credible. However, it was the Truman Doctrine speech that dramatized fantasy themes which chained out across the country and contributed greatly to the emergence of a global rhetorical vision of the world in the grips of a "Cold War." Truman's declaration of war projected the domestic drama of Red Fascism on the international scene and a total rhetorical vision was created in the minds of many Americans. In the next several years, an abundant number of here-and-now events would occur to sustain the Cold War rhetorical vision.

On July 2, 1947, Russia and all eastern European countries rejected the Marshall Plan. On October 5, the Cominform was created. On November 21, opposition parties in Poland and Hungary were dissolved. On December 24, Greek gorillas formed a provincial government. On February 16, 1948, the Czechoslovakian government fell. On June 20, the Berlin Blockade began. In 1949, the Russians exploded an atomic bomb and the Chinese People's Republic was proclaimed. In 1950, the Korean War began. As these events unfolded, the villains of the Red Fascism vision became villains of the Cold War rhetoric and most Americans were participating in the social reality plagued by these hosts of evil—communist conspirators.

## Cold War Rhetorical Vision

The Cold War fantasies became, by 1948, a total rhetorical vision which explained and justified American foreign policy for the next several decades. The rhetoric and action of the Truman Administration enlarged

[27]Karl E. Mundt, "The Mundt-Nixon Bill," *Vital Speeches,* July 1, 1948, p. 556.
[28]William C. Bullitt, "The Communist Creed," *Vital Speeches,* May 15, 1947, p. 463.

the Red Fascism vision to encompass the international scene. The Truman Administration's foreign policy rhetoric and the Red Fascism vision blended together to form fantasy themes that chained out through American audiences to create a coherent rhetorical vision—the rhetoric of the Cold War. Cold War fantasy themes chained out immediately after the Truman Doctrine speech. The newspapers and magazine commentators instantly participated in the drama of a declaration of war. Harrison Smith, in an editorial entitled: "The Die is Cast," included: "Our President has thrown down the gauge of battle. Our hat is in the ring and there must be no other end to it but success."[29] *The Chicago Tribune* reported: "Mr. Truman made as cold a war speech against Russia as any President has ever made except in the occasion of going before Congress to ask for the declaration of war."[30] The caption for James Reston's editorial on March 3, 1947, read: "Truman's Speech Likened to 1823 and 1941 Warnings."[31] Harold Chancellor's article on the European reaction to the Truman speech contained the subheading: "Diplomats in Paris Declare New Monroe Doctrine Must Force Soviet Showdown and Plan Would Have Halted Hitler."[32]

The World War II scenario of Hitler in nazi Germany was transposed to Stalin and Communist Russia. Chamberlain in England may have appeased Hitler at Munich but Truman in the United States would not appease Stalin in Greece and Turkey or anywhere else in the world, for that matter. The use of the Monroe Doctrine as a referent point forecasted critical elements of the Cold War vision. One element, the defensive posture in America, was quickly tagged "containment." Another element was the expansion of America's protective shield. Now the United States was not only the guardian of America's but of all the free people's of the world. Norman Graebner's argument that: "The assumption that Stalinistic behavior posed a moral rather than a physical challenge created the illusion that a sufficient response lay somewhere in the realm of verbal disapprobation."[33] The analogy to the Monroe Doctrine was clearly the appropriate reference.

The Cold War was a psychological rather than a shooting war but the traditional rhetorical visions of Americans contained a set of terms and fantasy themes with which to give meaning to war efforts. The most salient rhetoric, of course, came from World War II. Yet speakers felt a tension between the two. Thus, most speeches on the Cold War made an effort to define exactly what kind of war we were waging. James F. Byrnes stated: "We are engaged in a Cold War with the Soviet Republic. It is a

[29]Harrison Smith, "The Die is Cast," *The Saturday Review of Literature,* April 5, 1947, p. 22.
[30]*Chicago Tribune,* cited in "Extracts from American Editorial Comment on President Truman's Message, *New York Times,* March 13, 1947, p. 4.
[31]James Reston, "Truman's Speech Likened to 1923 and 1941 Warnings," *New York Times,* March 13, 1947, p. 3.
[32]Harold Callender, "Europe is Amazed by Blunt Warning," *New York Times,* March 13, 1947, p. 3.
[33]Norman A. Graebner, *Cold War Diplomacy: American Foreign Policy, 1945-1960* (New Jersey: D. Van Nostrand Co., 1962), p. 36.

clash between two ideologies—it is a battle for the minds of people. Communism must be fought on principle."[34]

Post-1948 rhetoric in the United States was dominated by dramas of war. Some typical titles on American foreign policy are: "We Declare War,"[35] "Waging the Cold War,"[36] "The United States Tactics and the Cold War: Gains and Losses,"[37] "One Way to Win the Cold War,"[38] and "We Can Win the Cold War."[39] The way in which the war would be fought was also commonly understood by 1948. The Red Fascism vision had already laid out the domestic policy. The Truman Doctrine, the Marshall Plan, and the "x" article not only legitimized the "red hunt" at home but formed the frame for international action. On the home front, we had to immunize ourselves against communism. As John Foster Dulles proclaimed, "Peace requires that the free societies be so healthy that we can repel communist penetration just as a healthy body repels malignant germs. That is the only way to prevent communistic dictatorships from so spreading that they will isolate us and eventually strangle us."[40]

On the international front, we would defend democracy from aggression. *The Saturday Evening Post* shows us how Red Fascism has been enlarged to become a new global vision. *The Post* saw that the Monroe Doctrine had been expanded to include all non-communistic nations, thus just as we protected the Western Hemisphere from foreignisms, now the free world would be behind the United States' protective shield.[41]

Walter Lippmann is generally cited as the person who first applied the phrase, "Cold War" to the United States-Soviet conflict.[42] He was successful in his efforts to frame a rhetorical stance somewhere between total peace and total war. However, the irony is that his term did not come to mean diplomacy in the sense of the Power Politics vision but came to summarize an ideological war that was in keeping with Red Fascism. Louis Halle indicates that prior to Lippmann's popularization of the term, the phrase "Cold War" was "loosely used in the 1930's to describe the activities of 'fifth columns'."[43] The term Cold War did not appear as a subject heading in the *Reader's Guide* until May, 1947. The *Reader's Guide* does not list any articles directly under the Cold War but refers the reader to other headings. The first reference to other headings was: "Psychological Warfare." Almost every speech on American foreign policy during the early part of the Cold War would present the cast of heroes and villains in the Cold War

---

[34]James F. Byrnes, "Preserve People's Rights," *Vital Speeches,* December 1, 1949, p. 100.
[35]"We Declare War," *Catholic World,* May, 1947, p. 97.
[36]R.G. Coroherd, "Waging the Cold War," *Current History*, December, 1948, p. 334.
[37]"U.S. Tactics in the 'Cold War,'" *U.S. News and World Report,* September 24, 1948, p. 11.
[38]"One Way to Win the 'Cold War,'" *U.S. News and World Report,* May 5, 1950, p. 52.
[39]Constantine W. Boldyreff, "We Can Win the Cold War," *Reader's Digest,* November, 1950, p. 9.
[40]John Foster Dulles, "Not War, Not Peace," *Vital Speeches*, February 15, 1948, p. 272.
[41]"Why the Truman Doctrine Makes Sense," *Saturday Evening Post,* July 5, 1947, p. 120.
[42]Louis J. Halle, *The Cold War as History* (London: Chatto and Windus, 1967), p. 136.
[43]*Ibid.*

drama, a vision in dramatic conflict. President Truman's inaugural address on May 20, 1949, is rather typical in its dramatic construction of democracy on the one hand and communism on the other. Although Truman's comparison of good and bad people is not nearly as vivid as most speeches of that day, the fact that it would constitute the main thrust of his inaugural indicates that the drama was widespread at the time.

> Communism is based on the belief that man is so weak and inadequate that he is unable to govern himself and therefore requires the rule of strong masters. Democracy is based on the conviction that man has to govern himself with reason and justice. Communism subjects the individual to arrest without lawful cause, punishment without trial, and forced labor as a chattel of the state.[44]

The hero of the Cold War was confronted with a dangerous villain. As one speaker said: "It is like an octopus—communism has stretched out its tentacles into our schools, into our sacred institutions, into our governmental bodies—even into some of our highest offices in the federal government."[45] Many American came to fear that if the octopus "fastened its blood-sucking tentacles upon many phases of American life the United States itself would be dragged down into a Red Sea."[46]

The American communist, like the rest of the communists in the world, were controlled from Russia "by desperate, ruthless, unscrupulous men who had no respect for human life; men who would not hesitate to plunge mankind into another bloodbath if we leave them any chance of winning world domination."[47]

The Cold War vision clearly presented an Orwellian nightmare should the hero lose the war to the communist villain. However, the vision of the Cold War contained an alternative to the war scenario. If the hero responded to the international conspiracy, the communists could be defeated and world peace could still be won.

America, due to her basic good nature, was not capable of starting a shooting war. Also, remembering Munich, she was not going to appease the villain. While this placed the American democracy at a disadvantage, she still had the assets that would eventually bring her victory. "We have tremendous advantages in the struggle for men's minds and loyalties. We have truth and freedom on our side."[48][7] Most Americans believed that the goodness of America, characterized by democracy and freedom, would ultimately prevail.[49]

The Cold War vision clearly contained in it the motive that "if we

---

[44]Harry S. Truman, "The Faith by Which We Live," *Vital Speeches*, February 1, 1949, p. 226.

[45]George N. Craig, "For This We Fight," *Vital Speeches,* October 15, 1951, p. 19.

[46]Thurman Sensing, "America Faces Destiny," *Vital Speeches,* April 15, 1948, p. 402.

[47]Styles Bridges, "American Foreign Policy and Communism," *Vital Speeches,* April 15, 1948, p. 393.

[48]Harry S. Truman, "The Faith by Which We Live," p. 228.

[49]*Public Opinion Quarterly,* Spring, 1950, p. 192.

dedicated ourselves to it with the same conviction and confidence that
marked our efforts from 1941 to 1945," we can win the war.[50]

As speech after speech chained out the character sketches of the
American hero, they created meaning, aroused emotions, and developed
motives that controlled a great deal of behavior of the American people, as
the Cold War drama unfolded in the 1950's and 1960's. For purposes of a
more detailed criticism, three major heroic character types existed in the
Cold War vision. The three types are the heroic missionary for freedom, the
heroic American facing the perils of the atomic age, and the heroic competitive America.[51] However, in this paper, I will focus on the Missionary
American hero as a means of illustrating the Cold War vision from 1948 to
1972.

## The Missionary American

The rhetorical vision that chained out in 1948 had defined the Cold War
as a war for the hearts and minds of men. Psychological warfare and propaganda were important weapons in this war. However, these words did not
set well with Americans. Psychological warfare seemed sneaky and
villainous. The dramas that stemmed from the Cold War thus often had as
their hero a man of truth. He was direct. He said exactly what he meant and
meant exactly what he said.

The hero as missionary for freedom was not only free himself but he was
a Christian and the Cold War vision was steeped in religious metaphors.
The hero did not propagandize the world rather he preached the truth and
with the zeal of a missionary he would convert the world to
"Americanism." The metaphor that came to connote America's role is a
religious crusade.

Americanism was the hero's brand of political religion. Rallying the
people for the cause of freedom could well have ended with the
refrain: "Bringin' in the sheaves." Political speeches containing the heroic
missionary sounded like a good sermon. The vision of the promised world
of peace and freedom reflected a millennial vision which has had a long
history in America. Like the religious zealots of the past, the hero was filled
with excitement. Convinced of his righteousness, the hero grew impatient to
see the word go forth. He could not contain himself. The Christian soldier
had to go onward to victory. The dominant emotional evocation was
righteousness and zeal.

The heroes of the dramas had twice before mobilized their economic and
military resources and set out to make the world safe for democracy.
However, the Cold War was different than the first and second world
wars. The Cold War was a battle for people's minds and it was a war in
which all motives had to be tempered with the reality of nuclear destruction.
Nevertheless, the urge to convert the world was so strong, the vision so

[50]William O. Douglas, "Our Political Competence," *Vital Speeches,* August 15, 1948, p. 649.
[51]See Cragan, "The Cold War Rhetorical Vision," pp. 112-135.

vivid, that the motives within the rhetoric of the Cold War generated four great crusades.

The first crusade for freedom to travel the land was an effort to renew America's faith in the Missionary hero of the Cold War. In May, 1947, the Truman Administration, at the urging of Tom Clark and J. Edgar Hoover, started the "Zeal for American Democracy" program which featured the Freedom Train.[52] Clark felt the Freedom Train was "a Paul Revere that would go around behind a modern engine" and create an "upsurge of patriotism."[53] The train traveled to over 200 American cities displaying such American documents as the Declaration of Independence, the Constitution, the Emancipation Proclamation, and the Truman Doctrine.[54] Thousands of Americans turned out to examine their sacred documents. School children sent away for replicas of the great Freedom Train and its parchment.

By 1949, Truman was calling for a second crusade. With their faith renewed, the American people would go forth and emulate the heroic Missionary American as presented in many Cold War scenarios. Truman asked for private groups to stand up and help "get the truth to other peoples."[55] Indeed, a very important group was being formed to help spread the truth. Joseph C. Grew, in consultation with George Kennan and with the approval of Dean Acheson, formed the National Committee for a Free Europe for the purpose of helping East European exiles, in June, 1949.[56]

Dwight Eisenhower, Henry Luce (Editor of *Time* magazine), DeWitt Wallace (Editor of *The Reader's Digest*), Francis Biddle, Adolf Berle, Jr., Allen W. Dulles, and General Lucious Clay soon became involved in the program. Although it initially started as an organization to find suitable employment for refugees, the Free Europe Committee soon "had for a goal the liberation of the captive nations."[57] From this Committee, the Radio Free Europe Program was started and in July of 1950, it went on the air. By the end of the year, Radio Free Europe was broadcasting to the peoples of Poland, Czechoslovakia, Albania, Hungary, Rumania and Bulgaria.[58]

On Labor Day, 1949, Eisenhower formally launched the Crusade for Freedom to raise funds for Radio Free Europe. Eisenhower's speech set in motion a crusade that was not unlike the great religious crusades of the past. Eisenhower stated:

[52]Richard M. Freeland, *The Truman Doctrine and the Origins of McCarthyism* (New York: Alfred A. Knopf Co., 1972), pp. 232-234.

[53]*Ibid.,* p. 233.

[54]*Ibid.*

[55]Harry S. Truman, "Fight False Propaganda With Truth," *Vital Speeches,* May 1, 1950, pp. 442-444.

[56]Robert T. Holt, *Radio Free Europe* (Minneapolis: University of Minnesota Press, 1958), pp. 9-11. Also see Allan A. Michie, *Voices Through the Iron Curtain: The Radio Free Europe Story* (New York: Dodd, Mead & Co., 1963) pp. 11-13.

[57]*Ibid.,* p. 14.

[58]*Ibid.*

In this battle for truth, you and I have a definite part to play during the crusade. Each of us will have the opportunity to sign the Freedom Scroll. It bears a declaration of our faith in freedom, and of our belief in the dignity of the individual who derives the right of freedom from God. Each of us, by signing the scroll, pledges to resist aggression and tyranny wherever they appear on earth. Its words express what is in all our hearts, your signature on it will be a blow for liberty.[59]

A ten-ton freedom bell, standing eight feet high, was built with the inscription: "That this world under God shall have a new birth of freedom." Eisenhower's Crusade for Freedom Committee placed the bell on a flatbed trailer truck and brought it from town to town as the main attraction at their rallies. Sixteen million Americans signed the Freedom Scroll that Eisenhower spoke of and $1.3 million was raised in the first year of the crusade.[60]

Eisenhower said the purpose of the crusade was: "To fight the big lie with the big truth."[61] He also stated that the program had been "hailed by President Truman...as an essential step in getting the case of freedom heard by the world's multitudes."[62]

While the "freedom bell" was chiming in West Berlin, the Cold War vision was jolted by two major events. China fell to the Communists and South Korea was invaded from the north. The rhetorical vision had to account for and give meaning to these here-and-now events. By August 19, 1950, 58% of the American people thought World War III had begun and only 28% thought the Korean War would stop short of another world war.[63]

In accounting for these sudden changes, the crusading motive of the vision was not diminished but rather intensified. The result was a third crusade. A more militant march for the liberation of the enslaved people began.

In June of 1950, David Lawrence proclaimed that Americans should cross the Rubicon and adopt an affirmative course of action. He went on to say:

We can have a people's peace — and it can be a peace without appeasing any of the despotic governments now lined up against us in the 'cold war'. It can be a peace of liberation for the masses of human beings now under the yoke of tyranny. They can be liberated by the moral force of mankind, which alone can direct and mobilize the material resources of the world and bring enduring peace.[64]

[59]Dwight D. Eisenhower, "The Crusade for Freedom," *Vital Speeches,* October 1, 1950, p. 747.

[60]Michie, pp. 15-17.

[61]Eisenhower, p. 746.

[62]*Ibid.,* p. 747.

[63]A.I.P.O. Polls, August 19, 1950, *Public Opinion Quarterly,* Winter, 1950-1951, p. 811.

[64]David Lawrence, "Liberation — Not 'Appeasement'," *U.S. News and World Report,* January 23, 1950, p. 56.

On February 11, 1951, two-hundred exiles from Europe signed a "Declaration of Liberation" at Independence Hall in Philadelphia. *Life* reported:

> The Declaration is framed in the language of Western freedom. It rings with echoes from the Declaration of Independence and from the U.S. Constitution, and it refutes the assumption of all too many Americans that their principles of freedom somehow cannot be 'exported' to others.[65]

Throughout the presidential campaign of 1952, and during the first years of the Eisenhower Administration, John Foster Dulles espoused a policy of liberation. In testimony before the Senate Foreign Relations Committee in 1953, he stated:

> ...we must always have in mind the liberation of these captive peoples. Now, liberation does not mean a war of liberation. Liberation can be accomplished by processes short of war...It must be and can be a peaceful process, but those who do not believe that results can be accomplished by moral pressures, by the weight of propaganda, just do not know what they are talking about.[66]

In 1956, the Hungarians revolted. In the midst of the Suez Crisis, many Americans sat and watched on their television sets the young defenders of Budapest as they were defeated by the Russian army. American public opinion had come face-to-face with a decision between life and honor. The motivation in the Cold War rhetoric stopped short of action that would bring atomic conflict. *The Reporter* magazine contained an editorial comment:

> We had better be humble and restrained in speaking about the agony the people of Hungary have endured and are still enduring...No matter what we thought or did or did not do, we *are* responsible to Hungarians. We have failed them this time—we have failed them and the other peoples of eastern Europe. Let's see to it that we do not fail them again.[67]

Richard Nixon pinpointed the reason for the failure and the source of the dilemma:

> The United Nations has no armies that it could send to rescue the heroic freedom fighters of Hungary. There were no treaties which would invoke the armed assistance of the free nations. Our only weapon here was moral condemnation, since the alternative was action on our part which might initiate the third and ultimate world war.[68]

The words of Patrick Henry had penetrated the Iron Curtain but his descendants dared not follow. In Guatemala, Lebanon, Cuba, Laos, Santa

[65]"For a Free Europe," *Life*, July 16, 1951, p. 26.
[66]"Dulles Reveals Policy on World for U.S.," *U.S. News and World Report,* January 23, 1953, p. 100.
[67]"Day of Atonement," *The Reporter,* November 29, 1956, p. 2.
[68]Richard M. Nixon, "In the Cause of Peace and Freedom," *Vital Speeches,* January 1, 1957, p. 163.

Domingo, and in Vietnam the Missionary American as hero would act to keep people free, but the "captive nations" would always be a source of anguish and shame. Even in the dying years of the rhetorical vision the Czechoslovakian Revolt would reopen the wounds.

Americans often chided themselves for empty rhetoric unaware of how rich with meaning their discourse really is. The rhetoric of liberation contained a crusading motive that was consistent with the character sketch of the hero when the original Cold War vision chained out in 1948.

The lesson on Hungary was not that Americans should change their rhetoric to fit their "real intentions," for the meaning and motives are in the rhetoric and the people participating in the vision will attempt to act them out. The lesson of Hungary was that the rhetorical vision of the Cold War contained conflicting motives in the drive for liberation with the desire to avoid nuclear war and that this choice-forcing tension would continue to produce more Hungarys as long as the rhetorical vision remained salient. The tension was painfully obvious in the failure of the rhetoric to account for American action in the rice paddies of Vietnam.

The Missionary Hero's desire to make the world safe for democracy brought him to the edge of the abyss and as he backed away from oblivion he became quieted and ashamed. The captive nations, then Cuba, and finally Vietnam, seemed to lie beyond the fringe. However, in the Cold War drama, the hero could barely tolerate and not long endure a world that was half free and half slave.

When "the spring thaw" took place in 1953 and when the danger of nuclear war posed by Korea was over and the uprising in Eastern Europe had subsided,[69] the call went out for yet another crusade. Speaking to a college audience in 1956, Richard Nixon indicated the role of the academic world in the new crusade. He stated that the Cold War is:

> ...basically a war for men's minds, a struggle for their allegiance, an effort to win them peacefully...
>
> In this struggle, ideas — not guns or aircraft — are the weapons.
>
> In this war, our armies wear the university cap and gown — not the uniform of the soldier.

Nixon then states the new object of the crusade:

> First, let us see what is at stake. Approximately 600 million people live in the so-called uncommitted or neutral nations. It is easy to see that the world struggle will be determined by what happens to these people.

Nixon then reassured his crusaders that the cause was just.

> May I make one point clear at this time? There is no question but that we have the better case to sell. Because basically we are on the right side.

[69]Andre Fontaine, *History of the Cold War,* Vol. 2 (New York: Random House, 1969), pp. 63-81.

> The side of freedom and justice, or belief in God — against the forces of
> slavery, imjustice, and atheistic materialism.

In the true spirit of a religious revivalist Nixon concluded by urging his audiences to action.

> You in the academic world are particularly fitted to serve in this contest.
> May I suggest that you graduates and you the faculty give thought to
> the part that you can play.
>
> Jointly you should embark upon a peaceful crusade for freedom.
>
> Some should volunteer for service abroad, just as soldiers volunteer for
> special missions.[70]

For a number of reasons that related to Khrushchev's visit, the launch of Sputnik, and the U-2 flights, the Nixon fantasy of educated Americans volunteering to serve in a "Peace Corps" abroad to win the neutral nations for the United States did not chain through the mass audience. However, when President Kennedy labelled the third world a "new frontier" the fantasy caught the public imagination.

With the leadership of a young, gallant warrior and under the banner of "Ask what you can do for your country," the call for the last great crusade was answered by a new generation of American patriots. By the end of 1962, 500 young crusaders had joined the Peace Corps. By mid-1963, 5,000 had signed up and by 1964, the Peace Corps swelled to 10,000.[71] But by then the music had died. In the words of a song, "We saw his widowed bride and something struck us deep inside — the day the music died."[72] Many of the new generation who were children when President Kennedy was assassinated lost the faith and as they dropped out of the vision they began to chain out new fantasies which dramatized the heroes of the Cold War as villains and the villains of the Cold War vision as heroes.

By the mid-1960's, the hero as missionary for democracy and freedom was no longer an attractive figure for many young Americans. The people who no longer participated in the drama refused to go forth with word or gun in behalf of the cause. For twenty years, the American public had been deep in the Cold War vision but the new generation coming of age in the 1960's had not witnessed the original miracle (the bomb), nor had they been to hell and back to defeat Germany, Italy and Japan. As time passed the vision grew dim for the second generation after the war. For twenty years the Missionary Hero had spread the word, first in his battle dress, then in a Brooks Brothers suit, and finally in his Peace Corps sweatshirt but a new generation rejected the Cold War rhetoric and chained out fantasies which impelled them to burn draft cards, spit on the flag, paint obscenities on their

[70]Richard M. Nixon, "The New Soviet Tactics," *Vital Speeches,* July 1, 1956, pp. 546, 547, 548.

[71]Richard J. Walton, *Cold War and Counter-Revolution: The Foreign Policy of John F. Kennedy* (New York: The Viking Press, 1972), p. 219.

[72]These lines taken from the song, "American Pie" by Don McLean, 1972.

bodies, and march forth under banners bearing the names of Fidel, Che, Mao, and Ho.

Communications across the rhetorical visions was all but impossible in the late sixties and early seventies.The person who saw Ho as the leading character in the drama of conspiratorial communism subverting South Vietnam to impose a totalitarian regime and the whole dramatic action as the latest act in a continuing conflict between freedom and slavery had little common ground with those who saw Ho as North Vietnam's George Washington leading a gallant struggle against the forces of capitalistic imperialism in battle in which the leading villain was the American GI, the American government, and by association the American people.

# Summary

The horrible destruction of World War II and Russian foreign policy initiatives synchronized with the Red Fascism rhetoric to create the rhetorical vision of the Cold War. The rhetoric and foreign policy decisions of the Truman Administration, provided the Red Fascism drama with an international scene and a new foreign policy rhetoric was born. The Monroe Doctrine was expanded and a protective shield was built around all non-communist nations. The communist conspiracy of the Red Fascism drama was present in both the domestic and international scenes. The United States was locked in the grips of Cold War. The Cold War rhetorical vision remained stable from 1948 to 1954. The Berlin Blockade, the Korean War, the Fall of China, the explosion of the atomic bomb by Russia, were the here-and-now events that sustained the drama for the vast majority of Americans. The loss of China and the end of America's atomic monopoly was accounted for by the conspiracy scenario of the Cold War rhetoric. The Truman Administration was voted out of office and Joseph McCarthy's popularity soared. In 1953, the Korean War ended and Stalin died. These events, combined with the Russian rhetoric of "peaceful coexistence" and the "spring thaw" of Eastern Europe produced a split in the Cold War vision. One string of Cold War rhetoric in the vein of Red Fascism continued to regard the domestic scene of America as the critical battle area. Americans who participated in the Red Fascism strain of the Cold War drama, continued to see attacks on Christianity and Capitalism as part of an international communist conspiracy. In 1958, the John Birch Society was established in an attempt to preserve the Red Fascism rhetorical vision. The Barry Goldwater Campaign of 1964 in part represented the last effort to elevate the domestic scene to its original level of visibility in the Cold War drama. The majority of Americans continued to participate in the international strain of the Cold War on through the 1950's and 1960's. However, major changes did occur. The Hungarian Revolt of 1956 stopped the Third Crusade of the Cold War and shifted the scene of the drama to the "third world."

During the Kennedy years, further changes took place. The missile confrontation between Kennedy and Khrushchev revitalized the personification of the Atomic American and transferred this persona from all Americans to the President. The Thomas Eagleton Affair indicates that this strain of the Cold War vision was still quite vivid in the 1970's. The rhetoric of the "new frontier" replayed the crusade drama for the last time and the Competitive American engaged in the space race. The death of John F. Kennedy and the moon landing seemed to dampen the zeal for crusades and made the space race trite. However, the Vietnam War appeared to be the here-and-now event that finally reduced the plausibility of international strain of the Cold War vision to the point where many people no longer found the drama believable.

The beginning of the 1970's may be regarded as the transitional period similar to the one that took place between World War II and the Cold War. In the 1970's, the American people were in the process of framing a new foreign policy rhetoric. On February 19, 1972, President Nixon boarded the "Spirit of '76" for his flight to the People's Republic of China. This was the first time an American President had visited China. On May 20, 1972, President Nixon departed on the "Spirit of '76" destined for the Soviet Union. This was the first time a President of the United States had traveled to Russia. These two here-and-now events were covered live over national television. They were historic events that could not be easily accounted for by Cold War rhetoric. The Nixon Administration seemed to have set in motion the beginning of a new rhetorical vision. The dramatic situation of the new drama was drawn from the Congress of Vienna of 1814.[73] Henry Kissinger was characterized as another Prince Metternich.[74] Foreign policy experts were discussing the validity of the analogy between the balance of power that existed among Austria, Prussia, Russia, France and England in 1815 and the current power relationships between the United States, Europe, Japan, the Soviet Union and China.[75]

The shorthand expression for this vision may well be he title of Kissinger's book, *A World Restored*.[76] The Nixon Administration interupted world events with a rhetoric that was in sharp contrast to the Cold War vision. Not only did it appear that the Nixon Administration was attempting to re-direct American foreign policy, it also seemed that they were in the process of creating a new foreign policy rhetorical vision to explain and sustain these policy initiatives. Nixon argues that: "Our alliances are no longer addressed primarily to the containment of the Soviet

---

[73]Alastair Buchan, "A World Restored?" *Foreign Affairs,* July, 1972, pp. 644-659.

[74]See for example. Paul Greenberg, "19th Century-style Diplomacy," *Minneapolis Star,* March 6, 1972, p. 6A.

[75]See for example, Stanley Hoffmann, "Weighing the Balance of Power," *Foreign Affairs,* July, 1972, pp. 618-643.

[76]Henry Kissinger, *A World Restored*, (New York: Grosset and Dunlap, 1964).

Union and China behind the American shield."⁷⁷ "The containment of
enmity is better than its release but is not enough as a permanent goal."⁷⁸ In
his televised toast to Premier Chou-en-lai at a banquet in Peking, Nixon
dramatically contrasted the Cold War rhetorical vision with the new visions
he hoped to create. "What legacy should we leave our children? Are they
destined to die from the hatreds which have plagued the Old World or are
they destined to live because we have the vision to build a New World."⁷⁹

With the Nixon Administration, we have the formal end of the Cold War
rhetorical vision. Whether the Power Politics vision that he and Kissinger
popularized can be nourished, sustained and developed is not clear yet, but
the Cold War vision held in the fifties and sixties is dead. Carter's foreign
policy rhetoric of human rights seems to be a polycentrism throw-back to
the Missionary American rhetoric of the Cold War. Therefore, we presently
seem to be in a transitionary rhetorical period much like the period between
the end of World War II and the beginning of the Cold War in 1948.

⁷⁷Richard M. Nixon, "United States Foreign Policy for the 1970's: The Emerging Structure of
    Peace," *Weekly Compilation of Presidential Documents, Monday, February 14, 1972,*
    (Washington: U.S. Government Printing Office, 1972), p. 238.
⁷⁸*Ibid.,* p. 411.
⁷⁹Richard M. Nixon, "The President's Toast," *Weekly Compilation of Presidential Docu-
    ments, Monday, February 28, 1972,* (Washington: U.S. Government Printing Office, 1972),
    p. 468.

# 5

# Rhetorical Strategy:
## A Dramatistic Interpretation and Application

## JOHN F. CRAGAN

Events of the last ten years have provided ample support for Douglas Ehninger's observation that "of all the arts, rhetoric is perhaps the most sensitive to the intellectual and social milieu in which it finds itself, and is constantly changing with the times."[1] However, the sixties produced so much change it seems as though ever since Edwin Black put "neo" in front of Aristotle we have been experiencing future shock.[2] New Rhetorics, methods, and generic forms have created a pluralism that makes assimilation and synthesis difficult.[3]

With the rejection of the well-understood neo-Aristotelian system, it was recommended that we classify rhetorics by situation.[4] Our focus did not shift from the speaker to the situation but instead to a swirl of message, ideology, and situation. Our shorthand for this change in emphasis was to attach ambiguous generic meaning to the phrase: "the rhetoric of." A cursory examination of our scholarship indicates that we have the rhetoric of Black Power, Black Revolution, and Radical Black Nationalism. We have

This article is based on a paper presented at the Central States Speech Convention, Milwaukee, April 5, 1974. The author wishes to thank Carl Moore for his assistance.

[1]Douglas Ehninger, "Campbell, Blair, and Whately Revisited," *Southern Speech Journal*, 28 (1963), 182.

[2]Edwin Black, *Rhetorical Criticism: A Study in Method* (New York: Macmillan, 1965). Black was not the only or the first critic of Aristotelian criticism but his rhetorical strategy of using the phrase "neo-Aristotelian" was most effective. For an example of an older attack on the traditional approach, see Albert J. Croft, "The Functions of Rhetorical Criticism," *The Quarterly Journal of Speech,* 42 (1956), 283-291.

[3]Robert L. Scott and Bernard L. Brock's book, *Method of Rhetorical Criticism, A Twentieth Century Perspective* (New York: Harper and Row, 1972), provides an analysis and organization of our current pluralism.

[4]Edwin Black suggests that "it is possible for us to construct an accurate and exhaustive topology of rhetorical situation" (p. 133). Also see Lloyd F. Bitzer, "The Rhetorical Situation," *Philosophy and Rhetoric*, 1 (1968), 1-14.

the rhetoric of:    Agitation,   Confrontation,   Abolition,   Women's
Liberation, and the Civil Rights Movement. We also have the rhetoric of:
Christian Socialism, the True Believer, the Death of God Theology, the
Radical Right, and the Medieval Rhetoric of Letter-Writing.[5]

Along with each "rhetoric of" we tend to discover a set of rhetorical
strategies that adhere to the rhetoric. For example, Arthur L. Smith
indicates that there are four special rhetorical strategies of revolutionary
rhetoric — vilification, objectification, legitimation, and mythication.[6]
John Bowers and Donovan Ochs present nine strategies that exist in the
rhetoric of agitation: petition of the establishment, promulgation, solid-
ification, polarization, non-violent resistance, escalation/confrontation,
guerrilla and Gandhi, guerrilla, and revolution.[7] In his study of radical
rhetoric James Klumpp discovered a strategy he labeled: "Polar-rejective
identification."[8]

An exhaustive list of the rhetorical strategies we have uncovered in the
last ten years would probably reveal two things. First, in the sixties we
tended to stress the differences as opposed to the similarities of rhetorics.
Second, without a paradigm or even a method, knowing a rhetorical
strategy when we saw it was no simple matter. As Thomas Kuhn explains:

> In the absence of a paradigm or some candidate for paradigm, all of the
> facts that could possible pertain to the development of a given science
> are likely to seem equally relevant. As a result, early fact-gathering is a
> far more nearly random activity than the one that subsequent scientific
> development makes familiar.[9]

[5]For examples of these rhetorics see:  Robert L. Scott and Wayne Brockriede, *The Rhetoric of
Black Power* (New York: Harper & Row Publishers, 1969); Arthur L. Smith, *Rhetoric of
Black Revolution* (Boston: Allyn and Bacon, Inc., 1969); Karlyn Kohrs Campbell, "The
Rhetoric of Radical Black Nationalism: A Case Study in Self-Conscious Criticism," *The
Central States Speech Journal*, 22 (1971), 151-160; John Waite Bowers and Donovan J. Ochs,
*The Rhetoric of Agitation and Control* (Reading: Addison-Wesley Publishing Company,
Inc., 1971); Robert L. Scott and Donald K. Smith, "The Rhetoric of Confrontation,"
*Quarterly Journal of Speech*, 50 (1969), 277-284; Ernest G. Bormann, ed. *Forerunners of
Black Power* (Englewood Cliffs: Prentice-Hall, Inc., 1971); Karlyn Kohrs Campbell, "The
Rhetoric of Women's Liberation," *Quarterly Journal of Speech*, 59 (1973), 74-86; Haig
Bosmajian and Hamida Bosmajian, *The Rhetoric of the Civil Rights Movement* (New York:
Random House, 1969); Paul Boase, *The Rhetoric of Christian Socialism*) New York:
Random House, 1969); Roderick P. Hart, "The Rhetoric of the True Believer," *Speech
Monographs,* 38 (1971), 249-261; Roger J. Howe, "The Rhetoric of the Death of God Theol-
ogy," *The Southern Speech Journal,* 37 (1971), 150-162; Dale G. Leathers, "Fundamental-
ism of the Radical Right," *The Southern Speech Journal,* 33 (1968), 245-258; and Peter E.
Kane, "Dictamen: The Medieval Rhetoric of Letter Writing," *The Central States Speech
Journal,* 21 (1970), 224-230.
[6]Smith, *The Rhetoric of Black Revolution,* p. 27. Also see, James W. Chesebro, "Rhetorical
Strategies of Radicals," *Today's Speech, 20 (1972), 37-48.*
[7]Bowers and Ochs, p. 17.
[8]James W. Klumpp, "Challenge of Radical Rhetoric: Radicalization at Columbia," *Western
Speech,* 37 (1973), 148.
[9]Thomas S. Kuhn, *The Structure of Scientific Revolutions* (Chicago: The University of
Chicago Press, 1970), p. 15. Also see, Scott and Brock, pp. 13-14.

Of course we should not abandon the task of identifying strategies that flow from our expanding list of rhetorical genres. However, we need to be about the building of a macro-theory so that we can make larger, more synthetic statements about rhetoric. This theory-building should also be rhetorical in origin and not borrowed from other disciplines.[10] Although at one level of analysis it may be useful to sort out rhetoric as it adheres to such things as the four political positions, it may also be helpful to classify rhetoric by means of our own schemata.

## A Dramatistic Theory

Ernest Bormann has developed a dramatistic method for sorting out and evaluating public discourse which may provide parameters and a rhetorical structure for the phrase, "the rhetoric of." The focus of the approach is not on the speaker, the audience, or the situation, but on the message. The method allows a critic to describe the rhetorical dramas that form a community's social reality and analyze the meanings, emotions, and motives that are contained in these rhetorical visions.[11]

A rhetorical vision is a blend of discursive material, "here and now" events, and fantasy themes which are woven together to form a drama that is credible and compelling. The contrasting rhetorical dramas of the abolitionists and the pro-slavers in the 1800's provide examples of what Bormann means by rhetorical vision. The northern abolitionists dramatized their view of southern whites in a vision of a vicious slaveholder sadistically beating the black man and lustily raping the women; *Uncle Tom's Cabin* is probably the best statement of this drama. The southern white, conversely, depicted slavery in the aura of beautiful white mansions filled with delicate southern belles, gallant men, and happy slaves; *Gone With the Wind* is one of the more popular statements of this drama.[12]

The rhetorical critic may examine man's symbolic reality and react to it in much the same way a film critic would respond to a motion picture. As we collect public discourse in the form of rhetorical dramas, certain redundancies will become apparent. We can label these as strategies and classify the strategies that are unique to each drama. In using Bormann's approach we should not be looking for strategies which adhere to certain kinds of people, or ideologies, or situations, but rather for strategies which are inherent to certain dramas.

The conspiracy drama has long been a popular rhetorical mode for

[10]Robert S. Cathcart, "New Approaches to the Study of Movements: Defining Movements Rhetorically," *Western Speech*, 36 (1972), 86.

[11]For a full explanation of this method see, Ernest G. Bormann, "Fantasy and Rhetorical Vision: The Rhetorical Criticism of Social Reality," *The Quarterly Journal of Speech*, 59 (1973), 143-159.

[12]Ernest G. Bormann, "Fantasy and the Rhetoric of Motives," unpublished paper, University of Minnesota, 1970, p. 2.

Americans to frame their social reality. From the "Anti-Papal" rhetoric in Colonial times through "McCarthyism" to the present "Watergate" drama, many Americans have tended to weave "here and now" events and fantasy themes into a conspiracy drama.[13] A brief description of a character and a motive contained in a conspiracy drama may help explain Bormann's method.

In analyzing a rhetorical vision that has a conspiracy plot line one predictable character contained in the drama is the "superhero." The hero is a character of such moral stature that he can defeat the conspiracy. He is usually a man who has dedicated his life to the careful study of the villain and over the years has developed the ability to spot the few available signs of the evil one — signs that the average person could easily overlook.

In conspiratorial religious dramas, the super-hero is usually a priest who has spent his life chasing the devil and knows the sacred rite of exorcism. The Dracula movies produced a heroic college professor who has read the ancient documents on the habits of vampires. In the crime and quasi-political mysteries it is the likes of Sherlock Holmes that carry the day. Science fiction dramas portray a scientist who understands the mystery of biochemical structures. Within the domestic scene of the Cold War drama, the character sketch of the Communist villain sets the stage for the appearance of such super-heroes as J. Edgar Hoover and Joseph McCarthy. In the Watergate conspiracy Judge John Sirica and Senator Sam Ervin emerge as super-heroes.[14]

The scenario of a conspiracy drama contains three predictable action lines or motives for the super-hero: (1) piecing together the conspiracy; (2) uncovering the secret plans or the secret hideouts of the villains; and (3) punishing the conspirator. One of the more exciting aspects of a conspiracy drama is the revealing of the secret documents. The public discourse of the late 1960's provides numerous examples in which this motive is present.

Within the vision of the criminal conspiracy, the FBI raided the Mafia headquarters. When the Black Panthers' "plan" became known, police raided their headquarters. When the military industrial complex conspiracy became a visible drama for some college students, the college president's office was raided by students in search of the "secret documents." In another drama, the radical revolutionary became the leading villain in a plot to overthrow the establishment. With this drama, the "plumbers" were ordered out by the White House to plug the establishment's pipeline so that important secrets would not drip down to the "underground," and this same conspiracy drama sent CREEP off to find the "secret documents" in the national offices of the Democratic Party.

[13]Examples of various conspiracy plots can be found in, Richard O. Curry and Thomas M. Brown, eds. *Conspiracy: The Fear of Subversion in American History* (New York: Holt, Rhinehart and Winston, Inc. 1972).

[14]For a more detailed discussion of the conspiracy drama and its occurrence in American foreign policy discourse, see John F. Cragan, "The Cold War Rhetorical Vision, 1946-1972." Unpublished diss., University of Minnesota, 1972.

A critic can describe a rhetorical vision such as the ones I have referred to and then make judgments about the quality of the drama based on an archetype or by comparing it to similar or competing dramas.[15] Finally, he may attempt to predict the behavior of people who are caught up in a rhetorical vision.

The role of a rhetorical critic is not analogous to the football coach who writes a book on winning football strategies. To be sure, as forensic coaches and as speech teachers, we explain manipulative communication theories and the strategies that flow from them. However, the role of a rhetorical critic is to make judgments about our symbolic social reality. While his comments might be reducible to a "how-to-do-it" book, it is not his purpose. Thus, although a critic may seek to predict, he does not seek to control.

Aristotle constructed a manipulative theory to help rhetors create persuasive speeches; his Rhetoric was not a theory of rhetorical criticism. We just assume that his advice to the speaker would work as a system for criticizing public discourse. As long as our focus as critics was only on the speaker and his speech, the assumption seemed valid. The use of the Aristotelian model by a rhetorical critic who wishes to expand the scope of his criticism beyond the speaker and his speech would be like using a theory of acting to criticize the whole play. In short, a theory of rhetorical criticism is not a mirror image of a persuasive theory for a speaker. Therefore, what are called rhetorical strategies for a speaker are not necessarily what a critic calls a rhetorical strategy.

A strategy assumes freedom of choice, generally connotes planning, and implies a system for categorizing the various options that exist. What we call rhetorical strategy depends on our notion of rhetoric, our choice of critical method, and our list of rhetorical genre. Thus we have strategies for developing persuasive messages; strategies that adhere to ideologies; and strategies that are inherent to situations. I propose that we examine the strategies which are contained in rhetorical visions.

In describing, interpreting, and evaluating a rhetorical vision, the term "rhetorical strategy" is the critic's term for labeling important options that exist in contructing a symbolic social reality. Since in most cases a rhetorical drama is created by the "chaining-out" of fantasies[16] which are created and repeated by many spokesmen through multiple communication channels, it is not important or many times even possible for the critic to determine if the people caught up in a rhetorical vision perceive the choices the critic has labeled or even if the spokesmen for a rhetorical vision have the same metalanguage as the critic. The important relationship is between the critic's reconstruction and evaluation of the public discourse and the critic's audience.

---

[15]Bormann outlines several sets of questions a critic might pursue once a rhetorical vision has been reconstructed. See, "Fantasy and Rhetorical Vision: The Rhetorical Criticism," 401-402.

[16]For a definition of "chaining out" of a fantasy, see ibid., 397.

## Application

Using Bormann's theory as a lens, I would like to focus on the public discourse surrounding the Indian occupation of the Bureau for Indian Affairs building in Washington, D.C. during the fall of 1972. The BIA occupation is but one scene in the Indian Movement drama and the Indian variation is but one drama we might collect under the label "The Movement." There is not space here to reconstruct The Movement rhetorical vision of the late 1960's, however, The Movement drama contains a dramatic situation, a scenario, and a set of rhetorical heroes and villains which are now so familiar that any third rate rhetor can reconstruct a version of the drama for the "cause" of his choice.[17]

In late August of 1972, members of the Rosebud Sioux Tribe and members of The American Indian Movement, in a series of group meetings, created the idea for the "Trail of Broken Treaties" caravan. In late September, a group of fifty Indians gathered at the New Albany Hotel in Denver, Colorado to refine the idea. It was decided that three auto caravans would depart from Seattle, San Francisco, and Los Angeles and arrive in St. Paul, Minnesota for the Wild Rice Festival. From St. Paul the caravan would proceed to Washington, D. C. The caravan was to cross historic Indian sites such as Sand Creek and Wounded Knee, stopping to offer prayers for the dead and the living. Once in Washington, they hoped to meet with congressmen and the President to plead their case.[18]

What might have started out to be a dramatic reconstruction of the Civil Rights marches of the early 1960's turned into a pathetic reproduction of the confrontation scene from The Movement dramas of the late 1960's. In fact, an examination of the rhetorical footage of the Trail of Broken Treaties tempts me to look at the credits to see if the "motion picture" was made in Italy. I say this not to ridicule or demean native Americans nor do I intend to be flippant. The Movement dramas of the sixties were gripped with tension and suspense. The dramatic division between hawks and doves, between gays and straights, and between men and women was credible both to the participants caught up in the dramas and the spectators who watched. Yet the Indian version of The Movement drama seems curiously out of sync, almost comical at times, despite the fact that the "here-and-now" reality of the Indian situation should have produced the best drama. The BIA occupation did not create either fear of red radicals or compassion for oppressed indians but instead generated a sort of sick humor that is inadvertently present in many Italian-made western movies.

One explanation for the failure could be the timing. By 1972, the novelty of such dramas may have worn thin; or maybe after years of watching Movement dramas the American public and press had a basis for judgment,

---

[17]By 1968, Robert L. Scott and Donald K. Smith had perceived the nature and form of the drama. See Scott and Smith, 277-284.

[18]The most complete discussion on the planning of "The Trail of Broken Treaties" caravan is contained in the Indian publication, *Akwesasne Notes*, (Early Winter, 1973).

and compared to other dramas the Indian version did not measure up. Although lateness and increased audience sophistication are important factors, the initial problem was the Indians' lack of experience in creating a compelling rhetorical drama that can be understood by white Americans. Ironically, this is in part true because of cultural differences.

In terms of cultural pluralism in the United States, the aboriginal peoples of North America are not a sub-culture but a distinctly different culture. Edward Spicer, in discussing the native Americans of the Southwest, states:

> At the end of 430 years, it was clear that, despite intensification of communication among all the peoples of the region, through the adoption of common language and a great deal of cultural borrowing and interchange, most of the conquered people had retained their own sense of identity. Moreover, there was little or no ground for predicting that even by the end of half a millenium of contact the native peoples would have ceased to exist as identifiable ethnic groups.[19]

After examining the Indians' illiteracy, poverty, suicide rate and the whole Federal Government-Indian relationship, Carl Degler concludes that one mistake white America makes is refusing "to recognize that the Indians are not like other minorities and particularly not like the blacks with whom they have so often been mistakenly compared."[20]

The problem of cross-culture communication is further complicated by the fact that most of the major spokesmen of the Indian Movement are urban Indians. They are removed from their own culture and have not assimilated into another. As Richard Oakes (the leader of an Indian group that occupied Alcatraz Island in 1969 explains: "They had grown up between two worlds—the world of their elders, which was dead to them, and the contemporary world where they could live with reconstructed Indian identities not yet born."[21]

The inexperienced Indian spokesmen clearly failed in their attempts to portray a convincing rhetorical drama before the eyes of white Americans. The most damning comment that can be made of a rhetorical drama is that it is really a theatrical drama, yet that was *The Wall Street Journal's* observation on the BIA occupation: "As much as anything else, that occupation seemed to be an exercise in play-acting—an effort by a relative handful of militants, claiming to speak for the broader Indian community, to occupy center stage within the 'Red Power' movement."[22]

A closer examination of the Indian discourse may reveal the parts of the drama that are responsible for the failure. One starting point for analysis is the dramatic situation in which a group of powerless, moral, courageous people are being oppressed by a larger, more powerful, decadent society. The confrontation is a "pseudo" event designed to amplify the oppressed/

[19]Spicer's remarks are contained in Carl N. Degler, "Indians and Other Americans," *Commentary*, November, 1972, p. 71.
[20]*Ibid.*
[21]"The Only Good Indian," *Ramparts,* December, 1972, p. 36.
[22]*The Wall Street Journal* (November 16, 1972), p. 26.

oppressor relationship. Each specific Movement drama has its own set of rhetorical analogies that work to give meaning, emotion, and motive to the confrontation scene.

For the Indian Movement drama, the accounts of helpless Indians being massacred by savage white soldiers are the salient historical facts that are repeated in speeches and painted on placards. At the height of the BIA Occupation, Russell Means (one of the leaders of the Occupation) proclaimed that: "two hundred Indians had taken a vow to fight to the death."[23] The Indians told reporters that this would be"another Wounded Knee —the famous 1890 battle in which an Army regiment massacred 250 to 300 Sioux Indians, most of them women and children."[24] This strategy did not work successfully for the Indians occupying the BIA primarily because the "here-and-now" setting was not consistent with the historical examples.

A downtown office building (even it is the BIA) in Washington, D.C. is not the best place to create a dramatic situation for confrontation between white and red Americans. Movement dramas place Black Panthers in urban ghettos; student revolutionaries on college campuses, and Indians in spacious Western settings. To see native Americans dressed in traditional costumes on Pennsylvania Avenue looked ridiculous instead of ominous. Ironically, Means stated: "We've been likened to the blacks but we watched them during the 60's and we noted their mistakes...The Indian is not going to make the same mistakes. He's not going to destroy his community."[25] However, it was not until the scene was set in the Indian community at Wounded Knee that the drama became authentic to spectator and participant.

When the setting is not correct for the drama, the rhetoric does not create social reality but instead the historical allusions help form what appears to be an epic stage play. Thus, newspaper accounts of the BIA Occupation did not focus on the present oppression of the American Indian but instead dwelled on historical events. Reporting of the Occupation on November 4th and 5th indicates this tendency. *The Washington Post* commented: "The beating tom-toms, the chants and dances of the young in the auditorium of the Indian Affairs building will bring back neither land nor brothers, but they receive the spirit and remind all who listen of former Indian glories."[26] The next day the same newspaper reported: "While tribal drums reverberated through the long halls of the building, the Indians prepared again to battle the white man. There was much joking but also anger and disbelief that this could be happening. It seemed out of the story books. There was much talk of Chief Big Foot and Wounded Knee."[27]

When the dramatic situation is not successfully created, the characters in

[23]*New York Times* (November 7, 1972), p. 36.
[24]*Washington Post* (November 5, 1972), p. A10.
[25]*The Times Reporter* (November 12, 1972), p. 1, Dover-New Philadelphia, Ohio.
[26]*Washington Post* 4 November 1972, p. A8.
[27]*Washington Post*, 5 November 1972, p. A10.

the drama are not believable. Sitting in an office building the Indians did not project the dramatis persona of a villainous revolutionary that we have come to expect from a good confrontation scene. *Ramparts* reports that during the occupation: "Seventh graders from the Fields School, a private school in Washington, visited the scene as part of a class project on Indians."[28] Reverend Karl McIntire, a conservative radio preacher, led two hundred of his followers to see the Indians "like a fifth grade class" that was viewing "zoo animals."[29]

Set in an urban scene, the Indian was not a threatening villain to the white establishment, particularly to Washingtonians who have had few experiences with Indians. Racial confrontation between red and white America is not an urban phenomenon in the minds of most Americans. Once the confrontation scene was restaged in South Dakota, which was a red-white setting which had experienced racial conflicts, the gaunt silhouette of an Indian with rifle in hand which appeared on television news programs seemed more credible to white Americans.

Not only did the Indians in the BIA building have difficulty portraying themselves as serious revolutionaries, they also failed in their attempts at creating a vivid characterization of their oppressor. This failure occurred in part because the Indian rhetorical drama has no Indian label for the establishment villain and no common set of adjectives to describe him. The Women's Movement has the label, "Male Chauvinist Pig," the Gay Movement has "Ugly Straight," and the Black Movement has "Honky" and "Whitey." Each villain, although generally a persona of the established power structure, is nonetheless unique and discernible. It is difficult to picture the villain in the Indian Movement and thus much of the power of the drama is lost. The Indian drama borrows too heavily from the Black Movement drama. The Indian terms for villain are "Honky" or "Whitey," while the "Oreo Cookie" becomes the "Red Apple." In general, the key rhetorical labels of the Indian Movement drama are trite and sometimes humorous, such as the slogans scribbled on the BIA walls, "Custer had it coming and so do some others," and "Kemo Sabe means Honky."[30]

The scenario of The Movement drama is basically a conspiracy plot line. The script calls for a villain who is not only an oppressor but who conspires to oppress. Thus, there is a strong motive for the heroic revolutionary to "expose" the plot primarily by uncovering the "secret documents" that prove the conspiracy. For example, the Pentagon Papers "exposed" the military conspiracy and the Nixon tapes "exposed" the Watergate conspiracy.

One successful rhetorical act that came out of the BIA Occupation was the predictable "exposure" of the Bureau of Indian Affairs as oppressors that had conspired against American Indians. This was effectively done by

[28]Eugene Meyer, "Bury My Heart on the Potomac," *Ramparts,* January, 1973, p. 12.
[29]*Ibid.,* p. 10.
[30]"Drums Along the Potomac," *Newsweek,* 20 November 1972, p. 37.

the "discovery" and release of "secret documents" that proved the conspiracy. *Newsweek* reported:

> Although the FBI mounted a nationwide search for the 7,000 cubic feet of paper the Indians carried off, the documents began to turn up instead in Anderson's column. According to Anderson, the printed excerpts showed that the government has violated treaties, sided with the land and timber barons to exploit water, timber, and mineral rights belonging to the Indians.[31]

The "here-and-now" fact that the U.S. government had cheated the Indians out of land, timber, and mineral rights has not been a well kept secret. Yet, the release of these facts in the context of a conspiracy, especially by the likes of Jack Anderson, did much to heighten the excitement and interest of Americans. If the Indians could have produced a "defector" (a white BIA worker who would testify that a conspiracy did indeed exist and that he had participated), the occupation of the BIA would have been more successful. As it was, the release of the "secret documents" was the only rhetorical act in the drama that "chained out" in the American press. However, it was balanced with a negative dramatization of the destruction of the BIA building. The *Washington Post* reported:

> Damage done to the Bureau of Indian affairs by protesting Indians... was the most extensive ever committed by U.S. citizens on a federal building... only two other incidents surpassed in cost... the burning of Washington by the British in 1814 and the destruction of government buildings in the San Francisco earthquake in 1906.[32]

The Indian Occupation of the BIA building in 1972 was a rhetorical and, as a consequence, a political failure. The urban setting was the wrong place to stage a confrontation scene from the Indian Movement drama. Because the historical allusions of Wounded Knee and the "here-and-now" setting in Washington, D.C. were not properly meshed the dramatic situation of the Indian drama was not projected in the media. As a result, the Indian radical looked humorous instead of dangerous. The Indian rhetorical drama in general and the rhetoric surrounding the BIA Occupation in particular lacks important symbols for depicting their oppressor. However, the selected release of "secret documents" and the subsequent occupation of Wounded Knee indicates that Indian spokesmen are improving in their ability to create a Movement drama. Yet, the Movement drama may be a rhetorical artifact of the 1960's. If this is so, native Americans may still find themselves frustrated in their attempts to portray their reality to white Americans.

## Conclusion

As the history of American public discourse is collected in the form of rhetorical visions, we will develop categories for classifying different kinds

[31]*Newsweek,* 12 February 1973, p. 46.
[32]*Washington Post,* 11 November 1972, p. A4.

of rhetorical dramas. For example, this article suggests that one major category may be the conspiracy drama of which The Movement drama of the late 1960's is but one subset. The Indian Movement drama would then be a subset of The Movement drama.

Using this approach we can then sort out rhetorical strategies that are inherent to each drama and the strategies that are common to all dramas of a given category. In this article an effort was made to indicate how this task might proceed with respect to the Indian Movement drama.

Bormann's rhetorical theory is aesthetically pleasing and its utility for the critic appears promising. Whether the method will become a paradigm is not a question that will soon be answered. Scott and Brock's prediction that "no paradigm will soon arise to gain the adherence that neo-Aristotelianism had in the 1930's and 1940's" is probably correct.[33] However, as our critical focus continues to shift from the speaker to the message Bormann's approach will become an increasingly valuable addition to our current pluralism.

[33]Scott and Brock, p. 404.

# 6

# Malcolm X's Black Unity Addresses:
## Espousing Middle-Class Fantasy Themes as American as Apple-Pie

### DONALD C. SHIELDS

A decade ago, including the time from March, 1964, when Malcom X intitiated his black nationalism movement to his assassination in March, 1965, few in this country would have been so bereft of mental faculties or so satirically cruel as to depict Malcolm X's black unity vision as mirroring the mainstream of traditional American values. Indeed, the prevalent view a decade ago placed Malcolm X at the forefront of radical black thought. At the inception of his black nationalism movement, popular portrayals contrasted markedly with the imagery of this essay's title.

In March, 1964, *U.S. News and World Report* blazed this story headline: "Brother Malcolm: His Theme Now is Violence."[1] *Newsweek* framed his face with the caption: "Malcolm X: Charm and Guns."[2] *Life,* replete with accompanying photos discussed: "The Ominous Malcolm X;"[3] and its *Ebony* counterpart provided photographic insight detailing the "Mystery of Malcolm X."[4] *U.S. News* concluded quite acrimoniously: "Now It's A Negro Drive for Segregation."[5] Such headlines comprised descriptions applied to Malcom X, not as spokesman for Elija Muhammad's Black Muslims, but as a leader of a newly formed black nationalism movement.

At the heart of this essay is the question of the universality of the above headlines in depicting Malcolm X. I shall attempt to demonstrate that the ideology and philosophy contained in the rhetoric advancing his new movement may be interpreted in another way. Rather than a lunatic urging separatism, violence, and racial hatred, Malcom X's preachments on black nationalism reveal a primary focus on persuading blacks to accept the main-

---

[1] *U. S. News and World Report*, 56:19 (March 23, 1964), 19.
[2] "Malcolm's Brand X," *Newsweek*, 63:22 (March 23, 1964), 23.
[3] Marc Crawford, "The Ominous Malcolm X Exits from the Muslims," *Life*, 56 (March 20, 1964), 40-40a.
[4] H. J. Massaquoi, "Mystery of Malcolm X: Fired Black Muslim Denounces Cult, Vows To Take Part in Rights Revolt," *Ebony*, 19 (September, 1964), 38-40 + .
[5] *U. S. News and World Report*, 56 (March 30, 1964), 38-39.

stream of American thinking and cónfirming his right to lead the black people.[6]

As could be expected from the leader of a new movement, Malcom X gave a number of talks aimed at gaining converts and building up the ranks. Although not all of these pro-black talks are extant and the exact titles and texts of these speeches varied, the central and most often reiterated theme stressed a plea for black unity. Representative of Malcom X's new black unity theme are his "Ballot or the Bullet" and "Black Revolution" addresses.[7]

To expedite the explanation of my thesis, I offer analysis of the addresses, drawing insights through the application of Professor Bormann's dramatistic concept of rhetorical vision.[8] I conclude by looking at the nature of rhetorical visions and suggesting that multiple rhetorics may function in the same message, thereby providing an explanation of why the media headlines, typifying as they did the prevalent view of Malcolm X,

---

[6]For elaboration of the pro-black rather than anti-white aspect of Malcolm's unity preachments, see: Wyatt Tee Walker, "Nothing But a Man," appearing in John Henrik Clarke, ed., *Malcolm X: The Man and His Times* (New York: Collier Books, 1969), 67.

[7]The word addresses refers both to the two titles, and to the fact that Malcolm X delivered each speech to more than one audience. A printed reproduction of his April 3, 1964 "Ballot or Bullet" address to the Cleveland Chapter of CORE is available in: George Breitman, ed., *Malcolm X Speaks* (New York: Grove Press, 1965), 23-44; as is an audio reproduction of his April 12, 1964 "Ballot or Bullet" address in Detroit sponsored by the Group on Advanced Leadership and the Freedom Now Party taped by the Afro-American Broadcasting Company, Detroit, Michigan. In these speeches, Malcolm X used many of the themes developed in his four Sunday night Harlem, New York rallies held to explain the philosophy of the new movement.

A third speech entitled "The Black Revolution" delivered April 8, 1964 to a three-quarters white audience in New York is available in: Breitman, 45-47; as is his March 18, 1964 talk to the predominantly white audience of the Leverett House Forum at Harvard University: Archie Epps, ed., *The Speeches of Malcolm X at Harvard* (New York: Wm. Morrow and Co., Inc., 1968), 131-160.

The development of the pro-black unification vision is generally the same in each of the above-named speeches. The content and approach is similar, differing only in the embellishment of particular ideas and examples, and I feel it to be fair to examine them collectively. The phrase "the ballot or the bullet" appears in all but the March 18 speech. For a discussion of the evolving nature of Malcolm X's ideas during the March-April period, see Breitman, *The Last Year of Malcolm X: The Evolution of a Revolutionary)* (New York: Schocken Books, 1967), 60-63.

[8]Ernest Bormann suggested the fantasy theme analysis of a collectivity's discourse to identify key characters, recognize scenarios, and determine important elements of the scene. For Bormann, characters, scenarios, and scenes interlock to form *rhetorical vision* to such "composite dramas that catch up large groups of people into a symbolistic reality" providing impetus and direction for human action. The fantasy themes depicting such elements show what events provide meaning for the vision's adherents, the emotions that the vision is likely to evoke, and the particular motives that are likely to inspire a people to action. See Ernest G. Bormann, "Fantasy and Rhetorical Vision: The Rhetorical Criticism of Social Reality," *The Quarterly Journal of Speech*, 59, 2 (April, 1973), 143-159. Also, see John F. Cragan's, "Rhetorical Strategy: A Dramatistic Interpretation and Application," *Central States Speech Journal*, 26, 1 (Spring, 1975), 4-12 for critical application of the method to the Indian occupation of the B.I.A.

could logically find violence in his rhetoric, rather than middle-class-white American values.

I

Malcolm X both participated in certain dramas as an individual and utilized certain dramas as rhetor to gain converts to his black nationalism movement. Given that Malcolm sought to become leader of a new movement, the dramas he participated in as an individual and the dramas he selected to motivate his audiences may well have been one and the same. As such, his rhetoric can be interpreted as reflecting those persuasive fantasy themes he deemed central in motivating black Americans to rally in support of his black-unity movement.

Thus, Malcolm X's vision of black nationalism can be viewed as drawing its persuasive power from what I call *modal societal* fantasy themes. That is, fantasy themes so intrinsic to our society that they exist as a general pattern among individuals stemming from long standing values, public dreams, and rhetorical visions.[9] For the most part, the fantasy themes present in Malcolm X's unity addresses may be interpreted as American as apple pie — as representing the symbolic reality of the white, democratic society.

In the black unity addresses, Malcolm X attempted to unify the black people to the common cause of raising their level of human dignity and physical well-being. The speeches concentrated their consciousness-raising efforts on a discussion of black political, economic, and social problems and solutions. Malcolm X sought to create a oneness among black people that would supersede lesser differences. He did this by calling for blacks to put aside old solutions in favor of a new view.

Malcolm X attacked both black separatism and integration as solutions to the black man's plight. His basis for unity was that "all blacks are in the same boat and are going to catch hell from the same man — the white man."[10] He depicted all whites, both liberals and conservatives, as unwilling to help alleviate black suffering. Thus, the black man must help himself. Although Malcolm addressed himself solely to the needs of the black people, he did not in his unity addresses advocate the establishment of a separate black nation, either in the United States or elsewhere. Rather, he derided the back-to-Africa movement.[11] So too, in developing his vision of

---

[9]Although some might draw subtle distinctions among values, dreams, and visions, the two former concepts appear as part of the third. For example, what is often spoken of as the *work ethic* represents a modal societal fantasy. The work ethic's roots lie in the Puritan's rhetorical vision regarding salvation. The work ethic, as a fantasy theme, has continued to be accepted for long periods of time by major — modal — segments of our society, even after the initial rhetorical vision, of which the work ethic was only a part, has diminished in impact.

[10]"Ballot or Bullet," Detroit tape; Cleveland address, 24. Subsequent quotations are from the Detroit tape, unless cited by footnote.

[11]"Ballot or Bullet," Detroit also, in "The Black Revolution" Malcolm said: "We don't want to be integrationists. Nor do we want to be separationists. We want to be human beings." (24)

black unity, he posited the futility of integration. In the Detroit ~"Ballot" address he spoke directly to the black audience: "You want me to integrate? Now, you are out of your mind..." Malcolm argued the fallacy of integration: "When blacks move into a white community, the whites move out, and the community becomes black again."

In the place of the old separatist or integrationist solutions, Malcolm X offered a self-enrichment program based on black unification and action to create the best of possible worlds where they were. Malcolm relied on three dominant fantasy themes, recurrent in each of the four speeches, to augment his new vision of black unity. Malcolm X spoke of re-education to gain political consciousness, re-education to create economic understanding, and legal maneuvering to gain social justice.

The education modal fantasy is a prevalent one in American culture. In the fantasy's broadest contest, education is depicted as a kind of cure-all-evil panacea. In the speech communication discipline, the educational modal fantasy may be seen in the scenario that a student, once he or she learns to judge the quality of evidence and analyze the cogency of arguments, can use rational skills to identify charlatans, shysters, and demagogues and improve the outcomes likely from the individual's choice-making and decision-making. The education modal fantasy exists as part of the symbolic reality of groups other than our discipline. Indeed, the roots of the education modal fantasy may be found in the longstanding agrarian, middle-class, white view that ignorance is the breeding ground for disease, poverty, and injustice. The fantasy holds that by educating the masses, society can eradicate disease, can eliminate poverty, and can create justice. The power of the education modal fantasy historically is such that it provided the impetus to enact state-supported public-education and create America's vast system of land-grant colleges.[12]

Malcolm X looked to "re-education"—his god-term—as the solution to both the political and economic problems of blacks. In the political arena, blacks needed to be re-educated about the power of the ballot box. Blacks had no power or voice according to Malcolm because of two short-comings in their behavior. First, blacks voted for the whiteman or his "Negro lackey," even though these men had no interest in the black community, "except at election time."[13] Second, the black voters did not realize the extent of their political power. In Malcolm's view, if blacks would only unify and demand results for their votes, they could decide an election and

[12]For a concise review of *education's* place in the rhetorical vision of the proponents of *Jacksonian Democracy* with their belief in the superiority of the *common man*, see John M. Blume, *et al. The National Experience: A History of the United States,* 2nd Ed. (New York: Harcourt, Brace, and World, Inc., 1968), 260-262.

[13]Also, he reiterates this theme in the Harvard Lecture of March 18: "When they want to get elected to office they come into the so-called Negro community and make a lot of promises they don't intend to keep." (133); and the theme appears in the Cleveland speech as he discussses "re-education" (38 and 39); as well as in the "Black Revolution" address when he describes the black man as: "A beggar economically, a beggar politically, a beggar socially, a beggar even when it comes to trying to get some education." (57).

gain improvements for themselves. For Malcolm X, re-education would make the blacks "politically conscious." Political consciousness would provide voter strength, and political maturity would keep the blacks from being "misled" and would allow them to vote for the person with the "good of the community at heart."[14]

Malcolm X's terms *politically mature* and *politically conscious* denote an association with the western democratic modal fantasy regarding the power of the ballot box. This fantasy theme orders the world by depicting people as controlling their fate and destiny through the intelligent use of the democratic process—registering to vote, getting to know the candidates and the issues, and voting for the person who seems likely to provide the best representation. Such a theme is intrinsic to Jacksonian democracy and holds that the common man possesses both common sense and ingenuity. These traits enable the manifestation of a collective political wisdom and generate the wherewithal for material advancement. Government, as seen from the perspective of Jacksonian democracy, is an agent of the people, and it is the people's duty to control government.[15]

Malcolm X described the economic problems of blacks as two-fold. Economically, he saw blacks in a "double trap." Either blacks spent their money in the white community or they patronized a white-owned store in the black community. Blacks, in Malcolm's eyes, had been misled into spending their money "with the man."[16] Hence, of their own volition, they had "bankrupted their community" and had brought on "ghetto conditions."

Again, Malcolm X presented re-education (enlightenment) as the solution. He argued that Blacks needed to own, operate, and control the economy of their own community. Such capitalistic enterprise would provide the additional benefit of creating jobs for blacks via the natural expansion of black businesses.

Malcolm X's vision of the economic aspects of black nationalism may be viewed as springing from a white American modal fantasy. Malcolm dreamed of a black community where blacks could own, operate, and control their economy. He argued in his unity addresses that black businesses could start out small and expand and expand until they rivaled General Motors in power and wealth. Malcolm vividly portrayed this view in his statement, "General Motors started out as a little rat-race type operation... You and I have to make a start—right here in the community where we live."[17] Again,

---

[14]See also the discussion of "politically mature" in the Cleveland address (26), and his discussion of blacks holding the balance of political power in the "Black Revolution" address (57); and blacks being in a politically "strategic position" in the Harvard talk (136, 137).

[15]For a succinct description of the rhetorical vision encompassing what we call Jacksonian Democracy, see Blume, *et al*. 222-225; and 229-231.

[16]See also his "economic philosophy" in Cleveland speech, (38-39); and his "Economic philosophy of Black Nationalism, in the Harvard Lecture, (142, 143).

[17]In the Cleveland talk, he said: "If we own the stores, if we operate the businesses, if we try and establish some industry in our own community, then we are developing to the position where we are creating employment for our own kind." (39).

Malcolm may be seen as tacitly associating his cause with a white modal fantasy theme, namely, the nineteenth century rags-to-riches, Horatio Alger dream that a hardworking entrepreneur could rise to the top.[18] Of course, the ironic corollary to this fantasy theme is that the competitive struggle weeded out the weak, the incompetent, and the unfit making slums and poverty the unfortunate but inevitable results of the competitive struggle.[19]

Malcolm's presentation of the social problems facing black people appeared less specific than his political and economic arguments. Basically, he appeared to view the social issue from the perspective of a "conspiracy" which kept blacks in slavery under the guise of "second-class" citizenship. Moreover, civil rights and the civil rights movement were viewed as "tools" manipulated by the government to control black people. Malcolm felt that in order to be free it was necessary to "expand from civil rights to human rights."[20] In Malcolm's view, as long as blacks concerned themselves with civil rights they would be denied freedom. For him, human rights could only be won by taking the United States government to the United Nations and World Court and charging the U. S. with physical, political, economic, and mental genocide. Malcolm stated that Uncle Sam was a hypocrite and a crook and "you don't take your case to the criminal—you take your criminal to court."[21]

Thus, in the social domain, Malcolm X described the scenario of united blacks rectifying their social ills through the appeal to a higher law, such as the United Nations and the World Court. Clearly, this scenario parallels a fairly dominant twentieth century white American modal fantasy, namely that the world brotherhood of man must logically become the ultimate authority in settling political disputes among peoples. The theme is akin to the world court idea of Woodrow Wilson and the one-world concept of Wendell Willkie.[22]

## II

In his black unity addresses, Malcolm X sought acceptance of himself as well as his ideas. He saw pluralist black leadership, and the pluralist black organizations as incapable of solving the black man's plight without a

---

[18]Horatio Alger wrote some 119 books during the late 19th and early 20th century filled with rags-to-riches heroes that young readers could emulate. Compare these stories to recent I.R.S. reports that there were 500 new millionaires last year.

[19]See Blume, et al.'s discussion of "The Gospel of Wealth," 451-454.

[20]Also in "Black Revolution," (54); Cleveland speech, (34); and the Harvard Lecture, (142-143).

[21]See also, Cleveland speech (35); "Black Revolution," (53-54).

[22]For a precise discussion of the world court idea, see Blume, et al., 648-711. The reader will note that the world court idea was not well received by the American Congress. To best understand Willkie, the reader is referred to: Wendell Willkie, One World (New York: Simon and Schuster, 1943).

common cause. He offered unity as the common cause, and himself as the supreme leader. His *Autobiography* offers two pertinent insights. He writes at one point: "One of the major troubles that I was having is building the organization that I wanted—an all-black organization whose ultimate objective was to help create a society in which there could exist honest white-black brotherhood—was that my earlier public image, my old so-called 'Black Muslim' image, kept blocking me. I was trying to turn a corner, into a new regard by the public, especially Negroes."[23] At another point in the *Autobiography* Malcolm provides the following disclosure: "I honestly evaluated my own qualifications to be worthy of presenting myself as an independent leader among black men."[24] Malcolm X employed two rhetorical strategies to effect the acceptance of a unitary black movement with himself as leader: (1) he engaged in pointed attacks upon the solutions offered by other black leaders; and (2) he sought to subsume black political and religious organizations under the black nationalism banner, thereby discounting differences among the organizations.

Malcolm felt that others' attempts to alleviate black problems had both "worsened" the blacks' plight and "increased blacks' humiliation." In the Detroit speech, Malcolm indicated that blacks had been "trapped, double trapped, triple trapped—in fact, solutions are just another trap."[25] In discussing the economic plight of blacks, Malcolm criticized the "ignorant and disgraceful boycotting of some white cracker trying to take his poor job...Anytime you have to rely on your enemy for a job, you're in poor shape."[26] An excerpt from the Cleveland speech is equally pointed: "I'm not going to sit at your table and watch you eat, with nothing on my plate and call myself a diner. Sitting at the table doesn't make you a diner unless you eat some of what's on that plate."[27] Both criticisms definitely belittled the potential of the early 1960's civil rights demonstrations to bring about a solution to the black's problems. Such attacks on solutions indirectly undermined the positions of the leaders who had proposed the solutions.

Other attacks were more to the point, and more stinging. Malcolm stated that there was too much singing of "We Shall Overcome" and that the whole sit-down philosophy "castrated" the blacks. He indicated that the march to Washington in 1963 was a "fiasco" and implied that Martin Luther King was either "duped by the whites" or maybe "in cahoots with them."[28]

---

[23]Malcolm X, with the assistance of Alex Haley, *Autobiography* (New York: Grove Press, 1964), 374-375.

[24]*Autobiography*, 312.

[25]In the Cleveland speech Malcolm X says: "He's got us in a vise." (39).

[26]In the Cleveland talk he says: "Once you gain control of the economy of your own community, then you don't have to picket and boycott and beg some cracker downtown for a job in his business." (39).

[27]"Ballot or Bullet," Cleveland address, 26.

[28]In the Cleveland talk he refers to "handkerchiefheads" "dilly-dallying and pussyfooting and compromising..." (31). In the "Black Revolution" Malcolm X berates James Farmer, the head of CORE, for "barking up the wrong tree" by thinking his having coffee with President Lyndon Johnson would help the blacks (56).

Just as Malcolm X's black nationalism platforms may be viewed as containing modal societal fantasies instrinsic to white society, so too, his reasons for accepting a new leadership persona can be interpreted as reflecting Apple-Pie America. Malcolm cautioned his black brothers to be watchful of the white man's subversive attempts to divide and conquer, and implied that blacks must search out those black leaders who are in cahoots with the white man—a conspiracy scenario that appears in each of the black unity addresses.[29] Of course, the conspiracy scenario is a prevalent and longstanding drama traditionally associated with the white majority's attempts to subjugate minorities, be they racial, religious, or political.[30] Some may see irony in Malcolm X's use of the conspiracy drama to motivate blacks toward unification.

Malcolm X's second strategy for establishing himself as an independent leader among black men called for all existing black organizations to be subsumed beneath the all-encompassing black nationalism movement. In the "Ballot" speeches, Malcolm draws an analogy between the proposed black nationalism movement and the "white nationalist" movement of Billy Graham. He indicated that Graham overcomes the "jealousy and suspicion" of local leaders by "preaching the gospel of Christ and telling the converts to go to any church that is organized around Christian concepts." To Malcolm, this strategy enables Graham to be "non-threatening," thus enabling the local church leaders to cooperate with Graham in support of his cause.

In the Cleveland "Ballot" speech, Malcolm stated:

> We're going to take a page from his (Graham's) book. Our gospel is black nationalism. We're not trying to threaten the existence of any organization, but we're spreading the gospel of black nationalism. Anywhere there's a church that is preaching black nationalism, join that church. If the NAACP is preaching and practicing the gospel of black nationalism, join the NAACP. If CORE is spreading and preaching the gospel of black nationalism, join CORE. Join any organization that has a gospel that's for the uplift of the black man.[31]

Malcolm X attempted more than a mere analogy between the black nationalism movement and the Graham Christian evangelizing movement. His words contained the tacit assumption that his role in the black movement paralleled the position held by Graham; that is, inspired, inspiring, messianic leader. Malcolm articulated his position when he confided in his *Autobiography* that he "was not attempting to teach Negroes a new direction."[32]

[29]"Ballot or Bullet," Detroit tape; Cleveland speech, 30; and "Black Revolution," 55.
[30]A number of conspiracy plots can be found in, Richard O. Curry and Thomas M. Brown, eds., *Conspiracy: The Fear of Subversion in American History* (New York: Holt, Rinehart and Winston, Inc., 1972). The book focuses attention on the tendency of American political leaders and their followers to view the world in conspiratorial terms.
[31]Malcolm X, "Ballot or Bullet," Cleveland, 41.
[32]Malcolm X, *Autobiography*, 366.

Malcolm X tried to advance his desire for black unity by discounting differences among the black religious groups. He avoided denigrating black religious leaders for their religious beliefs and centered his attacks upon the solutions to the black man's plight which had been posited by these same leaders. However, activist civil rights leaders were not alone in receiving the brunt of Malcolm X's criticism. By discounting religious and religious beliefs as peripheral to the struggle for black freedom, Malcolm X struck directly at the root strength of Elijah Muhammad's Black Muslim movement.

His strategy of debunking other black leaders and solutions served to legitimatize the acceptance of the new vision and sanctioned his claim to leadership.

Still another sign pointing toward Malcolm X's proximity to Apple-Pie America comes in the selection of the Graham Christian Crusade as the ideal organizational framework, the ideal institution to emulate. Blacks were asked to channel their new-found consciousness within the organizational patterns of evangelizing white America.

Clearly, the values Malcolm X sought to promulgate were not unlike white, middle-class values; the fantasy themes selected as persuasive were akin to those ingrained in the white culture; and the organization and persona identified for modeling behavior epitomized the success qualities of a white leader and his white organization.

## III

So, fantasy theme analysis indicates that Malcolm X's rhetoric may be viewed as drawing upon white modal fantasies in developing a program of black nationalism, and using appeals similar to those ingrained in the white culture to elicit support for the goal of black unity. But how does fantasy theme analysis explain the imagery of the *bullet* and of *black revolution*? Weren't both images implied *threats*? My answer is yes if, as critic, one concentrates on the discursive and ignores the dramatistic. But, with the concept of rhetorical vision comprising the critical lens, the critic becomes aware that in any message, a rhetor may be seen as a function of a number of themes, a number of rhetorics in process. To this point, I've examined the themes that reflect middle-class-white values and demonstrated how they appear to be present in Malcolm X's black unity addresses. But what of the violent themes? The Bormann critical lens, as it captures and reveals the dramatic vision in which Malcolm X appeared to participate, helps to explain how Malcolm X could use violent themes along with deepseated white cultural themes without internal dissonance.

Malcolm X, as a Black Muslim, participated in the Muslim vision regarding the nature of God; or, as I prefer to label it, the Puritan vision regarding the nature of God.[33] Malcolm X believed in a *just* God who by His nature would let a base unrepentant sinner receive his due. Similarly, Malcolm X believed that God, because He was just, would bestow atrocities on America for the sins committed against the black man. Moreover, time was running out; God's patience was wearing thin. Consequently, Malcolm X saw revolution, violence, and bloodshed as America's just reward unless the black man was allowed his rightful place in society. Moreover, he believed that God helped those who worked to receive His righteousness. Thus, Blacks must awaken—must help themselves—lest they miss the opportunity that God had given them. These two strains, that the time was here for Black awakening and that time was running out on America, since God's patience was wearing thin, pointed up the expediency of the moment to Malcolm X. It followed that if white Americans denied the blacks political, economic, and legal consciousness, then, for sure, 1964 would be the year of the black revolution, the year of the bullet. Justice from God—the bullet and revolution.

Of course, the Puritan vision of the nature of God is familiar to students of public address. Recall that Abraham Lincoln, in his "Second Inaugural Address," relied on the modal fantasy of a *just* God to explain why the scourge of the Civil War has been visited on America.[34] Like the Puritans, Malcolm X believed that time was of the essence, because a just God might bestow his wrath at any moment. Malcolm's participation in the Puritan-like drama regarding the nature of God explains why he made continual references in his unity addresses to America sitting on a "powder keg" and 1964 being the most crucial year ever—the year of the ballot or the bullet; the year of the black revolution.

Artistically, the phrases "Ballot or bullet" and "black revolution" pinpointed definite militant imagery. Nonetheless, application of the dramatistic lens belies the singularity of the militant view. Whereas application of a discursive critical lens contributes to the evaluation of the imagery as conflicting, or ambiguous, or implying a veiled threat,[35] the use

[33]For a glimpse into Malcolm X's religious rhetorical vision, listen to his "The Wisdom of Malcolm X." Other insights are scattered throughout his *Autobiography*. For example, he writes "I believe that God is giving the world's so-called 'Christian' white society its last opportunity to repent and atone for the crimes of exploiting and enslaving the world's non-white peoples. It is exactly as when God gave Pharaoh a chance to repent. But Pharaoh persisted in his refusal to give justice to those whom he oppressed. And, we know, God finally destroyed Pharaoh." (370). Of course there are key differences between the Puritan and Muslim visions when one considers aspects other than the nature of God—for example the pro-black, anti-white element in the Muslim dogma of Elija Muhammad.

[34]See the dozen or so lines beginning: "The Almighty has His own purposes..." and ending "...'The judgments of the Lord are true and righteous altogether'." Abraham Lincoln, "Second Inaugural," appearing in *Inaugural Addresses of the Presidents of the United States from 1789-1969* (Washington, D.C.: U.S. Government Printing Office, 1969), 127-128.

[35]For a critical essay relying on a discursive critical lens, see: Peggy Reynolds, "The Ballot or the Bullet: One-Man Dialectic," appearing in Paul O. Weiss and Bernard B. Brock, eds., *Current Criticism* (Delta-Sigma-Rho/Tau-Kappa-Alpha, 1971).

of the rhetorical vision dramatistic lens indicates that the imagery may be interpreted as being consistent within the logic of the Puritan-like rhetorical vision regarding the nature of a just God and the baseness of mankind.[36]

## IV

In the introduction to this essay, I made the statement that a decade ago few in this country would have been so bereft of mental faculties or so satirically cruel as to depict Malcolm X as being as American as apple pie. As indicated previously, popular portrayals contrasted markedly with the imagery of this essay's title. To test the accuracy of the popular portrayals, I applied fantasy theme analysis to the rhetoric relating to Malcolm X's black nationalism movement. The analysis showed that Malcolm X's black dominant fantasy themes may be interpreted as reflecting longstanding white-middle-class modal fantasies. Given the fantasy theme analysis of Malcolm X's rhetoric, what led the media to portray him as a lunatic fanatic? Some, of course, might answer that the media portrayed him as a radical to make news; others, that the media failed to recognize his changing philosophy and continued to characterize him as he had appeared as spokesman for Elijah Muhammad.

I believe that fantasy theme analysis provides another, perhaps richer explanation of why the headlines were amiss than either media expediency or media naivete. Malcolm's talks did not occur in a rhetorical vision vacuum. Other fantasies existed at the same time. Fantasy theme analysis of other existing modal fantasies fosters the conclusion that some of Malcolm X's lesser fantasy themes (lesser in terms of characterizing his program) worked at cross-currents with the primary focus of his black unity talks. For example, the modal fantasy of the *field slave uprising*, where the laborer fieldhands would unite, throw off their shackles, and wreak havoc on the plantation system that kept them in slavery, had been present since before

---

[36]In a similar vein, I believe the rhetorical vision lens, a dramatistic model, offers insights that diverge from those to be gained via the application of the more familiar dramatistic stance labeled Burkean. To analyze the pieces via division, identification, mystery, and hierarchy places the rhetorical emphasis of the pieces as a reflection of society. To say that social forces operate in dramatistic terms is quite different than saying individuals cognitively assimilate information dramatistically. Thus, a Burkean critic is quite likely to miss the operating rhetorical visions that bind individuals into a collective symbolic reality and instead concentrate on description of the hierarchy, acceptance and rejection, and guilt, purification, and redemption from a mass societal perspective. Similarly, specific use of the pentad to aid in the identification of the individual's motives will miss the mark and yield different interpretations. For example, there is nothing in act, scene, agent, agency, and purposes that would indicate directly from Malcolm's black unification speeches the existence of the Puritan-like rhetorical vision of the Black Muslims to which Malcolm ascribed.

Although I personally think the rhetorical vision analysis the better method in that we can subsume Burkean and rational methods within it, such a claim is not important. What is important is that the rhetorical vision lens provides a means of analyzing aspects of rhetoric that were previously missed by both the rational and Burkean approaches.

the time of Nat Turner.[37] The primary force precluding the uprising was the
absence of a slave leader capable of inciting action. Thus, the militant black
spokesman who could inflame an uprising was feared by both the
house slaves who didn't have to toil in the fields, and the slave owners, who
would suffer both financial loss and bodily harm were a slave uprising to
occur.

One interpretation, using the lens of rhetorical vision, is that the drama
of the field slave revolt could have been more dominant in the minds of the
American people, white and black, than were the other themes that
Malcolm X used to further his program. Similarly, the intensive anti-white
fantasy themes contained in the rhetorical dogma or vision of those
participating in the Black Muslim religion with which Malcolm X had
associated could have been so dominant in the minds of whites and blacks
that Malcolm X's new vision, even though it rejected the anti-white themes,
could not gain acceptance.

On the other side of the spectrum, the more militant whites and blacks
also picked up on Malcolm X's occasional references to violent imagery.
Such references, even though oblique to Malcolm X's central thesis, served
to crystalize militant consciousness and chained out as part of the new
militant rhetorical vision depicting the necessity for immediate
revolutionary change. Having already given up on the ballot, the pro-
militants assumed they could only resort to the bullet. Moreover, by
assimilating these fantasy themes that fit their militant vision, they erron-
eously heard Malcolm X telling them that militancy was the only way.[38]

It is ironic that Malcolm X turned on the one hand to longstanding white
modal fantasies to promote his vision of black nationalism, and at the same
time his periodic use of fantasy themes relating to the vision of a slave
uprising conflicted with the ability of those positive white modal fantasies
to catch up his audiences—to be persuasive.

The preceding fantasy theme analysis provides an interpretation at
variance with the news headlines. The media, like most of Malcolm X's
audience, may have chained-out on the revolt themes rather than the themes
of democracy, work-ethic, free enterprise, legal solutions, and the nature of
God.

# V

Malcolm X's vision of black nationalism meant black unity here in
America, especially on political and economic issues. Such a view, on the
surface, appeared highly ethnic and for many people engendered images of

[37]In August, 1831, Southampton County, Virginia, a bondsman, Nat Turner, led the South's
bloodiest slave insurrection in which sixty whites and scores of Negroes were killed.
[38]Indeed, James Farmer sensed the problem, claiming that militant, violent blacks would dis-
tort Malcolm X's doctrine and use it as "An excuse for generalized and indiscriminant
violence." See George Breitman, *The Last Year of Malcolm X* (New York: Schocken
Books, 1967), 82.

black separatism and volatile radicalism.[39] However, as I illustrated, Malcolm X's vision of black nationalism rejected nihilism and accepted existing political and social institutions as necessary to ensure future improvement for black people. That Malcolm advocated working within the system may seem incongruous to the many who knew him solely through media portrayal.[40] I chose not to belabor this point. Rather, I presented an aberrant view drawn from the application of fantasy theme analysis to the unity addresses of Malcolm X.

My argument points to the utility of Bormann's construct of rhetorical vision and his critical method of fantasy theme analysis. In the absence of such a dramatistic perspective, the rhetoric of Malcolm X's black nationalism addresses would clearly be the rhetoric of a fanatic employing veiled threats. With this method, Malcolm X's rhetoric may be interpreted in terms of fantasy themes relating to traditional majority American dreams and religious thinking.

The essay indicates that by examining the rhetoric through fantasy theme analysis, one could identify the rhetorical dramas that had impact for Malcolm X. Startlingly, this analysis found that the rhetorical dramas were white-middle-class dramas.

Finally, the essay indicates that if one is using dramatism as rhetor, one must take precautions to preclude what seems to be irrelevant or subsidiary fantasy themes from cognitively triggering a persuasive drama that is at odds with the rhetor's purpose.

[39]Malcolm X knew of his mis-interpretation, but seemed unable to preclude it. Instead, he blamed the press for the problem. At one point in the *Autobiography* he writes: "Largely, the American white man's press refused to convey that I was now attempting to teach Negroes a new direction;" (366). At another point: "I want you to just watch and see if I'm not right in what I say: that the white man in the press is going to identify me with 'hate';" (381) and again, "You watch. I will be labeled as, at best, an 'irresponsible' black man." (381).

[40]I refer the reader to the articles cited in footnotes 1-5. The all-encompassing nature of the press's epitomization of Malcolm X is reflected in *Newsweek's* eulogy to his death, entitled: "Death of a Desperado," 65 (March 8, 1965), 24-25.

# 7

# The Eagleton Affair:
## A Fantasy Theme Analysis

## ERNEST G. BORMANN

The 1972 presidential campaign was an exciting one for the rhetorical critic who wished to concentrate on the emotions and motives inherent in the symbolic action which was creating, no matter how momentary, a social reality for the American electorate. In a recent issue of the *Quarterly Journal of Speech* I described a Fantasy Theme approach to the discovery and analysis of rhetorical visions in the persuasion of campaigns and movements.[1] Examining the campaign of 1972 from the critical viewpoint reveals that the rhetoric provides an intriguing case study in the ways in which political unknowns become widely known persona.[2] In addition, the emotional evocation of dismay and frustration and the motivation commonly called *apathy* which characterized the chaining fantasies of those

*Quarterly Journal of Speech*, 59 (1973), 143-159. Reprinted with permission from The Speech Communication Association.

[1]Ernest G. Bormann, "Fantasy and Rhetorical Vision: The Rhetorical Criticism of Social Reality," *Quarterly Journal of Speech*, 58 (Dec. 1972), 396-407.

[2]I am using the term *persona* in a relatively traditional way as the characters in a dramatic work, the speaker or voice of a poem or other literary work (although not necessarily the author), and the public personality or mask that an individual uses to meet a public situation. Since a fantasy theme analysis emphasizes the dramatizing aspects of rhetoric a critic needs a term to distinguish the public mask or personality of individuals from other aspects of their personality. The commonly used term *image* is unsatisfactory because it has been used for so many different concepts that it no longer communicates much of anything. Not only do professional persuaders tend to use the term *image* for such diverse purposes as to describe the overall general impression of a public figure, of institutions and of products, but scholarly commentators have also used the term to indicate a wide range of symbolic events. See for example, Daniel Boorstin, *The Image: A Guide to Pseudo-Events in America* (1961; rpt. New York: Harper and Row, 1964). See also Kenneth Boulding, *The Image* (Ann Arbor: Univ. of Michigan Press, 1956). *Persona*, as I use the term, is restricted to the character a public person plays in a given dramatization. When the same persona acts in a series of fantasy themes that chain through the public, the cumulative dramatizations create a more generalized character or persona as part of the rhetorical visions of the various rhetorical communities. The concept of *image* also tends to be static whereas fantasy theme analysis requires a term which conveys the dynamic notion of action and also connotes the potential for change.

who earlier had been excited and impelled by the dramas of the New Politics rhetorical vision are illuminated and clarified by a fantasy theme analysis of the campaign rhetoric of late summer and early fall. Finally, a critical analysis of the major fantasies that chained through the American electorate reveals the awesome power of the electronic media to provide, in the form of breaking news, the dramatizations that cause fantasies to chain through large sections of the American electorate and that thus provide the attitude reinforcement or change that results in voting behavior which elects a president and a vice president.[3]

No political campaign begins with a blank slate. Each party in a campaign has a well-defined rhetorical vision which gives its members a sense of identity and which provides the basic assumptions upon which the party campaigns. On occasion a campaign will see the rise of a rhetorical vision that is either based upon elements from the older visions reshaped into a new pattern or one which rejects the older visions entirely. Often the emergence of a rhetorical vision is indexed by the term *new*. Such labels as the "New South," the "New Deal," and the "New Left" are shorthand ways of referring to rhetorical visions which have emerged clearly enough so people can refer to them and understand the basic elements of the vision when they are so characterized. As a new vision takes shape interested observers will often discuss and debate the meaning of a label. The rhetoric surrounding a new label when a vision is emerging is often couched in definitional terms but the real question at issue is essentially the character of the rhetorical vision indicated by the terms. A critic can often locate the period in history when a new rhetorical vision is emerging by searching for commentary relating to the meaning of the labels such as "Black Power" and "New Left." Once the vision has clearly emerged and is well understood the discussion of definitions tends to die out. The campaign of 1972 is of particular interest because it saw the rise of and the demise of a rhetorical vision in the form of the "New Politics."

What I propose to do in the brief confines of this essay is to concentrate on only one side of the campaign of 1972. I will begin with a capsule summary of the New Politics rhetorical vision of George McGovern and then move to a description and evaluation of one major fantasy that chained through the American electorate. My current estimate is that there were four major news events which provided the dramatization needed to start fantasies chaining through the communication system associated with the cam-

---

[3]There is a whole literature of "voting studies" which can be interpreted to prove that the electronic media do not influence voting behavior. The survey studies of voting behavior are apparently at odds with another large body of research literature which indicates that relatively short persuasive messages can change scores on attitude scales. For a summary of some of the conflicting studies see Carl I. Hovland, "Reconciling Conflicting Results Derived from Experimental and Survey Studies of Attitude Change," in Richard V. Wagner and John J. Sherwood, eds., *The Study of Attitude Change* (Belmont, California: Wadsworth Publishing, 1969), pp. 184-199. The problem with the voting studies is that the research designs tend to encourage the collection of data so gross that they miss the impact of television messages on the symbolic reality of the American electorate.

paign of 1972. They were the Watergate Affair, the Eagleton Affair, the McGovern plan to give people 1,000 dollars, and the peace negotiations of late October and early November. I will examine only the Eagleton Affair. The Eagleton fantasy theme was largely ignited and fueled by the mass media, particularly by television, and was an important factor in the dying out of the New Politics rhetorical vision.

Prior to the primary in California the McGovern character was a shadowy one in the fantasy themes of the general public. He was identified, if at all, as a dove, a stock antiwar persona. The pro-McGovern people, however, were deep into a rich rhetorical vision which contained powerful emotional evocations and compelling motives to action. The McGovern rhetorical vision had much in common with the over-reaching traditional Democratic Party rhetoric, particularly in its view of the Republicans as the party of the rich and the privileged oriented toward big business. Like the traditional democratic vision, the New Politics rhetoric saw the persona of Richard Milhous Nixon as essentially that of Tricky Dick. The slogan that catches the persona in both visions is: would you buy a used car from him? Despite the similarities, the McGovern vision has some crucial differences with the traditional Democratic Party rhetoric.

The rhetorical strategy which undergirded the McGovern vision was an emphasis upon the drama of character. The style and tone of the vision was that of a high drama verging from melodrama to tragedy. The New Politics was more than politics according to its rhetoric; it was a movement that encompassed all of life from aesthetics to social style. Or, put another way, politics was elevated in the vision of the McGovernites into the fundamental and all important drama of life. The fantasy themes contained little humor, little irony, little satire. Potentially the scenario was one of tragedy or of glorious redemption in the mode of the mythic drama of the Christian religion. The rhetoric spoke of a turning point in history, of a "last chance," of no hope should the movement fail.[4]

The fantasy themes of the New Politics tended to be character sketches which stressed the moral superiority of the heroes and the evil nature of the villains. The vision had its roots back to the persona of clean Gene McCarthy and the 1968 campaign. The motives embedded in the rhetoric included a personal attachment to a persona of high ethical character for whom a participant would work and strong impulses to strive for such goals as ending the war, aiding the poor, the women, and the minorities. The emotional evocations of the vision were powerful and included admiration for a persona almost saintly in motivation and a hatred of the villainous devil figures. The McGovern rhetoric created a social reality which saw such villainous characters as Lyndon Johnson, Richard Daly, and Hubert Humphrey as the enemy. The vision saw both major parties as essentially

[4]For a study of the New Politics rhetorical vision see Linda Putnam, "The Rhetorical Vision and Fantasy Themes of McGovern Campaign Planners," *Moments in Contemporary Rhetoric and Communication*, 2 (Fall 1972), 13-20. The entire issue of *Moments* is devoted to the campaign.

corrupted by the war, both as racist and closed. The dream was of a purging of the Democratic party which would oust the bosses, the minions of the military-industrial complex, and the racist elements from all of society but particularly from the South.

As the McGovern campaign grew more and more successful until its final triumph at the Miami convention, the vision solidified and the emphasis on villains became sharp and clear in the fantasy themes of the movement. The arch-enemy was Tricky Dick and his laughable hatchetman Spiro Agnew but these persona hovered in the background. The more tangible villains, the ones that were the main characters in the fantasy themes, were those symbolized by the Chicago convention of 1968 and these included the devil figures of Lyndon Johnson, Richard Daly, and Hubert Humphrey, all of whom stood for a closed convention, barricaded behind barbed wire, protected by police, a convention which barred the young, the poor, the blacks, the Chicanos, the Indians, and the women. Now the leadership of McGovern backed by the army of the formerly disenfranchised would defeat the old politicians.

The participants in the New Politics rhetorical vision saw themselves as a coalition of various liberation movements that would open the party and give power to the people. The style of the New Politics was openness, participation, community and cooperation while the style of the old politics was closed, barricaded, unresponsive. The persona of McGovern in the vision of his followers before and during the Miami convention was that of St. George on a crusade. He was not really a politician. He was an honest, sincere, decent man who just happened to be in politics. The fantasy themes presented McGovern patiently working for party reform, opening it up to the people, standing courageously against the Vietnam war, and forging a dedicated and mighty army of hard-working volunteers who finally were to get their chance within the system. One salient scenario presented those who had been outside the walls in Chicago as on the floor in Miami.[5]

After Senator McGovern received the nomination the usual reconciliation of factions within the party in preparation for a campaign was made more difficult because of the collision of key elements of the old rhetorical vision of the Democratic Party with the rhetorical vision of the New Politics. The old vision saw labor at the core of the party; in the new vision, labor bosses such as George Meany were among the villains of the old politics. The labor movement was racist, conservative, and closed off from the poor and the minorities. In the old vision party regularity was a virtue. After all, the party was a coalition and the New Deal fantasy themes dramatized keeping the ethnic groups, the blacks, labor, and the South all under an umbrella. The new vision saw party regulars such as Mayor Daly of Chicago as the enemy. The new vision would sacrifice the racist South (symbolized in the

---

[5]*Time* reported this version: "Ted Pillow, 20, Iowa, vividly recalls the 1968 Democratic Convention in Chicago. He was one of the protesters outside the hall, taunting police, throwing rocks, breaking windows and fleeing down side streets. Last week in Miami Beach he was sitting inside the convention hall as a member of the Iowa delegation." (24 July 1972), p. 27.

persona of George Wallace) for the sake of the minorities. If the party was not purged the participants in the new vision were ready to leave the ranks.

Clearly, however, success at the polls required a new rhetoric which would transcend the two competing visions within the party. Unless the rhetoricians within both visions could find a strategy to fashion a coherent drama on the basis of the common materials within the two visions, one undergirded by the old mythic assumptions of the traditional rhetoric, the party had little possibility of winning the election in November.

The McGovern leadership group began the rhetorical effort at the convention itself. Fantasy themes began to chain through the McGovern delegations around the theme of *pragmatism*. Involving the ultimate legitimizer of more political party visions, that is, winning an election, a move was made by the McGovern forces to create a unifying rhetoric.

How could a new vision be fashioned to transcend the competing visions within the party? The McGovern campaign strategy was to continue to emphasize *persona*. In an article entitled, "St. George Prepared to Face the Dragon," *Time* magazine noted, "The McGovern Campaign will be similar to the personality-oriented, almost evangelical appeal for faith in a candidate that was unsuccessful for Edmund Muskie."[6] Why did the rhetoricians of the New Politics decide to emphasize fantasy themes based on persona? Certainly they knew that the Muskie candidacy had foundered and that the reports of Muskie's lashing out at a newspaper publisher and breaking down in tears had dramatized a fantasy theme which chained through the American electorate and severely damaged the Muskie persona. Emphasis on persona is a risky strategy unless the heroes can remain, in the words of presidential candidate Eisenhower when Richard Nixon was accused of double dealing in 1952, as "clean as a hound's tooth." What alternatives were open to the planners of the McGovern persuasion? They could have chosen to emphasize *scene*. The refrain of McGovern's acceptance speech was, after all, "Come home America." They could have emphasized *action* which was the strategy adopted by official Republican campaign rhetoricians.

In many respects the emphasis on persona is understandable. The rhetorical strategy had worked in the primaries and brought success at Miami. The nature of the opposition indicated that an emphasis on persona was a strong rhetorical ground. If the challenger selected action as a strategy he would be at a distinct disadvantage since the president is, by the nature of the office, where the action is. Then, too, the breaking news surrounding the Nixon persona during the 1970's presented the president in action scenarios. The Nixon persona had withdrawn troops from Vietnam, signed an arms limitation agreement with Russia, agreed to seating Red China in the United Nations, traveled to China, and traveled to Russia. In the campaign, many fantasy themes were available to dramatize the

[6](24 July 1972), p. 9.

president as persona in action.[7] In addition, the scenarios in which the president was the leading actor were not all that unattractive. The persona of Nixon, on the other hand, seemed a good target for attack. Certainly those who participated in the New Politics vision and hated the persona would be tempted to frame rhetorical dramas in which Richard Milhous Nixon was the center of attack.

The unifying rhetoric at the Miami convention began first with the emphasis on a villainous persona. Bad as Mayor Daly might be, and bad as Hubert Humphrey might be, still, those deep in the New Politics vision ought to join forces with their old enemies within the party in order to defeat Nixon. As much as the old politicians disliked the new, would it be worth four more years of Nixon to carry on the internal battle. Senator McGovern developed the theme in his acceptance speech. "Now to anyone in this hall or beyond who doubts the ability of Democrats to join together in common cause I say never underestimate the power of Richard Nixon to bring harmony to Democratic ranks."[8]

The second rhetorical strategy which began at the convention was to find a new symbolic persona who could bridge the competing visions. Traditionally the nomination of a vice president serves as a symbolic welding of the disparate visions within a party. The McGovern team began its search with Theodore Kennedy who would have been ideal except the Kennedy persona was so potent it might have overshadowed the candidate himself. When Kennedy would not accept, the McGovern forces turned to an attractive young senator with strong ties to the competing Democratic rhetorical vision, strong with labor, strong with the regulars but also young and attractive, much in the mold of the Kennedy persona. Senator Thomas Eagleton seemed to provide a personality which could be fashioned into a transcending figure.

With the decision in Miami to select Senator McGovern the campaign for the votes of the electorate got under way in all seriousness. Now the fantasy themes that would chain out through the American public would carry with them the motives to go or not to go to the polls and, just as importantly, to vote for either the Nixon persona or the McGovern. For many the McGovern public figure was vague and shadowy at this stage; even the professionals of the media had not formed a clear rhetorical vision of that portion of the campaign dominated by McGovern. The traditional rhetorical vision of the professional news person and political commentator was that of politicians as essentially ambitious people out to get elected, scrambling about for political advantage, generally hypocritical. Wise inside-dopesters such as professionals never were taken by appearances and

[7]Which is precisely what many of the paid political announcements produced by the Committee to Reelect the President did do. Their persuasion on television tended to show montages of the President at work in the White House, walking along a beach with his wife, walking on the Great Wall of China, meeting with the Russian leaders, and so forth.

[8]CBS Network Coverage of the Convention, 14 July 1972.

never took a politician's words for anything more than smokescreen.[9]

The Miami convention provided the first big chance for newsmen to chain out on the dramatic action of events. One of the first fantasies to spread through the media was that of the McGovern machine. Some media reports dramatized the New Politics as just the Old Politics honed to a sharper than usual edge.[10] Larry Hart and Frank Mankiewicz emerged as characters in the drama; for some reporters, they were the able people who had harnessed the high idealism of a lot of students and new leftists and poor people to a volunteer organization that had outmachined Richard Daly himself.

In a sense the fantasy fit in well with the media vision where no politician is as virtuous as he or she maintains and the ultimate legitimatization for politics is winning. They had miscalculated McGovern's chances for many months. Now he had won. Now he was legitimatized. The fantasy accounted for their miscalculation and also put St. George the self-righteous in his place. They had miscalculated because they had not realized that the McGovern machine had such a thorough and effective grass roots organization. As the McGovern forces crushed all attempts to seat the contested delegates from the opposition and as it began to play down issues like women's liberation, abortion reform, and amnesty, the fantasy began to chain through the media that McGovern had worked a miracle and that he just might be ruthless enough and his machine might be well organized and disciplined enough to pull off a second miracle and unseat the President.

McGovern and the television cameras went to Sylvan Lake in the Black Hills of South Dakota to rest and plan for the campaign. The American public had every reason to pay more attention to the McGovern persona as

[9]The concept of inside-dopester is explained in detail in David Riesman, Nathan Glazer, and Reuel Denney, *The Lonely Crowd: A Study of the Changing American Character* (1950; rpt. Garden City, N.Y.: Doubleday Anchor Books, 1953), pp. 210-217.

Riesman, Glazer, and Denney note, "There are political newsmen and broadcasters who, after long training, have succeeded in eliminating all emotional responses to politics and who pride themselves on achieving the inside-dopesters' goal: never to be taken in by any person, cause, or event." (p. 211) For further discussion of the media professionals' vision and its motive which causes them to seek out the dramatic, see David Berg, "Rhetoric, Reality, and Mass Media," *Quarterly Journal of Speech,* 58 (Oct. 1972), 255-263. Richard Dougherty, McGovern's press secretary during the 1972 campaign, bitterly castigated the press because they gave McGovern "a hell of a beating." He was referring to the Eagleton Affair. He concluded, "The man they offered up for the people to judge was a caricature of the real man, and more reporters knew it. I would guess that 90 percent of the news people who covered McGovern voted for him. Why, if that was their ultimate personal judgment of him, could they not pass that judgment on to the public? Hard news wouldn't let them. It wouldn't have been objective reporting. You can write about a candidate who is being sneaky and bumbling: that's objective reporting. But you can't write about a candidate who is being kind and forgiving: that's editorializing." "The Sneaky Bumbler," *Newsweek,* 8 Jan. 1973, p. 7.

[10]*Time* magazine, for example, headlined its convention cover story: "Introducing...the McGovern Machine" (24 July 1972), p. 18.

it was portrayed by the media for he was not a potential president. The confident nominee had barely time to be seen on the television screens enjoying a well-earned rest in the serene mountains when a dramatic news story broke.

On Tuesday, July 25, 1972, Senators McGovern and Eagleton called a press conference in the Black Hills. That evening, Roger Mudd, sitting in for Walter Cronkite, asserted that an obviously "nervous" Eagleton had told the press of his mental health problems. The producers cut to a film clip of McGovern and Eagleton walking with a parade of supporters, workers, and newsmen to a building where the press conference was to be held. The film cut to Eagleton's statement which included the crucial phrase, "on three occasions in my life I have voluntarily gone into hospitals as a result of nervous exhaustion." As the press conference continued, the network producers cut to shots of Mrs. Eagleton and Mrs. McGovern, to Senator McGovern watching Senator Eagleton, and to the questions and answers of both senators. In answer to the question, Senator McGovern said, "I don't have the slightest doubt about the wisdom of my judgment in selecting him as my running mate nor would I have any hesitancy at all in trusting the Unites States Government in his hands." The producers cut back to Roger Mudd who said that the decision to hold a press conference "obviously followed a major crisis in the McGovern camp and apparently was precipitated by persistent rumors that Senator Eagleton had a possible drinking problem."[11]

The story of Senator Eagleton's nervous exhaustion was top priority news on all three major television networks. Key excerpts from the press conference were shown to the huge audiences that watch the dinner time and late evening news. David Brinkley on his journal on NBC mentioned electric shock therapy and noted that "it has been a long time since the office of the vice president got so much attention."

The story had the human interest required to chain out in all directions through the American electorate. Millions of people who had little impression of the McGovern persona and less of the Eagleton presence were suddenly attending to both. How far would the fantasy chaining process go? How compelling would the drama become for the majority of the American people? The answer to such questions depended partly upon new developments or, in dramatic terms, new complications and partly upon the rhetorical art with which the drama was presented.

Senator McGovern had expressed support of Senator Eagleton in the first press conference. In long film clips on all networks reporters questioned McGovern again and again about the nature and extent of his support for Senator Eagleton. ABC News on July 26th featured an interview between Harry Reasoner and George McGovern. They were pictured seated at a picnic table beside Sylvan Lake. Reasoner asked, "Can you flatly say that if

[11]My reconstruction of the network newscasts is based upon videotape recordings of the broadcasts. I will identify the date and the network in the text.

you had known this before you selected him your decision would have been the same?'' McGovern, "Absolutely. There would have been no difference.'' A bit later in the interview Reasoner asked, ''Suppose Senator Eagleton in the face of whatever reaction there is to this announcement wanted to leave the ticket, what would your attitude be, sir?'' McGovern answered, ''I would...I would discourage that. I don't want him to leave the ticket. I think...uh...I think we're going to win the election. I think he's going to be a great vice president. If anything were to happen to me I think he would make a great president. I will do everything I can to discourage any move on his part to leave the ticket. He's not considering that, though, by the way.'' Later in the same newscast, Howard K. Smith asserted, ''In the chat with reporters today McGovern escalated numerically his support of Eagleton. He was, he said, '1,000 percent resolved to keep Eagleton as a running mate'.''

Where is the rhetorical dimension of the Eagleton Affair? Assuming, as I do, that rhetoric is an art, where is the artistry? Both the strategists for McGovern and for Nixon made rhetorical choices affecting the dramatizations that were presented to the American people. The media professionals also made rhetorical programs on July 25, 26, 1972, were joint artistic efforts of the Nixon, McGovern, and media rhetoricians. (The same process was, of course, operating in radio, newspapers, and magazines.)

The age of mass communication has seen the rise of a unique mass rhetoric fashioned by groups of artists of strangely mixed objectives and approaches. Both McGovern and Nixon publicists had a clear persuasive objective and a general notion of how they would have liked to have their position presented on network television news. The two antagonistic groups had to make their rhetorical choices with an eye both to the symbolic responses of the other and to those of the "objective" media professionals. In one sense, if the Nixon forces gained, the McGovern forces would lose, and vice versa, but the essentially zero-sum game of the two campaigns was mediated by the electronic journalists with their own intent and the success or failure of each candidate's rhetoric was to some extent dependent upon the cooperation of the media professionals. The fact that the network news seldom dramatizes events as advocates wish they would accounts for some of the anger and disillusionment with the media.

McGovern's people made some of the more important early rhetorical choices. They decided to hold a press conference. Since their man was a newly nominated presidential candidate they could, if they were skillful in the way they planned and conducted the news briefing, assure themselves of free television time and of a very large audience.

The McGovern strategists certainly could select the scene for the drama. They might select, as they did, Sylvan Lake in the Black Hills of South Dakota; they could have chosen Washington, D.C., or Barnes Hospital in St. Louis. The strategists could also select the persona of the drama. Should, for instance, the McGovern persona take center stage with the

Eagleton persona standing silently by? Should the McGovern persona be separated in space, for example, Senator Eagleton holding a press conference in Washington, D.C., with McGovern simply answering reporters' questions in the Black Hills? Should other persona be present? To indicate the extent of the rhetorical choices, one possible alternative for the McGovern rhetoricians could have been to have Senator Eagleton make his announcement from Barnes Hospital with a battery of doctors who would testify as to his medical record and to the present state of his mental health. The McGovern persona might then have stayed in South Dakota and expressed noncommital concern.

The contemporary strategist for mass audiences needs to be skilled at estimating the response of the mediating professionals and should draft messages, select time, scene, and persona with a view to getting the fantasy themes most likely to chain dramas persuasive to his position on prime-time evening television. In estimating the responses of the professionals and in their decisions as to persona, scene, and dialogue, the McGovern forces made some rhetorical errors of the first magnitude. They selected as the scene the Black Hills vacation retreat of Senator McGovern and they had the McGovern persona at the Eagleton press conference. Not only that, but McGovern made a strong statement supporting Senator Eagleton.

Everything about the setting, the persona, and the lines they spoke reinforced the support of McGovern for the Eagleton persona and his identification with it. In addition, no other major persona of the Democratic Party was on the scene to lend symbolic unity and support to the decisions.

On television the media reporters appeared delighted if a bit incredulous about the McGovern support and kept prodding for clear and unequivocal expressions of such commitment. Clear expressions of positions in risky situations are rare in political campaigns but they are good news just because of that fact.

Having gotten the McGovern persona, epitome of the New Politics, to express unequivocal support, the rhetoricians of the media went to work to create a good news story. The media professionals evaluate a good story as one having the ability to hold the interest of the audience. Human interest stories dramatizing fantasies that chain out through the public raise television ratings.

When the McGovern forces called the news conference and staged the opening scenes of the Eagleton Affair they, of course, lost control of the story. They could affect future symbolic events but they could not completely control them as they could with the dramatizations they presented during the television time they purchased.

The stage was now set for dramatic action from the Nixon persona. In line with the overall Nixon rhetoric of playing down persona and emphasizing action, the Nixon decision came quickly and was delivered by the surrogate persona of MacGregor. On July 26th, film clips of MacGregor appeared on several network newscasts. On CBS MacGregor claimed that the Republicans knew about Eagleton's health record but, even before the announcement, had received "a mandate and directive from the President that no one connected with him governmentally or politically would have any comment whatever to make."

The Nixon rhetoricians would keep the persona of the President out of the drama. By doing so they gained little but they also risked little. In a situation where the public opinion polls indicated that Nixon was ahead, the temptation to take a conservative position and not gamble was strong. The Nixon forces had, however, taken the same rhetorical stance in the much closer campaign of 1960 in regard to the religion of his opponent, John F. Kennedy. On that occasion the rhetoricians for Kennedy had set a scene in Houston, Texas and provided the Kennedy persona with dramatic antagonists in the form of a group of protestant ministers. Kennedy made a strong direct defense of his religion and its role in his functioning as a president should he be elected. The fantasy theme of the Kennedy confrontation apparently chained out to the advantage of the Senator. His campaign organization subsequently bought time to show an artistic dramatization of the scene in the form of a documentary film on television stations throughout the country. In 1960 the low-risk decision nonetheless cost the campaign of Richard Nixon votes because of the artistry with which the skillful Kennedy rhetoricians presented the media and the public with further dramatizations.[12]

After the news conference announcing Eagleton's medical history the media rhetoricians had their turn. They operated under stringent time limitations. Their dramatic format was that of an "anchor man" with star status, the Walter Cronkite, Roger Mudd, David Brinkley, John Chancellor, Harry Reasoner, Howard K. Smith persona, playing the leading role and the lesser reporters serving as narrative voices, a mass media chorus, speaking from the scene of action. The narrator convention serves to tie the events that are dramatized into some sequence and fit them into an interpretive frame. The convention of narrator generally requires that the persona of the reporter be an "objective" voice.

The illusion of objectivity is created by the device of having the narrator attribute all editorial comments, unverified statements of fact, and opinion statements to others. Thus when the narrator chorus began to assert that pressure was building up on McGovern to dump Eagleton, the narrators always attributed the information to others. For instance, NBC reporter Bob Clark mentioned from South Dakota (July 26th) that the Democrats were keeping a calm public face but "off the record, a number of Democrats agree with most Republicans that the Eagleton disclosures have hurt the McGovern ticket." NBC reporter John Dancy asserted (July 27th) that "one of McGovern's top aides privately calls the disclosure a blow to their chances." ABC reporter Sam Donaldson maintained (July 28th) that the "Senator's top staff men are deeply worried about the Eagleton affair." Reporter Stephen Geer of ABC added, "McGovern's advisors are concerned because he has been on the defensive." Since the narrators present an objective voice they seem removed from partisanship and thus, in a political campaign, are often more credible sources than most of the partisan campaigners.

The dramatistic structure of the network news in presenting an event such as the Eagleton developments consists of a lead-in by the star persona, a narrative commentary with short film clips of dramatic action presented either by the star or one of the lesser reporters, and transitional material usually provided by the anchor man. The media rhetoricians' artistry in selecting from the materials presented by the campaign rhetoricians and their skill in weaving new materials of their own manufacture into an interpretative frame has much to do with the way the story catches on and chains through the public (or fails to do so) and with the persuasive impact of the chaining fantasy. Whether the drama as it chains through the general public contains motives to vote for Nixon or for McGovern or for neither is of less importance to the media rhetoricians than that it does chain widely. The charge that the media are liberal or conservative or systematically biased in their dramatizations is too simple, in my estimation. The media rhetoricians are hard-headed dramatists more interested in success at the box office than in partisan political persuasion.

A drama to be compelling required plausibility, action, suspense, and sympathetic characters. Developing audience interest in a drama which emphasizes character takes time and time is in short supply on the evening news (as contrasted, say, with daytime television dramas where time is in long supply and where the dramas tend to emphasize character at the expense of action). Because of the shortage of time of the evening news the skillful media professional tends to go for conflict and suspense. The McGovern rhetoricians thus were operating under a handicap because of their decision to emphasize character when it came to utilizing one of the most credible outlets of television, that of the network sponsored newscasts.

Now the professional news people began the artistic interpretation of the events. The day after the original press conference several networks interviewed a former alcoholic, Senator Hughes of Iowa, identified as Senator Muskie's vice presidential choice had the Maine Senator received the nomination. Hughes was supportive of Eagleton's staying on the ticket and asserted that the American people had "outgrown this immaturity" in regard to mental health. The Hughes persona was one of the few characters selected by the media rhetoricians which fit the fantasy that Eagleton's mental health problems were no drawback for the ticket and that, indeed, the American people would be sympathetic to him. Early in the breaking news the fantasy theme that Eagleton should stay on the ticket and demonstrate the maturity of the electorate appeared to be a viable one. For the most part, however, the professional journalists sought to dramatize the conflict.

CBS News on July 27th did an able and artistic job of finding and presenting the controversy. Roger Mudd began by listing all of the major newspapers which had come out for Eagleton's withdrawal. Reporter Duke interviewed Mankiewicz and Hart and both reiterated that the decision to keep Eagleton had been made and that it was irrevocable. Next CBS cut to an interview with Howard Metzenbaum, identified as a Cleveland attorney and millionaire fund raiser for McGovern. Metzenbaum was sought out to dramatize the story that the Eagleton disclosures were hurting fund-raising for the McGovern campaign. Metzenbaum was of the opinion that Eagleton would do the right thing and resign. He said, "unfortunately the American people don't comprehend the nature of psychiatric treatment." If Eagleton would resign, he felt, the election might still be won because, fortunately, "in time people do forget." Henry Kimmelman, identified as finance chairman, also appeared briefly, but took no firm stand.

Next the CBS News cut to a long interview with an articulate and attractive persona identified as Matthew Troy, Democratic leader in Queens, New York, and strong McGovern supporter. Troy asserted that people "are really scared that you're giving the power possible to a man to ...to...to destroy this world with a nuclear holocaust if he buckles under the pressure of the presidency." Troy had urged McGovern to drop Eagleton. What did McGovern reply? "He told me he was standing by Senator Eagleton and he would not walk away from him."

When a fantasy begins to catch on with a large group of people the evidence of public interest tends to draw outsiders into the social reality for self-serving reasons. Thus an unexpected outside complication is often a component of a major fantasy drama.

On July 27th an unexpected and dramatic complication entered the Eagleton affair when the crusading reporter persona, Jack Anderson, charged that Senator Eagleton had a record of arrests for drunken driving. Another press conference was arranged for Senator Eagleton and again he received extensive coverage on the three major networks. On ABC News Eagleton testified that he had no record of arrests for drunken driving. Eagleton said, "Mr. Anderson's statement to that effect is, in blunt but direct English, a damnable lie." The camera cut to a tight face shot catching the Senator from the hairline to just below the chin. He passed the test of the closeup lens. Clear-eyed, with jutting jaw, he reaffirmed his innocence and his firm resolve to stay in the race and vindicate himself and his record. "I have never been more determined in my life about any issue than I am today about remaining on this ticket. I'm not going to bow to Mr. Anderson. I'm not going to let a lie drive me from this ticket."

The Eagleton rhetoricians had responded brilliantly to the Anderson complication. The Senator's denial, his demeanor during the newscasts, his statements of resolve were appealing. The problem, of course, was the possibility that the crusading reporter was right. For the McGovern rhetoricians the new complication was probably extremely traumatic.

The media peoples' decisions to interview certain individuals (and not

others) and then feature these interviews as part of the dramatizations gave
them considerable control over the cast of the drama. Picking the cast gave
the electronic journalists some control over the action line and the conflict
and suspense that resulted and, thus, over the potential of the story to be a
big one--that is, to catch the attention of many people and remain in
featured position of the evening news for a number of days. The media
production people cast such individuals as Hart, Mankeiwicz,
Metzenbaum, and Troy into the fantasy as it unfolded. Some of the
breaking news was, of course, beyond the control of media production
crews. They were restricted by the nature of the material presented by the
McGovern and Nixon persuaders. They were also restricted by such
intrusions as Jack Anderson's charges. Nonetheless, the room for artistry
and the options available are very large and much larger than a rhetorically
naive viewer watching the hard news unfold at dinner time is likely to
realize. They chose to feature the Troy persona which emerged on television
as an attractive, articulate, and dramatic antagonist to keeping Eagleton on
the ticket. The Metzenbaum persona was less articulate and less attractive
but presented the more "pragmatic" and cynical political position most
effectively.

Clearly the fantasies chaining through the media professionals, given
their rhetorical vision of politics, influenced their selection of persona.
Although I do not have copies of all segments of all network's newscasts
covering the Eagleton Affair, I do have the bulk of them. In none of the
segments that I have studied do the networks present a medical authority on
Senator Eagleton's health. His doctor never appeared on network news. In
many other dramatizations regarding the health of a president, vice
president, or candidate for those offices, the reporters often go to medical
men. When President Eisenhower had his heart attack medical material was
a prominent part of the news. When Lyndon Johnson was a national leader
his health was often discussed. In the instance of the Eagleton candidacy,
however, the networks featured the drama of pressure from within the
Democratic Party for his resignation.

On July 28th the ABC News showed Eagleton saying, "I'm not quitting.
I'm not getting out...No, you're not going to get me out of this
race...never..." Howard K. Smith reported that Eagleton was considering
taking his case to the people on television as Richard Nixon had in 1952. On
NBC News an excerpt from Eagleton's press conference showed Eagleton
alluding to the fact that John Kennedy had taken the case of his Catholicism
to the people and won and that maybe Eagleton would do something to lay
to rest the mental health issue.

By the 28th, fantasy themes which would be supportive and contain
sympathetic emotional evocations were beginning to chain out in the media
in regard to Eagleton's candidacy. Like Richard Nixon in 1952, he might lay
to rest another bigoted political prejudice. On his evening commentary,
Howard K. Smith urged McGovern to keep Eagleton since he had expressed 1,000 percent support for his running mate and "a switch now

would give a wishy-washy impression that would be bad for a presidential candidate.'' Smith noted that Abraham Lincoln and Winston Churchill had suffered from spells of melancholia which probably should have been treated professionally and yet one had been the greatest president ever and the other had been the greatest prime minister. Eagleton's colleagues in Washington found him to be, "outstandingly vigorous and easy to work with. Moreover, a couple more undocumented charges like Jack Anderson's yesterday and there is going to be a big backlash of sympathy for Eagleton. McGovern would look pretty bad disowning him just as the public may be about to turn for him.''

Clearly, some media professionals were beginning to interpret the drama in ways which presented McGovern-Eagleton as heroic figures striking a blow for public understanding of mental problems. The blunder of the McGovern rhetoricians was one of timing in that they temporized and allowed the drama to unfold for too long in this age of electronic media. Here the symbolic role of money in a political campaign in the United States played an important part in the developing rhetoric. In the vision of many citizens, partisans, media professionals, and independents, the drama of politics is rife with monetary implications. In some visions elections can be bought but in most, campaigns require money. The election of 1972 saw the great preoccupation with campaign contributions and financing. The media decision to dramatize the impact of the Eagleton medical record on campaign contributions is indicative of the interpretive frames of the visions. Money symbolizes both the potential for success and for corruption; it symbolizes both the potential for the selling of a president and the selling out of a presidential candidate.

Now the McGovern rhetoricians had to accommodate to the fantasies chaining out from the media dramatization to the effect that their campaign was doomed because, already behind, they would find the sources of campaign funding drying up. At this juncture, I have no evidence of the extent to which the fantasy chained through those groups with the greatest likelihood of contributing to the campaign. Should the fantasy have chained out through those groups, however, it contained motives that would, indeed shut off contributions. Thus fantasy theme analysis provides a clue to the mechanism by which the oft-noted phenomenon of the self-fulfilling prophecy comes about. The media, by dramatizing the possible impact of the Eagleton Affair on contributions, could trigger fantasy chains among potential contributors which would cause opinion leaders among potential contributors (such as Metzenbaum) to report to the McGovern headquarters that contributions would dry up.

Having allowed the drama to unfold to the point where the fantasies about monetary support were moving through the public, the potential loss of funds became a factor that the McGovern rhetoricians had to deal with on several levels. They had to estimate what, indeed, would happen to the flow of money if they decided to keep the Eagleton persona, which had by now been invested with great symbolic power, power to work either for or against their drive to persuade the American electorate to vote for McGovern. They also had to anticipate what would happen to American public opinion if they severed the powerful Eagleton persona from the ticket. Finally, if they removed Eagleton, could they find a suitable persona to replace him? Could they find a persona with the potential to repair the damage to their rhetoric of character? (Notice that I am phrasing all issues and options in rhetorical terms and such important questions as the ability of the candidate as administrator are bypassed. My analysis focuses on symbolic action. If rhetorical decisions clash with other considerations then a campaign organization might, of course, make a poor rhetorical decision in order to achieve other goals. For instance, if McGovern's forces had had evidence that Senator Eagleton's health was such that he could not assume the duties of president, they might decide to remove him from the ticket even if the Eagleton persona had become so attractive that the decision would have deleterious rhetorical effects.)[13]

The suspense continued to build up over the weekend. On July 30th, Jean Westwood said she thought Eagleton should resign. Eagleton continued to assert his decision to stay in the race. The news reporters intensified their reports of inside information and rumors of pressures and counter pressures.

On July 31st, CBS News reported that Senator McGovern would announce a final decision soon and that he would meet with Senator Eagleton. Bruce Morton of CBS asserted that Eagleton would argue to stay and McGovern would urge him to leave. The dramatization of CBS News of July 31st, however, clearly was based upon the theme that Eagleton would leave the ticket. CBS carried a feature of how the new vice presidential candidate would be chosen and reported rumors of who the new candidate might be. The commentator, Barry Serafin reported that Eagleton was receiving many supportive letters. Eagleton said he had a good case to present but, according to Serafin, in McGovern he would have a difficult jury.

ABC News reported a poll of Democratic state chairmen and vice chairmen in which eighteen voted to keep Eagleton, seventeen voted to have him step down, and ten refused to comment. NBC News features a three-way discussion with Chancellor asking questions of Fred Briggs who had been with Eagleton, and John Dancy who had been with McGovern. Chancellor asked Dancy why did not McGovern ask Eagleton to step down immediately? Why has it gone on this long? (Actually the first report came on the 25th so the Eagleton Affair had been before the public less than a week. Yet when one views the recordings of the television news shows for the week, the saturation coverage does give the impression that the drama has gone on for a long time.) Dancy answered that at first they were going to try to "tough it out" and, of course, that had not worked.

Howard K. Smith's commentary assumes that Eagleton will be dropped and Smith dramatizes a fantasy theme most damaging to McGovern's

[13]This is a purely hypothetical possibility; I have no information indicating this to be the case.

persona. Eagleton had hardened his resolve to stay. "McGovern, 1,000 percent resolved to keep Eagleton, in his phrase, turned to marshmallow and let his national chairwoman tell the public Eagleton had to go," Smith said. He further asserted that McGovern's reputation for leadership has been "sullied by too much yielding to pressure. His 1,000 dollar welfare plan went the way his 1,000 percent support of Eagleton did."

Tuesday, August 1st, 1972, just a week after it had opened, the drama of the Eagleton Affair came to a close. John Chancellor opened the NBC Evening News with, "Good evening on a day that will make at least an important footnote in American history; for the first time ever, a vice presidential candidate has resigned." The CBS Morning News that day had featured an interview between Barry Serafin and Senator Eagleton. Eagleton said, "I've come out of it stronger than I went in. I'm...I'm at peace with myself...This may be the most important week of my life. I did the job. I took the heat and I endured."

Tuesday was highlighted by dramatic irony. CBS featured a news conference with Eagleton and Jack Anderson. The crusading reporter had checked and found his charges were unsubstantiated. He had done the Senator an injustice. "I owe him a great and humble apology." Eagleton made no comment on the film clip but the narrator asserted that Eagleton had said the books were closed on the matter.

Senator McGovern cancelled a talk he had scheduled to give the American people on television in regard to the matter of his decision to drop Eagleton.

David Brinkley, in his journal feature, delivered a bitter attack on politicians without mentioning any candidates by name. But straight out of the inside-dopester vision of the media professional, Brinkley asserted that most people do not believe politicians, that the public had turned sour on politics and politicians.

Eric Sevareid editorialized on CBS to the effect that Eagleton's career at the political summit had been one of the shortest on record but in the course of it he had become a household word and created thousands of friendly sympathizers. Sevareid used the term "Eagleton Affair" in his commentary. He asserted that Eagleton was burned by a fire started by the press and that a fire started by the press could be very hot indeed but that in the long run it was cleansing. Certainly, Sevareid concluded, the affair indicated that the press was not biased in a liberal direction as some had charged.

Sevareid was right. Much of the dramatization (the fire) was an artistic creation of the media. The impact of the media selection of characters and action lines upon the fantasy themes was considerable. When the announcement came of Eagleton's departure from the ticket the dramatic suggestion that McGovern had bowed to pressure for the crassest of political reasons, namely, loss of campaign financing from big contributors, was very strong. Certainly the emphasis on characters relating to financing and allusions to financing on NBC were most important.

The most sympathetic character in the drama turned out to be Tom

Eagleton.[14] He came through the network news as an open, cleancut, if intense, young man. He recounted his medical problems in some detail. When he decided to stay in the race he was forthright and forceful in his statement about the American people being intelligent and sophisticated about mental health and ready to be understanding about his problem.

The Anderson charges which Eagleton denied put the characterization of Eagleton to the test. If Anderson had proved his charges then the Eagleton persona would have received a damaging blow to its credibility; then all of Eagleton's other testimony, no matter how convincingly portrayed on television, might be wrong also. With a discredited Eagleton persona in the drama, McGovern might not have appeared as the "heavy." When Anderson publicly admitted the charges were untrue, however, the Eagleton character increased its credibility and the halo effect of a man falsely accused increased the sympathy one felt about his earlier statements regarding his mental health.

Finally, as the pressure mounted, Eagleton remained adamant that he would stand firm and fight the charge through to ultimately win the election and thus justify his faith in the American people. A dramatic protagonist who has a clear and sympathetic goal and is willing to stand firm and fight for it, even at a personal sacrifice, is sympathetic. When the Eagleton persona was finally cut down, it was by the one force in the drama he could not fight, the presidential candidate himself.

The persona of Jack Anderson as presented in the Eagleton drama is important not only because it emerged as the antagonist but also because it was a key character in other fantasies relating to the campaign and to the drama of corruption within the Nixon Administration. Jack Anderson had been playing the role of the fearless investigative reporter discovering hidden deals and secret papers. The Anderson character was thus a kind of hero in the rhetorical vision of the New Politics. Now, he was playing the part of an antagonist. As the breaking news presented Anderson as an unethical opportunist trying to gain personal advantage by making unsupported charges, his persona was tarnished. Certainly, within the vision of the New Politics with its emphasis on high ethical standards for persona, the revelations were damaging to Anderson. The tension within the vision came from the role that Anderson was already playing in the fantasy themes related to other matters such as the I.T.T. Affair. If Anderson was lacking in credibility in the Eagleton Affair, could he be a hero in the I.T.T. Affair? How much the loss of credibility of the Anderson persona had to do with the apparent difficulty of the media and the McGovern campaign to make the Watergate Affair chain through the general public in a way that damaged Nixon is an interesting question beyond the scope of this essay. Certainly, however, the Watergate Affair deserves extended criticism from a fantasy theme frame of analysis.

[14]On July 28, 1972, Howard K. Smith on ABC reported results of a poll showing 60% sympathetic to Eagleton although there was a 30% negative response to McGovern for being caught unaware of Eagleton's past medical history.

The greatest damage of all the persona came, of course, to that of George McGovern. First there was his rather offhand response. The matter, he said, was really not very imprtant but the decision was made to stop rumors. The persona asserted strong and unequivocal support for his vice president. The persona reiterated that support. The question, however, was never closed. The possibility apparently lingered. The continued rumors of possible "dumping" and then the indirect story that McGovern had signalled Eagleton that he would like a resignation persisted. Eagleton stood firm. Finally, after what seemed like pressure from his more unsavory supporters, the persona made his decision to remove Eagleton for apparently base political motivations.

What motives were embedded in the scenario for those who chained into it? For the New Politics vision the fantasy of Eagleton was more than the rhetoric could absorb in plausible fashion. The leading character in a rhetorical vision which had emphasized persona was revealed as a politician acting in expedient fashion. The motivational pivot went out of the vision. The only remaining spur to action was hatred for the villainous personae such as Nixon and Agnew, but that was much less impelling by itself than when coupled to admiration for a persona of high ethical power. Some continued to work for the candidacy of George McGovern, but for many with less inertia and momentum, the motivation was replaced with *apathy*. Thus the rising tide of apathy can partially be accounted for by the disillusionment of those who participated in the New Politics, responding after the Eagleton Affair. For those who had little impression of George McGovern before the Eagleton Affair became staple fare on television, the fantasy brought reactions of distrust and lack of confidence in the persona.[15]

The viewer who came to sympathize with Eagleton would have every reason to distrust the McGovern character. Eagleton had placed trust in McGovern in a situation of considerable personal risk. The McGovern persona had promised support in Eagleton's time of trial and then when the situation came to a dramatic climax, had "dumped" him. Inconsistency was a highlight of the dramatic action.

The one major piece of prepared campaign persuasion which tapped into the legacy of the Eagleton Affair was produced by the Democrats for Nixon and is, I believe, possibly the most skillful piece of persuasion produced during the campaign. Although the short spot announcement does not mention Eagleton by name, the suggestion connects very strongly

Columnists Evans and Novak reported a late October poll by interviews in three San Fernando Valley, California precincts selected by elections analyst Richard Scammon. They interviewed 118 voters and found twenty-four registered Democrats decidedly for Nixon. The basic reasons given were the perception that McGovern was ideologically extreme and "habitual complaints about McGovern's inconsistency." *The Minneapolis Star,* 1 Nov. 1972, editorial page. The Harris Survey reported in early November to the effect that McGovern's credibility problem still plagued him. By 61 to 29 percent, a majority agreed with the statement that "he does not inspire confidence as a president should." *The Minneapolis Star,* 6 Nov. 1972, p. 1A.

with the residue of the Eagleton fantasy. McGovern's picture is presented on a weather vane-like stand. McGovern's position of a question is mentioned, the picture swings to face in the opposite direction and the narrator asserts that McGovern has shifted his position. Several shifts of the picture from left to right ensue until at the end of the announcement the picture is twirling in circles. The power of the announcement comes from its skillfully tapping into the rhetorical visions created by chaining fantasies such as the Eagleton Affair.

Coming at a strategic time in the campaign, capturing prime-time television for long film clips of the characters of the drama, the fantasy chained throughout the electorate and the role that the McGovern persona played in the fantasy as it was participated in by large segments of the American public was one of an inconsistent, inept, untrustworthy and politically expedient politician. Since the original dramatization was played out on the network evening news, on radio, and in the supposedly objective columns of the print media, the credibility of the presentation was high. The damage done to a rhetoric based on persona was considerable. Other breaking news events were subsequently interpreted along the same lines and the New Politics rhetorical vision lost its power to generate commitment and action and to attract new converts.

# PART III:

## Using the Theory to Analyze and Manage Political Campaigns

# III:  Using the Theory to Analyze and Manage Political Campaigns

Sociologists, psychologists and political scientists have developed instruments to analyze American politics quantitatively from their theoretical perspective. This section reports research that developed instruments and procedures for quantifying dramatistic rhetorical communication in political campaigns.

In the first piece, Cragan and Shields report research procedures for systematically building competing rhetorical dramas into one research instrument--a structured Q-sort. This accomplishment allowed them to validate Bormann's theory and ground its major concepts in empirically observable reality. They also developed a procedure for generating a computer written dramatistic speech that was pre-tested to please the most and offend the least members of a political audience.

In the second piece Rarick, et. al., reports that their research provides evidence "to support the hypothesis that mass media campaign events influence voters because listeners come to share the fantasies in their face-to-face discussions."

In the third piece, Bormann, et. al., argue that their research indicates the subjects in their study formed three major rhetorical groups that "with a few exceptions voted as a rhetorical critical analysis of the vision anticipated they would." They further report their study provided "evidence in support of the argument that fantasy theme analysis of rhetorical visions forms a potential basis for communication theory which will combine the 'humanistic concerns of the dramatist and the symbolic interactionist with the rigor of behavioral models'."

In the fourth piece, Shields and Cragan sketch out a quantitative procedure for running a dramatistic communication based political campaign using Bormann's theory as the basis for building three dimensional matrices (cubes) that capture the symbolic reality of the voting populace. In addition, the essay illustrates the use of the technique in managing five campaign communication events.

The final entry in this section contains six media critiques of the dramatistic based, computer generated political speech that evolved from Cragan's and Shield's examination of the foreign policy communication dramas that played in Peoria in Campaign '76. These pieces of political journalism further amplify the utility of Bormann's theory as a lens for examining political communication.

# 8

# Foreign Policy Communication Dramas:
## How Mediated Rhetoric Played in Peoria in Campaign '76

## JOHN F. CRAGAN and DONALD C. SHIELDS

In 1972 Ernest G. Bormann set forth a dramatistic communication theory.[1] The starting point for his theory is not the speaker, the audience, the channel, nor the situation, but the message. To him, the message is dramatistic in form, filled with heroes, villains, scenarios, and scenes. Bormann argues that large groups of people get caught up in shared symbolic dramas or visions and that since the meaning, emotion, and motive for action are contained in the drama, the object of study is not the people but the message.

The utility of using Bormann's theory as a lens for describing, interpreting, and evaluating rhetorical discourse has been demonstrated by a number of scholarly works. Bormann applied his theory to the Eagleton Affair, Kidd to interpersonal communication in popular media, Hensley to religious rhetoric, Cragan to radical Indian rhetoric, and Bantz to the rhetoric of network news.[2] However, the major concepts and structure of the theory have yet to receive empirical verification. In the absence of empirical objectivity, the possibility exists that the reconstructed visions are merely the product of the filtering process of the critic's mind. As with any

*Quarterly Journal of Speech*, 63 (1977), 275-289. Reprinted with permission from The Speech Communication Association.

This research was made possible through grants from Illinois State University and the University of Missouri-St. Louis. We wish to thank the Peoria Chamber of Commerce for their cooperation.

[1]"Fantasy and Rhetorical Vision: The Rhetorical Criticism of Social Reality," *Quarterly Journal of Speech,* 58 (1972), 396-407.

[2]Ernest G. Bormann, "The Eagleton Affair: A Fantasy Theme Analysis," *Quarterly Journal of Speech*, 59 (1973), 143-159; Virginia Kidd, "Happily Ever After and Other Relationship Styles: Advice on Interpersonal Relations in Popular Magazines, 1951-1973," *Quarterly Journal of Speech*, 61 (1975), 31-39; Carl Wayne Hensley, "Rhetorical Vision and the Persuasion of a Historical Movement: The Disciples of Christ in Nineteenth Century American Culture," *Quarterly Journal of Speech*, 61 (1975), 250-264; John F. Cragan, "Rhetorical Strategy: A Dramatistic Interpretation and Application," *Central States Speech Journal*, 26 (1975), 4-11; Charles R. Bantz, "Television News: Reality and Research," *Western Speech*, 39 (1975), 123-130.

filter, some elements pass through. Others remain excluded. The result may be highly artistic and creative. Yet, the objectivity of the reconstruction may be dependent on the bias of the filter and not the form of the object. Indeed, the possibility exists that the personal reconstruction of a communication drama is more a product of the critic's mind than the social reality of the collectivity being studied.

Consequently, in 1974, Donald C. Shields conducted research that demonstrated the feasibility of validating empirically Bormann's dramatistic communication theory.[3] Using William Stephenson's Q-Methodology and N. Van Tubergen's Quanal program for Q-type factor analysis, Shields took one of the theory's concepts (heroic personae) and validated it.[4] Nevertheless, the basic task of grounding the dramatistic theory remained. In order to provide empirical confirmation that people framed reality and cognitively assimilated events in dramatistic form, rich rhetorical dramas in competition with one another were required. John F. Cragan's reconstruction of American foreign policy dramas (Cold War, Neo-Isolationism, and Power Politics) that appeared in the media between 1946 and 1972 identified the competing dramatic visions needed for validating the theory's major concepts and structure.[5]

To us, the three foreign policy dramas combined with Q-Methodology and Q-type factor analysis provided a mechanism for designing a study to ground Bormann's communication theory, while at the same time creating a rich descriptive frame for analyzing American foreign policy mediated messages.

In light of our concerns as communication theorists and considering our pragmatic rhetorical interests in the political rhetoric of Campaign '76, a useful question for us to ask was, "How do American foreign policy mediated messages play in Peoria?"[6] In addition to providing a literal answer to this question, we hoped our research would shed light on two additional questions: (1) do people process foreign policy mediated messages dramatistically; and (2) is public opinion data gathered in rhetorical form via a small sample research technique useful in political campaigns?

---

[3]"The Fire Fighters' Dramatis Personae: A Study of Private, Projected, and Public Character From the Perspective of Rhetorical Vision" Diss. Univ. of Minnesota 1974.
[4]*The Study of Behavior: Q-Technique and Its Methodology* (Chicago: University of Chicago Press, 1953): N. Van Tubergen, "Q-Analysis (Quanal)" University of Iowa, undated manuscript.
[5]"The Cold War Rhetorical Vision, 1946-1972," Dissertation University of Minnesota 1972.
[6]We selected Peoria as the test site for both poetic and sampling reasons. Since the days of vaudeville, the expression "How does it play in Peoria?" has been taken to mean that if an act played well in Peoria, it would play anywhere, and the Watergate tapes gave this expression political meaning. In market research, this metaphor also has held true. Peoria is a midwestern test market for several national corporations because Peoria's general characteristics in population, employment, family incomes, age, and education are almost identical with U.S. averages.

# Procedure

In doing a field study to discern whether the foreign policy dramatizations that occur in the media also exist in the heads of Peorians, we first build a structured Q-sort matrix derived from the foreign policy discussions in the media from January to July, 1976 with the structure of the dramas coming from Cragan's analysis of American foreign policy rhetoric from 1946-1972.[7]

The top of the structured matrix (columns) contains three archetypal foreign policy dramas: Cold War, Neo-Isolationism, and Power Politics. Cragan argued in his initial research that the Cold War drama is a vision that portrays the international scene as a struggle between the free world and communism. In this drama, America's role is to defend the free world from communist aggression. The Neo-Isolationism drama depicts a world in which the United States cannot be the policeman of all conflicts. America's role in this vision is to provide the world with an example through the great experiences of democracy, but America should not impose our system on other people. Reason must replace force or we will perish. The Power Politics drama describes a world in which a balance of power among the major nations must be stabilized and managed. America's role in this vision is to provide world stability through the diplomatic successes of its statesmen, who use a combination of military power and negotiation to maintain world order.[8]

The side of the structured matrix (rows) includes elements of the dramatic structure, dramatic situations, and issue scenarios. We selected the categories for the side of the matrix through the use of an intuitive strategy that led us to examine more than 150 foreign policy articles cited in the *Reader's Guide* for the period January to July, 1976. The items, selected from content appearing in the media, provided representative dramatizations of here-and-now foreign policy phenomena proportionately

---

[7]The use of a structured Q-matrix as a means to validate a theory has been established by Stephenson, *The Study of Behavior* and by Jack Block in *The Q-Sort Method in Personality Assessment and Psychiatric Research* (Springfield, Ill.: Charles C. Thomas, 1961). Fred Kerlinger observes that Stephenson's most important contribution may well be the notion of systematically constructing a Q-sort to represent a theory or part of a theory and thereby bridging the gap between nomothetic and ideographic research. See Kerlinger's "Q-Methodology in Behavioral Research," appearing in *Science, Psychology, and Communication: Essays Honoring William Stephenson,* ed. Stephen R. Brown and Donald J. Brenner (New York: Teachers College Press, 1972), pp. 3-38. We followed these scholars' thinking and started with the dramatistic theory and built the theory into our structured Q-sort in the attempt to see if the subjects replicated that structure (and thus the theory) in their choices of salient rhetorical messages.

[8]For a more extended depiction of the attributes of these visions, see Cragan, "The Cold War Rhetorical Vision," Chs. II and III.

across the three dramas.[9] Thus, we built twenty Q-cards for each drama producing a sixty-item structured Q-deck.[10] The foreign policy matrix appears as Table I.

Late in July, 1976, we conducted a pilot study involving thirty Illinois State University students. The students sorted the dramatizations on a forced choice continuum from most reflective to least reflective of their view of U.S. involvement in foreign affairs. Our sixty-item forced distribution was 2-3-6-11-16-11-6-3-2 for a nine-category sort.[11] The administration of the pilot study indicated that the sixty items could be sorted and recorded in under sixty minutes and that two researchers were needed to administer conveniently the Q-sort to groups of ten to fifteen respondents.

The structured Q-deck provided the *observations* about American foreign policy when considered from the perspective of Q-type factor analysis. Two different sets of thirty Peorians constituted the *variables* in the study.[12] A stratified sample of Peorians comprised our variable. The subjects in each group mirrored four demographic characteristics of urbanized Peoria: sex, education, occupation, and income. For example, urbanized Peoria contains fifty percent blue collar workers. Thus, our sample did too. Since it takes forty-five minutes to sort the sixty foreign policy messages, we rejected going door-to-door to gather our data. Instead we asked the cooperation of the Peoria Chamber of Commerce in securing subjects to sort the cards at central locations. The data was gathered in Peoria on August 11 and 12, 1976.

The use of the two groups of thirty Peorians provided a simple design consideration to enable a determination of the construct validity of the Q-analysis factor types by comparing the factor solutions and the derived Q-arrays from the sorting behavior of the two groups. Data were factor

[9]Items were tested for internal consistency within each vision generally following the procedure outlined by Block in *The Q-Sort Method*. Basically the procedure consists of using experts in the discipline (in this case, political communication and foreign policy) to sort the 60 item deck into three stacks that correspond to the three dramas. This procedure allowed us to identify several messages that were not discreet across visions. These cards were rewritten until they were consistently sorted as part of the applicable drama.

[10]The procedure of going to the *Reader's Guide* and selecting relevant articles for building a Q-sort on foreign policy has been previously used and reported by Stephenson in "Application of the Thompson Schemata to the Current Controversy Over Cuba," *Psychological Record*, 14 (1964), 275-290. The rationale for using this intuitive strategy for building the left side of the matrix is provided by Lewis R. Goldberg in his "Parameters of Personality Inventory Construction and Utilization: A Comparison of Prediction Strategies and Tactics," *Multivariate Behavioral Research Monographs*, 73 (1972), 1-59.

[11]For a discussion of how to administer a forced-choice structured Q-deck, see William D. Brooks, "Q-Sort Technique," appearing in Philip Emmert and William D. Brooks, *Methods of Research in Communication* (Boston: Houghton-Mifflin, 1970), pp. 165-181.

[12]When doing Q-type factor analysis, items and people are treated the opposite of what they are in R-type factor analysis. In Q, people are variables and items are observations. Moreover, Q-observations (messages) must exceed Q-variables (people) by at least a 2:1 ratio. For a detailed discussion of these points, see Raymond B. Cattell, "The Meaning and Strategic Use of Factor Analysis," appearing in *Handbook of Multivariate Experimental Psychology*, ed. Raymond B. Cattrell (Chicago: Rand McNally, 1966), p. 237.

analyzed by means of Tubergen's Quanal Program for Q-analysis, providing the Principal Components Solution with Varimax rotation to simple structure and a Weighted Rotational Analytical Procedure that ranked dramatizations for each factor by means of descending z-scores.

**Table I**

Structured Q-Matrix:  Foreign Policy Messages;
Involvement in Foreign Affairs

Archetypal Dramas (columns) and Elements (rows)

| Dramatic Structure: | Cold War | Neo-Isolationism | Power Politics |
|---|---|---|---|
| **Plotline** | | | |
| Dramatic Scene | 1a | 1b | 1c |
| Hero Persona | 2a | 2b | 2c |
| Villain Persona | 3a | 3b | 3c |
| **Main Actors** | | | |
| U.S. Self-Image | 4a | 4b | 4c |
| Russia | 5a | 5b | 5c |
| **Supporting Players** | | | |
| Kissinger | 6a | 6b | 6c |
| CIA | 7a | 7b | 7c |
| **Situations:** | | | |
| Africa | 8a | 8b | 8c |
| Angola | 9a | 9b | 9c |
| China | 10a | 10b | 10c |
| Latin America | 11a | 11b | 11c |
| Mid-East | 12a | 12b | 12c |
| Panama | 13a | 13b | 13c |
| Vietnam Lesson | 14a | 14b | 14c |
| **Issues:** | | | |
| Arms Control | 15a | 15b | 15c |
| Detente | 16a | 16b | 16c |
| Grain | 17a | 17b | 17c |
| Intervention | 18a | 18b | 18c |
| NATO Troops | 19a | 19b | 19c |
| Terrorists | 20a | 20b | 20c |

## How the Mediated Messages Played

Factor analysis of our data provided a composite picture describing how foreign policy messages played in Peoria and graphically illustrated the interplay between the three foreign policy dramas. In general, the computer analysis revealed that the dominant drama in the minds of Peorians is Power Politics. Peorians clustered about this drama as the major factor-type. The second largest factor-type presented the Cold War drama, but those loading on this factor type were polarized. As many respondents rejected the Cold War drama as accepted it. Neo-Isolationism played to some extent, but the factor-type that resembled it was very small and somewhat diffused.

Specifically, the factor analyses of the two sets of Peorians produced Principal Components solutions accounting for 52.4 percent and 51.0 percent of the total variance in sorting behavior. Both solutions included six factors and the three major factors in each solution accounted for 76.6 percent and 74.3 percent respectively of the variance within each six factor solution.

The factor type accounting for more than 30 percent of the variance in Peorian's sorting behavior in both factor solutions was Power Politics. The view of foreign policy mediated messages reflective of persons who loaded highest on the Power Politics type is reported in Table II. Table II contains the fifteen cards most reflective of the view of foreign affairs of the people loading highest on this factor and the fifteen cards least reflective of the view of foreign affairs of the people loading highest on this factor.

Clearly, the sorting behavior represented by the data in Table II indicates that this factor-type is accurately labeled Power Politics. The top two messages in the typical array for this factor depict the dramatic scene and dramatic hero of Power Politics. Those messages read respectively: *Today's international scene is one in which the major powers have reached military parity. What we must do is manage and stabilize our relationship with each other and maintain the balance of power. In a nuclear age we cannot escape the responsibility to build a safe future through wise diplomacy;* and *America's major role in foreign affairs is to provide world stability through the diplomatic successes of its statesmen who use a combination of military power and negotiation to maintain world order.*

Henry Kissinger was the player enacting the heroic role within the Power Politics drama. It therefore followed that he and his policies should have received at least token support by Peorians participating in the Power Politics drama. As can be seen from Table II, Henry Kissinger was applauded politely (ranked twelfth) as his policies received a standing ovation. Detente is ranked third, Middle East is ranked fourth, and Arms Control is ranked fifth.

The villain of the Power Politics drama was basically the uninformed emotional citizenry that either crusades to make the world safe for democracy or retreats into isolationism. So, it is not surprising that Peorians

## Table II

### Factor Type I
### Power Politics Drama
Accepted Messages (ranked 1-15)   Rejected Messages (ranked 46-60)

| | Cold War | Neo-Isolationism | Power Politics |
|---|---|---|---|
| **Dramatic Structure:** | | | |
| Plotline | | | |
|   Dramatic Scene | | | 1 |
|   Hero Persona | 55 | 7 | 2 |
|   Villain Persona | | | 10 |
| Main Actors | | | |
|   U.S. Self-Image | 51 | 46 | |
|   Russia | | | 14 |
| Supporting Players | | | |
|   Kissinger | 59 | 54 | 12 |
|   CIA | | 48 | |
| **Situations:** | | | |
|   Africa | | 52 | |
|   Angola | | | |
|   China | | 56 | 13 |
|   Latin America | | | 9 |
|   Mid-East | 47 | | 4 |
|   Panama | 50 | | 8 |
|   Vietnam Lesson | 15 | | |
| **Issues:** | | | |
|   Arms Control | 57 | | 5 |
|   Detente | 60 | | 3 |
|   Grain | 58 | 11 | |
|   Intervention | 53 | | 6 |
|   NATO Troops | | | |
|   Terrorists | 49 | | |

participating in this drama would reject with equal vigor elements of the Cold War drama and the Neo-Isolationist drama. The data in Table II support this expectation. For example, Peorians loading highest on the Power Politics factor rejected an American hero who is the defender of the free peoples of the world and at the same time rejected the Neo-Isolationist position on dismantling the CIA. A typical Cold War situation card that the Power Politics type rejected is the one pertaining to Panama. It reads: *The*

*Panama Canal Zone is not a colonial possession. It is sovereign U. S. Territory, every bit the same as Alaska and all the States that were carved from the Louisiana Purchase. The U.S. has no obligation to relinquish the Canal Zone to Panama.*

The data in Table II indicates that Peorians loading highest on this Power Politics factor-type did not strongly reject any Power Politics mediated messages. However, they did strongly accept two Neo-Isolationist messages and one Cold War message. It is not surprising that Power Politics Peorians would deviate from their vision with respect to the sale of grain to Russia. Peorians did not want agricultural products used as strategic weapons; they wanted to sell their products to the highest bidder. Finally, the Peorians in this factor-type accepted the Cold War interpretation of the lesson of Vietnam, which is that we rightfully tried to stop the spread of communism but acted indecisively.

A second factor-type accounting for an average of nearly 30 percent of the variance in Peorian's sorting behavior across the two samples was Cold War. The view of foreign policy mediated messages reflective of persons who loaded highest on the Cold War type is reported in Table III. Table III displays the fifteen messages most reflective of the view of foreign affairs of the people loading highest on this factor and the fifteen messages least reflective of the view of foreign affairs of the people loading highest on this factor.

The sorting behavior represented by the data in Table III illustrates that this factor type is accurately labeled Cold War. Three of the four top-ranked messages in this typal array depict the dramatic villain, dramatic scene, and dramatic hero of the Cold War drama. These messages read respectively: *The major obstacle to world peace is still the Communist ideology which is bent on world domination; and Today's international scene is still a Cold War. It is a struggle between the free world and Communist domination. A struggle for the minds and hearts of the peoples of the world. A struggle that we must not lose;* and *America's major role in foreign affairs is to defend ourselves and the free peoples of the world from Communist aggression.*

Peorians loading on this factor strongly defended the CIA. The media message the Cold War Peorians ranked second states: *Open attacks on the CIA seriously harm America's capability for conducting a covert fight against the spread of Communist power. The destruction of the CIA demoralizes the anti-communist forces, threatens the freedom and independence of other countries, and endangers freedom here at home.*

Since the dramatic structure of the Cold War drama depicts the international scene as a bipolar world with the U. S. as an active defender against Communist expansion, it is not surprising that Cold War Peorians rejected the Neo-Isolationist drama and view isolationist mediated messages antagonistically. For example, Peorians loading highest on the Cold War factor rejected the message calling for dismantling the CIA, and rejected the view that America should sign a new Panamanian Canal Zone treaty bringing our troops home, thereby staying out of the affairs of Panama. Indeed, the Peorians loading highest on the Cold War type felt so strongly about Panama that they also rejected the Power Politics message that the U.S. should negotiate a new treaty in the best interests of both parties. The fact that the Peorians strongly accepted the Cold War mediated message on Panama, and strongly rejected the Neo-Isolationist and Power Politics mediated messages confirm the strength of the Panama issue and the

### Table III

#### Factor Type 2
#### Cold War Drama

Accepted Messages (ranked 1-15) Rejected Messages (ranked 46-60)

| Dramatic Structure: | Cold War | Neo-Isolationism | Power Politics |
|---|---|---|---|
| Plotline | | | |
|   Dramatic Scene | 3 | | |
|   Hero Persona | 4 | | |
|   Villain Persona | 1 | | |
| Main Actors | | | |
|   U.S. Self-Image | | 48 | |
|   Russia | 10 | 55 | |
| Supporting Players | | | |
|   Kissinger | | | |
|   CIA | | ＼ | |
| **Situations:** | | | |
|   Africa | | 49 | |
|   Angola | 11 | 57 | |
|   China | | 52 | |
|   Latin America | 12 | | |
|   Mid-East | | | 51 |
|   Panama | 5 | 59 | 50 |
|   Vietnam Lesson | 8 | 54 | 13 |
| **Issues:** | | | |
|   Arms Control | 15 | 53 | 9 |
|   Detente | | | |
|   Grain | | 7 | 58 |
|   Intervention | | 46 | |
|   NATO Troops | 47 | 56 | 14 |
|   Terrorists | 6 | | |

intensity of the Cold War position for the respondents loading highest on this factor type. Another situation message stemming from the Neo-Isolationist drama that the Cold War type rejected was one pertaining to Angola. It reads: *The U. S. should stop fighting on the side of oppression in places like Angola, and instead provide a model of democracy and decency. The U.S. should dramatize our commitment to African Anti-Colonialism by avoiding both overt and covert interventions into civil wars like Angola.* Peorians participating in the Cold War drama wanted the U. S. to maintain a worldwide commitment.

The data in Table III indicate that Peorians loading highest on the Cold War factor type did not view the Power Politics mediated message antagonistically. Negotiation is often viewed as a holding action, and sometimes the Cold Warriors interpret the military moves of the Power Politician as supporting their cause. For example, their reaction to the NATO troops, and Arms Control issues as well as the lesson of Vietnam reflect adherence to the "stick" Power Politics position. However, the Cold War Peorians did deviate from the expected on the issue of grain, in a manner similar to the Power Politics Peorians factor type reported above. Once again they accepted rather strongly the Neo-Isolationist message on grain. Foreign markets for grain appear more important than grain as a negotiating tool or strategic weapon.

It is important to note that the Cold War factor-type was a *reflected* factor. Reflected means that it was extracted with a nearly equal number of persons correlating highly positively and highly negatively with the essence of the factor. In the description above, the positive depiction is reported. But it must be remembered that other Peorians who loaded highest on the factor rejected it and what it represented. Thus, the Cold War drama was a polarizing drama in Peoria, and Cold War mediated messages, while creating intense feeling, may have created as much repulsion as acceptance in Peoria.

A third factor type accounting for an average of about 15 percent of the variance in Peorians' sorting behavior across the two samples was Neo-Isolationism. The view of foreign policy mediated messages reflective of persons who loaded highest on the Neo-Isolationism type is reported in Table IV. Table IV contains the fifteen messages most reflective of the view of foreign affairs of the people loading highest on this factor and the fifteen messages least reflective of the view of foreign affairs of the people loading highest on this factor.

The sorting behavior represented by the data in Table IV indicates that this factor type is less clearly labeled Neo-Isolationism, in that the sorting behavior is not entirely attributable to a classical isolationist position. What we mean by this is that some Power Politics and Cold War mediated messages were accepted by what is otherwise a Neo-Isolationism type. Nevertheless, the Peorians loading highest on this factor type did accept the dramatic scene and dramatic hero of Neo-Isolationism and rejected the dramatic heroes of both the Cold War and Power Politics dramas.

## Table IV

### Factor Type 3
### Neo-Isolationism Drama

Accepted Messages (ranked 1-15)  Rejected Messages (ranked 46-60)

| Dramatic Structure: | Cold War | Neo-Isolationism | Power Politics |
|---|---|---|---|
| Plotline | | | |
| Dramatic Scene | | 1 | |
| Hero Persona | 46 | 11 | 59 |
| Villain Persona | | | |
| Main Actors | | | |
| U.S. Self-Image | 52 | 50 | |
| Russia | | | 12 |
| Supporting Players | | | |
| Kissinger | 51 | 13 | |
| CIA | | | |
| Situations: | | | |
| Africa | | 14 | |
| Angola | 55 | | |
| China | | 6 | |
| Latin America | 58 | | |
| Mid-East | 7 | 53 | 4 |
| Panama | 15 | | |
| Vietnam Lesson | 48 | 8 | |
| Issues: | | | |
| Arms Control | 56 | 5 | |
| Detente | 57 | | 2 |
| Grain | 54 | 3 | 60 |
| Intervention | | | 10 |
| NATO Troops | 49 | | |
| Terrorists | | 9 | 47 |

A fourth factor type accounting for an average of only 10 percent of the variance in Peorian's sorting behavior across the two samples was small but worth reporting. It is worth reporting because it does not fit the typology underlying the foreign policy dramatistic matrix. There are two possible interpretations for the sorting behavior of people loading highest on this factor. Either our research instrument did not test these people or the dramatistic communication theory as represented by these three foreign policy dramas cannot explain their behavior. The instrument used in this study demands a high level of literary and an extended period of concentration (approximately 45 minutes) that some subjects may not have been capable of with respect to foreign policy mediated messages. On the other hand, the Peorians in this factor may have sorted the messages on foreign policy from a dramatic vision not encompassed by our topology. Whatever the case, Table V presents the data for the factor type. Two examples illustrate the difficulty in interpreting this factor. For one, it is difficult for us to understand how the three mediated messages on the CIA

**Table V**

Factor Type 4
Unknown Drama

Accepted Messages (ranked 1-15) Rejected Messages (ranked 46-60)

| | Cold War | Neo-Isolationism | Power Politics |
|---|---|---|---|
| Dramatic Structure: | | | |
| Plotline | | | |
| Dramatic Scene | 1 | | |
| Hero Persona | | 2 | |
| Villain Persona | | 53 | 4 |
| Main Actors | | | |
| U.S. Self-Image | | | 49 |
| Russia | 9 | | |
| Supporting Players | | | |
| Kissinger | 57 | 58 | 48 |
| CIA | 6 | 11 | 8 |
| Situations: | | | |
| Africa | | 14 | 13 |
| Angola | | | |
| China | | 10 | |
| Latin America | | 3 | 59 |
| Mid-East | | | |
| Panama | | | 47 |
| Vietnam Lesson | 5 | | |
| Issues: | | | |
| Arms Control | 54 | | 46 |
| Detente | 55 | 51 | |
| Grain | 56 | | |
| Intervention | 60 | 50 | 15 |
| NATO Troops | 52 | | |
| Terrorists | | 7 | 12 |

could all be reflective of one viewpoint, especially since we had pretested them for their discreetness. Also, the acceptance and rejection of various mediated messages appear almost random across the three foreign policy dramas.

The fifth and sixth factors in both factor solutions do not deserve an extended report. They did not account for much variance and they are merely variations of the previously reported factors of Power Politics and Cold War. They differ from the reported factors only in the intensity and kind of foreign policy messages they reject.

## Theoretical Implications

Our rhetorical question guiding this research was: do people process foreign policy mediated messages dramatistically? The data provides strong support for an affirmative answer. The factor solutions for both samples clearly resemble the three dramas underlying the structured Q-deck matrix as the above explanation of Tables II and III indicated. Furthermore, in terms of statistical verification it is important to point out that the Tubergen Quanal program provides three tests for the discreteness of the factor solutions. One is the use of orthogonal rotation itself which means that the extracted factors are independent since the vectors in factor space are rotated at 90 degree angles. Second, the program also computes Pearson Correlation Coefficients between the factors within a solution. In our first sample of Peorians the correlation between the Power Politics factor and Cold War factor was .089 and in the second sample, .048. These very low correlations suggest the degree of the factors' independence. Finally, the program searches for consensus items, i.e., items that are viewed similarly across the factor solution. There were no consensus messages in the first sample, and only two in the second.

We took two samples of thirty Peorians primarily to assess the invariance of the derived factors. The Principal Components Solution extracted six factors in both samples, and both solutions accounted for nearly equal percentages of variance. Also, the major factor in both studies was Power Politics, the second factor was Cold War, and the third factor was Neo-Isolationism. We computed Spearman *rho* Coefficients on the rank-order z-scores in the typal arrays of the major factors and found positive correlations hovering around .65 between the corresponding factors in both solutions. These are high correlations given the fact that the computation is based on the rank-order variation of the sixty messages. When one looks at the messages in terms of what drama they represent there is an even better fit between the two solutions. For example, the Power Politics factor in both samples can be compared by a simple table that illustrates message placement on the basis of dividing in half the descending array of z-scores. The top half includes accepted messages; the bottom half rejected. As Table VI indicates, both factor solutions reflect similar message distribution. In

**130**                              Applied Communication Research

both solutions the base majority of the twenty Power Politics cards are accepted, while the vast majority of Cold War messages are rejected.

However, Tables IV and V display data that may indicate that our three-part typology cannot account for all major foreign policy dramas. Our Neo-Isolationism factor is not as coherent as one might expect and our fourth factor is simply not comprehensible when interpreted via our typology.[13] It may be that more than three dramas could be included in our typology in order to explain the remaining variance in sorting behavior.

In validating our foreign policy typology we have necessarily provided strong evidence that people process messages dramatistically. There is a close empirical fit between the major factors in both samples and the typology. By this we mean the subjects in the study had free choice and could have sorted the cards so that the dramas were not represented by the factors, but they did not. Also, the respondents' acceptance of the dramas is confirmed across two independent factor analyses. Other evidence that the Peorians did not have to sort the messages in such a way as to replicate the three foreign policy dramas is indicated by the presence of a quite random

## Table VI

### Comparison of Power Politics Factor

| | Sample A Factor 1 | | | | Sample B Factor 1 | | |
|------|--------|--------|------|------|--------|--------|------|
| | Accept | Reject | | | Accept | Reject | |
| P.P. | 16 | 4 | (20) | P.P. | 15 | 5 | (20) |
| C.W. | 3 | 17 | (20) | C.W. | 4 | 16 | (20) |
| N.I. | 11 | 9 | (20) | N.I. | 11 | 9 | (20) |
| | (30) | (30) | N = 60 | | (30) | (30) | N = 60 |

(although significant) factor in both samples. Additionally, the factors representing the typology appeared in the same order in both solutions and there were high correlations between the placement of messages within each comparative factor across the two samples. The factors representing the three foreign policy dramas account for approximately 75 percent of the variance in sorting behavior within each six factor solution. In the Power Politics and Cold War factors in both solutions, the mediated messages representing the dramatic structure of the dramas took precedence over the situation and issue messages. Such evidence suggests that the relationship

[13]In the pilot study of college students we did find a strong Neo-Isolationism drama, so another explanation may be that there is simply not a strong Neo-Isolationism drama playing in the minds of Peorians at this time.

between the theory and the subjects' sorting behavior is quite strong. Thus, this research appears to provide empirical confirmation that people frame reality and cognitively assimilate events in dramatistic form

Of course, the validation of this theory does not preclude the validation of other communication theories to explain human behavior. Our design did not build in alternative communication theories to see which one better explains human behavior, but this is certainly an intriguing design for future research.

## Rhetorical Applications

The combination of Bormann's dramatistic communication theory, Stephenson's Q-sort technique, and Tubergen's Quanal program for Q-type factor analysis has several applications to speech making. Through this approach rhetorical messages can be directly tested for their persuasiveness. Other widely used approaches such as semantic differential scales, Likert scales, or single response polling techniques gather data about targeted audiences, attitudes, and beliefs without testing the primary relationship between the message and the audience. Thus, the data must be converted to rhetorical messages and the messages themselves remain untested. The possibility exists that the speech writer's intuitive analysis of such data will produce messages that are not related to the symbolic reality of the targeted audience. Currently, the most popular way for correcting the disparity between the speech writer's reality and the audience's reality is a trial-and-error method such as the revising of campaign speeches during the primaries. However, this approach risks the integrity of the speaker for the rhetor can be easily accused of inconsistency.[14]

Although any communication theory can be used for building structured Q-decks of rhetorical messages, this paper concerns itself with the benefits of using Bormann's dramatistic communication theory. There are two direct applications of this approach. First, rhetorical messages can be tested to determine how well they play, and second, a factor analysis produces a composite picture resembling an effective speech since the thematic ingredients are rank-ordered and compared across dramas.

Our structured Q-deck of three foreign policy dramas essentially provided three different dramatic interpretations of twenty pieces of phenomena on foreign policy. Using the raw data derived from respondents' sorting behavior, a speech writer can compare different rhetorical treatments of the same phenomena. The data gathered in Peoria provides an example of how such an analysis might proceed. Table VII displays six of the twenty items from our 3 × 20 matrix.

---

[14]In the 1976 presidential campaign, the terms "flip-flopping" and "waffling" were used to describe the inconsistencies arising from such experimentation.

## Table VII

### Frequency of Message Placement:
### Raw Data Test for Saliency*    N = 60 Respondents

|                    | Cold War  | Neo-Isolationism | Power Politics |
|--------------------|-----------|------------------|----------------|
| Dramatic Structure |           |                  |                |
| Hero Persona       | + 8,  − 6 | + 10,  − 1       | + 15,  − 2     |
| CIA                | + 10,  − 7| + 3,  − 12       | + 7,  − 1      |
| Dramatic Situation |           |                  |                |
| Mid-East           | + 6,  − 6 | + 3,  − 4        | + 9,  − 1      |
| Panama             | + 1,  − 12| + 4,  − 7        | + 4,  − 10     |
| Dramatic Issue     |           |                  |                |
| Arms Control       | + 5,  − 8 | + 2,  − 7        | + 10,  − 1     |
| Grain              | + 4,  − 10| + 9,  − 2        | + 1,  − 11     |

*Saliency determined by extreme ranking in top two cells (N = 5) or bottom two cells (N = 5) of nine-celled distribution of 60 messages.

− numbers for times rejected

+ numbers for times accepted

An analysis of the table quickly reveals a number of ideas that would be valuable for a speech writer who is preparing a candidate's speech on foreign policy for delivery before a Peorian audience. For example, the speech writer would not want to depict the CIA as an immoral agency that should have its covert powers stripped away (Neo-Isolationism, + 3, − 12), but should take the position that a covert response stands between a do-nothing policy and nuclear confrontation and thus is a necessary part of our diplomacy. (Power Politics, + 7, − 1). However, the speech creator could identify with the Neo-Isolationsim hero of the U.S. as a moral model of democracy (+ 10, − 1) at an idealistic level and still argue the practical Power Politician heroic role of providing world stability through the diplomatic success of its statesmen (+ 15, − 2). A similar analysis could proceed with regard to dramatic situations and dramatic issues. The speech writer would avoid the Neo-Isolationist dramatization of Panama (+ 1, − 12), while strongly emphasizing the Power Politics depiction of the Middle East (+ 9, − 1). The speech designer would not describe American grain as a strategic weapon (Power Politics, + 1, − 11), but would accentuate our negotiated posture with respect to arms control (Power Politics, + 10, − 1). Finally, on these six items, the speech writer would avoid the Cold War dramatic interpretation of American foreign policy because of the polarizing reactions that are in evidence.

Although the raw data analysis of the Q-sort responses provides a speech writer with a way of avoiding mistakes of specific themes, it doesn't enable an assessment of how the specific themes are arranged within a drama or the overall configuration of competing dramas. The combination of Stephenson's Q-technique with Tubergen's Quanal program for factor analysis provides the means to such an assessment.

We felt that the best way to demonstrate the second application of this approach to speech making was to write a speech that is essentially created from the computer printouts that the Weighted Rotational Analytical Procedure of the Quanal program provides. The WRAP phase of this program arrayed the sixty messages on the basis of z-scores from most accepted to most rejected for each of the factors. In addition it used z-score differences to compare individual messages across the factors for their similarities and differences.

Since we were trying to build a foreign policy speech that would please the most and offend the least, we took the messages appearing in the dominant vision receiving the highest Z-scores and combined them with the messages scoring high in the other factors of Cold War and Neo-Isolationism, but not strongly rejected by the Power Politics drama.

The computer-derived speech contained in Table VIII is presented to show the utility of building the rhetorical messages into the audience analysis instrument. In this case we simply "glued together" the successful messages as indicated by the Q-type factor analysis and WRAP phase of the Quanal program. Since the elements of this speech have already been pretested for their acceptance by the targeted audience (Peorians), via the construct validated factor analysis, it is reasonable to assume that the derived speech would also be successful if presented to that audience.

## Conclusions

The use of message-centered dramatic communication theory in conjunction with Q-sort technique and factor analysis allowed us to build and test a message-centered foreign policy inventory that contained three dramatic interpretations of U. S. involvement in foreign affairs: Cold War, Power Politics, and Neo-Isolationism. The inventory contained mediated messages for each of twenty foreign policy items across the three dramas, producing a sixty message structured Q-matrix. The mediated messages came from an analysis of 150 articles on U. S. foreign affairs listed in the *Reader's Guide* for the period January to July, 1976. The Q-deck was administered to two sets of thirty Peorians and the data obtained was construct validated via Q-type factor analysis to determine what foreign policy mediated messages played in Peoria.

## Table VIII

## Computer-Derived Foreign Policy Speech

I'd like to take this opportunity here in Peoria to set forth clearly and specifically my position on foreign policy. In order to do that I'd like to explain how I
see the world today and indicate to you what I believe America's role in world
politics should be. First of all let me say that the U. S. is not a failure. For 200
years we have provided the world, through the great experience of democracy,
a model — a model that the world is free to follow, but one that we will not
impose. Ideally, we would prefer merely to be this model. Unfortunately, the
pragmatic realities of the international scene force us to play other roles.

The international scene today is highly complex. In some ways it is still a
struggle between the free world and communism. For despite all claims to the
contrary, Russia is still a communist state. But, 1976 is not 1956. Russia has
acquired nuclear and conventional military parity with us — and China and the
Middle East make all dealings with the Russians more difficult. Therefore, in
day-to-day affairs of world politics, we must strive to manage and stabilize
our relationships with other major powers. In a nuclear age we cannot escape
the responsibility to build a safe future through wise democracy.

Now please do not misunderstand me. A policy of detente with the Soviet
Union does not mean that we're "Uncle Sucker." I recognize that it's foolhardy to unilaterally disarm, but I also know that it's easy to talk in a mock
and tough way and run the risk of war. Neither response reflects my position.
Detente means to me a state of affairs marked by the absence of significant
tension that could lead the U. S. and Russia into a nuclear confrontation.
Detente does not mean that all differences will be resolved, or that Russia
will not attempt to expand her influence. It does mean that peaceful co-exis-
tence is the only rational alternative.

I don't intend to "flip-flop" on any foreign policy issues. Nor do I intend to
speak in glib generalities. I came here to talk specifically about American
foreign policy and that's what I mean to do. First of all, the lesson of Vietnam.
The lesson of Vietnam is one of indecision. The U. S. was not wrong in the
purpose for which we fought. While South Vietnam was not totally a free government, they still enjoyed more liberty than any communist regime in Eastern
Europe allows. Our mistake was in not moving decisively when we first militarily intervened to discourage further communist aggression in that country.

Which brings me to the issue of possible future U. S. interventions. I believe
that intervention is a diplomatic tool that is needed even if it is only a threat to
maintain a balanced international scene. Intervention is not right or wrong.
But, it may be used rightly or wrongly.

Of course, we cannot talk about intervention without talking about the CIA.
I do not believe that we should dismantle the CIA, for many times it is the
CIA's covert capability that stands between a do-nothing policy and nuclear
confrontation. I oppose unnecessary secrecy, but I believe in a strong national
defense. And, unfortunately, in today's world, the CIA is needed.

There has been a lot of talk about Europe in this campaign. Let me again state
my position. The NATO alliance and the "trip-wire" presence of American

troops stationed in Germany are important parts of America's defense. It would be foolish to withdraw American troops from the Continent of Europe without negotiating a similar withdrawal of Russian troops from Eastern Europe.

The Middle-East is again in a no-war, no-peace stalemate and is likely to remain so for some time. Step-by-step diplomacy, treating all parties with an even hand, is the only means for maintaining a delicate peace in the Middle East.

The United States must ground its China policy in morality. We should work to improve our relationships with her. The People's Republic of China is a sovereign state, but we must not forget to support our ally, The Republic of China, on Taiwan. I believe both governments can learn to live with the reality of each other.

In Africa, a specific American presence is necessary if we are to prevent further communist inroads and a tarnishing of America's influence on this awakening continent. The communists should know that we are prepared to come to the defense of sovereign nations and the Africans should know that we stand ready to help them negotiate a peace among themselves.

In Latin America, we should avoid "big stick" tactics, but we should not stick our heads in the sand to what's going on down there. With respect to Panama, the U. S. neither owns nor has sovereignty over the Canal Zone. But, Panama granted us rights by a 1903 treaty. We should re-negotiate a new treaty that protects America's vital interests in the Canal Zone.

On terrorists, my positon is clear. International terrorism, such as bombings and hijackings is deplorable. Yet, the U. S. should not put itself in a position committed to meet such actions whenever and wherever they might occur. I will go to the United Nations and get an international law against terrorism.

I should not leave Peoria without stating my opinion on grain sales. First of all, I think the embargoing of food is immoral given the starving millions in the world. Second, whether we sell or do not sell grain to Russia will not alter her behavior in international affairs.

As I stated in my opening remarks, the U. S. is not a crippled giant. We have not lost confidence in ourselves. We are a proud democratic nation that must play a major role of leadership in international affairs. I trust you will agree that my foreign policy is based on a realistic and mature view of how to maintain world order and peace.

The Power Politics drama was the most accepted rhetorical vision in Peoria. Cold War was a close second, but it appeared to polarize Peorians. Neo-Isolationism was a distant third. The most accepted foreign policy mediated messages might be said to be somewhere between a hard Power Politics and soft Cold War position.

Theoretically, this research provides empirical verification not only for the typology of foreign policy dramas, but for Bormann's dramatistic communication theory. It appears that the utility of Bormann's theory of rhetorical vision goes beyond its use as a descriptive schemata for critiquing rhetorical communication. It may provide us with a *why explanation* of communication phenomena that is predictive. This research grounds the dramatistic concepts. Subsequent research might work toward prediction.

Pragmatically, the design used in this study indicates that rhetorical messages may be tested for their persuasiveness, producing a direct relationship between message production and audience analysis, without risking the credibility of a speaker.

Also, the study demonstrates the utility of using a Q-type factor analysis of dramatic themes as means for writing pretested dramatic speeches.

# 9

# The Carter Persona:

## An Empirical Analysis of the Rhetorical Visions of Campaign '76

DAVID L. RARICK, MARY B. DUNCAN
DAVID G. LEE, and LAURINDA W. PORTER

The campaign strategy which characterized President Carter's ten-year rise from the obscurity of Plains, Georgia through the Governor's mansion in Atlanta to the White House illustrates the increasing importance of candidate personality of "image" and highlights the possible usefulness of the dramatistic approach for analyzing presidential campaigns. In 1972, Carter had commissioned his chief aide, Hamilton Jordan, to draw up a prospectus for a 1976 presidential bid.[1] Jordan's main conclusion was that "most voters would be inclined more favorably toward a candidate stressing personal qualities such as integrity and confidence than those emphasizing ideological stands on the issues."[2] Not only did the Carter campaign strategy carry through on Jordan's suggestions, but much of the Ford publicity and media coverage featured Carter in portrayals which were predominately character sketches rather than action scenarios. The personality of Carter dominated so much of the campaign in 1976 that we selected the Carter persona as the focal point for this investigation.

A number of political scientists, sociologists, and rhetorical scholars have noted the importance of how campaign organizations and the media dramatize a political campaign in relation to how the voters come to see the

*Quarterly Journal of Speech,* 63 (1977), 258-273. Reprinted with permission from The Speech Communication Association.

Mr. Rarick is Assistant Professor and Ms. Duncan, Mr. Lee, and Ms. Porter are doctoral candidates in the Department of Speech-Communication at the University of Minnesota. Mr. Lee is also Assistant Professor of Speech-Communication at Bethel College, and Ms. Porter is visiting Instructor in Speech-Communication at Concordia College. The authors express their appreciation to Professor Ernest G. Bormann for his assistance in development of theoretical rationale and instrumentation for the study.

[1] Jimmy Carter, *Why Not the Best?* (New York: Bantam Books, 1975). See especially Chapter 15, "Presidential Plans."

[2] "Brassy Gamble by Jimmy Carter Looks Like Solid Gold," *Minneapolis Tribune,* 13 June 1976, p. 16A. The strategy was also discussed at length in Fred McMorrow, *"Jimmy"—The Candidacy of Carter* (New York: Whirlwind Book, 1976).

political process, the candidates, and the issues.[3] Les Cleveland, for example, outlines the following dramatistic approach to politics: "Political events are presented to mass publics in ways which closely resemble the stock situations of general literature. No matter what the intentions of political actors and celebrities, the parts they play before their audiences cannot differ greatly in formal, aesthetic terms from the roles enacted by the heroes and villains of popular entertainment."[4] Dramatistic analysis thus focuses on the ways political actors "strive to present themselves in the public drama, what identities they characteristically seek to construct for themselves, how they are typecast by their audiences, and what terms they use to delineate the public issues."[5]

Cleveland argues that such analyses can be carried out by looking at documentary records of political actions, such as those presented in the mass media. He cautions, however, that dramatistic analysis has pitfalls as well as strengths. "The operational defects of this essentially ideosyncratic procedure make it impossible for anyone else to replicate the analysis of another investigator with any precision, but its very freedom from the rigidities of scientific method may be its greatest advantage."[6] He continues, "It is one thing to assert that we respond to symbolic stimuli, another thing to measure their exact qualities, or even to describe them systematically."[7]

Cleveland is right in that studies of the media as purveyors of dramatic action tend to use the techniques of humanistic scholarship. Despite the increasing awareness of the importance and complexity of the symbolic participation by the public in campaign persuasion, few investigators have used the rigor of behavioral science to study the way the voter symbolically structures the campaign process. Meanwhile, rhetorical critics have been making increasingly sophisticated analyses of the symbolic structure, complexity, and potential function of campaign persuasion.[8] However, rhetorical critics have neglected the study of audiences' perceptions of such messages.

[3]See Dan D. Nimmo, *Popular Images of Politics* (Englewood Cliffs, N.J.: Prentice-Hall, 1974), Chapter 6; Joseph R. Gusfield, *Symbolic Crusade* (Urbana: Univ. of Illinois Press, 1966); James N. Rosenau, *The Dramas of Politics* (Boston: Little, Brown, 1973).
[4]Les Cleveland, "Symbols and Politics: Mass Communication and the Public Drama," *Politics: Australiasian Political Studies Association Journal* 4 (1969), 186.
[5]*Ibid.*
[6]*Ibid.*, 188.
[7]*Ibid.*, 189.
[8]For a representative collection of such writers see *Drama in Life: The Uses of Communication in Society,* ed. James E. Combs and Michael W. Mansfield (New York: Hastings House, 1976). See for example, the essays on the 1972 Presidential Election in *QJS*, 59 (1973), particularly Edwin Black, "Electing Time," 125-129; Walter R. Fisher, "Reaffirmation and Subversion of the American Dream," 160-167; Herbert W. Simons, James W. Chesebro, and C. Jack Orr, "A Movement Perspective on the 1972 Presidential Campaign," 168-179; see, also, Robert O. Anderson, "The Characterization Model for Rhetorical Criticism of Political Image Campaigns," *Western Speech*, 37 (1973); 75-86; Barbara A. Larson, "Criticism and the Campaign Concept of Persuasion: A Case Study Analysis of Method," *Central States Speech Journal*, 24 (1973), 52-59.

# Purpose

We began with Simons' notion that the richness and complexity of the humanistic study of rhetorical genres can and should be validated by evidence gathered by observing audience response to the rhetoric.[9] Combining a method of rhetorical criticism (fantasy theme analysis) with an empirical method (Q-methodology), we examined the link between a rhetorical analysis of the Carter persona in the 1976 Presidential campaign and empirically-generated data on audience perceptions of Carter's persona. We investigated three questions:

1. What were the major dramatic themes by which the Carter persona was presented to the public by the Carter and Ford campaigns, and by the news media?

2. How did audience members perceive the themes and visions of the Carter persona in Campaign 1976?

3. How did audience members' perceptions of the Carter persona relate to their expressed voting intentions and to their actual voting behavior?

Our purpose was not to validate a method of rhetorical criticism nor to map the patterns of public opinion during the campaign. Our study is preliminary to such investigations. Rather, our purpose was to discover if audience responses are in line with expectations developed from a rhetorical criticism of campaign messages. If such a link can be established, we can provide an explanation of campaign communication which has more validity than the explanations provided by critical studies alone.

## Recent Conceptions of "Candidate Image"

A growing number of empirical studies on the personal qualities (or image) of political candidates indicate that: (1) voters perceive candidates on many complex subdimensions,[10] (2) voters' perceptions of candidates change during campaigns,[11] and (3) voters' perceptions of candidates can

[9]Herbert W. Simons, " 'Genre-alizing' About Rhetoric: A Scientific Approach," paper presented at Kansas Conference on Significant Form in Rhetorical Criticism, June 1976.

[10]See Dan Nimmo and Robert L. Savage, *Candidates and Their Images* (Pacific Palisades, Cal.: Goodyear, 1976), pp. 45-80: Roberta S. Sigel, "Effect of Partisanship on the Perception of Political Candidates," *Public Opinion Quarterly*, 28 (1964), 485.

[11]See Nimmo and Savage, pp. 127-160; John H. Kessell, *The Goldwater Coalition* (Indianapolis: Bobbs-Merrill, 1968), pp. 274-76; The American Institute for Political Communication, *The 1968 Campaign: Anatomy of a Crucial Election* (Washington, D.C.: American Institute for Political Communication, 1970); for findings on mass media effects on voting and candidate image, see Robert D. McClure and Thomas E. Patterson, "Television News and Political Campaigns: Information, Gratification and Persuasion," Chapter 6 in *Current Perspectives in Mass Communication Research*, ed. F. Gerald Kline and Phillip J. Tichenor (Beverly Hills: Sage Publications, 1972).

significantly influence their voting behavior, especially when they do not vote on the basis of their party loyalty.[12] Because the research on the dimensions of candidate image is the most relevant for our study of the Carter persona, we will discuss only this line of research in more detail.

In perhaps the most comprehensive study of candidate images to date, Nimmo and Savage focus on "what attributes a candidate publicizes to appeal to the voter and the attributes the voter sees in the candidate, which comprise the voter's image of the candidate."[13] Based on prior studies and their own research, Nimmo and Savage analyze candidates in terms of their political and stylistic roles. Each of these roles contains a cluster of candidate traits or attributes, which when combined, make up the candidate's "image." A candidate's political role includes his leadership qualifications, his role as a spokesperson for his party, and his stands on the issues. The candidate's stylistic role includes his ability to impress voters with his capabilities through his performance in media or personal contact settings, and his personality traits (his honesty, compassion, appearance, and the like).[14] Most relevant to our study of the Carter persona is the series of investigations Nimmo and Savage did on candidate image using Q-methodology.[15] In a study of the 1972 Nixon-McGovern campaign, they asked voters to evaluate the two candidates by ranking a set of general statements descriptive of candidate political and stylistic roles. Voters were asked to rank the statements twice; first they ranked them from most to least like McGovern. A number of groups of voters were identified, each group perceiving the candidates in different ways. For example, one group saw Nixon as a strong "partisan campaigner" who lacks empathy and integrity. Another group saw Nixon as a "great statesman," who put the interests of the country above partisan politics with much conviction and integrity.[16]

Although Nimmo and Savage's concept of candidate image and their use of Q-methodology provided useful background for our study of Jimmy Carter, their definitions and operationalizations of candidate image are different from the concept of "persona" we employ. Nimmo and other researchers tend to test rather static dimensions of candidate personality, leadership qualities, issue stands, and the like. For example, Nimmo and Savge's image tests are composed of trait-like items, such as "hardworking leader" and "shady politician," or brief descriptive sentences like "He has the highest degree of honesty, integrity, and intelligence," or "He can unite people in support of his policies."[17]

---

[12]See Nimmo and Savage, pp. 34-44; Richard W. Boyd, "Presidential Elections: An Explanation of Voting Defection;" *American Political Science Review,* 63 (1969), 498-514; Ithiel de Sola Pool, Robert P. Abelson, and Samuel L. Popkin, *Candidates, Issues and Strategies* (Cambridge, Mass.: MIT Press, 1964).

[13]Nimmo and Savage, p. 8.

[14]*Ibid.*, p. 46.

[15]*Ibid.*, pp. 55-80, 113-159.

[16]*Ibid.*, pp. 69-73.

[17]*Ibid.*, pp. 66-73. On these pages are lists of items used in the Nimmo and Savage Q-sort studies.

In contrast, we define persona as "the character a public person plays in a given dramatization."[18] This definition emphasizes the dynamic process of the candidate acting in a setting, often responding to others who participate with him in the dramatic scene. Our persona is a character in process who evolves because of the scenarios in which he is involved. In this view, the candidate is presented to voters much like a character in a play is presented to the audience: through what he says and does and through the responses of others to his actions.

## A Dramatistic Approach to the Study of Campaigns

Bormann has developed an approach which provides a way systematically to describe the propagation of campaign dramas through the electorate.[19] Drawing upon the work of Bales, Bormann accounts for the process by which group members share dramatic fantasies. In 1970 Bales published his discovery of a process called group fantasy in which group members introduce dramatic messages in the form of stories or anecdotes to illustrate a point.[20] If the fantasy is shared by other group members, they respond with signs of approval (laughing, nodding, commenting, and the like), and relate similar experiences of their own. When this occurs, the fantasies are said to be "chaining out" through the group. Bormann adapted this approach for use in rhetorical criticism. He provided a method by which the components of group fantasy messages are analyzed in detail to provide an account of the common beliefs, values, and motives of group members who share the fantasy.[21] According to Bormann a shared fantasy contains "characters, real or fictitious, playing out a dramatic situation in a setting removed in time and space from the here-and-now transactions of the group."[22] Such fantasies are structured, plausible, and interpretative,

[18]Ernest G. Bormann, "The Eagleton Affair: A Fantasy Theme Analysis," *QJS*, 59 (1973), 143.

[19]The method is outlined in Ernest G. Bormann, "Fantasy and Rhetorical Vision: The Rhetorical Criticism of Social Reality," *QJS*, 58 (1972), 396-407. Examples of rhetorical criticism of political campaigns based on this approach are William D. Semlak, "A Rehtorical Analysis of George S. McGovern's Campaign for the 1972 Presidential Election," Diss. Univ. of Minnesota 1973; Bill Henderson, "An Evaluation of the October, 1972 Rhetorical Strategy of the White House Which Chose to Attach the *Washington Post* Coverage of Watergate: A Fantasy Theme Analysis of Rhetorical Situation," Diss. Univ. of Minnesota 1975; Charles R. Bantz, "Television News: Reality and Research," *Western Speech,* 39 (1975), 123-130.

[20]Robert F. Bales, *Personality and Interpersonal Behavior* (New York: Holt, Rinehart, and Winston, 1970).

[21]Bormann's definition of fantasy differs from other common definitions which see fantasy as an inventive work which deals with supernatural, fanciful, or unreal characters and events. Bormann says the largest number of political campaign dramatizations are depictions of living historical persons acting out documented events. Fantasy in this sense does parallel another common definition of fantasy as a mental image fulfilling a psychological need and containing motives for action.

[22]Bormann, "Fantasy and Rhetorical Vision," 397.

whereas actual events are often experienced as chaotic and confusing.

Bormann argues that the dynamic process of fantasy sharing may also account for the ways in which fantasies get transmitted through the mass media to larger publics in campaigns. Two main sources provide the messages which dramatize a political campaign for the public. First, small groups of policy makers plan the main themes of the candidate's campaign, and the main arguments and dramatizations which provide the substance for the campaign.[23] They then plan a strategy whereby they insert these themes and dramas into the campaign through campaign advertising, campaign tours, and "news events" staged for the benefit of reporters.[24] Second, professional media journalists and commentators select and inerpret campaign events through discussions in work groups and talks with colleagues. They thus come to share common fantasies and dramatize the campaign in particular ways.[25] The journalistic fantasies often depict the candidate less favorably than do the candidate's paid political announcements. The advertisements of the opposition candidate may also generate competing dramatizations damaging to the persona of a candidate.

Finally, some members of the audience pick up these competing dramas and repeat them in face-to-face discussions with family and friends, where the fantasies may again be shared.[26] The outcome of this sharing process is the generation of distinct "rhetorical visions," which are composites of recurring themes and dramas which have been formulated by each of the major producers of campaign messages. Bormann defines rhetorical visions as "the composite dramas which catch up large groups of people in a symbolic reality...just as the fantasy themes chain out in a group to create a unique group culture so do the fantasy dramas of a successful persuasive campaign chain out in public audiences to form a rhetorical vision."[27]

## Method

This study used the critical method of fantasy theme analysis[28] to identify the key themes and rhetorical visions which characterized the Carter

[23]Many descriptions of how political campaign policy groups generate campaign themes and appeals may be found in Robert Agranoff, *The Management of Election Campaigns* (Boston Holbrook Press, 1976). See especially chapters 6, 7, 12, 13, 14.

[24]Recent trends in campaign media strategies are discussed in Robert Agranoff, *The New Style in Election Campaigns,* 2nd ed. (1972; Boston: Holbrook Press, 1976).

[25]Timothy Crouse notes that when reporters covering a political candidate travel, eat, gamble, and work together they come to generate similar images of the campaign and tend to write similar news stories. Crouse calls this "pack journalism." See Timothy Crouse, *The Boys on the Bus* (New York: Random House, 1973), pp. 3-15.

[26]For a review of research on the influence of interpersonal and group communication on audience perceptions and uses of mass media messages see Steven H. Chaffee, "The Interpersonal Context of Mass Communication," in *Current Perspectives in Mass Communication Research,* pp. 95-120.

[27]Bormann, "Fantasy and Rhetorical Vision," 398.

[28]See Bormann, "Fantasy and Rhetorical Vision" for a discussion of the method.

persona in the 1976 campaign. Then a structured Q-sort was constructed and administered to a sample of audience members to discover whether or not they shared the fantasies and visions discovered by rhetorical criticisms of campaign messages.

## Rhetorical Criticism

The first step in the study was to conduct a fantasy theme analysis of the rhetoric of Campaign 1976. Following Bormann's procedure, we collected campaign materials (articles containing news and commentary, video tapes of newscasts and candidate ads, campaign literature, etc.) which had been generated by the media journalists, and the Carter and Ford campaigns from September 1 to October 25, 1976. Three of us independently analyzed these materials. We discovered many dramatic incidents in which the persona of Jimmy Carter played a major role. We paid particular mention to the characterization of Carter in the incidents, his reported values and motivations, his actions, and the settings in which the incidents occurred. From this analysis we identified twenty major dramatic incidents (or themes) from the Carter campaign, twelve from the Ford campaign, and fourteen from the media journalists. From these we selected eight thematic areas which had appeared in all three campaign sources (Carter and Ford campaigns, media journalists). For example, the thematic areas included fantasies about Carter's record as governor of Georgia, Carter's *Playboy* interview, and Carter's response to voter apathy in the campaign. Our criteria for selecting thematic areas included: frequency of appearance in the campaign and news materials, range of media in which the themes appeared, the dramatic content of the themes. After selecting the eight thematic areas richest in fantasizing about Carter, we returned to the original rhetoric in the campaign and news media materials and wrote three separate fantasies of Carter for each. The three fantasy portrayals generated for each thematic area reflected the way the Carter campaign, the Ford campaign, and the media journalists dramatized the Carter persona. In conducting the rhetorical analysis and selecting the themes and fantasies we felt were most salient in the campaign, we had implicitly made some hunches that the audience would share these fantasies.

## Empirical Analysis

We used Q-methodology to discover how members of the electorate perceived various dramatizations of Carter in the campaign.[29] The procedure allows persons to respond to a set of statements by rank ordering them on a continuum from those they agree with to those they disagree

[29]For a description of Q-methodology see William Stephenson, *The Study of Behavior* (Chicago: Univ. of Chicago Press, 1953).

with. Thus in Q-sorting, persons can express comparative feelings about many subcomponents (i.e., concrete fantasies) comprising their vision of the Carter persona in a manner that allows for careful statistical comparisons of individual responses.[30] The procedure allows us to discover which dramatizations of the Carter persona voters accept or reject. Therefore, we could operationally define a person's participation in a rhetorical vision of the Carter persona in terms of his or her sorting of Q-items along the accept-reject continuum.

From each fantasy portrayal of Carter developed in our rhetorical criticism we wrote two Q-sort items. Each of the items described the Carter persona acting in one of the eight thematic incidents[31] and depicted him from the point of view (vision) of: the Carter or Ford campaigns, or the media journalists. The resulting structured Q-sort instrument had 48 items (i.e., 8 thematic areas × 2 items for each thematic area × 3 visions; Carter, Ford, media = 48.)[32] Each item (25-50 words long) was typed on a card. The items were written in dramatistic form and each presented the Carter persona acting in a campaign scenario, in a specific scene.[33]

We drew a quota sample of 26 voting age adults from diverse age, socio-economic, and political backgrounds.[34] Table I presents demographic

[30]Nimmo and Savage explain why Q-methodology is an appropriate technique for studying the complex subdimensions of candidate image in "The Q-Sort as a Procedure in Candidate Image Research," Appendix A of Nimmo and Savage, *Candidates and Their Images,* pp. 213-225.

[31]The eight thematic areas or incidents which provided the fantasies around which our Q-sort items were developed were: Carter's standing in the polls, Carter and the *Playboy* interview, Carter's response to public apathy, Carter as governor of Georgia, Carter's personality, Carter's performance in the TV debates, Carter as leader, Carter on the issues.

[32]By structuring our Q-sort this way, we could systematically test how different persons perceived Carter in terms of how the various subdimensions of his persona interacted with one another. That is, we would assess how persons structured the eight thematic areas in relation to how the areas were presented by the Carter or Ford campaigns or by the media journalists.

[33]The following are three of the six Q-sort items drawn from the thematic area relating to the personality of Carter:

item 38.  Jimmy Carter is a peanut farmer. He is at home walking his fields in rural Georgia. Rosalynn and Jimmy Carter worked hard, scrimped and saved and made a success of their peanut warehouse. He is committed to his family and believes in honest hard work.

(Carter campaign vision)

item 17.  Mr. Carter has played fast and loose with the facts when debating and when campaigning. Many voters are afraid of him. Mr. Carter seems to be all smiles and promises without much backing it up.

(Ford campaign vision)

item 19.  Mr. Carter teaches Sunday school and says he is a peanut farmer, but when he campaigns for political office he is a tough fighter. He drives hard. In Carter, love and kindness mix with a hunger to prove himself in combat.

(Media Journalists' Vision)

[34]The sample was purposively drawn from four neighborhoods in the Minneapolis-St. Paul metropolitan area, and Buffalo, Minnesota, a small agricultural community (population 3,200) in central Minnesota, and from a pool of undergraduate and graduate students in communication classes at the University of Minnesota and Concordia College.

# Table 1

## Demographics of Person-Sample and Corresponding Factor Loadings on Four Factor/Types — Varimax Rotation

| Person # | SES | Sex | Ages[a] | Party Preference[b] | Planned Vote[e] | Actual Vote | Simple Structure Matrix Type I (N=14) | Type II (N=6) | Type III (N=2) | Type IV (N=3) |
|---|---|---|---|---|---|---|---|---|---|---|
| 1 | White Collar | M | 2 | I | C | C | .755 | .247 | -.359 | -.074 |
| 2 | White Collar | F | 3 | D | C | C | .737 | -.117 | .200 | .266 |
| 3 | White Collar | F | 3 | D | C | C | .359 | .449 | .411 | .027 |
| 4 | Professional | M | 3 | D | C | C | .820 | -.162 | .051 | -.090 |
| 5 | Professional | F | 2 | D | C | C | .830 | -.065 | -.314 | -.032 |
| 6 | Professional | M | 3 | D | C | C | .859 | -.131 | .076 | -.179 |
| 7 | Student* | M | 1 | None | C | C | .742 | -.213 | -.026 | -.085 |
| 8 | Student | M | 2 | D | C | C | .785 | .007 | .081 | -.243 |
| 9 | Student | M | 1 | D | C | C | .486 | .451 | .191 | .109 |
| 10 | Student | F | 2 | D | C | C | .620 | .467 | .135 | -.162 |
| 11 | Student | F | 1 | D | C | C | .690 | .193 | -.038 | .028 |
| 12 | Student* | F | 1 | D | C | N.A. | .718 | .306 | .154 | -.034 |
| 13 | Student* | F | 2 | D | C | C | .621 | .105 | -.312 | .112 |
| 14 | Student* | F | 1 | D | C | F | .458 | .213 | .117 | -.244 |
| 15 | White Collar | M | 4 | R | F | F | .021 | .113 | .711 | .101 |
| 16 | White Collar | M | 4 | None | F | F | -.166 | .799 | -.046 | .095 |
| 17 | Professional | F | 4 | R | F | C | .208 | .486 | .306 | .010 |
| 18 | Student | F | 2 | D | F | F | -.462 | .300 | .433 | .458 |
| 19 | Student | M | 1 | None | F | F | .335 | .629 | .280 | .143 |
| 20 | Student | F | 2 | I | F | F | -.151 | .628 | .221 | .156 |
| 21 | Student* | F | 1 | R | F | N.V. | -.138 | -.176 | -.520 | .068 |
| 22 | Blue Collar | M | 2 | D | U | C | .534 | .145 | .211 | -.021 |
| 23 | Blue Collar | F | 2 | None | U | F | -.456 | .204 | .519 | .250 |
| 24 | White Collar | F | 2 | I | McC | F | .008 | .559 | .110 | .519 |
| 25 | Professional | M | 2 | N.A. | U | F | .001 | .098 | -.070 | .727 |
| 26 | Student | F | 1 | O.P. | O.C. | O.C. | -.189 | .251 | .394 | .551 |

a. Age Codes
1 = 18-25
2 = 26-35
3 = 36-50
4 = 50+
* = black respondent

b. Party Codes
D = Democrat
R = Republican
I = Independent
O.P. = Other Party
N.A. = No Answer

c. Vote Codes
C = Carter
F = Ford
McC = McCarthy
O.C. = Other Candidate
N.V. = Did not vote

information relating to the party preference, socio-economic status, sex, and age of the persons in the sample. Although the group is diverse it is small and not a random sample. We emphasize that we did not select our subjects in order to draw inferences about a parent population.[35]

We conducted personal interviews with the respondents from October 29 through November 1, 1976.[36] The late date assured that most of the significant campaign themes had been discussed by various information sources and that respondent perceptions of the campaign and candidates were well established. In the interviews, the researchers read a 625-word set of instructions to the respondents which asked them first to read all 48 items, then to sort them in three piles representing (1) those statements which "express most closely your own views of the Carter campaign or Carter the presidential candidate," (2) those statements which "are least like your own thinking on Carter and the campaign," and (3) those statements which mean nothing to you or you are unsure about." Respondents then subdivided the three piles into nine piles according to the quasi-normal distribution as shown in Figure 1.

## Figure 1

| | Least Like | | | | | | | Most Like | |
|---|---|---|---|---|---|---|---|---|---|
| Pile Number: | 1 | 2 | 3 | 4 | 5 | 6 | 7 | 8 | 9 |
| # of items in pile: | 2 | 3 | 5 | 8 | 10 | 8 | 5 | 3 | 2 |

After the Q-sorting the investigators asked each respondent to fill out a short questionaire to get information relating to his/her intention to vote, candidate choice if any, and political party preference. While the respondent filled out the questionaire the investigator filled out a demographic report relating to sex, age, race, and SES. One week after the presidential election, we asked the subjects to fill out a confidential questionnaire indicating how they actually voted.

Data analysis was conducted using Van Tubergen's QUANAL program

[35]Stephenson says Q-methodology is an inductive approach based on R.A. Fisher's small-sample doctrine. It is designed to (1) discover patterns inherent in the subjective perceptions of persons and (2) test variables of a theory as they operate in Q-sorting. He argues therefore, that large random samples are not needed for Q-studies. See William Stephenson, *Play Theory of Mass Communication* (Chicago: Univ. of Chicago Press, 1967), pp. 17-22.

[36]For all interviews, the investigators introduced themselves as University of Minnesota researchers conducting a study "so we can understand what people are thinking about the current presidential campaign and the candidates running for president." One of the five trained interviewers used in the study conducted interviews with eight of the students in our sample in a university classroom. Other interviews consisted of one researcher administering the Q-sort to one or two people in the respondents' homes.

on a CDC Cyber 74 Computer.[37] The program correlated the Q-sort data of each person with the date of every other person, and factor analyzed the resulting correlations. The factors represent groups of persons, each of the groups containing persons who responded to the Q-sort items similarly. Thus, persons in each group structure the fantasies about the Carter persona in similar ways.

The ways in which persons sort the items should provide a test of whether or not they have come to share the campaign fantasies which we discovered from our rhetorical criticism of the campaign messages. Since the criticism identified eight themes in three distinct rhetorical visions, we would expect our respondents to cluster into distinct groups, each of which is characterized by a significant acceptance of one of the rhetorical visions of Carter and rejection of another. This finding would tend to support the convention that the themes and visions identified in our rhetorical criticism were in fact paralleled by voter perceptions. This contention would be supported further if persons actually voted in line with the way our rhetorical criticisms anticipated they would. That is, we would expect persons who accept the Carter vision of Carter to vote for Carter, and persons who accept the Ford vision of Carter to vote for Ford.

With 26 persons sorting 48 items, the possible outcomes are many. Respondents may not cluster into groups at all. Or persons may cluster into groups, but they may cluster on the basis of sorting which does not reflect any perceived distinctions between our identified rhetorical visions. Finally, the actual voting of the groups may be inconsistent with their response to the rhetorical visions. These outcomes would fail to support a link between our critical analysis of the campaign rhetoric and audience response to that rhetoric.

## Results

The factor analysis of the Q-sort data revealed four factors which accounted for 57.5 percent of the total variance.[38] (Hereafter, the factors are referred to as "types," or clusters of persons, each having similar perceptions of the Carter campaign.) Table I presents the results of the

[37]QUANAL correlated the Q-sort data of every respondent with that of every other respondent, resulting in a 26 × 26 person-person correlation matrix. This matrix was then factor-analyzed via the principal components method. The resulting factor matrix was subjected to varimax rotation (orthogonal solution). The analysis extracted all factors with eigen values greater than 1.0. The bipolar splitting criterion was set at 30%, indicating a factor must be at least 30% negative for the program to split it into two types. Analysis was completed using Van Tubergen's WRAP procedure which weighs factor loadings for persons in each factor, and computes standardized Q-arrays indicating the response patterns of persons in each factor to the 48 items. Statistical procedures are detailed in Norman Van Tubergen, "Q-Analysis (QUANAL)," Mass Communication Research Bureau, School of Journalism, University of Iowa (N.D.), mimeo.

[38]The Correlations among the Q-arrays of the four types are negative to slightly positive (−2.40 to .377), indicating that the four types are relatively dissimilar.

varimax rotation and indicates how each of our 26 respondents loaded on each factor-type.[39] Table I also indicates the planned and actual voting behavior, political party preference, as well as demographic characteristics of the respondents. Note that 25 of the 26 persons loaded significantly on at least one type, and that the four types strongly discriminated the Carter voters from the Ford voters.

## Analysis of Types

We developed the type descriptions which follow from the standardized Q-arrays computed from the rotated factors. Each type represents the composite response patterns of the persons in the factor type to each of the 48 items in the Q-sort. Table 2 summarizes the z-scores assigned to each of the items by the persons in each of the four types. A high positive z-score indicates that persons in the type perceived the item as "most like their views on the Carter campaign or the candidate Jimmy Carter." A strong negative z-score indicates that persons in the type perceived the item as "least like their views on the Carter campaign or candidate Jimmy Carter." Those items with low z-scores (positive or negative) can be seen as neutral or of low salience for persons in the type.

Type I "Carter Convert," Type I is the strongest factor identified, accounting for 30.3 percent of total variance and 52.7 percent of variance within the four factor solution. Fourteen persons loaded highest on this type. Table 2 presents a numerical indication of which Q-sort items were accepted and rejected by Type I. The rehetorical vision from which each item was drawn is identified in the "vision code" column of the table. Table 2 indicates that the most salient fantasies accepted by Type I portray Carter's personal leadership qualities winning him the nomination despite the fact that he was unknown before the primaries. Further, the dramas depict the Carter persona as achieving success without becoming beholden to any special interest groups. Carter is a man who can restore the people's faith in government after the Watergate trauma and once again make government responsive to their will. Carter will overcome the voter apathy which is a legacy of Watergate and Vietnam. Participants in the "Carter Convert" vision see his persona as that of a good man, loving, kind, religious, but also as a tough, driving and determined political combatant.

Type I sees Carter's *Playboy* interview as an attempt on his part to reach a new audience and to explain his religion and basic humanity. However, the members of Type I do view the interview as a problem for the Carter campaign. Finally, the "Carter Converts" chain into the media drama of a tightening campaign with Carter losing a big lead in the polls as election day

[39]To be significantly loaded on a factor, persons had to have a loading of at least .43 on that factor. See Mary Jane Schlinger, "Cues on Q-Technique," *Journal of Advertising Research*, 9 (1969), 56-57.

**Table 2**

Item Descriptions and Z-Scores for Four Identified Types

| Item | Theme Code[a] | Vision Code[b] | Item Descriptions | Type I | Type II | Type III | Type IV |
|---|---|---|---|---|---|---|---|
| 1 | 3 | 3 | People don't care about election because of Carter's empty promises. | −1.3 | −.1 | −.9 | .3 |
| 2 | 4 | 3 | Carter was lackluster as governor. | −1.2 | .3 | 1.7 | .1 |
| 3 | 8 | 3 | Carter flip-flops on issues if it is to his advantage. | −1.4 | .0 | −.2 | 1.0 |
| 4 | 6 | 3 | Ford was too much for Carter in the debates. | −2.2 | −1.2 | −.6 | −.3 |
| 5 | 1 | 1 | Carter couldn't confront Ford, power of the president makes polls. | .3 | −2.0 | −.0 | −.3 |
| *6 | 7 | 2 | Carter was a leader at his church when he voted for a civil rights worker. | .4 | −.4 | .4 | .4 |
| *7 | 1 | 2 | If Carter loses he will have blown a huge lead. | −.3 | .5 | −.4 | .3 |
| 8 | 6 | 2 | Carter lost the first, but won the second and third debates. | .9 | −.4 | −.4 | −.5 |
| 9 | 5 | 3 | Carter will say anything to get elected. | −2.0 | −1.2 | .8 | .7 |
| *10 | 8 | 2 | Carter asked for trust from the voters. | .3 | .8 | 1.1 | .8 |
| 11 | 4 | 2 | Carter told old bosses in Georgia discrimination was over. | .8 | −.7 | 1.3 | −.5 |
| 12 | 1 | 2 | A shoo-in became a horse race. | .5 | 1.1 | .8 | 2.4 |
| 13 | 8 | 1 | Carter is clear, but media has not reported his positions. | .8 | −1.5 | −.4 | −.5 |
| 14 | 7 | 1 | Carter was unknown, but his leadership qualities won nomination. | 1.6 | −.6 | −.2 | .4 |
| 15 | 3 | 1 | Carter understands the voters and will restore faith in government. | 1.5 | .1 | −.4 | −1.3 |
| 16 | 6 | 3 | Carter should have said "Mr. President" in the debates. | −.9 | −1.5 | .8 | .1 |
| 17 | 5 | 3 | Carter played fast and loose with the facts. | −1.3 | 1.3 | .6 | 1.3 |
| 18 | 3 | 2 | Voters don't care because Carter and Ford are not on the issues. | −.3 | 1.5 | −1.5 | .3 |

| | | | | | | | |
|---|---|---|---|---|---|---|---|
| 19 | 5 | 2 | Carter is a Sunday school teacher, farmer, and a tough fighter. | 1.0 | .4 | .6 | − 1.2 |
| 20 | 7 | 3 | Carter is a typical democrat and will throw money away. | − 1.5 | 1.1 | .4 | .0 |
| 21 | 6 | 1 | People were not happy with Carter in Georgia. | − 1.3 | − .9 | .2 | .1 |
| 22 | 6 | 1 | Carter came through the debates with flying colors. | − .2 | − 2.3 | − 1.9 | − .7 |
| 23 | 2 | 1 | Carter followed others lead in giving *Playboy* an interview. | .5 | − .9 | .2 | 1.4 |
| 24 | 6 | 2 | After the debates, people are still not sure about Carter. | .1 | 1.8 | 2.3 | 1.3 |
| 25 | 2 | 2 | Carter got in trouble with the *Playboy* interview. | .9 | .9 | .4 | − 1.1 |
| 26 | 2 | 1 | Carter did *Playboy* to reach a new audience. | 1.2 | .9 | .4 | − .8 |
| 27 | 3 | 2 | Apathy is due to unexciting candidates. | .5 | 2.1 | − .2 | .9 |
| 28 | 1 | 3 | Carter is losing steam while Ford is gaining. | .4 | .5 | − .0 | 1.2 |
| 29 | 7 | 1 | Carter is beholden to no one. | .9 | − .8 | − 1.1 | − 2.3 |
| 30 | 4 | 1 | Carter's plan eliminated bad spending in Georgia. | .5 | − .5 | − 1.9 | − 1.1 |
| 31 | 1 | 1 | Carter expected race to tighten, only poll counts November 2. | 1.4 | 1.1 | − .0 | .7 |
| 32 | 7 | 2 | Carter as president would work late, pray, be on attack, keep in touch. | − .1 | − .8 | − 1.3 | − 1.0 |
| 33 | 5 | 2 | Carter is good, has a quick mind, steel will, genius for politics. | .9 | − .3 | 1.1 | .5 |
| 34 | 3 | 3 | Carter was not able to inspire confidence which Ford did. | − 1.2 | − .4 | 1.5 | − .3 |
| 35 | 8 | 1 | Carter gets to know people, has position papers for issues. | .7 | − .3 | − 1.3 | .7 |
| 36 | 6 | 1 | Carter won the debates by surpassing those who thought he was weak. | .2 | − 1.3 | − 1.7 | − 1.0 |
| *37 | 2 | 2 | Voters didn't like Carter saying "lust" and "screwing" in *Playboy*. | − .1 | .7 | .2 | .2 |
| 38 | 5 | 1 | Carter works hard, is committed to family, and a peanut farmer. | .1 | .7 | − .4 | 1.1 |
| 39 | 2 | 3 | Carter showed lack of judgment in giving *Playboy* interview. | .8 | .7 | .8 | − 2.2 |

| *40 | 4 | 2 | Carter did a lot for welfare, but not much for budget in Georgia. | −.2 | .1 | .6 | −.3 |
|-----|---|---|----------------------------------------------------------------------|-----|-----|------|------|
| 41 | 2 | 3 | It is hard to imagine what Carter tried to prove in *Playboy*. | −1.0 | −.1 | .8 | −1.4 |
| 42 | 3 | 1 | Carter listens and wants to make government responsive to the people. | 1.4 | −.6 | −1.5 | −.3 |
| 43 | 7 | 3 | Carter people have no experience, ran a shifting campaign, and are a sign of poor leadership. | −1.6 | −.5 | −.8 | 1.5 |
| 44 | 8 | 2 | Carter programs are hard to pin down. | −.0 | 1.0 | 1.9 | .9 |
| 45 | 5 | 1 | Carter is a compassionate man who cares. | .8 | −.9 | −1.1 | −.9 |
| 46 | 1 | 3 | Carter is losing momentum and Ford is gaining on the polls. | .3 | 1.3 | .2 | 1.0 |
| 47 | 8 | 3 | Carter stands against U.S. interests in foreign affairs. | −1.2 | 1.1 | −.0 | 1.3 |
| 48 | 4 | 1 | Carter streamlined government in Georgia and made Georgia government responsive. | .8 | −.1 | −1.3 | −.9 |

NOTE:  Item descriptions are condensed considerably.

*Consensus items

a.  Theme Codes

1 — Carter and polls
2 — Carter *Playboy* interview
3 — Carter and public apathy
4 — Carter as governor of Georgia
5 — Carter personality
6 — Carter and TV debates
7 — Carter as leader
8 — Carter and the issues

b.  Vision Codes

1 — Carter vision of Carter
2 — Media vision of Carter
3 — Ford vision of Carter

approaches. However, they also accept the interpretation of the Carter publicists that the only poll that counts is the one taken on November 2.

The people in Type I strongly reject the fantasies about the Carter persona drawn from the Ford rhetorical vision. All of the fourteen items in the Q-array most rejected by "Carter Converts" are from the Ford vision of Carter. For example, Type I reject the characterization of the Carter persona as one who plays fast and loose with the facts, says anything to get elected, and who, despite his anti-Washington stance, is really an extravagant Democrat. They strongly disagree with the scenario of Carter running a flip-flopping campaign, surrounded by Georgia "good-old-boys." Type I also strongly rejects the fantasy that Ford, with his experience in foreign and domestic policy, was too much for Carter in the debates. Also rejected is the Ford campaign's portrayal of campaign apathy. According to the Ford vision, apathy resulted because Carter is an uninspiring, poor campaigner who makes empty promises.

The finding that Type I strongly accepts the Carter vision of the Carter persona and rejects the Ford and media interpretations is revealed in Table 3. Chi-square analysis reveals that the differences between the acceptance of the Carter fantasies on the one hand and rejection of the Ford and media fantasies on the other is highly significant ($x^2$ = 21.83, d.f. = 2, p < .001, 13.82 required).

Table 3 does indicate a moderate admixture of media fantasies in Type I but it also indicates that over one third of the media fantasies were rejected by the members of Type I.

**Type II — "Media Spectator Seeing Ford as Lesser of Two Evils."** Type II accounts for 17.5 percent of total variance, and 31.5 percent of variance within the four-factor solution. Six persons loaded highest on this type. Type II participates in a mixed vision composed of dramas from both the Ford and media visions of Carter. Table 2 indicates that the persons who are members of Type II most strongly accept a scenario which depicts a largely apathetic voting public which does not care about the election because both candidates are unexciting. According to the scenario the Ford persona is a weak leader and Carter's persona raises doubts about its judgment and personality. Both candidates fail to address the real issues in the country.

Given a group of people who participate in fantasies about unexciting, inept candidates and apathetic voters, Type II individuals appear drawn to the campaign primarily by the drama created by the preelection polls. Despite apathetic voters, the scenario contains some excitement for Type II because Carter is losing momentum while Ford is gaining in the polls. What looked like a "shoo-in" for Carter has become a real "horse race" and could end in a photo finish by November 2.

Coupled with the "Media Spectator's" apparent interest in poll results is an underlying uncertainty about candidate Carter. People who load strongest on Type II accept the portrayal of Carter as a smiling person who cannot be trusted and who is promising more in the campaign and the debates than he can deliver. In addition, individuals in Type II participate in fantasies which characterize Carter as lacking knowledge about Yugoslavia and Korea, as a president who would increase Federal spending, and as a candidate who shifted positions on the issues.

When we look at the end of the Q-array which indicates the items most strongly rejected by individuals in Type II, the coherence of the vision becomes clearer. They most strongly reject items depicting Carter as victor in the debates. Type II individuals, however, reject the notion that Carter was unfair, too aggressive, and disrespectful of the President in the debates.

Finally, the "Media Spectator" rejects the efforts of Carter campaigners to dramatize Ford as hiding in the White House, and to blame Carter's slippage in the polls on a lack of opportunity for Carter to confront the President publicly. Type II also rejects the Carter campaign characterizations of Carter as a consistent and honest campaigner whose positions on the issues only appeared to be unclear or flip-flopping because of poor media reporting and Republican campaign distortions.

Table 3 indicates that Type II participates predominantly in a media vision of the Carter persona with a strong mixture of fantasies from the Ford vision. The Chi-square approaches statistical significance ($x^2 = 6.17$, d.f. = 2, p<.05, 5.99 required).[40]

## Table 3

### Frequency of Acceptance and Rejection of Carter, Ford, Media Media Visions for all Types[a]

|  | Type I Vision | | | Type II Vision | | | Type III Vision | | | Type IV Vision | | |
|---|---|---|---|---|---|---|---|---|---|---|---|---|
|  | C | F | M | C | F | M | C | F | M | C | F | M |
| # of items accepted: | 15 | 2 | 10 | 4 | 8 | 11 | 2 | 10 | 11 | 4 | 12 | 10 |
| # of items rejected: | 1 | 14 | 6 | 12 | 8 | 5 | 14 | 6 | 5 | 12 | 4 | 6 |
|  | N = 48 | | | N = 48 | | | N = 48 | | | N = 48 | | |

Type II's uncertainty about both Ford and Carter visions is illustrated in Table 3 which shows as many Ford vision items are rejected as accepted. The Carter vision fantasies are more frequently rejected, but note that all items in Type II's Q-array with z-scores of $-1.0$ or less are from the Ford and Carter visions. Overall, the pattern of the Type II Q-array suggests that "Media Spectators" do not participate strongly in the rhetorical visions of either candidate. Instead, they share the fantasies of the media with some mild participation in a few of the Ford dramas.

**Type III—"Anti-Carter Media Convert."** Type III acounts for 5.4 percent of total variance and 9.3 percent of variance within the four-factor solution. Only two persons had their highest loadings on this type. Table 2 indicates that five of the seven items with z-scores $+ 1.0$ are from the media vision of Carter. Table 2 also indicates that Type III individuals strongly accept dramas portraying public uncertainty about Carter and his positions on the issues. Typical are depictions of Carter promising more than he could deliver in the debates, and Carter shifting his issue-positions in public while

[40]Many researchers are reluctant to place confidence in such results based on Q-data unless they reach the .01 level of significance. See Fred N. Kerlinger, *Foundations of Behavioral Research,* 2nd ed. (1964; New York: Holt, Rinehart, and Winston, 1973), p. 595.

extolling the goodness of the American people. Type III "Media Converts" accept the scenario of public apathy caused by Vietnam and Watergate. They feel, however, that Ford, not Carter, has the potential of overcoming the alienation of the people from their government. Although persons in this type accept the idealism of Carter (as demonstrated when he defied the old southern bosses in 1970), they are disappointed in Carter's inability to deliver what he had promised as governor of Georgia. Type III also accepts the good, intelligent, religious, and determined persona of Carter but clearly rejects Carter's actual record in the debates, his record as governor, and his capabilities as a leader.

Two items strongly rejected by Type III dramatize Carter's elimination of wasteful spending in Georgia, and his success in reducing bureaucracy thereby making Georgia government more responsive. Type III also rejects the scenario of Carter winning the debates by revealing Ford's weakness as a leader, and surprising those who thought Carter was weak on foreign policy. These "Media Converts" also reject the notion that voter apathy was caused by lack of discussion of issues by the candidates.

Table 3 reveals that Type III rejects more items from the Carter vision than any other type. Chi-square analysis indicates Type III's strong rejection of the Carter vision and acceptance of the Media vision ($x^2 = 12.18$, d.f. = 2, p<.005, 10.59 require). Overall, Type III responds to aspects of Carter's idealism but feels Carter has not and cannot deliver on his promises.

**Type IV—"Marginal Ford Participant."** Type IV is the weakest type identified, accounting for only 4.3 percent of total variance and 7.5 percent of variance within the four-factor solution. Three persons are significantly loaded on the type. Like Type II, this type accepts the dramatizations of the campaign as a horse race in which Carter lost an early lead due to serious mistakes. Other strongly-accepted items dramatize Carter losing steam in the polls and Ford gaining. Although Type IV accepts the Carter persona of a hard-working family man and a farmer, he also accepts items that depict Carter's shifting campaign, his tendency to play fast and loose with the facts, and his lack of information on foreign affairs. Finally, Type IV accepts the explanation of Carter publicists that Carter only did what other politicians had previously done in granting an interview with *Playboy*. In addition, the items most strongly rejected by Type IV depict the Ford and Media vision explanations of the *Playboy* interview. This type, however, rejects aspects of Carter's persona which depict him as beholden to no one, understanding of voters, and effective as governer of Georgia.

Table 3 indicates that Type IV accepts the Ford campaign vision of Carter with more frequency than any other type. The Media vision of Carter is also highly accepted by this type. Chi-square approaches statistical significance ($x^2 = 8.73$, d.f. = 2, p<.025; 7.38 required).

**Consensus Items**—Items having a z-score difference among types no greater than 1.0 are consensus items. All five such items identified in the study reflect the media vision of Carter (see Table 2). Interestingly, one such item reflects a dramatization of voters reacting negatively to Carter's revelations about "lust" and references to "screwing" in the *Playboy* interview. The other item depicts Carter voting to admit a black to his church. Despite the fact that both events were well publicized, our four types relegated the items to the middle (neutral) sections of their Q-arrays.

**Typal Membership and Actual Voting**—Table 1 reveals that of the 14 persons who loaded highest on Type I ("Carter Convert"), 13 actually voted for Carter, and one did not report her actual vote. Of the six persons loading highest on Type II ("Media Spectator—Ford Lesser of Evils"), five voted for Ford, one voted for Carter. Both persons in Type III ("Media Convert") voted for Ford. Of the three persons in Type IV ("Marginal Ford Participant"), one voted for Carter, one for Ford, one for another party candidate. Interestingly, only one of our 26 respondents did not load significantly on any type. This person was the only respondent who did not vote in this election.

Another interesting finding of this study is that in some cases, a person's membership in our four types appeared to be a better predictor of the person's actual voting than his/her stated voting intentions a week before the election. Of the three persons who said they were undecided before the election, two voted for Ford (one was in Type III, one in Type IV), and one voted for Carter (he was in Type I). One person who intended to vote for McCarthy actually voted for Ford (she was in Type II). In summary, of the 24 persons who voted and reported their actual vote, only three voted in a way contrary to their expressed participation in one of the three rhetorical visions of Jimmy Carter.[41]

## Discussion

The results of this study provide some evidence in support of a link between rhetorical critical analyses of political campaign persuasion and audience responses. Specifically we discovered preliminary evidence to support the hypothesis that mass media campaign events influence voters because listeners come to share the fantasies in media dramas much as members of groups come to share fantasies in their face-to-face discussions. Particularly intriguing in this regard is our discovery of two groups of voters (i.e., Types I and III) whose responses to the Q-sort closely matched the rhetorical visions we discovered in our rhetorical criticism. In no instance did we find a voter group who in Q-sorting mixed items drawn from all three visions in random order.

---

[41]Two of these persons had the lowest factor loadings of any of the persons in their respective types. The usefulness of the Q-arrays for understanding voting behavior is also noted in the fact that for Type II, four of the seven items having z-scores $< -1.0$ were from the Carter vision. For Type III, eight of the ten items having z-scores $< -1.0$ were from the Carter vision, and for Type IV, three of seven items with z-scores $< -1.0$ were from the Carter vision.

We did, however, find some overt groups whose visions of the Carter persona were composed of both media and candidate interpretative fantasies. These mixed visions appear to have almost as much power to anticipate actual voting behavior as the relatively pure vision of the "Carter Convert" which so closely matched the rhetorical vision we discovered in our critical analysis of 1976 campaign rhetoric. One hypothesis generated from this study is: persons who have a mixed rhetorical vision indicating their acceptance of a media vision as well as the vision of a candidate will vote for the candidate whose vision is represented. The degree to which a candidate's vision must be represented in such a mixed vision in order to predict the vote for that candidate remains an empirical question inviting further research. Our finding that Types II and IV (both composed of mixed candidate and media visions) strongly rejected items associated with the Carter campaign vision and tended to vote for Ford (or against Carter) is an interesting discovery. Further research should investigate the relationship between persons' strong rejection of a particular candidate's rhetorical vision and those person's tendency to vote against that candidate.

In attempting to apply Q-methodology to the analysis of rhetorical visions in Campaign '76, we encountered several methodological problems. First, the explanatory and predictive power of this kind of research is strongly dependent upon the sensitivity of researchers to campaign rhetoric. The validity of the Q-sort items is dependent upon the ability of the critic researcher to accurately assess and then express the essence of the campaign dramas in very brief verbal statements. We found it was difficult fully to capture vivid and complex dramas in a fifty-word verbal item. Thus, the challenge of item generation is to produce a representative sample of items which in toto capture the full range of characters, scenarios, and themes contained within a rhetorical vision.

The second methodological problem we discovered was that many of the scenarios and dramas of the campaign changed very quickly, sometimes daily. To identify accurately when audiences are participating in a vision, the substructures of that vision must be empirically tested when they are salient in a campaign. We found that many of the themes which were salient very early in the campaign were no longer important in the later stages of the campaign, and thus had to be disregarded in this study.

Finally, this research has suggested areas in which empirical tests of rhetorical criticisms of campaign communication might usefully be extended. Q-sorts could be developed for testing during different stages of a campaign to discover shifts in voter perceptions of candidates' personae over the course of the primaries, conventions, and the final weeks of the campaign. This kind of analysis could be combined with a study in which the most significant Q-sort items identified from small-sample critical/empirical studies such as ours might be administered in a briefer form to persons via large-sample surveys.[42] Thus, one might discover the degree to which the rhetorical visions we identified have been propagated through the entire electorate.

[42]Nimmo and Savage did this in a study of voter perceptions of candidates who exemplified the Old and New Politics. They first tested the images of the candidates using Q-sorts administered to a sample of 100 voters and identified four voter types. Then the most important candidate traits identified in the Q-study were tested in a large sample survey of 400 voters. The distribution of voter types in the large sample survey was similar to those types found in the earlier Q-study. See Nimmo and Savage, pp. 112-125.

# 10

# Political Cartoons and Salient Rhetorical Fantasies:

## An Empirical Analysis of the '76 Presidential Campaign

ERNEST G. BORMANN, JOLENE KOESTER,
and JANET BENNETT

A number of political scientists, sociologists, and rhetorical scholars have argued that how the media dramatize a political campaign influences how voters come to see the political process, the candidates, and the campaign.[1] In this study we take an explanatory account of political communication drawn largely from rhetorical criticism and using the rigor of behavioral models seek to find empirical support for that account. We used the method of fantasy theme analysis for a rhetorical criticism of political persuasion and the news coverage of the 1976 presidential campaign. We selected the key dramas discovered by our criticism and investigated the way they were portrayed in political cartoons. We then sought to test audience response to the media dramas in cartoon form using an empirical method (Q-methodology).

Our theoretical rationale suggest that voters respond to fantasy themes in media campaigns and news reports in the same way that participants in small groups respond to dramatizing messages. Specifically we investigated the question of whether the political cartoon functions in mass political persuasion like the "inside joke" in a small group, as an indicator of a salient shared fantasy. To investigate this question we asked three subsidiary questions:

*Communication Monographs,* 45, (November, 1978). Reprinted with permission from The Speech Communication Association.

Mr. Bormann is professor, Ms. Koester and Ms. Bennett are doctoral candidates in speech communication, University of Minnesota. The authors express their appreciation to Professor David Rarick for assistance in the development of the Q-sorts and the design of the investigation.

A Q-analysis of cartoons published during the campaign provides evidence of the complex patterns of shared fantasies among various types of voters, and the relationships between these fantasies and those dramatized by various groups during the political campaign.

[1]Les Cleveland, "Symbols and Politics: Mass Communication and the Public Drama," *Politics,* 4 (1969), 186-196; Joseph R. Gusfield, *Symbolic Crusade: Status Politics and the American Temperance Movement* (Urbana: University of Illinois Press, 1963); Dan D. Nimmo, *Popular Images of Politics* (Englewood Cliffs, N.J.: Prentice-Hall, 1974): James N. Rosenau, *The Dramas of Politics* (Boston: Little Brown, 1973).

1. What were the major fantasies portrayed in political cartoons during the 1976 presidential campaign?

2. How did the voters' perception of the saliency of the shared fantasies as revealed by the Q-sort compare with our estimate of the importance of the fantasies based upon rhetorical criticism of the messages?

3. How did the sharing of the salient fantasies relate to the audience's expressed voting intentions and actual behavior in the 1976 presidential election?

Our purpose was neither to validate our method of rhetorical criticism nor to guage public opinion. Rather we sought to gather preliminary evidence bearing on the question of whether there is a link between fantasy theme analysis and audience response. If such a link could be found we would have a better explanation of political persuasion than could be provided by rhetorical criticism or audience response studies alone.

## Theoretical Rationale

### The Concept of Group Fantasy

Since our study investigates some of the concepts of fantasy theme analysis we need to explain our specialized use of the terms "fantasy" and "group fantasy" in this study.[2] The common definition of fantasy that comes closest to our technical meaning for the term is that it is the creative and imaginative interpretation of events which fulfills a psychological or rhetorical need. Fantasy, as we define it, includes the creative interpretation of historical events as well as the more fanciful fictitious portrayal of imaginative characters. Indeed, the largest number of campaign fantasies tends to be depictions of living human beings or historical personages acting out documented events.[3]

[2]Two other technical terms are important in the method. A *fantasy type* is a recurring scenario in a body of discourse. During the campaign of 1976 a number of sources portrayed President Ford as a bumbler in scenarios such as the one where he stumbled on some steps, bumped his head when leaving a helicopter, and so forth. Taken together these fantasy themes formed a fantasy type. For a study which uses fantasy type as the master concept see Ernest G. Bormann, "Fetching Good Out of Evil: The Rhetorical Uses of Calamity," *Quarterly Journal of Speech,* 63 (1977), 130-139. A *rhetorical vision* is a coherent integration of various shared fantasies which presents a broader view of a campaign or issue. The fantasy types and themes of a specific campaign are often integrated by a master trope or analogy which pulls the elements of the vision together. When a coherent rhetorical vision emerges during a campaign it is often indexed by a label such as the New Populism, the New Politics, the New Frontier, or the New Deal.

[3]The rhetorical criticisms which we made of the 1976 campaign in preparing the design of this study revealed that the majority of dramatizations were portrayals of historical events and personages.

Our concept of group fantasy stems from empirical work of Bales[4] followed by Bormann.[5] Further studies building on Bales's work were reported in the *Analysis of Groups.*[6]

These and other investigations discovered that a group fantasy results from the joint participation of two or more people in one or a series of dramatizing messages within a communication context. Participation includes sharing the tone and interpretation of the portrayal. The messages which spark the sharing of fantasies in a group are those which dramatize fictitious or non-fictitious characters enacting a dramatic incident at some place and time other than the here-and-now.

Investigators have discovered that not all dramatizing messages result in sharing. In order for people to share a fantasy they must respond appropriately. If the drama is humorous they must laugh along with rather than at the narrator. If the speaker presents a leading character in a sympathetic way, then the others must sympathize with the character in order to share the fantasy.

One important kind of evidence that fantasies are shared by a mass audience might be analogous to what occurs when an "inside joke" is told in a small group. An *inside joke* is a cryptic allusion to an element of a dramatic situation which sparks a strong reponse from the other group members. When a member makes the cryptic allusion, nonparticipant observers often find the response to be out of proportion to the apparent importance of the stimulus. Group members, when asked to explain, indicate that the response relates to something important which happened to the group and only someone who was there at the time could fully understand it. When the investigators go back into the tape recordings of previous meetings to discover the context for the inside joke they frequently find a shared fantasy which was alluded to in the inside joke.

## Group Fantasy and Political Campaigns

Our theoretical perspective is based upon an analogy which sees mass communication events creating shared fantasies in larger publics by means of the same dynamic psychological processes which create shared fantasies in small face-to-face groups.

The messages which come to the public during a campaign are a mixture of what the campaign organization sends, what is sent by the subsystem controlled by the media professionals, and what arises spontaneously from the general public.

[4]Robert F. Bales, *Personality and Interpersonal Relations* (New York: Holt, Rinehart and Winston, 1970).
[5]Ernest G. Bormann, *Discussion and Group Methods: Theory and Practice,* 2nd ed. (New York: Harper & Row, 1975).
[6]Graham S. Gibbard, John J. Hartman, and Richard D. Mann, eds., *Analysis of Groups* (San Francisco: Jossey-Bass, 1974).

An important question is the process by which the vision of the campaign and the candidates is propagated. Our hypothesis is that campaign strategists develop their plans in a series of intensive small group discussions during the course of which they share the fantasies that come to form a rhetorical vision for their campaign. Then they work these fantasies into their campaign messages.[7] In a similar way professional journalists come to share fantasies as they discuss the campaign and then dramatize the news in a particular way because of their common vision.[8] Members of the media audiences come to share some of the fantasies as they read, hear, or watch them. A given individual may share predominately in the fantasies of one of the contending candidates or of the professional journalists or in some idiosyncratic combination. The viewers who participated in mass media fantasies may retell the story in small group conversations with friends, family, coworkers, and others. If the members of such groups participate in the dramatizations, they come to share the media fantasy second hand but within the supportive climate of the small group.[9] Only the empathic participation of large numbers of people results in such shared fantasies which come to compose the public's various rhetorical visions of the campaign. Our concern in this study was with ways to verify whether a fantasy was shared by the voters and to discover the possible impact of shared fantasies upon voting behavior.

## Method

In searching for the mass media equivalent of the inside joke in small groups we decided upon the political cartoon.[10] A political cartoon contains personae in at least an implied dramatic action, is cryptic, and tends to allude to a single fantasy. A cartoon which depicts candidate Carter in a little boat shooting an ineffectual popgun at a large ship named the Mayaguez

[7]For an analysis of the way a small group of strategists share fantasies in preparing public relations campaigns see Laurinda W. Porter, "The White House Transcripts: Group Fantasy Events Concerning the Mass Media." *Central States Speech Journal,* 27 (1976), 272-279; for examples of such dramatizations of scenarios in the 1976 presidential campaign see Fred McMorrow, *Jimmy — The Candidacy of Carter* (New York: Whirlwind Book Co., 1976).

[8]For a study outlining the way groups arise and function among reporters during the normal course of covering a political campaign see Timothy Crouse, *The Boys on the Bus* (New York: Random House, 1973). Interestingly, our rhetorical critical studies in preparation for this investigation discovered a relatively coherent common vision of the campaign reflected in the fantasies of the "hard news" reports of the media.

[9]For a definitive treatise on the role of interpersonal and group communication in the mass communication process see Eliott Friedson, "Communication Research and the Concept of the Mass," *American Sociological Review,* 18 (1953), 313-317.

[10]Among the few studies we have been able to find regarding the rhetorical function of political cartoons is Matthew C. Morrison, "The Role of the Political Cartoonist in Image Making," *Central States Speech Journal,* 20 (1969), 252-260.

means little to the individual who did not share in the media fantasies relating to the Mayaguez incident.

We used Q-methodology to discover how members of the electorate perceived the various cartoons relating to the campaign of 1976.[11] Q-methodology allows persons to respond to a set of items such as cartoons by rank ordering them on a continuum from those they accept to those they reject. Our choice of method was guided by several factors. First, it had to accommodate the special visual nature of the cartoon. Second, we needed a technique which would provide an index of the degree of strength of saliency of response on each subject to each fantasy. Saliency was important because we wished to discover whether some fantasies were more important to voters than others and, if so, whether such forceful fantasies could be evaluated on qualitative grounds. In reporting the results of one poll, the polling organization argued that the dramatizations which portrayed Gerald Ford as having bumbled again in regard to his statement in the second television debate concerning Soviet influence in Eastern Europe were of great importance in influencing voters in the concluding days of the campaign.[12] By gathering data on saliency we hoped to be able to evaluate the conclusions of analysts and pollsters regarding the importance of such interpretative fantasies as those relating to Ford's statements about Eastern Europe.[13] Finally, Q-methodology allows persons to express comparative judgments on many items and provides a way to group persons on the basis of similar responses to the items. An individual's comparative sorting of items such as cartoons is useful for discovering the extent to which a person shares in a complex social reality such as a rhetorical vision.

Assuming that a successful political cartoon was a key to salient shared fantasies we collected cartoons from the major newspapers and magazines published during the height of the 1976 political campaign.[14] We made a systematic search of cartoons published after Labor Day until two weeks before the election. We categorized each of the cartoons according to the fantasy about the campaign for which it served the "inside joke" function. From our categorization we selected sixteen most frequently alluded to fantasies, including six dramas which were critical interpretations of Carter,

---

[11]The method is described in William Stephenson, *The Study of Behavior* (Chicago: University of Chicago Press, 1953).

[12]*Gallup Opinion Index*, Report 137, December 1976, pp. 7-8.

[13]The Q-sort procedure allows respondents to rank order a set of cartoons on a continuum from those which most resemble their own position on the campaign to those which are least like their position. Thus, in sorting a Q-deck, individuals can express comparative feelings about the cartoons in a way which allows for statistical comparisons of individual responses. We argue that in discovering how far from the mean an individual placed a given cartoon we have evidence as to how salient the cartoon was for the individual.

[14]We searched representative major metropolitan newspapers from all regions of the United States. We selected the 48 cartoons to construct the Q-sort from a total of approximately 150 cartoons.

six critical of Ford, and four critical of the campaign in general.[15] We then constructed a Q-sort instrument of 48 cartoons in which each of the sixteen fantasies was represented by three different cartoons.

We drew a quota sample of 29 voting-age adults of different ages and from different socio-economic and political backgrounds. The group was diverse but small and not intended to be a random sample from which we could draw inferences about a parent population. Our sample enabled us to evaluate our explanatory account of how mass media political persuasion works. We wanted to see if our sample responded to the campaign fantasies as our previously conducted rhetorical criticism anticipated they would, and whether they would sort the Q-items as though they shared group fantasies of the campaign. We argue that sorting the cartoons in similar ways, hence loading heavily on the same factor, provides evidence that individuals share the same fantasies and thus a common rhetorical vision of the campaign.

We conducted personal interviews with the subjects from October 29 through November 1, 1976. The late date assured us that most of the significant campaign themes had been portrayed and that the voters had already participated in the most important fantasies relating to the campaign.

## Results

The Q-analysis resulted in four factors which accounted for 45.4 percent of the total variance.[16] (Hereafter, we will refer to the factors as *rhetorical groups*.) If we set a level so that a person had to have a loading of at least .45 to be significantly associated with a group, 23 of the 29 persons shared significantly in at least one rhetorical group. However, of the six individuals

[15]The six anti-Carter fantasies were: Carter and the *Playboy* interview; Carter slipping in the polls; Carter's religion; Carter revealing ignorance in tax reform program; Carter's smile and nice-guy image hiding a tough politician; and Carter making a political error in attacking ex-president Lyndon Johnson. The six anti-Ford fantasies were: Ford's receipt of corporate gifts; Ford's bungling of the Butz affair; Ford as figurehead and Kissinger as the real power in foreign affairs; Ford politically embarrassed by downturn in economy; Ford's use of the Mayaguez affair for public relations revealed by new information; Ford bungling in comment about Soviet domination of Eastern Europe. The four media fantasies regarding the election were: public outcry about Carter's *Playboy* interview reveals hypocrisy of voters; the campaign is mediocre because candidates do not deal with issues; the debates were dull and meaningless; and the mediocre campaign results in voter apathy.

[16]The statistical procedures we used are detailed in Norman Van Tubergen, "Q-Analysis (Quanal)," Mass Communication Research Bureau, School of Journalism, University of Iowa (n.d.), mimeo. The analysis extracted all factors with eigen-values greater than 1.0. The bipolar splitting criterion was set at 30%, indicating that a factor must be at least 30% negative for the program to split it into two types. Analysis was completed using Van Tubergen's WRAP procedure which weights factor loadings for persons in each factor and computes standardized Q-arrays indicating the response patterns of persons in each factor to the 48 items. We got seven factors but the last three accounted for so little variance that we included only those factors which accounted for 5% or more of the total variance.

who did not load at least .45, three loaded .34 or higher on at least one
group and another individual loaded at .30 or higher. Membership in the
four groups strongly discriminated the Carter voters from the Ford voters
even when we used factor loadings of .30 as a criterion for membership.[17]

**Analysis of Rhetorical Groups**

We developed a description of the rhetorical vision associated with each
of the four groups on the basis of Q-arrays expressed in standardized z-
scores. We interpreted items with low z-scores (positive or negative) as
having little salience for a person in a given rhetorical group and items with
high z-scores as having a great degree of salience.

**Type I, "The Group of Media-Sensitive Carter Supporters"** The first
rhetorical group is the strongest type identified by the Q-analysis accounting
for 24 percent of the total variance and 55 percent of variance within the
four-factor solution. Seven people loaded strongest on this factor with
loadings of .45 or higher. In their Q-sorting, members of this group
accepted as most expressing their position 24 cartoons, nine of which tended
to ridicule the campaign in line with the fantasies of professional media
journalists, and 13 of which alluded to anti-Ford fantasies.

We found both the cartoons accepted and rejected by members of the
first group to be equally important in analyzing the vision. Group I
indicated that 16 of the 18 anti-Carter cartoons least expressed their
position. In particular, they strongly rejected those cartoons which
portrayed Carter as taxing the poor, goofing on the *Playboy* interview in
discussing lust and in making unwise political comments about former
President Lyndon Johnson.

If we assume that the cartoons acted as an "inside-joke" to tap into the
individual's emotional responses and motivations then we can infer the
following rhetorical vision of the campaign held by persons in the first
rhetorical group. The media-sensitive Carter supporters saw the campaign
as lacking in excitement, inadequate in terms of discussing the issues, and
exemplified by the dull and meaningless debates in which a bumbling
Gerald Ford, despite prompting from Henry Kissinger, revealed his
ineptness in foreign policy by comments about Soviet domination in
Eastern Europe.

**Type 2, "The Committed Partisans"** Type 2 accounted for 9 percent of
total variance and 16 percent of the variance within the four-factor
solution. In many respects the response patterns of the persons in Type 2 are
the most interesting of our analysis. The second type is bipolar because
persons in this type responded to the 48 cartoons in opposite ways. One
group saw certain cartoons positively while another group saw the same

[17]For a discussion of the significance of factor loadings see Mary Jane Schlinger, "Cues on
Q-Technique," *Journal of Advertising Research*, 9 (1969), 56-57. In our subsequent interpretations of the data we will indicate when we are discussing the 22 subjects who loaded at
the .45 level or better or when we are including the four who loaded between .30 and .45. A
complete table of z-scores for each type on each cartoon can be obtained from the senior
author.

cartoons negatively. Five persons loaded greater than or equal to $+ .34$ on this group, and four loaded less than or equal to $- .45$ on it. These nine people can be seen as two rhetorical groups whose visions of the campaign are mirro-images of one another.

We shall refer to one end of the bipolar Type 2 as "Carter Partisans" and the other end as "Ford Partisans." The Carter Partisans found a resemblance to their views in cartoons which portrayed the Ford connection with big business interest, his mishandling of the Butz incident, his ignorance on Eastern Europe, his using the Mayaguez incident for public relations purposes, and his inability to deal with the economic situation. They disliked the cartoons portraying Carter as taxing the poor, caught in a compromising situation in the *Playboy* interview, slipping in the polls, and shedding his "nice-guy" image.

The Ford Partisans accepted cartoons which portrayed Carter as taxing the poor and making a major error on tax reform, revealing his hypocrisy in the *Playboy* interview, shedding his nice-guy image and revealing himself to be an unscrupulous politician, slipping in the polls, and making a political error in his references to former President Lyndon Johnson. Ford Partisans rejected the cartoons which portrayed Ford as inept in economic matters, a figurehead for Kissinger in foreign policy, a captive of big business, a bungler in the Butz affair, or as having used the Mayaguez incident for public relations purposes.

Eight cartoons were strongly salient (that is, strongly accepted or rejected) by both the Carter and Ford partisans; these eight cartoons are important indexes of the mirror nature of the groups in bipolar Type 2. The Carter Partisans sorted four of the eight most salient cartoons into their "expresses-most-closely" end of the Q-sort and the Ford Partisans sorted the same four cartoons towards the "least expresses" end of the Q-sort. Another four cartoons were sorted into the Carter Partisans' "least expresses" positions, while they were sorted into the Ford Partisans' "expresses-most-closely" end of the Q-array.[18]

---

[18]The four anti-Carter cartoons which were most salient for both poles were: two derelicts standing on a street corner on skid row and the caption "Carter wants to impose more taxes on us and give them to the poor"; Carter with boxing gloves on and his robe hanging behind him labeled "nice guy image, honesty, vagueness" and the caption "Coming-Out Party"; Carter with a *Playboy* bunny on his back and the caption "Ford has a monkey on his back with Watergate!"; a moth labeled "Carter" flying through the flame of a candle labeled "Income Tax Issue." The four anti-Ford cartoons included: two set on the golf course, in one Ford is crammed into a golf cart with a number of other players, the cart is labeled "Big Corporations," the caption is "Easy Rider," and in the other Ford is on the putting green with a group of people each bearing the label of a large corporation and the caption is "Concentrate On Your Game, Jerry! We'll Worry About Other Things Later!"; one with Ford placing a bouquet of roses labeled "Ford Stalling on Butz Case" in a garbage can and the entire cartoon captioned "Latest Rose Garden Ceremony"; one of Ford and Kissinger standing outside a theatre with a poster featuring them in cowboy outfits bellied up to a bar and the billboard in front of the theatre entitled "The Mayaguez Triumph" and Ford and Kissinger saying "We can lick any Cambodian in the house!" The caption for the cartoon reads "It's Not Playing the Way It Did Last Year."

The traditional Republican Party rhetorical vision contains, as a central type, the drama of fiscally irresponsible Democrats. Two of the eight mirror-image cartoons make allusions to anti-Carter fantasies in which he is portrayed as fiscally irresponsible. The traditional Democratic Party rhetorical vision features a central fantasy type of Republican as a friend of big business. Two of the eight cartoons were anti-Ford depictions which portrayed the then President as hobnobbing with corporations. Thus, four of the eight salient cartoons were allusions to partisan political rhetoric with roots going back at least as far as the New Deal of Franklin Roosevelt.

The remaining four mirror-image cartoons alluded to interpretative fantasies relating to media events associated with the 1976 campaign. The cartoons dealt with Ford's handling of the Butz affair, Carter shedding his "nice-guy" image and becoming a hard-hitting politician, Carter's *Playboy* interview, and the Mayaguez incident.

The way people who were positively or negatively loaded on Type 2 sorted the cartoons alluding the Mayaguez fantasy was particularly significant in our estimation. The Mayaguez fantasies had moved rapidly through the media and apparently through large segments of the public at the time of the final withdrawal of American troops from Vietnam. The Gallup poll reported an 11 percent rise in popularity for President Ford immediately after the affair and indicated that it was the sharpest rise in Presidential ratings since the Gallup organization began taking such soundings of public opinion. The pollsters attributed the rise largely to the Mayaguez incident.[19] For people who loaded strongly on bipolar Type 2 the Mayaguez fantasies were still potent dramas more than a year after the event. The dedicated Ford Partisans in Type 2 in our sample rejected the cartoon portraying the Mayaguez incident as a public relations ploy. The Carter Partisans sorted the public relations cartoon as expressing their own position. Interestingly, the members of Type 1 found the Mayaguez incident less compelling, sorting it into a neutral position in their Q-array.

Unlike Type 1, members of Type 2 rejected cartoons portraying fantasies of a meaningless, mediocre campaign resulting in voter apathy. When we couple this finding with the fact that the mirror-image cartoons included several which made cryptic allusions to widely and strongly held traditional Republican and Democratic fantasy types, we conclude that Type 2 persons were more involved political partisans than those of Type 1. Type 2 voters responded strongly to more fantasies relating to different personae and actions such as the Mayaguez incident and, thus, seemingly participated in a more thickly textured rhetorical vision and the fantasies were more compelling and salient than was the case for individuals in Type 1. We, therefore, decided to call them "Committed Partisans." Compared to Type 1 persons the Committed Partisans were much less influenced by interpretative fantasies of the news media.

[19]*Gallup Opinion Index*, Report 120, June 1975, p. 1.

**Type 3, "The Group of Disillusioned Democratic Regulars"** The third type accounted for 6.4 percent of total variance and 14 percent of variance within the four-factor solution. Eight persons loaded at .30 or higher on Factor 3 and seven at .45 or higher.

The rhetorical group comprising Type 3 resembles Type 1 in its acceptance of media dramas which portrayed the campaign as avoiding the issues and the debates as meaningless, and in its acceptance of anti-Ford cartoons. However, there are substantial differences between the two groups. Type 3 people tended to accept cartoons which emphasized Ford's failures in economic matters much more strongly than did Type 1. Both groups found allusions to Ford's slip in regard to Soviet domination of Eastern Europe salient.

Even more interesting was the nature of the other cartoons to which members of the two groups reacted differently. Type 1 Carter voters rejected the dramas which alluded to the *Playboy* interview as revealing Carter's hypocrisy and bad political judgment, but Type 3 Carter supporters tended to accept them. Type 3 accepted the cartoons portraying Carter as shedding his "nice-guy" image and battering down the door to Ford's defenses much more than did Type 1 supporters. Type 3 rejected the fantasy of the Mayaguez as "White House public relations" while Type 1 Carter supporters tended to be neutral about it. Type 3 also strongly rejected the cartoons which implied a disparagement of Carter's born-again religious position and the fantasy which saw the general public as hypocritical in establishing a double standard in regard to candor when it related to a discussion of sex and lust in the *Playboy* magazine.

The rhetorical vision of Type 3 Carter supporters, thus, seems to be a cynical one about the election and the electoral process to some extent, resembling Type 1 and differing from Type 2 in that regard. The third group is much more preoccupied with economic matters than the other two groups of Carter voters. The third group is also supportive of Ford's efforts in the Mayaguez affair and dislikes the attempts to ridicule Carter's religion. One tentative conclusion suggested by the data is that members of Type 3, while ostensibly cynical about politics and politicians, are nonetheless supportive of the United States in foreign policy, upset by Carter's comments in *Playboy* magazine, and disturbed because Ford was not more "hard-nosed" about Soviet domination in Eastern Europe.

Thus, the people in Type 3 can be viewed as cherishing some fantasies about the sanctity of religion and sex, participating in the remnants of the "Cold War" vision, viewing the political process with some cynicism, and approving Carter's adoption of a get-tough attitude toward Ford and the campaign. They also seem to be preoccupied with domestic economic conditions and view Ford as essentially inept in this area.

**Type 4, "The Enigma"** The fourth type accounted for 5 percent of total variance and 11.5 percent of variance within the four factor solution. The three individuals who loaded most heavily on Type 4 were a student without party preference who voted for Carter, a blue collar independent voter who voted for Ford and a white collar worker without party preference who anticipated voting for Ford but for whom we have no voting data.[20]

These three people might as well have been at the opposite end of the continuum from the committed partisans in Type 2. Two of the three had no party preference and one identified himself as an independent.

We have been unable to find a plausible interpretation of the sorting behavior of the subjects in Type 4. They rejected cartoons which alluded to Ford's connection with big business as well as those portraying Carter as a hypocrite on the *Playboy* interview. They also sorted the cartoons which put down Carter's religion as "least expressing" their own views. They participated in the apathy dramas of the media, the fantasy of Carter taxing the poor, and Ford making a major slip in his comment on Soviet domination of Eastern Europe.

Perhaps the few individuals in Type 4 were more confused than our other respondents by the campaign or, perhaps, they were skeptics who discounted much of the media coverage and the partisan persuasion.

**The Overall Rhetorical Landscape**

We can plot the symbolic reality of the presidential campaign of 1976 for our 29 subjects in the following manner. Figure 1 presents a graphic representation of the way the various rhetorical groups distributed themselves around the core rhetorical visions of the Ford and Carter Partisans of Type 2. At either end of the bipolar Type 2 were the committed people who participated in the traditional visions of the Republican or Democratic Parties. At the one end the Committed Carter Partisans consisted of one female and four male Democrats. Moving out from the core vision of the committed was the rhetorical group of Type 3, which consisted of seven female Democrats and one anomalous blue-collar male with no party preference in the oldest age bracket ( + 50). As the core vision of the committed Type 2 Carter Partisans moved into the region of Type 3, the basic traditional Democratic party fantasies were mixed with some of the media dramas of apathy and campaign mediocrity. The vision of Type 3 involved salient fantasies relating to the domestic economy as well as foreign affairs.

Still in the region of the Carter voters were members of Type 1. The first group consisted of seven females, five of whom were students, and all under thirty-five years of age with five under twenty-five. Members of Type 1 were less homogeneous as to political preferences than were the other people in the region of the Carter voters. Four members of Type 1 were Democrats, two had no party preference, and one was a Republican. Type 1 participated more strongly in the media fantasies of apathy, mediocrity of

---

[20]One other subject loaded heavily on Type 4 although she loaded even more heavily on Type 1. She was one of the few subjects who demonstrated such an unusual sorting pattern. She was a young student who was a Republican but voted for Carter.

# Figure 2

## Plot of Rhetorical Landscape 29 Voters 1976 Campaign

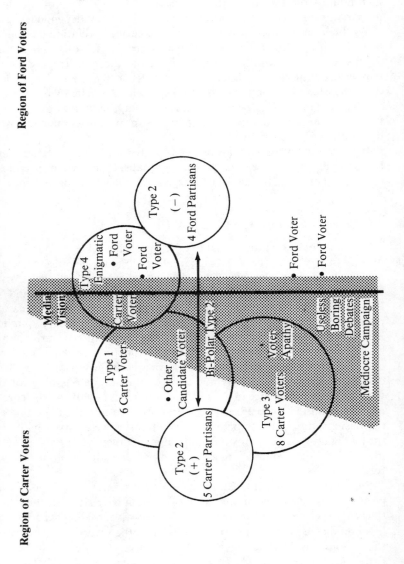

Region of Carter Voters

Region of Ford Voters

the campaign, and uselessness of the debates than did the members of Types 2 and 3. Members of Type 1 did not accept fantasies relating to the economy of the Mayaguez incident, although they did tend to accept cartoons portraying Henry Kissinger as manipulator of foreign policy.

At the opposite end of the bipolar Type 2 was the community of committed Ford Partisans consisting of one female and three male Republicans. The five remaining members of our sample fall somewhere between the Committed Ford Partisans and the region of the Carter voters. Three of the five formed the enigmatic Type 4 and two did not load significantly on any of the four types. One of the two people who did not load significantly on any type was a middle-aged, white collar, female Democrat who voted for Ford and the other a young student, male Democrat who voted for Ford. All five seem to fall into a rhetorical no-man's land where the fantasies do not form a coherent rhetorical vision.

One of our interesting discoveries was the way the political cartoon Q-sort worked to discriminate rhetorical groups which turned out to be highly homogeneous on such demographic characteristics as age, occupation, and political preference.

Certainly the rhetorical communities identified by the cartoon sort anticipated voting behavior with success. The sorting behavior of our respondents even anticipated accurately the voting behavior of those individuals who were undecided before the election. Six of the seven members of the first group voted for Carter, the seventh member voted for a third candidate. All of those who loaded positively on Type 2 voted for Carter, all of the members of the third group voted for Carter, all of those who loaded negatively on Type 2 voted for Ford. Only the enigmatic Type 4 failed to distinguish the Ford from the Carter voters. Of the 24 respondents who loaded .30 or more on types 1, 2, 3, 23 voted in line with their membership in a given rhetorical group.

**The Salient Fantasies**

We anticipated that the three most salient shared fantasies relating to the campaign of 1976 would be, in order of prominence, Jimmy Carter and the *Playboy* interview, Gerald Ford and the Soviet domination of Eastern Europe, and Gerald Ford and the Butz affair. We further expected that the three least salient fantasies would be Carter's political error in reference to President Lyndon Johnson, the Mayaguez drama, and fantasies which portrayed the hypocrisy of the voters and the Ford campaigners in regard to their double standard as revealed in their responses to Carter's *Playboy* interview.

To compute saliency of fantasies we used the raw z-scores for all three of the cartoons alluding to each of the fantasies. Table 1 presents the fantasies ranked from first to sixteenth in total raw z-scores. On this basis of Carter in an unfavorable light on the *Playboy* interview turned out to be a highly salient fantasy as we anticipated. Contrary to our expectations, however, the Ford comments on Eastern Europe were only moderately salient. The fantasy of Ford making a major "goof" in the debates ranked ninth of the sixteen fantasies. We were even further off in our anticipation that the Ford handling of the Butz resignation was a salient fantasy. The Butz resignation ranked at the very bottom of the list in terms of saliency.

## Table 1

### Saliency of Shared Fantasies Rankings On Basis of Raw Z-Scores

| Rank — Fantasy Theme | Raw Score[1] | Comment |
|---|---|---|
| 1. Carter on Taxation | 17.8 | |
| 2. Playboy Interview Major Carter Error | 17.0 | |
| 3. Ford Embarrassed by Downturn in the Economy | 16.4 | Salient for Type 3 positive and Ford Partisans Type 2 negative. Least significant for Type 1. |
| 4. Ford's Corporate Connection | 13.1 | Salient for Type 2, Carter Partisans positive, Ford Partisans negative. Moderate response for Types 3 and 4. |
| 5. Carter's Religion | 12.5 | Salient for Type 3 and 4 negative. Moderate response for Type 1. |
| 6. Mayaguez | 12.3 | Salient for Types 2 and 4. |
| 7. Anti-Debates | 12.0 | Salient for Type 1. |
| 8. Anti-Campaign | 11.9 | Salient for Type 1, Moderately salient for Types 3 and 4. |
| 9. Ford Misstatement on Eastern Europe | 11.8 | Salient for Types 1 and 3, and Carter Partisans Type 2. |
| 10. Kissinger as Power Behind the President | 11.6 | |
| 11. Voter Apathy | 11.2 | Salient for Types 1 and 4. |
| 12. *Playboy* Interview Hypocrisy of Public and Ford Campaign. | 10.0 | Salient for Type 2 Carter Partisans, positive. |
| 13. Carter and LBJ Error | 9.6 | Salient for Type 1. |
| 14. Butz Resignation | 9.3 | Salient for Type 2 Carter Partisans Positive, Ford Partisans negative. |
| 15. Carter Losing Nice Guy Image Really Tough Politican | 9.3 | |
| 16. Carter Slipping in Polls | 9.3 | Salient for Type Ford Partisans, positive. |

[1]Raw score was computed by adding z-scores across all types for all three cartoons relating to each fantasy theme. Negative z-scores were made positive.

In terms of the dramas we anticipated to be of low potency, the Carter statements in regard to Lyndon Johnson did rank low on the list, in the thirteenth position; the fantasy which portrayed the voters and Ford campaigners as hypocrites on the *Playboy* interview was twelfth; but the Mayaguez fantasy, ranked sixth, was more salient than we anticipated.

Examining the sharing and salience of group fantasies in terms of their general distribution throughout our sample of 29 subjects, however, is somewhat misleading since we discovered that the rhetorical landscape of the 1976 campaign was much more complicated than such a simple analysis would indicate. We discovered that fantasies were shared and salient for some of our communities and not for others. Sometimes a comparison of important shared fantasies of rhetorical groups provided insight into the rhetorical vision of a community. For example, the major *Playboy* interview fantasy was one which stimulated strong acceptance or rejection from members in all four of the rhetorical groups. In contrast, the drama of Ford's gaffe on the Butz resignation was not salient for the people in Types 1,3, and 4, but was salient for the bipolar Type 2. Likewise the Mayaguez fantasy was not important for members of Types 1 and 3 or for the Ford Partisans of Type 2, but the Carter Partisans of Type 2 and Type 4 members found it important.

One interpretation of sorting patterns in regard to the Mayaguez drama is that the participants in the traditional Democratic Party rhetorical vision (Type 2) were particularly rankled by the favorable fantasies associated with Ford's handling of the Mayaguez affair. That drama still had saliency for them, and, thus, they happily accepted a cartoon which alluded to a fantasy portraying the Mayaguez incident as a bungled affair cleverly turned into a public relations ploy to hoodwink the American people. The members of Type 4, on the other hand, may have participated in the fantasies at the time of the incident which put a favorable interpretation on America's strength and dramatized Ford's action as an American President finally doing something to reassert the power of the United States. They, thus, did not accept cartoons which debunked the president's handling of the Mayaguez incident.

Among the more interesting of our discoveries in terms of the saliency of fantasies was that the drama of Carter on taxation was one of the most salient across all four types.

## Conclusions

This study, along with those of Cragan and Shields and Rarick et al. is part of a coordinated research program which is beginning to provide evidence of the relationship between the fantasies dramatized by various groups during the course of a political campaign and the rhetorical visions which voters come to share and which serve to form their political social reality. All three studies began with rhetorical criticism from which the investigators developed a Q-sort. Cragan and Shields studied foreign policy persuasion in the campaign of 1976 and concluded that the theory of shared fantasies "goes beyond its use as a descriptive schemata for critiquing rhetorical communication. It may provide us with a *why explanation* of communication phenomena that is predictive."[21] Rarick et al. studied the persona of Jimmy Carter and reported that their study provided "some evidence in support of a link between rhetorical critical analyses of political campaign persuasion and audience responses."[22]

One of our major findings was that our respondents shared fantasies in much more complex patterns than we had anticipated. In setting up our expectations of their most salient fantasies we made a tacit assumption whose importance was not clear to us until we began interpreting our data. We had assumed a strong audience response, whether positive or negative, to those fantasies which appeared repeatedly in the media. Perhaps we made the tacit assumption because of the recent research on the agenda-setting function of the media which argues that although the media do not tell the American voter *what to think* they do tell the public *what to think about*. Our sample did respond to two cartoons as we tacitly assumed they would to all. All four types of respondents either strongly accepted or rejected the Carter on taxation and the Carter making a major error in the *Playboy* interview fantasies. But the respondents accepted, were neutral towards, or rejected the other cartoons in complex patterns which varied from type to type.

Our theoretical rationale includes a composite panoramic view (rhetorical vision) of the campaign featuring some central fantasy types and other fantasy themes in a more peripheral postion. Our rhetorical criticism of the media messages failed to provide us with the nuances relating to the comparative strength of acceptance or rejection that Q-methodology provided. Our findings furnish an empirical clarification of the nature of our audience's rhetorical vision which went beyond that discovered by rhetorical criticism.

The purpose of this study was to investigate the possible link between shared fantasies in small groups and the sharing of media fantasies in political campaigns. To achieve this purpose we discovered what seemed to us to be representative cartoons which alluded to the major dramatic fantasies presented to the public during the 1976 presidential campaign. Our major findings were (1) that the cartoon did function as the mass media equivalent of the inside joke for our sample of respondents, (2) that the people in our sample divided into three major types according to patterns of shared fantasies which formed coherent visions of the campaign, and

[21]John F. Cragan and Donald C. Shields, "Foreign Policy Communication Drama: How Mediated Rhetoric Played in Peoria in Campaign '76," *Quarterly Journal of Speech,* 63 (1977), 289.

[22]David L. Rarick, Mary B. Duncan, David G. Lee, and Laurinda W. Porter, "The Carter Persona: An Empirical Analysis of the Rhetorical Visions of Campaign '76," *Quarterly Journal of Speech*, 63 (1977), 272.

(3) that the members of the three major rhetorical groups, with few exceptions voted as a rhetorical critical analysis of the vision anticipated they would. Our study thus provides evidence in support of the argument that fantasy theme analysis of rhetorical visions forms a potential basis for communication theory which will combine the "humanistic concerns of the dramatists and symbolic interactionists with the rigor of behavioral models."[23]

[23]This recommendation is from James E. Combs and Michael W. Mansfield, eds., *Drama in Life: The Uses of Communication in Society* (New York: Hastings, 1976), p. xxix.

# 11

# A Communication Based Political Campaign:
## A Theoretical and Methodological Perspective

DONALD C. SHIELDS and JOHN F. CRAGAN

This essay begins from the assumption that there is utility in making the crucial decisions of a political campaign from a communications, as opposed to a psychological, sociological, or political science, perspective. Such utility exists whether one is a practitioner, researcher, or critic of political campaigns. Consequently, this essay explores a design and research perspective for conducting a communication theory based political campaign.

Ernest Bormann's dramatistic rhetorical theory is the communication theory we recommend for forming the basis of a communication based political campaign. In this theory, Bormann argues that meaning, emotion, and motive are as much in the rhetoric as they are in people. His dramatistic theory makes the rhetorical message the object of study as the theory explains human behavior by examining the dramatistic form that is present in discourse. Bormann argues that such an explanation will indicate that large groups of people share symbolic dramas that are filled with characters, scenarios, and scenes. The dramas are made credible by their linkage to compelling here-and-now events.[1]

The methods used to draw the implications flow from our applied communication research with government agencies and private

---

[1]A description and evolution of the theory may be found in the following articles by Ernest G. Bormann: "Fantasy and Rhetorical Vision: The Rhetorical Criticism of Social Reality," *Quarterly Journal of Speech,* 58 (1972), 396-407; "The Eagleton Affair: A Fantasy Theme Analysis," *Quarterly Journal of Speech,* 59 (1973), 143-59; and "Fetching Good Out of Evil: A Rhetorical Use of Calamity," *Quarterly Journal of Speech,* 63 (1977), 130-39. Also see, John F. Cragan, "Rhetorical Strategy: A Dramatistic Interpretation and Application," *Central States Speech Journal,* 26 (1975), 4-11.

corporations.[2] Together, the theory and methods detailed in this essay provide insights at the macro and micro levels of campaign management. They enable control of the campaign as a total communication event and provide for the structuring of necessary communications for the day-to-day campaign.

The ability to conduct a communication based campaign has been precluded in the past by both methodological and theoretical barriers. Barrier 1 was the absence of a message-centered communication theory that focused on the symbolic reality of rhetoric that catches up large collectivities of people. Barrier 2 was the reliance on research techniques and concepts that were rooted in other disciplines. Barrier 3 was the dichotomizing of research as either large sample or small sample, quantitative or qualitative, with the resultant inability to bridge the gap between nomothetic and ideographic research.[3] Barrier 4 was the inability to quantify people's participation in competing rhetorical visions. Barrier 5 was the inability to determine and quantify the demographic, psychographic, sociographic, and politicographic characteristics of people participating in a given rhetorical vision. What follows is a design for overcoming these barriers as techniques are described for applying Bormann's theory to the totality of a political campaign.

## Viewing Communication as Primary

The main requisite for conducting a communication theory based political campaign is sufficient dramatistic data from the candidate's potential constituency. Thus, the first place to start a campaign is with the

---

[2]See Donald C. Shields, "The Fire Fighters' Dramatis Personae: A Study of Private, Projected, and Public Character from the Perspective of Rhetorical Vision," Diss. University of Minnesota 1974; and his "The Self-Image, Projected-Image, and Public-Image of the Fire Fighters," *Fire Command,* 41 (1974), 26-7; and see John F. Cragan and Donald C. Shields, "Foreign Policy Communication Dramas: How Mediated Rhetoric Played in Peoria in Campaign '76." *Quarterly Journal of Speech,* 63 (1977), 274-89; and their "The Identifying Characteristics of the Public Fire Educator," The National Fire Protection and Control Administration, Department of Commerce, U.S. Government, 1977 (mimeo); also see, Shields, "Hog Producer Focus Group Interviews on Shell's XLP-30, a Gestation Litter Conditioner," Animal Health Division, Shell Chemical Company, Houston, Texas, 1978 (mimeo); and Shields and Cragan, "Marketing Farm Management Services," Doane Agricultural Service, St. Louis, Missouri, 1978 (mimeo); and their "Market Segmentation Study of Cattle Producers," Market Research Division, Upjohn Corporation, Kalamazoo, Michigan, 1978 (mimeo).
[3]For a discussion of the problem brought about by such dichotomizing, see Gerald Miller's, "Humanistic and Scientific Approaches to Speech Communication Inquiry: Rivalry, Redundancy, or Rapproachement," *Western Speech Communication,* 39 (1975), 230-39; and Shields and Cragan, "Miller's Humanistic/Scientific Dichotomy of Speech Communication Inquiry: A Help of Hindrance?" *Western Speech Communication,* 40 (1976), 278-281. Also see, Robert L. Scott, "Evidence in Communication: We are Such Stuff," *Western Speech Communication,* 42 (1978), 29-36.

candidate's audience. The goal is to research and retrieve the rhetorical dramas about issues and candidates in which voters participate. Data retrieval necessitates the choice of appropriate instruments. Typically, instruments for gathering voters' ideas are not communication derived. As a result, they tend to operationalize psychological, sociological, or political science concepts like "attitude," "status," or "liberal." Data retrieved through such instruments becomes a benchmark, not the necessary communication within a campaign, but for pre-existing characteristics and attributes of voters. The assumption in utilizing such instruments is that communication is never primary in the campaign. What is primary are such things as situation, attitudinal state, and past voting behaviors. These instruments, and the research approaches they represent, assume that meaning, emotion and motive are in people and not in the rhetoric. As a result, the function of the campaign communication specialist is to create rhetorical messages to fit the particular demo/psycho/socio/politico graphic variables. Here the non-communication variables are primary and the duty of the communication specialist is to translate such variables into rhetorical postures. The only time that communication even appears to be primary is when emphasis is placed on selection of communication channels, or efforts at enhancing a candidate's rhetorical style, or efforts at promoting a candidate's image. Yet, the initial research approach to the campaign, and its concommitant data base, forces the rhetorical assessments to stem from non-communication orientations and instruments. Again, the communication specialist is diminished to the role of campaign traffic manager regarding the desired channels of communication, or cosmotologist for the candidate's image, or ghost writer for the candidate's speeches.

As history points out, the 18th Century "rhetorics" were properly called "managerial," in as much as the canon of invention had been usurped from the rhetorician by logicians, theologians, and philosophers. The result was that the rhetorician was stripped of the right to create and invent argument and was left only to "manage" arrangement, style, and delivery.[4] The 20th Century saw invention once again leave the province of rhetoric. This time psychology, sociology, and political science controlled this crucial activity because it was audience analysis:

Using Bormann's theoretical perspective for describing a campaign, one necessarily starts with the assumption that meaning, emotion, and motive for action are in the dramatic structure of the rhetoric. Thus, people's rhetorical dramas and not their attitudes, or past voting record, or socio-economic status, are the phenomena that need to be studied, researched, and analyzed. Here, communication is primary in the campaign. The goal is to piece together a campaign based on the symbolic realities in which the

[4]For a discussion of 18th Century rhetoric as managerial see, Douglas Ehninger, "Campbell, Blair, and Whately Revisited," *Southern Speech Journal,* 28 (1963), 169-182; and Vincent M. Bevilacqua, "Philosophical Origins of George Campbell's *Philosophy of Rhetoric,*" *Speech Monographs,* 32 (1965), 1-13.

constituents participate. All that is needed are procedures to capture these rhetorical realities. Just as Likert scales and semantic differential scales lend themselves to operationalizing concepts like attitude, and belief, and public opinion, so too, there are instruments and procedures that lend themselves to operationalizing and quantitatively capturing and measuring the symbolic reality manifested through rhetorical dramas.

## Determining Symbolic Reality

The pivotal methodological activity in the gathering of dramatistic data for a political campaign is the building of three dimensional matrices that depict the competing rhetorical visions of important macro issues in the campaign. In single variable research we are used to plotting the relationship of one variable to another by means of two coordinates ($X$ and $Y$). Here we are talking about adding a third coordinate ($Z$) and conceptualizing the axes as occurring perpendicular to each other within a cube. One axis will represent vision, one axis will represent the dramatic structure, salient themes and issues, and the third axis will represent demo/psycho/socio/politico graphic variable. (See Figure I.)

The three procedures necessary to build the matrices are thematic analyses of any previously captured rhetorical statements, thematic analysis of personal interview data, and thematic analysis of dramatistic focus group interviews. The two instruments necessary to actuate the three dimensional matrix are structured Q-sorts that include the salient visions and themes, and a questionnaire that collects the relevant demo/psycho/socio/politico graphics. The latter can later be attached to the specific visions thus indicating the kind of person who participates in a given rhetorical drama.

The richness and accuracy of the dramatizations contained in the three dimensional matrices are crucial to the effectiveness of this approach to directing political campaigns. Thus, it is necessary to discuss in detail the three procedures for gathering the dramatistic rhetorical phenomena that will comprise the structured matrix for each macro campaign issue.

The first research effort is an indepth rhetorical criticism using fantasy theme analysis of existing printed, video, and audio material. In doing these rhetorical criticisms, we have found that a thematic analysis which groups like themes and organizes them in some scematic display by content area proved most useful. In our research on how foreign policy dramas played in Peoria, we analyzed the dramatistic content of 150 articles on foreign policy cited in the *Reader's Guide* for the period January to July, 1976. Through this analysis, we found thirteen here-and-now situations and issues (e.g., grain, terrorists, lesson of Vietnam, Panama Canal), that combined with seven dramatic structure themes present in three overall foreign policy visions (Cold War, Neo-Isolationism, Power Politics) to produce a 3 × 20 fantasy theme by vision matrix. To clarify how a specific issue is viewed within the competing visions, we present the foreign policy rhetorical

# Figure I
## Foreign Policy Macro Issue
## Three Dimensional Matrix

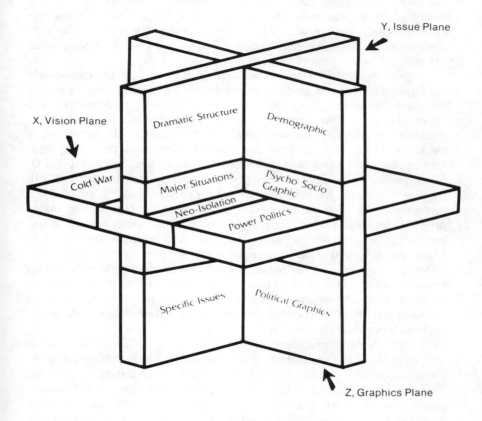

statements on the issue of the Panama: (Cold War) *The Panama Canal Zone is not a Colonial possession. It is sovereign U.S. territory, every bit the same as Alaska and all the States that were carved from the Louisiana Purchase. The U.S. has no obligation to relinquish the Canal Zone to Panama;* (Neo-Isolationism) *A new treaty would remove the only major problem between the U.S. and Panama. Panamanians should control the Canal Zone and America should return its troops home and stay out of the internal affairs of Panama. The U. S. must avoid "Big Stick" tactics;* (Power Politics) *The U. S. neither owns nor has sovereignty over the Canal Zone. Panama granted us rights by a 1903 treaty. We should re-negotiate a new treaty that protects America's vital interests in the Canal Zone.* The ability of these statements to reflect unique visions stems from the discreetness of the visions, the artistry with which vision adherents represented the fantasy theme, and the intuitive and artistic strategies used to build structured Q-decks.[5]

The second research effort is personal interviews with the candidate's constituents. These can be done on the phone, but face-to-face interviews are better. The objective in conducting these interviews is to determine what "here-and-now" phenomena about the particular macro issue being discussed, trigger fantasies and scenarios important to the interviewee's rhetorical vision. For example, in doing market research for an agri-business company using Bormann's theory and Stephenson's structured Q-technique, we discovered that interviewees ventilated their frustrations with the time consuming problem of observing for estrus in order to use artificial insemination in their cattle operations, by saying: "One of the major problems in the use of artificial insemination is heat detection. Heat just can't be detected in my operation and still maintain profitability. Therefore, my hired hands in charge of heat detection are my bulls." In order to determine whether these personal comments were manifestations of an overall drama in the beef cattle industry, its chaining effect needed to be checked via dramatistic focus group interviews and ultimately through the analysis of the Q-sorting behavior of a stratified random sample of 400 beef cattle producers in the U. S.

The third research procedure is the dramatistically structured focus group interview. Here, an examination of the fantasies that have "chained-out" in the media analysis and the fantasies that were depicted during the personal interviews are combined to structure a scenario based outline. This outline which contains both negative and positive fantasy themes, and even multiple ways of describing the same subject issue, is used to stimulate interaction among small groups of constituents discussing the macro issue

---

[5]We used this procedure in developing the matrix for our Peoria study as did Wil Stephenson in his Cuban Missile Study. See, Cragan and Shields, "Foreign Policy Communication Dramas," 276; and William Stephenson, "Application of the Thompson Schemata to the Current Controversy over Cuba," *Psychological Record,* 14 (1964), 275-90.

in face-to-face interaction.[6]

The three dimensional matrix is represented in the form of two instruments: A structured Q-deck (visions by fantasy themes) formed out of the collected rhetorical data, and a questionnaire (demo/psycho/socio/political graphics) that can be used in distinguishing participants in one vision from those in another.[7] William Stephenson popularized the use of Q-sorts in doing communication research.[8] Since his primary objective in using the technique was gathering rich data from individuals by operationalizing their subjectivity, he became an outspoken advocate of small sample research.

We followed his advice in our study of how mediated foreign policy rhetoric played in Peoria in as much as we used only sixty subjects and compared two factor analyses of thirty respondents each to validate the factor structure. However, in attempting to determine the identifying characteristics of public fire educators for the National Fire Protection and Control Administration, we decided to break from Stephenson's tradition and use Q-decks of dramatic subjectivity in a large sample research design;[9] thus, we had a stratified random sample of 400 fire fighters sort a sixty-item Q-deck. This large sample allowed us to accomplish two important objectives: (1) stabilize the factor structures across a dozen separate factor

[6]The art of conducting these interviews is important. At one level the group moderator needs to lead the group through the issues and elicit their reactions and embellishments of certain scenarios. At another level, the moderator cannot be so intent on leading the participants through the discussion outline that he/she misses important fantasy events or squelches fantasy events prematurely. The moderator is not only responsible for the agenda but participates and indeed gets caught up in the discussions. Consequently, tape recording for subsequent thematic analysis of the group interviews is needed. For a more complete discussion of the use of dramatistic focus group interviews, see Donald C. Shields, "Group Communication and Focus Group Interviews," paper presented to Doane Agricultural Service's Annual Market Research Seminar, St. Louis, Missouri, March, 1974.

[7]The process of building a three dimensional matrix is a laborious and artistic effort. In building three dimensional matrices, the top of the matrix (columns) represents the salient competing rhetorical visions, the left side of the matrix (rows) contains the key competing dramatic elements such as dramatic structure and the "here-and-now" incidents that trigger or call forth the dramas. The back side of the matrix contains the relevant demo/psycho/socio/politico graphic variables. For more specific information on how to build structured Q-decks and administer them to subjects, see our "Foreign Policy Communication Dramas," 275-77; and see, William D. Brooks, "Q-Sort Technique," appearing in Phillip Emmert and William D. Brooks, *Methods of Research in Communication* (Boston: Houghton-Mifflin, 1970, pp. 165-81).

[8]*The Study of Behavior: Q-Technique and Its Methodology* (Chicago: Univ. of Chicago Press, 1953).

[9]In general, we have built sixty-statement, $3 \times 20$ decks for three reasons: (1) sixty statements that project dramatistic action-oriented scenarios of approximately forty words each require about one hour for respondents to sort (which comes close to reaching the maximum number subjects can reach to in one setting); (2) in building five Q-decks on wide ranging subjects, we have found it difficult to discover enough rhetorical material to systematically structure more than three rhetorical visions in competition with each other; and (3) analysis of previous studies revealed that most respondents adhered to one of the three major visions representing a given subject.

analyses, enabling us to place a high degree of confidence in the derived
rhetorical visions; and (2) gather nineteen demo/psycho/socio graphic
variables about each fire fighter sorting the deck, enabling us to do a
discriminant analysis to determine the characteristics of the fire fighters
who were participating in each of the different competing rhetorical visions
about fire public safety education.[10]

A rhetorical analysis of published fire fighter literature, selected
interviews with fire fighters, and several focus group interviews with fire
fighters in midwestern cities, generated sufficient dramatistic rhetorical
statements to allow us to determine the three major rhetorical visions in
which fire fighters participate regarding their view of how we might best
reduce property and life loss due to fire. The *Suppression* vision projected
the well-trained suppression fire fighter as the best means to control fire and
thus reduce the loss from its occurrence. The *Inspection* vision
characterized the stringent enforcement of fire codes as the primary means
of fire loss reduction. Finally, the *Fired Education* vision dramatizes the use
of fire education in the schools, community, and the media as the best
means of reducing fire loss. An example of a rhetorical statement from a
suppressionist viewpoint that was rejected by public fire educators read:
*Fire Education helps public relations for the fire service, but I have
my doubts if fire education can really reduce fire loss. People are just
careless no matter what you tell them.*

The factor analysis of the sorting behavior of 400 fire fighters allowed us
to capture empirically the fire fighters' rhetorical visions and enabled us to
successfully discover the variables (demo/psycho/socio graphics) that were
predictors of a given fire fighter's participation in a given rhetorical vision.
Specifically, college education, photography or art as a hobby, and high
scores on two standardized tests of creativity predicted a fire fighter's
participation in the rhetorical vision most acceptable to the National Fire
Protection and Control Administration.[11] In this way, we had joined
together a detailed description of the rhetoric that a given collection of fire
fighers shared with easily recognizable attributes and characteristics which
could be used to identify a fire fighter as a participator in a given drama.

What this means in terms of political rhetoric is that it is now possible to
quantitatively capture rhetorical visions of large collectivities of people,and
simultaneously determine the identifying characteristics of age, sex,
economic level, education, etc., that will signpost a person who is
participating in a given drama. Knowing such signposts, constituents may
be located and messages may be targeted directly to them. Our subsequent
replication of the above procedure in two market research studies for

[10]The Q-factor analysis program we used was Norman Van Tubergen's "Q-Analysis
(QUANAL)" University of Iowa, undated manuscript (mimeo). The regression programs
were current SPSS programs for both direct and step-wise discriminant analysis using
options 1, 5, 6  7 and 8 coupled with statistics 1, 2, 4 and 5.
[11]Cragan and Shields, "Fire Educator," 10-18.

private corporations has convinced us that the utilization of dramatistic structured Q-sorts and graphics questionnaires in political surveying is both feasible and necessary in creating a communication based political campaign.

What this procedure does is make rhetorical visions the controlling variable in a political campaign. One can discover the rhetorical reality in which people participate and then find out if the people in a given vision tend to be mostly liberal, or democrat, or poor, or rural or whatever other descriptors might help in identifying them so that a campaign's messages may be targeted. Furthermore, the Q-cards that are used to represent two of the dimensions of the matrix are dramatistic rhetorical statements concerning the salient issues within the relevant dramas. Once respondents' reactions to those statements are retrieved and empirically analyzed, the political campaign practitioner is armed with collections of rhetorical material, i.e., "dramatic topoi," that should be predictable favorable to a targeted audience. This is particularly so since the audience, through their previous reaction to the items on the Q-sort, has in essence pre-tested them. For example, in our Peoria study we discovered that even though the majority of Peorians accepted a Power Politics vision of foreign policy with some Cold War overtones, nearly everyone, regardless of their political party, age, or educational background, accepted the Neo-Isolationist position of grain sale exports. The Neo-Isolationism grain card read: *The Russian government has survived for sixty years without U. S. grain. Whether we sell or do not sell grain to them will not alter their behavior in international affairs. However, the Russians should pay the market price for grain.* Clearly, this degree of specificity in terms of audience acceptance of a rhetorical message makes a communication based approach to political campaigns superior to previous approaches.

To direct the political campaign from a communication perspective, it is necessary to build a number of three-dimensional matrices representing the macro issues of the campaign. The substance of these matrices are unique and the required number will vary from campaign to campaign. In a national political campaign for the presidency, some five or six macro issues will be present and thus five or six matrices will need to be constructed. Construction and analysis of each matrix will follow the above procedures. Once the output for each of these macro issues is available, a *composite* matrix must be developed. For purposes of illustration, assume that there are four macro issues in the campaign: foreign policy; domestic policy; social lifestyle; and candidates' personae. After building the four macro issue matrices, administering the energizing instruments (Q-sorts and graphics questionnaire) to a stratified national sample, factor analyzing the data, defining the breaker vision for each macro issue, and conducting a discriminant analysis to pinpoint predictive variable that indicate vision participation, the campaign practitioner could then construct the composite matrix, the composite Q-deck, and the composite graphics questionnaire. Upon completing administration and analysis of the macro issue matrix, the practitioner would have available a quantitative version of the major parts of the rhetorical vision that would be used for the campaign. These could be put together to form a composite vision. The composite vision might only last the length of the campaign, but in so doing, it would serve to rally both campaign workers and voters as it provided a coherent perspective through the election.

This composite matrix would contain on the left side the winning dramatizations of each of the initial macro issue matrices, e.g., foreign policy, domestic policy, social lifestyle, and personae fantasy themes. The backside of the composite matrix would contain all of the graphic variable that had proven predictive in any of the other macro issue matrices. The top of the composite matrix would then be "discovered" through factor analysis. The major factor coming out of the factor analysis of people's sorting behavior over the sixty to eighty composite matrix issues represents a prioritizing of the separate micro issues that had been called forth from people's sorting of each macro issue matrix. In other words, the sorting of the composite Q-deck would suggest a structure for knitting together the dispersed dramatizations of the various macro issues into one large rhetorical vision.

The analysis of the respondents' reaction to the composite matrix Q-deck would help to determine which collection of fantasy themes should predominate in the campaign. For example, such data would determine whether Middle East fantasy themes should take precedence over domestic taxation themes, or whether the candidate's persona as a humanist should predominate. Furthermore, the computer analysis of the Q-sorting behavior of the voter sample would help point to a coherent linkage of the winning foreign, domestic, social, and persona issues.

In summary, five procedures and instruments must be developed and administered to a stratified random sample of constituents in order for the audience to be analyzed in a fashion that will allow the key messages in the campaign to be successfully designed from one coherent communication theory. The initial instrument is thematic analysis of relevant print, audio, and video material which forms the basis of a rhetorical criticism. The data from the rhetorical criticism is used to produce a personal interview outline. In turn, the data from these two sources is used to develop a scenario based outline for collecting the universe of rhetorical phenomena from people through dramatistic focus group interviews. Essentially, the focus group interviews determine what mediated fantasies and personal fantasies related to each of the macro issues "chain-out" in live groups. All of the rhetorical phenomena captured by the above three procedures are then used to build a three-dimensional matrix for each of the relevant macro issues. When this macro issue deck is administered to constituents it will capture similarities in rhetorical space over large groups of people with respect to both the macro issues of vision participation and the micro issue of reaction the "here-and-now" rhetorical phenomena. The final procedure is to sort people out based upon their participation in a given rhetorical vision concerning a macro issue. This is done by determining what graphics (retrieved for each respondent via a questionnaire) adhere to respective rhetorical visions that discriminate the people participating in one vision from those in others. When these procedures are followed in the building of each needed macro issue matrix, plus the composite matrix, the resultant data should be sufficient to generate a communication based political campaign.

## Creative Dramatistic Campaign Rhetoric

There are five major groups of communication activity that should be structured and organized from the "facts" that have been gathered by the above procedures for collecting and analyzing political rhetorical visions.[12] These activities are: (1) the building of the campaign "Bible"; (2) the writing of major position papers; (3) the structuring of campaign rallies; (4) the production of mass media releases and commericals; and (5) the creation of major public addresses.

### The Campaign "Bible"

Scholars of political campaigns have recognized the importance of an "insider's" document that details the candidate's position on major and minor issues.[13] The developed macro issue matrices and the composite matrix will form the data base for building a vision centered campaign "Bible." Not only will the blocked-out positions be in dramatistic form, but the empirical analysis of the constituents' sorting behavior for the composite matrix will indicate the form and content of the campaign rhetorical vision. In keeping with Nimmo's suggestion that the campaign should have a central theme, the dramatizations from the composite matrix will provide insight into the central thrust of the campaign rhetorical vision.[14] Not only is the vision centered campaign Bible essential for indicating the central campaign rhetoric that will catch up large groups of people, it is equally important in the consciousness-raising of the

---

[12]Most handbooks on managing political campaigns describe the interpersonal and mass media channels but do not discuss the design of messages for the campaign. See for example, Arnold Steinberg's two recent books, *The Political Campaign Handbook: Media, Scheduling, and Advance* (Lexington, Massachusetts, 1976); and *Political Campaign Management: A Systems Approach* (Lexington, Massachusetts, 1976). Even political scientists who focus on persuasive communication as central to political campaigns treat the speechmaking activity as matters of style and image and discuss mass communication primarily in terms of media channels. See for example, Dan Nimmo, *The Political Persuaders: The Techniques of Modern Election Campaigns* (Englewood Cliffs, New Jersey: Prentice-Hall, 1970), especially 118-22; and his *Popular Images of Politics* (Englewood Cliffs, New Jersey: Prentice Hall, 1974); and Nimmo and Robert L. Savage's, *Candidates and their Images: Concepts, Methods, and Findings* (Santa Monica, California: Goodyear Publishing, 1976).

[13]Mirroring the position of Theodore White, Dan Nimmo in his *The Political Persuaders* discusses the importance of the campaign document.

[14]Nimmo, *The Political Persuaders*.

candidate's workers.[15]

Consciousness-raising sessions serve to heighten the worker's socio-political identity with the candidate. Similarly, CR sessions aid in the refinement and attractiveness of the campaign rhetorical vision. Indeed, it is during these sessions that key dramatic one-liners tend to chain-out and serve as major slogans and signposts for the campaign drama. Examples of the chaining-out of such slogans from recent political campaigns include John Kennedy's "Ask not what the country can do for you...," George McGovern's "Come home American," and Richard Nixon's "The silent majority." In addition, these sessions often produce the tabular phrase for the entire campaign rhetorical vision, such as "New Deal," "Square Deal," "New Frontier," and "Great Society."

**Position Papers**

An expected and necessary part of any political campaign is the building of detailed position papers on the major issues in the campaign. In a communication based political campaign, the position papers are built from the respondents' reactions to the themes comprising the macro issue matrices on foreign policy, domestic policy, social lifestyle, and candidate's persona. The item displays from the quantitative analysis will allow vivid in-depth portrayals of the candidate's position on the big issues. The campaign manager will know what here-and-now events are most salient for energizing people's emotions, meanings, and motives, and can target specific messages that reflect these issues at the voting constituency. For example, in our research on how foreign policy dramas played in Peoria we found that people participating in the Cold War drama were more likely to intensify their participation in that drama if the here-and now event of "tough response to terrorist action" were used, as opposed to using the theme of "the horrors of communist participation in NATO through successful elections in Italy."[16]

By knowing the demo/psycho/socio/politico graphics of participants in the various visions, the campaign manager can vary the here-and-now events that chain out essentially the same rhetorical vision and target these events to different clusters of voters. For example, in our Peoria research, the Neo-Isolationist foreign policy vision was called forth with equal saliency by the here-and-now event of "grain sales to Russia" and by the dramatization of "America as a heroic example of democracy who does not intervene in the internal affairs of other nation states."[17] Furthermore, a segmentation of Neo-Isolationist voters by demographic and sociographic

[15]James Chesebro, John F. Cragan, and Patricia McCullough, "The Small Group Technique of the Radical Revolutionary: A Synthetic Study of Consciousness-Raising," *Speech Monographs* (1973), 136-46, outline the four steps necessary for consciousness-raising. Use of this process heightens the workers' social-political identity with the candidate inasmuch as the candidate is the heroic persona of the campaign rhetorical vision.
[16]See the complete discussion of this in Cragan and Shields, "Foreign Policy Dramas," 280.
[17]See Cragan and Shields, "Foreign Policy Dramas."

characteristics may have indicated that the Neo-Isolationist view of grain sales to Russia triggered participation by agrarian midwestern voters, while the dramatization of America as isolationist hero ignited participation on the part of college educated, eastern urbanites. The ability to make such segmentation of the basis of specific issues, allows the campaign manager to build targeted position papers which emphasize the same vision but use different here-and-now phenomena to trigger the emotions, motives, and behavior of demographically diverse constituencies.[18]

## Political Rallies

In a political campaign the essential scene is the rally. When viewing this event through Bormann's lens, message and situation intertwine to form a critical aspect of the symbolic reality of the political campaign. The rally is the event that the media will turn to as its source for personifying the candidate as hero or villain, impending victor or vanquished challenger. The following prescriptions serve as a guideline for producing a communication based political rally, and illustrate the characteristics of a dramatistically controlled speaking event. In order to make the rally authentic for the mass media and the audience. the manager must first set a scene that is consistent with the campaign's rhetorical vision. This requires three steps. First, the building must be small, but not too small. If 10,000 people gather in a stadium that holds 60,000 even the best drama will not play well, nor will it be interpreted as playing well. Whereas, if the auditorium holds 8,000, overcrowding will charge the air with anticipation. Second, the placards and music must be compatible with the vision. The rallies for Richard Nixon's 1968 law and order drama would not have been stages well if Joan Baez provided the musical interludes and placards depicted celebrations of Woodstock. On the other hand, one would expect country and western music, uniformed Alabama State Troopers, and anti-Washington placards to set the scene for George Wallace's "Send a Message to Wahington" populist rhetorical vision in 1968. Third, the audience should contain certain stereotypic participants that ground the drama to the here-and-now realities of the electorate. Narrowly focused political campaign dramas produced an easily identified stereotypic participant in recent national campaigns. Thus, the 6 o'clock news portrayed the straw-hatted, affluent, suburban woman of the Goldwater campaign, the country red-neck and

---

[18]Preparing position papers via fantasy theme analysis also helps the campaign manager in planning the overall strategy for the campaign. If the candidate has a safe, comfortable lead (due perhaps to his/her incumbent status) and the objective is to avoid the "big mistake," the arrays of data from the quantitative analysis that bring the rhetorical visions into sharp focus will indicate the safe, yet interesting examples to utilize in writing prepared position statements. On the other hand, if the candidate is behind in the election, the fantasy data will indicate in quantitative rhetorical form the here-and-now events that will most likely point up the tensions and polarizations among competing rhetorical visions. It is these dramatizations that are most likely to be picked up and played out in the mass media since media people prefer to force candidates toward rhetorical stasis.

down-home populist of the Wallace and Carter campaigns, and the come-clean-with-Gene youth of Eugene McCarthy's campaign. Conversely, Lyndon Johnson's 1964 campaign rhetorical vision required the rally to be filled with such diversity as to defy the label of a narrow constituency. Thus, his rally audiences stereotyped the conception of a pluralistic electorate forming together in a great society.

Once the set is designed and built and the audience is placed and poised, the curtain opens on Scene 1 of a One Act Rally.[19] Scene 1 is the "John the Baptist" scene. John the Baptist comes before and is loved, but he is not the beloved. The "baptizers" at political rallies tend to be lesser politicians, movie stars, or sports heroes. For example, Paul Newman and Warren Beatty warmed audiences for McGovern in 1972, while Bob Hope and Frank Sinatra warmed audiences for Richard Nixon. Again, just as music and slogans must be consistent with the campaign's vision, so too must the John the Baptist, Thus, John Wayne and not Woody Allen could baptize for Ronald Reagan.[20]

Scene 2 spotlights the superstar. The candidate is usually late but not too late. The drama is heightened when the candidate is just late enough to bring the crowd to a sense of ecstasy that their awaited superstar has arrived. This ecstasy is promoted by the placards and music and the overflow standing-room-only crowd. Thus, the scene is set for the candidate to demonstrate superstar qualities as the heroic persona of the campaign's rhetorical vision.

Two dramatic plotlines assist the candidate in demonstrating superstar qualities. The candidate can portray an heroic persona of either devil-slayer or miracle-worker. If a devil-slayer, the candidate's dramatistic objective is to cast out the demons, slay the opposition, or exorcise and purge the forces and ideas which appear to work against the campaign's rhetorical vision. Thus, Richard Nixon's law and order vision of 1968 often found him opening his rally address by shouting down the hecklers or protesters and having his ushers escort them from the hall. Such symbolic action was crescendoed by the dramatic one-liner of, "Are we the silent majority going to let the vocal minority run this country?"

If the approach is that of miracle-worker, the scenario is for the crippled to be healed and the blind to see. In political rallies the future economic or social or foreign policy heavens are dramatized so vividly that the assembled people feel transported into the vision's joyous fulfillment. John F. Kennedy's "new frontier" rallies and Martin Luther King's "I Had a

---

[19]The reason we describe the rally as being One Act, Three Scenes is that rallies sometimes fail because more than one act is staged with more than one superstar. Such failures occurred frequently during the movement rhetoric of the late 1960's when a number of diverse causes of various oppressed peoples were allowed a place on the stage at the same time. This tactical error regularly occurs in local political rallies when a number of candidates for various offices seek a place in the same limelight.

[20]For a thorough discussion of the scenic contribution of the warmup artist, see Art James, "Warming Up Game-Show Audiences," *TV Guide*, 26, 17 (1978), 28-30.

Dream'' Washington rally are examples of miracle-working.

Whether devil-slayer or miracle-worker, the effect is achieved through the candidate's prepared speech. The organization of speech is in essence a stringing together of the dramatic topoi that have emerged from the composite matrix factor analysis, having been refined through CR sessions with campaign workers, and having been audience tested and further refined with each succeeding rally. This string of dramatizations is generally arranged to produce crescendo. Once the speech is completed, the devil slayed or miracle occurred, the audience awaits the final scene.

Scene 3 is the chorus. In Christian religious rallies the call goes forth for the audience to physically move down to center state and accept the miracle or participate in the exorcism. In rock rallies, the chorus scene is the final audience participation song that allows the audience to act out the central mood of the rally's vision. In political rallies both procedures are accomplished usually with the assistance of music, the changing and vocalization of campaign slogans, and the customary pressing of flesh and kissing of babies.

Obviously, each rhetorical vision based political campaign will do variations on the above prescriptions for a political rally. Nevertheless, all dramatistic communication based campaigns should be conceived from the basic assumption that rallies are important dramatic situations. Their goal is to highlight the heroic persona of the candidate and pinpoint the important fantasy themes of the candidate's rhetoric.

**Media Releases**

The collection of messages that the campaign communication team prepared for direct release to the mass media serves to emphasize several aspects of the campaign rhetorical vision. Perhaps the most widely discussed and documented function of TV-radio commercials and print ads is the building of the candidate's persona.[21] Although the impact of such persona building commercials is a matter of considerable disagreement, it is difficult to conceive of a modern political campaign that could risk ignoring their use. These persona commercials could achieve a higher degree of consistency if they were based upon the systematic quantification of dramatic themes of one campaign vision. Other scholars appear to support this notion. For example, beneath the label of candidate's image, Nimmo and Savage have experimented with techniques similar to ours to specify the specific composition of storyboards and ad layouts.[22] Rarick, et al., using

---

[21]The general importance of persona building commercials for a successful campaign has been discussed widely over the past two decades. Some of the more memorable discussions are contained in Joe McGinnis, *The Selling of the President 1968* (New York: Trident Press, 1968); Robert MacNeil, *The People Machine* (New York: Harper and Row, 1968); Joseph Napolitan, *The Election Game and How to Win It* (Garden City, N.Y.: Doubleday and Co., 1972); and Gene Wyckoff, *The Image Candidates* (New York: Macmillan Company, 1968).

[22]See Nimmo and Savage, *Candidates and Their Images*.

Bormann's theory and our design for structuring competing dramatistic material into Q-decks, demonstrated the viability of designing messages based upon constituents' sorting behavior of attributes of the 1976 presidential candidates' heroic persona.[23]

Although persona building is one important function of media releases, past political campaigns lead us to conclude that probably the most effective kind of spot commercials are the ones that attempt to chain-out negative fantasy themes of the opponent's campaign rhetoric and heroic persona. One is hard-pressed to recall memorable TV spots that attempt to build a candidate's image. However, we all have our collection of favorite commercials that appear to devastate the heroic persona of some candidate. While we don't know of any commercials that build positive images of candidates that were requested to be removed from the airways, there are a number of commericals that chained-out negative fantasies of candidates with such impact that cries went up for their removal from the air. Prominent examples are a 1952 Republican commercial attacking the persona of the democratic party to the futility of the Korean War, a 1964 democratic commercial discrediting Goldwater's position on testing nuclear weapons using the "Daisey Girl" and the "Ice Cream Girl," and a 1968 Republican commercial attacking Humphrey's persona of the "Happy Warrior" to Vietnam and urban rioting.[24]

The importance of such spots is their ability to become more than a TV commercial. Their impact stems from their becoming a here-and-now "news" event that produces discussion in the mass media, thus enhancing the impact of the negative fantasy theme.[25] While paid political spots and print ads are necessary communication events in a political campaign, the building of the heroic persona of the candidate in "hard news" stories is really the more important objective.

**Speeches**

Of all the campaign events, the one most familiar to the rhetorician is the political speech. Armed with the dramatistic proofs from both qualitative and quantitative fantasy theme analysis, the rhetorician is in a unique position to create a truly artistic speech for the campaign. Essentially there are four categories of campaign speeches. The first type is the *airport* speech. In the day of the train, this was the "whistle stop" speech, and before that it was the "stump" speech. Although the speech is created and

---

[23]David H. Rarick, et al., "The Carter Persona: An Empirical Analysis of the Rhetorical Visions of Campaign '76," *Quarterly Journal of Speech*, 63 (1977), 258-73.

[24]For a more thorough discussion of such commercials see Nimmo, *Political Persuaders,* pp. 150-151.

[25]The 1976 presidential election produced a refinement in this tactic. The Democrats produced a political commercial that was nothing but a replaying of President Ford's televised talk on pardoning Richard Nixon. It was difficult to call for the removal of this commercial, when it was Ford who chose to televise and thus dramatize his here-and-now decision to pardon Nixon on the public airways.

presented as a whole, it is intended to be pragmatically capable of dispersion in bits and pieces for diffusion through the print and electronic media. Some versions will be picked up by the local paper, or the local news service. Others will be reported in short thirty-second or one-minute TV news segments. As such, each brief dramatizaiton must be pre-tested to please the most and offend the least number of constituents in the given electorate. The quantitative procedure for pre-testing and generating the speech, as well as an example of a computer derived airport speech, is presented elsewhere.[26] Whether one uses a computer to write the speech or merely clusters the themes from raw data observation, the principle of the airport speech is that it is designed for fragmentation.

The second speech type is the *rally* speech. The rally speech which was described above, works not only on the principle of fragmentation but on the principle of synergy. It swirls dramatic topoi in ever-tightening circles until it pushes out the dramatic persona of the candidate as inescapably the force that will lead the constituents to the nirvana of the campaign rhetorical vision. In long, drawn-out campaigns, the fantasy themes that swirl around the candidate must be made fresh and refashioned with a variety of here-and-now events that will reliably produce the same dramatization. The resource for such refashioning is the carefully gathered dramatic topoi that have been prioritized and assessed for similarity of impact via the quantification of the many three dimensional matrices that were used to analyze the constituency. For example, if one key dramatization of the candidate is the ability to act firmly in foreign affairs, the campaign manager must have several international scenes and a number of scenarios for them that have been pre-tested and demonstrated to be part of the same rhetorical vision. Such variety is necessary because the media people covering the campaign will become cynical toward the same dramatization recurring in rally after rally. As their cynicism sets in they will start to report exceptional or unusual behavior instead of the behavior the candidate wishes to be portrayed to the public. Carter's discussion of

[26]Cragan and Shields, "Foreign Policy Dramas," 288. Although this computer derived airport speech was never delivered in Peoria, its mere creation became a hard news event that "chained-out" in the national and international press. However, the mediated fantasy was essentially negative in impact inasmuch as the media dramatized us and the computer as villains for having created such a speech. This experience leads us to the realization that there is a need for an ethic to guide the dramatistic computer based political campaign. For some of the sources that picked up and chained out fantasies on our computer written airport speech see: Mark Starr, "Politics by Computer," *Chicago Tribune,* April 13, 1977, 1; Bob Greene, "Computer Creates Peoplespeak," *Chicago Sun Times,* January 17, 1977, 6; Harper Barnes, "Political Speech Would Play Well in Peoria," *St. Louis Post-Dispatch,* October 28, 1976 1F; Ann Dooley, "Speech Experts Use DP to Write Rhetoric Echoing Voters' Views," *Computerworld,* March 21, 1977, 18; Reuters News Service, "Computer Can Write a Political Speech," *Christian Science Monitor,* May 11, 1977; Jaan Kangilaski, "Perfect Political Speech," *The Bulletin of the American College of Physicians,* 18, 11 (1977), 13-14; and Diane K. Shah and Richard Manning, "Machine Candidate," *Newsweek,* August 20, 1979, p. 83.

ethnic purity and Ford's reference to a free Poland are examples of this exception principle occurring during the 1976 Presidential campaign.

The third speech type is the *ad personam* speech. Ad personam speeches are unplanned at the inception of the campaign. They become necessary because of an extraordinary event that happens during the campaign that gets dramatized via the media and chains-out as a new fantasy theme. This new theme is one possessing great power which works havoc on the campaign rhetorical vision and clearly villifies the persona of the candidate.[27] When this situation occurs, the speech writer is called upon to generate an ad personam speech. Many times the candidate vocalized responsibility for the fashioning of this speech. Some of the more famous ad personam speeches of contemporary political communication are Richard Nixon's "Checkers," John Kennedy's "Bay of Pigs," Ted Kennedy's "Chappequidic," Lyndon Johnson's "Resignation," Wilbur Mills's "Fanny Foxx," Gerald Ford's "Pardon Nixon," and Jimmy Carter's "Bert Lance Resignation" speech. The commonality of these speeches may not be the apologetic nature of them, or their seeming refutative form, but that they seek to squelch and *neutralize* a chaining fantasy form that cuts to the core of the heroic persona of the candidate.[28]

Although the pre-campaign audience analysis does not prepare the rhetor for the ad personam speech, Bormann's dramatistic theory does provide some basic guidelines for its creation. The most important guideline is that the commonly accepted reality links or here-and-now events of the negative fantasy theme need to be reinterpreted and dramatized in such a way that they highlight a hitherto unknown but laudable dimension of the heroic persona. When one is successful in such reinterpretation, the negative fantasy theme is not only stopped, but the reinterpretation provides fuel for igniting an even larger and more invincible heroic persona.[29]

The final speech form for the political campaign is the *oration*. This speech form is the one we most often anthologize, criticize, and eulogize. It is the culminating campaign communication event. It calls upon all of the

[27]For a case history of the power of such a negative fantasy theme, see Bormann, "The Eagleton Affair."
[28]For an indepth portrayal of these speeches as apology, see B.L. Ware, and W.A. Linkugel, "They Spoke in Defense of Themselves: On the General Criticism of Apologia," *Quarterly Journal of Speech,* 59 (1973), 273-83.
[29]Nixon's "Checkers" speech provides a familiar example of a classic ad personam speech. A negative fantasy of Richard Nixon had been spreading through the media, dramatizing the Vice-Presidential candidate as a person who was stashing campaign monies in his private accounts. To counter this negative fantasy theme, Richard Nixon spoke on national TV on September 23, 1952, in defense of himself. His key rhetorical strategy concerned the dramatization of two here-and-now facts — a dog, Checkers, and Pat's cloth coat. Both here-and-now phenomena dramatized aspects of the Nixon persona that had not been previously disseminated in the public arena. Checkers enabled Nixon to project himself as a man who would give up the Vice-Presidency before he would give up his children's dog (a campaign gift). Pat's now famous "cloth coat" and the symbolic frugality it represented, allowed him to thwart directly the issue of taking campaign funds, and high-lighted his pesona as coming from a humble background and being of modest means.

resources and artistry present in the campaign rhetorical vision. Its objective is to depict clearly and dramatically the scenes and scenarios in which the candidate is personified as the only real choice of the electorate. This speech generally occurs late in the campaign, and is carried by all radio and television networks. It is generally reprinted in newspapers in its entirety, and it is the subject of leading editorials and commentaries.

While the airport speech and the rally speech maintain their freshness through the inclusion of a variety of acceptable dramatic topoi, the oration must focus on the specific choices of dramatic topoi that the candidate will stand by. For the oration, the mere acceptability of the dramatization is no longer the standard. The dramatic topoi included in the oration must be the best and the most salient for catching up large groups of people. Previous monitoring of the various airport speeches and rally speeches, coupled with a thematic analysis of campaign news stories, ought to indicate the dramatic topoi that should comprise the oration. In essence, the previous speechmaking in the campaign has been a pretest of the universe of acceptable dramatic themes for determining the best material from which to build the oration.

The form or dramatic structure behind the inclusion of dramatic topoi is also crucial to the success of the oration. The technical plot used to build the oration ought to include the several thematic elements that depict: (1) the scenic choices of the vision; (2) the overall plotline of the vision; (3) the character attributes that make the candidate the vision's superhero; (4) the action oriented scenarios that are unique and salient to the vision; (5) the vision's sanctioning agent and motive for action; (6) the vision's villain; and finally, (7) the action necessary to defeat the villain and achieve fulfillment of the vision.[30]

## Summary

The development of Bormann's dramatistic communication theory and the line of research and applications reported in this essay indicate that a communication based political campaign is now possible. The procedure for conducting such a campaign begins with the collection and quantification of dramatistic rhetoric that catches up large groups of people. The computer analysis of that rhetoric then allows campaign rhetors to design dramatistic messages that are pretested to stimulate various targeted audiences. This procedure involves five communication instruments: (1) rhetorical criticism; (2) personal interviews; (3) dramatistic focus group interviews; (4) structured dramatistic Q-decks; and (5) graphic questionnaires.

[30]Some of the pitfalls to be avoided when constructing the oration may be found in Cragan's, "Rhetorical Strategy."

These instruments enable the building of the relevant macro issue three dimensional matrices and the composite campaign vision matrix necessary to conducting the political campaign. When the instruments that operationalize these matrices are administered to a stratified random sample of the candidate's constituency, the resultant data enables the development of campaign messages that are linked directly to the voters' symbolic reality.

The campaign communication manager can then systematically construct the candidate's campaign messages from a common rhetorical perspective and research data base. The five most important campaign communication events are: *the campaign Bible* which is the basic fantasy theme schemata that is used to train campaign workers and stimulate consciousness raising sessions among them, *the macro issue position papers* which flow from each of the three dimensional matrices and lay out in rich detail the candidates selected stance; *the three scene, on act rally* which celebrates the candidate as miracle worker or devil slayer; the dramatistic media releases which either attack the opponent's persona or build the candidate's persona; and *the campaign speeches* of which there are four types: airport, rally, ad personam, and oration.

# 12

# Media Critique of the Dramatistic Based, Computer Generated, Political Speech

DONALD C. SHIELDS and JOHN F. CRAGAN

Since 1976 scores of journalists have been reporting how our computer generated speech on foreign policy "played in Peoria." This research report contains a sampling of their editorials and essays. Although the news coverage of our research does provide a sign argument that points to the effectiveness of combining a dramatistic communication theory with quantitative methods for writing speeches, the journalists' rhetoric that describes the "news story" is probably a more telling argument in support of the viablity of Bormann's theory.

A fantasy theme analysis of the following newspaper articles reveals that the professional journalists, working at different news agencies and papers, over the lapsed time of several years, independently created essentially the same drama to explain the reality of the computer generated speech. It is also our observation that the many broadcast journalists that devoted special programs to our research on radio and TV consistently developed the same rhetorical drama in their attempt to interpret our discovery to the American people. We conclude from the fantasy theme analysis of the journalistic essays and programs that the print and broadcast journalists were chaining out and getting caught up in the same rhetorical vision.

We suggest that a reading of the news stories reprinted here should reveal dramatic descriptions of the characters, scenarios, scenes, and sanctioning agent that form one drama. Note especially the villain, the dramatic scene and the future dramatic world that these journalists portray. It appears that Bormann's theory is a rich lens for describing and critiquing the "objective" news reporting in our mass media channels. Also, these editorials underscore what can happen to an applied political communication researcher when his or her *means* for inducing political cooperation through persuasion become the objects of a national news story, instead of the candidate for whom he or she is writing speeches.

*A 1979 Computer Gives Us PeopleSpeak\**

by

**Bob Greene**

*S.F. Sunday Examiner & Chronicle,*
Sunday Punch,
April 29, 1979

The next time you hear a candidate talking to you out of your television set, remember this column.

Two speech scientists, working with an IBM computer, have devised a method of producing the "perfect" political speech that may have chilling consequences in future U.S. elections.

The speech experts—Dr. Donald C. Shields of the University of Missouri at St. Louis and Dr. John Cragan of Illinois State University—devised and tested their technique during the 1976 presidential campaign, and feel that their methods may be copied and used by political candidates as soon as word of their research gets out. Dr. Shields said that he and Dr. Cragan will be "available to advise" both national and local candidates.

Here is how the Shields-Cragan technique was formulated:

The two scientists wanted to come up with a political speech that would be effective for a "Middle American" audience—in other words, a speech that would "play in Peoria."

They took the phrase literally. They went to Peoria, Illinois and tested a cross-section of the citizenry on a number of statements relating to foreign policy. The respondents were instructed to rank each foreign policy statement on a scale from "most reflective" of their views to "least reflective."

The professors had no political axes to grind in their research. They simply wanted to find out what the electorate being tested wanted to hear. In addition to finding out the respondents' substantive stands on foreign policy, the survey also determined in what kind of language—specific phrases—the respondents like to hear their opinions presented.

All of the Peoria data was fed into an IBM 370 computer. The computer was then directed to turn the information into a 7-to-9-minute speech on foreign policy.

"Our idea was to come up with a speech that a candidate could deliver at a typical airport rally," Dr. Shields said.

The computer wrote the speech. Some excerpts:

*The United States is not a failure. For 200 years we have provided the world, through the great experience of democracy, a model—a model that the world is free to follow, but one that we will not impose. Ideally, we would prefer merely to be this model. Unfortunately, the pragmatic realities of the international scene force us to play other roles.*

*The People's Republic of China is a sovereign state, but we must not forget to support the Republic of China on Taiwan. I believe both governments can learn to live with the reality of each other. "*

*Bombings and hijackings are deplorable. Yet the U.S. should not put itself in a position committed to meet such actions whenever and wherever they might occur. I will go to the United Nations and get an international law against terrorism.*

The possible ramifications of the Shields-Cragan technique are obvious. A national political candidate, guided by no principle other than the desire to win, could pre-test citizens in key communities all across the country, have the computer write him speeches telling the citizens exactly what they want to hear — and wait for the votes to roll in.

"The only factor left out of our system is a good delivery by the candidate," Dr. Shields said. "With the possible messages pre-tested, we know exactly what message will work. With the language pre-tested, we know exactly how the candidate should say what he's going to say. There is no guesswork involved. We know what the specific audience wants to hear, and the computer is programmed to give the audience exactly that. All that is needed is a candidate with an attractive manner of delivery."

Asked if the method would be perfected in time for use during the 1980 presidential campaign, Dr. Shields said:

"Yes. Not to mention 1984."

### Political Speech Would Play Well in Peoria*
**Harper Barnes**

*St. Louis Post-Dispatch*
October 28, 1976

"I'd like to take this opportunity here in Peoria to set forth clearly and specifically my position on foreign policy... First of all let me say that the U. S. is not a failure. For 200 years we have provided the world, through the great experience of democracy, a model — a model that the world is free to follow, but one that we will not impose. Ideally, we would prefer merely to be this model. Unfortunately, the pragmatic realities of the international scene force us to play other roles..."

That speech sounds familiar, doesn't it? Was it Ford or Carter? Dole? Mondale? George Jessel? Let's listen to a little more of it.

---

*Reprinted with permission from Editor, *St. Louis Post Dispatch*.

"...despite all claims to the contrary, Russia is still a Communist state. But, 1976 is not 1956. Russia has acquired nuclear and conventional military parity with us...In a nuclear age we cannot escape the responsibility to build a safe future through wise diplomacy...Now please don't misunderstand me. A policy of detente with the Soviet Union does not mean that we're Uncle Sucker..."

Henry Kissinger? Henry Cabot Lodge? Henry Ford? Henry Aaron? Henry VIII? Patrick Henry?

Actually, the speech was written by an IBM 370 computer, with considerable help from two college communications professors, Donald C. Shields of the University of Missouri at St. Louis and John F. Cragan of Illinois State University, plus a cross-section of the population of Peoria, Illinois.

"...I don't intend to flip-flop on any foreign policy issues. Nor do I intend to speak in glib generalities...The lesson of Vietnam is one of indecision. The U. S. was not wrong in the purpose for which we fought. While South Vietnam was not totally a free government, they still enjoyed more liberty than any Communist regime in Eastern Europe...Our mistake was in not moving decisively when we first militarily intervened to discourage further Communist aggression in that country..."

The speech has never been given in Peoria, but Shields says there is no reason to give the speech there — he already knows that the reaction would be overwhelmingly favorable. The speech was put together, after an extensive survey, to stress those foreign policy statements that most Peorians agreed with and to avoid those foreign policy statements that they strongly rejected.

Why Peoria? Partly, Shields conceded, for "poetic reasons" — taking into account the old theatrical question, "Will it play in Peoria?" which means, in effect, is the work under discussion too sophisticated for Middle America?

But, Shields said, there was a statistical reason as well — national corporations use Peoria as an area to test new products because its population does provide a good cross-section of the nation's population — if the speech plays in Peoria, it should play elsewhere.

"...Which brings me to the issue of possible U. S. interventions...Intervention is not right or wrong. But, it may be used rightly or wrongly... Shields explained, "We came up with three categories representing three types of foreign policy. The categories were Cold War, Power Politics and Neo-Isolationism.

"The categories don't exactly correspond to the classic liberal-conservative labels. The Cold War position would be represented by someone like Ronald Reagan, Power Politics, of course, is Henry Kissinger — the politics of pragmatism and expediency."

The Neo-Isolationism position, he said, could be thought of as the position of Eugene McCarthy in 1968 and George McGovern in 1972.

"...The Middle East is again in a no-war, no-peace stalemate and is likely to remain so for some time. Step-by-step diplomacy, treating all parties with an even hand, is the only means for maintaining a delicate peace in the Middle East . . .''

Shields and Cragan chose 20 areas in which the Cold War, Neo-Isolationism and Power Politics positions would differ significantly. They went through political speeches and newspaper articles and editorials for the first half of this year, selecting what they called "messages" — paragraphs that seemed to express those positions well. For instance, the messages defining the three positions on the Middle East read as follows:

**Cold War:** "The U. S. is the sole defender of Israel. As the ultimate guarantor of Israel's freedom, we have an obligation to defend her from attack. We should not force Israel into concessions that weaken her militarily and strengthen Communist influence in the Middle East."

**Power Politics:** "The Middle East is again in a no-war, no-peace stalemate and is likely to remain so for some time. Step-by-step diplomacy, treating all parties with an even hand, is the only means for maintaining a delicate peace in the Middle East."

**Neo-Isolationism:** "Secret diplomacy is not the road to a lasting peace in the Middle East. The American people must know the kinds of commitments made to the Mid-Eastern nations. The Administration has moved from crisis to crisis dragging us dangerously close to war, a war that Congress may not even have an opportunity to vote on."

Shields and Cragan discovered that, in this case and in general, Power-Politics positions were the most popular, with Cold-War positions a close second and Neo-Isolationism positions a distant third. So, in the case of the Middle East, the Power Politics message was translated into the quotation from the speech given above.

But the choosing of messages was much more complicated than a simple yes-no, like-dislike decision, and that is where the computer was required. There were nine possible choices for each of the messages, ranging from strong approval through neutrality to strong disapproval.

Shields explained, "We took the messages in the dominant category, Power Politics, and told the computer to take the messages in that category that were strongly agreed with and intersperse those with negative comments on those messages that were strongly disagreed with from the standpoint of Power Politics.

"Then, we told the computer to intersperse with those two kinds of messages a third type — various strongly accepted statements from the Isolationist and Cold War positions that were not strongly rejected by the Power Politics people.

"So what you have is a computer-written speech most likely to be accepted and least likely to be rejected by Peorians. All a human being had to do was add the transitions, introduction and conclusion. It was already tested — you got the Power Politics people, who were the dominant group, and at the same time could pick up supporters from the other two groups without offending your political base in Power Politics."

Shields, a young man with a bushy moustache, leaned back in the chair of his office at UMSL and grinned.

"There are different applications. Let's say a candidate is going to speak at an American Legion covention. In that case, he could make the Cold War position dominant, but using the computer to choose those Cold War messages that would be least likely to be strongly rejected by the other two points of view. And he could throw in a few Power Politics and Isolation messages that had been shown would not make the Cold War folks mad."

One thing Shields and Cragan discovered during the survey was that some dominant Cold War messages tended to be highly divisive—in other words, they turned off as many people as they attracted.

"For example, we think that Reagan's Cold War position on the Panama Canal got him a lot of support from that group, but tended to make members of the other group mad. From a standpoint of gaining the widest possible appeal and still conveying an essentially Cold-War viewpoint, other subjects would have served better."

"...In Latin America, we should avoid 'big stick' tactics, but we should not stick our heads in the sand...With respect to Panama, the U. S. neither owns nor has sovereignty over the Canal Zone. But Panama granted us rights by a 1903 treaty. We should renegotiate a new treaty that protects America's vital interest in the Canal Zone..."

Shields said the project, which was sponsored by the two universities and the National Speech Communication Association, was strictly an "academic exercise," at least this time around. "We agreed not to give it to anybody, or rather to release the speech and thus give it to everybody. But next time, who knows?

"I can certainly see practical applications in future races."

Is it unethical? he was asked.

He hesitated for a second. "I think it is an extension of public-polling techniques. To the extent that they are unethical, it is unethical, and they are generally accepted. They attempt to get inside the minds and viscera of the people. We do the same. We just do it better, I think."

Shields has given the speech once, to a communications class. "It's eerie," he said, "Read it and think of Ford's voice then of Carter's voice and it works for either one of them."

The speech ends this way:

"...I should not leave Peoria without stating my opinion on grain sales. First of all, I think the embargo of food is immoral given the starving millions in the world. Second, whether we sell or do not sell grain to Russia will not alter her behavior in international affairs. Russia should pay the market price for grain just like anyone else.

"As I stated in my opening remarks, the U. S. is not a crippled giant. We have not lost confidence in ourselves. We are a proud democratic nation that must play a major role of leadership in international affairs. I trust you will agree that my foreign policy is based on a realistic and mature view of how to maintain world order and peace."

How did his students react to the speech? Shields smiled again. "They gave me a standing ovation."


### Perfect Political Speech*
### Jaan Kangilaski

The Bulletin of the American College of Physicians
Vol. 18, No. 11
November, 1977

I have always suspected that there was something not quite human about political speeches and now I've finally found the proof that I had been looking for.

Computers are probably still incapable of the give-and-take of extemporaneous conversation (programming, after all, is a form of training the beast), but in the more stereotyped forms of discourse the electronic devices do rather well. For instance, they have been taking medical histories for some time.

They can also make up political speeches. An IBM-370, in fact, is credited with authoring the "perfect political speech," with some help from two Midwestern speech specialists who were inspired to that effort by the hoopla of the 1976 political campaigns.

This breakthrough en route to the brave new world by the computer, John Cragan, Ph.D., and Donald C. Shields, Ph.D., was first described in *Spectrum/Report*, a publication of the University of Missouri, and in greater detail, in the *Quarterly Journal of Speech*. For some reason, the report has failed to achieve the wide distribution it deserves, so the *The Bulletin,* with the gracious permission of the editor of the *Quarterly Journal of Speech,* would like to make some input into the public mind.

Dr. Shields, associate professor of speech at the University of Missouri-St. Louis, and Dr. Cragan, associate professor of speech at Illinois State University, Normal, went about the work in true scholarly fashion. First they culled the utterances of politicians. Then they pretested the product by recording the reactions of a group of Peoria, Ill., residents to various statements. The Peorians were asked to rank the statements on a scale ranging from "most reflective" to "least reflective" of their views and their answers provided the raw data for the computer in coming out with the perfect speech, i.e., the speech that was least offensive to the most respondents.

A perfect speech sticks to one subject, and Drs. Cragan and Shields choose foreign policy. It is to be hoped that the masterfulness of the

*Reprinted with permission from Editor, *Forum on Medecine* (formerly *The Bulletin of the American College of Physicians)* and *The Quarterly Journal of Speech.*

result will inspire some workers to produce a perfect speech on national health policy in the near future.

Enough of this buildup! Seeing is believing; here is the speech in its entirety:

"I'd like to take this opportunity here in Peoria to set forth clearly my position on foreign policy. In order to do that I'd first like to explain how I see the world today and indicate to you what I believe America's role in world politics should be. First of all, let me say that the U. S. IS NOT A FAILURE. For 200 years we have provided the world, through the great experience of democracy, a model — a model that the world is free to follow, but one that we will not impose. Ideally, we would prefer merely to be this model. Unfortunately, the pragmatic realities of the international scene force us to play other roles.

"The international scene today is highly complex. In some ways it is still a struggle between the Free World and Communism. For despite all claims to the contrary, Russia is still a Communist state. But, 1976 is not 1956. Russia has acquired nuclear and conventional military parity with us — and China and the Middle East make all dealings with the Russians more difficult. Therefore, in the day-to-day affairs of world politics, we must strive to manage and stabilize our relationships with other major powers. In a nuclear age we cannot escape the responsibility to build a safe future through wise diplomacy.

"Now please do not misunderstand me. A policy of detente with the Soviet Union does not mean that we're 'Uncle Sucker'. I recognize that it's foolhardy to unilaterally disarm, but I also know that it's easy to talk in a mock and tough way and run the risk of war. Neither response reflects my postion. Detente means to me a state of affairs marked by the absence of significant tension that could lead the U.S. and Russia into a nuclear confrontation. Detente does not mean that all differences will be resolved, or that Russia will not attempt to expand her influence. It does mean that peaceful coexistence is the only rational alternative.

"Now please do not misunderstand me. A policy of detente with the Soviet Union does not mean that we're 'Uncle Sucker'. I recognize that it's easy to talk in a mock and tough way and run the risk of war. Neither response reflects my position. Detente means to me a state of affairs marked by the absence of significant tension that could lead the U. S. and Russia into a nuclear confrontation. Detente does not mean that all differences will be resolved, or that Russia will not attempt to expand her influence. It does mean that peaceful coexistence is the only rational alternative.

"I don't intend to 'flip-flop' on any foreign policy issues. Nor do I intend to speak in glib generalities. I came here to talk specifically about American foreign policy and that's what I mean to do. First of all, the lesson of Vietnam. The lesson of Vietnam was one of indecision. The U. S. was not wrong in the purpose for which we fought. While South Vietnam was not totally a free government, they still enjoyed more liberty than any Communist regime in Eastern Europe allows. Our mistake was in not moving decisively when we first militarily intervened, to discourage further Communist aggression in that country.

"Which brings me to the issue of possible future U. S. interventions. I believe that intervention is a diplomatic tool that is needed even if it is only a threat to maintain a balanced international scene. Intervention is not right or wrong. But, it may be used rightly or wrongly.

"Of course, we cannot talk about intervention without talking about the CIA. I do not believe that we should dismantle the CIA, for many times it is the CIA's covert capability that stands between a do-nothing policy and nuclear confrontation. I oppose unnecessary secrecy, but I believe in a strong national defense. And, unfortunately, in today's world, the CIA is needed.

"There has been a lot of talk about Europe in this campaign. Let me again state my position. The NATO alliance and the 'trip-wire' presence of American troops stationed in Germany are important parts of America's defense. It would be foolish to withdraw American troops from the Continent of Europe without negotiating a similar withdrawal of Russian troops from Eastern Europe.

"The Middle East is again in a no-war, no-peace stalemate and is likely to remain so for some time. Step-by-step diplomacy, treating all parties with an even hand, is the only means for maintaining a delicate peace in the Middle East.

"The United States must ground its China policy in morality. We should work to improve our relationships with her. The People's Republic of China is a sovereign state, but we must not forget to support our ally, The Republic of China, on Taiwan. I believe both governments can learn to live with the reality of each other.

"In Africa, a specific American presence is necessary if we are to prevent further communist inroads and a tarnishing of America's influence on this awakening continent. The Communists should know that we are prepared to come to the defense of sovereign nations and the Africans should know that we stand ready to help them negotiate a peace among themselves.

"In Latin America, we should avoid 'big stick' tactics, but we should not stick our heads in the sand to what's going on down there. With respect to Panama, the U. S. neither owns nor has sovereignty over the Canal Zone. But Panama granted us rights by a 1903 treaty. We should re-negotiate a new treaty that protects America's vital interests in the Canal Zone.

"On terrorists, my position is clear. International terrorism, such as bombings and hijackings is deplorable. Yet, the U.S. should not put itself in a position committed to meet such actions whenever and wherever they might occur. I will go to the United Nations and get an international law against terrorism.

"I should not leave Peoria without stating my opinion on grain sales. First of all, I think the embargoing of food is immoral given the starving millions in the world. Second, whether we sell or do not sell grain to Russia will not alter her behavior in international affairs. Russia should pay the market price for grain just like anyone else.

"As I stated in my opening remarks, the U.S. is not a crippled giant. We have not lost confidence in ourselves. We are a proud democratic nation that must play a major role of leadership in international affairs. I trust you will agree that my foreign policy is based on a realistic and mature view of how to maintain world order and peace."

One last request. In the spirit of the whole thing, please rate the above speech on a scale of A to H on the following basis:

A = very reflective of your thoughts,
B = moderately reflective of your thoughts,
C = somewhat reflective of your thoughts,
D = not entirely reflective of your thoughts,
E = generally unreflective of your thoughts,
F = downright against the grain of your thoughts,
G = no opinion,
H = none of the above.

### Now a Computer Can Write a Political Speech*

**Reuters**

*The Christian Science Monitor*
May 11, 1977

Most politicians hire someone else to write their campaign speeches, but the ghost writers usually in demand for such duty may be in danger of losing their jobs — to computers.

An IBM 370 computer has written a foreign-policy speech guaranteed to please the greatest number and offend the fewest in the legendary land of "middle America."

The computer did its research in the stereotypical American city of Peoria, Illinois, well aware of the modern politicians most pressing question: "Will it play in Peoria?"

From arms control to detente, from Vietnam to the Middle East, the 1,000-word speech is guaranteed to satisfy that magical 51 percent majority coveted by all would-be office-holders.

### Basic Philosophies

If you don't agree with the following excerpts, you'd be out of step in Peoria:
- "We should work to improve our relationships with (China)...The People's Republic of China is a sovereign state, but we must not for-

*Reprinted with permission from Reuters News Service.

get to support our ally, the Republic of China, on Taiwan. I believe both governments can learn to live with the reality of each other."

- "Detente does not mean that all differences will be resolved or that Russia will not attempt to expand her influence. It does mean that a peaceful coexistence is the only rational alternative."
- "I do not believe that we should dismantle the CIA...I oppose unnecessary secrecy, but I believe in a strong national defense. And unfortunately, in today's world, the CIA is needed."
- "The lesson of Vietnam is one of indecision. The United States was not wrong in the purpose for which we fought...Out mistake was not moving decisively when we first intervened to discourage further Communist aggression in that country."
- "I will go to the United Nations and get an international law against terrorism."

The computer got a helping human hand in its literary efforts from two communications experts Dr. John Cragan, of Illinois State University and Dr. Donald Shields of the University of Missouri.

During the first six months of 1976, while the presidential election campaign was in full swing, the two researchers culled statements from the news media on 20 specific foreign-policy issues.

For each issue, statements were selected that epitomized what they considered the nation's three dominant foreign-policy philosophies: the "power politics" of former Secretary of State Henry A. Kissinger, "classic Cold War" and "neo-isolationism."

The 60 statements were taken to Peoria and perused by a representative sample of Peorians. The computer sorted through the citizens' likes and dislikes, and came up with the speech.

"Power Politics" was found to be the dominant philosophy, with "Cold War" a close second, and "neo-isolationism" a distant third.

"It was simply a more sophisticated approach than the public polling techniques politicians are already using in a less systematic way," Dr. Shields told Reuter.

"President Carter's advisers are sitting down, trying to put together public opinion polls and surveys to find out what's happening out here in the 'hinterlands'. Well, they're probably pretty accurate, but they might as well use a computer," he said.

Dr. Cragan agreed, adding: "You can get very, very scientific about the phraseology of your statements."

He continued: "Since Vietnam there's been a tendency by politicians to take the broad ambiguous stand calculated not to offend the majority of voters.

"For instance, in the last campaign the stress was on minimizing errors — being tactful, not alienating large groups, making sure your rhetoric didn't mess you up."

They said their pre-testing technique works best with broad, highly complex issues such as foreign policy, the national economy, and the environment, where it's possible to talk for some length while saying very little.

Said Dr. Cragan: "Carter seems to have a good feel for what we're talking about. His presidency's been highly symbolic, good 'PR'."

His colleague added: "He could have used our technique to find out which parts of his new energy policy would need the biggest "sell on the people."

Both researchers dismissed the suggestion that politicians could adopt their methods and carry to extremes the present practice of "selling" a candidate.

"Our technique is just a higher form of offensive weapon already being used by politicians," Dr. Cragan said. "If we could explain how it works, it might not work anymore. It will be effective only until people learn how it works."

The need now, they said, was for the public and the media to look beyond a politician's public statements.

"The kind of question we must ask is how they're manufacturing the rhetoric they're reading before the cameras and microphones," Dr. Cragan said.

### Now It's Politics by Computer:
### Machine Writes Speech that Will 'Play in Peoria'*

**Mark Starr**

*Chicago Tribune*
April 13, 1977

In American politics, the bottom-line question facing a new program or idea is, "Will it play in Peoria?"

John Cragan and Donald Shields know how to come up with an answer.

Cragan, associate professor of information sciences at Illinois State University, and Shields, assistant professor of speech communication at the University of Missouri—St. Louis, have been researching a method of pretesting political messages.

In doing so they have developed a politician's dream: the foreign policy campaign speech that will play better in Peoria, the quintessential symbol of middle America, than any other foreign policy speech.

And neither Cragan nor Shields had to write a single word. The entire 900-word speech, which runs the gamut from arms control to grain sales to Angola, was developed through an IBM 370 computer.

What Cragan and Shields did was simple. They chose 20 major foreign policy issues and scored newspapers and magazines for statements on each issue that epitomized what they felt are today's three major foreign policy philosophies — Kissinger power politics, classic Cold War, and neo-isolationism.

They then took those 60 foreign policy messages to Peoria and tried them out on a random sample of Peorians.

"What you're looking for are the messages that will please the most people while at the same time offend the least," Cragan said.

By pretesting their statements, politicians theoretically can avoid making the big mistake.

Traditionally, they did so by slipping a new idea or policy position onto a relatively insignificant speech in order to gauge popular reaction with minimum risk.

However, that tactic is no longer practical. With most politicians closely watched by the omnipresent media, every speech becomes a big speech, and a gaffe one place will quickly become a nationwide joke, courtesy of the evening news.

Shields says that pretesting would have spared former President Gerald Ford the embarrassment and political damage resulting from his statement on Russian domination of Eastern Europe.

Ronald Reagan is another 1976 presidential candidate whom the research indicates would have benefited from pretesting. For example, his hardline Cold War view on American control of the Panama Canal pleased a significant number of people, but it offended as many.

The computer indicated that if Reagan had chosen international terrorism to represent his get-tough policy ("The newest threat to the security of the world is international terrorism. The U.S. must take the lead from Israel and meet bombings and hijackings with force whenever and wherever they occur."), he would have pleased the same people while alienating hardly anyone.

The research disclosed that Kissinger's legacy, power politics, is the most acceptable foreign policy view in Peoria.

The most strongly rejected messages in Peoria were attacks on Kissinger as being "too soft in his dealings with Communists," and on detente as meaning "'All give on the U.S.' part and 'all take' on the side of the Communists."

For each issue, the computer discovered something that will play well in Peoria. At the urging of the professors, the IBM 370 belched out the following words of wisdom guaranteed to offend the fewest:

- On detente — "Detente does not mean that all differences will be resolved, or that Russia will not attempt to expand her influence. It does mean that peaceful coexistence is the only rational alternative."

- On the CIA — "I do not believe that we should dismantle the CIA, for many times it is the CIA's covert capability that stands between a do-nothing possibility and nuclear confrontation."

- On the Middle East — "Step-by-step diplomacy, treating all parties with an even hand, is the only means for maintaining a delicate peace in the Middle East."
- On Vietnam — "The lesson of Vietnam is one of indecision. The U.S. was not wrong in the purpose for which we fought. While South Vietnam was not a totally free government, they still enjoyed more liberty than any communist regime in Eastern Europe allows. Our mistake was in not moving decisively when we first militarily intervened to discourage further communist aggression in that country."

"With the message and language pre-tested, we know exactly what to say and how to say it," Shields added. "The only factor left out of our system is a good delivery by the candidate."

Computerized speech making would be a good system if the politicians wanted to mirror their electorate, but it wouldn't be very good on a leadership level, Cragan said. He feels the use of computers in political campaigns should be closely examined.

"We called up some local politicians just to see what they would say about it. They denied any interest in such a technique, but the press should be aware of the questions to ask, anyway," he said.

Although the political response has been guarded, seven or eight marketing firms have shown interest in the technique, he added.

The professors conducted the research as purely objective if somewhat cynical observers and said they would be "available to advise" any interested political candidates.

### Speech Experts Use DP to Write Rhetoric Echoing Voters' Views

**Ann Dooley**
*Computerworld**
*March 21, 1977*

Peoria, Ill. — Politicians will be able to win elections before long by using a computer to analyze the subgroups within their constituencies and tailor their political rhetoric to match, according to two speech experts.

Dr. Donald C. Shields of the University of Missouri at St. Louis and Dr. John Cragan of Illinois State University claim to have proved this during last year's Presidential campaign.

During the primaries, Cragan and Shields became interested in writing a speech that would "play in Peoria" — that is, appeal to "Middle America."

And they did exactly that. They tested a cross-section of Peoria citizens on 20 issues relating to foreign policy. The respondents ranked actual foreign policy statements taken from newspapers according to how they reflected their views, Cragan explained.

The statements were loosely classified into three views of American foreign policy. One view represented the "Cold War warrior" typefied by Ronald Reagan, the second was a neo-isolationist view represented by Sen. Eugene McCarthy and the third was a balance of power stance portrayed by Henry Kissinger, according to Cragan.

Besides finding out citizens' views on foreign policy, the survey also determined the most effective style and specific phrases in which the respondent liked to hear his opinions expressed.

### DP — Written Speech

The ranked statements were keypunched on cards and entered into an IBM 370/145 at Illinois State University here. Through factor analysis and linear equation programs, the computer wrote a seven- to nine-minute speech that "would please the most and offend the least" number of people, he said.

An example from their all-American speech goes: "The People's Republic of China is a sovereign state, but we must not forget to support our ally the Republic of China on Taiwan. I believe both governments can learn to live with the reality of each other."

"It's a bland speech; no one's going to march down the road with you," Cragan said. But when the speech was presented before a Peoria audience, it received an ovation.

### Nothing Controversial

Since the speech says nothing controversial, it will help to avoid the "big error," such as the one former President Ford made in reference to Poland during the second Presidential debate, Cragan said.

"We used essentially the same process that speechwriters use, although they are not as scientific," he said. "In the last campaign, it was referred to as 'flip-flopping.'"

### *Machine Candidate**

### Diane K. Shah and Richard Manning

*Newsweek Magazine*
August 20, 1979

"First of all," intones the speaker, "let me say that the United States is not a failure. I recognize that it's foolhardy to unilaterally disarm, but..." So begins an upbeat, let's-look-at-the-record foreign-policy speech that could well be the kickoff of the 1980 primaries. The speaker, however, is not Jimmy Carter, Ted Kennedy or even Howard Baker, but a fresh political voice from the Midwest. The name? IBM-370.

The slick-tongued computer-orator is the brainchild of two communications professors who believe that getting elected to public office is becoming more a matter of manipulating campaign symbols than dealing with substance. To prove their thesis, they set out to program the IBM-370 to write the "perfect" foreign-policy speech — one guaranteed, that is, to appeal to the most and offend the fewest in any given audience. "We figured that if we did the proper market-type research and programmed the computer to write a speech reflecting the findings, the speech would end up sounding pretty much like the genuine article churned out by a pack of poll-watching speechwriters," says John Cragan of Illinois State University.

'DRAMA': To begin with, Cragan, 35, and partner Donald Shields, 34, of the University of Missouri — St. Louis, theorized that all a politician need do to get elected is recognize that voters generally subscribe to one of three "dramatic" views of the world, then play to the most widespread of the views. Set in a foreign policy context, these three attitudes translated into cold-war, neo-isolationist and power-politics mind-sets. On the Panama Canal, for instance, the cold-war view held that the U.S. ought not to surrender the Canal Zone, the neo-isolationist view dictated that the U.S. get out of Panama and the power-politics view supported the negotiation of a new treaty to protect U.S. interests in the zone.

The professors picked twenty such issues to be covered by the speech. They culled newspapers and magazines for months, jotting down quotes that reflected all three positions on all twenty issues, then transferred the quotes onto 60 index cards. Finally, they went to — where else? — Peoria, Ill., to see how the opinions played. Sixty Peorians were asked to sort the cards in order of preference, from those most reflective of their views to those least reflective. Then the subjects rearranged the cards to show how important each issue was to them.

1984-ISH: Cragan and Shields fed the results into the computer and instructed it to write a speech based on the most prevalent opinions, complete with adverbs and adjectives. They pushed a button and out came the hypothetical candidate's carefully considered opinion on how best to handle U.S. foreign policy — for Peorians. "The point," says Cragan, "is that you can take any idiot, parade him around the country for twelve months, and get him elected."

But the ultimate purpose behind this slightly 1984-ish project, say the two professors, is to force politicians out of the business of manipulating symbols and back into the business of governing. To that end, their IBM-370 is about to churn out perfect speeches in 1980," says Cragan, "we hope it will spark enough controversy for someone to ask the candidates why their speeches sound so much like our computer's. Maybe that will get them to say what they really think for a change."

So far, that message hasn't got through. Instead of coming clean, six political aspirants, including a candidate in a gubernatorial primary and a mayoral contender, have already called on Cragan and Shields for a little help from their computer. All were turned down — and lost their races.

The importance of pretesting is revealed in the Vietnam sentiment which, despite the power-politics disposition of Peoria, is clearly a Cold War message.

While Shields and Cragan concede that the computer speech-writing concept is somewhat frightening and 1984ish,'' they say it is the logical extension of the modern phenomenon of packaging political candidates.

Cragan maintains that the computer process is more honest than the current camouflaged packaging of candidates.

"If the whole thing is really just packaging paragraphs, let's be efficient about it," he said.

Fears over their computer project Shields says, only reflect the basic distrust of politicians because the same methodology could be used by "a candidate who was really ethical and sincere and wanted to find the best way to present his ethical and sincere message."

He admits that the process could be a dynamic tool for "a candidate with a lot of money who wants to be manipulative," but adds, "I don't see how hiding the monster helps."

Cragan criticizes the naivete of the press in covering the substance of speeches and neglecting to report the process by which a speech evolved.

To be forewarned is to be forearmed, the professors feel.

So the next time you hear a politician say, "A policy of detente with the Soviet Union doesn't mean that we're 'Uncle Sucker.' I recognize that it's foolhardy to unilaterally disarm, but I also know that it's not easy to talk in a mock and tough way and run the risk of war," remember — Out of the mouth of a politician may come the words of a computer.

# PART IV:

## Using the Theory to Investigate Organizational Communication

# IV: Using the Theory to Investigate Organizational Communication

Since people get caught up in dramatistic symbolic reality at the small group and societal level, it stands to reason that members of an organization should participate in a common organizational drama(s). As well, it stands to reason that in a given organization there may be competing organizational dramas vying for supremacy. Various members of the organization may then participate in these competing dramas. The studies which follow demonstrate our application of Bormann's theory to the study of organizations.

The first study was commissioned by the U. S. Department of Commerce. They wanted to know how to identify more accurately fire fighters who might become good public fire education officers. In addition to characterizing the dramatistic reality and the key demographic, psychographic, and sociographic characteristics of good public fire educators, this study illustrates our first attempt at using a new procedure for doing applied dramatistic communication research. Here we abandoned William Stephenson's commitment to small samples when using Q-sorts. This allowed us to use fire fighters' participation in a given drama—as determined by their sorting behavior—as a *breaker variable* for assessing the predictive demo/psycho/socio graphics that identify fire fighters participating in one drama from those participating in another. We also employed this procedure in the Doane Farm Management Study and the Upjohn Lutalyse Market Segmentation Study.

Using participation in a rhetorical vision as the basis for doing regression analysis was an important breakthrough. By using Q-type factor analysis to quantitatively assess a person's participation in a rhetorical drama, a researcher knows that a person's dramatistic cognitive space differs from that of people assessed to be quantitatively participating in other dramas. Then by comparing the observable and measureable demo/psycho/socio graphic characteristics, the researcher can easily identify at a predictive level people likely to participate in a given communication drama. Once the researcher knows these sorts of things about an audience or market, he or she is set to design the content of political messages or product advertisements to fit directly the drama of the targeted audience.

In the second study in this section, Shields demonstrated how the theory and a quantitative procedure may be used to study the image, both public and private, of an organization. In this research of the St. Paul Fire Service, Shields reports on the initital attempt to quantitatively capture and empirically assess rhetorical visions. In so doing, he provided the initial concurrent and construct validation for the theory of rhetorical vision.

In the final study in this section, by Cragan, Shields, and Nichols, the theory and methods are applied to the problem of self-identification of employees with an organization, and its product. The Doane company wished to identify the make-up of its farm management service. Since the product as a service was the people who provided the service, the identification problem was essentially an assessment of both the heroic persona of Doane Farm Managers and the dramas in which they participated. This description then formed the basis for recommendation concerning the division's organization and the marketing of the service.

# 13

# The Identifying Characteristics of Public Fire Safety Educators:

## An Empirical Analysis

JOHN F. CRAGAN and DONALD C. SHIELDS
with
Chief Lawrence A. Pairitz and Inspector Lonnie H. Jackson

Fire prevention through fire safety education is and will continue to be a primary function of local fire departments. The fire education officer, as he develops and guides the fire prevention effort in the local community, is the central figure in educating the public he serves about the needs and means to achieve fire prevention. Such officers appear to be the key component in the creation of any systematic national program of fire saftey public education. Nevertheless, despite the importance of the job, our knowledge of the attributes and characteristics of the typical fire public education officer is quite limited.

A cursory examination of local fire safety education programs reveals that for every successful program there is a *sparkplug*, a creative fire education officer who is the driving force and in many cases the sole reason for the program's existence. Such an examination also reveals that when such key people in a local area leave the fire service their programs seem to degenerate. Thus, an intensive, thriving, successful public education program lays dormant as it awaits the arrival of another *sparkplug*. Sometimes such a person is forthcoming, at other times, and in all too many cases, such a person is not.

Given the continuing need for public fire safety education at the local level, and given the likely dependence of any systematic national program on the local fire education officer, it is important that the fire service knows more about the fire fighter who functions as the fire safety educator.

Do public fire educators have a consistent view of public fire education and if they do, how is it similar or different from the view of public fire education held by others in the fire service? What are the identifying characteristics of a public fire educator and how are these characteristics like or not like the characteristics of others in the fire service? With the encouragement and financial support of the National Fire Prevention and

This study is partially reported in *Fire Chief Magazine,* October, 1978, 44-50.

Control Administration and the Associate Administrator, Richard Strother, we set out during the summer of 1977 to conduct research that would provide answers to these basic questions.

## Research Procedures and Design

The procedures for conducting this research contained five steps: (1) case studies of public fire educators; (2) construction and administration of a sixty-statement structured Q-deck instrument containing three basic attitudes toward public education; (3) construction and administration of a survey questionnaire concerning fire educator demographics and psychological orientation; (4) selection of subjects; and (5) multivariate statistical analysis of the data.

The first procedure provided information to help us understand the professional make-up of public fire educators. Initially, we constructed interview questions to provide in-depth case studies on eight public fire educators who the NFPCA identified as having active, successful programs. The eight were: Lt. Tom O'Connell, Chicago Fire Department; Ms. Nancy Dennis, Fire Service Training, Oklahoma State University; Inspector Ken Mitchell, Santa Ana (California) Fire Department; Mr. Mathew Maley, Shriners' Burn Institute, Cincinnati; Mr. Rich Friedt, Seattle; Mr. Emil Jensen, Palatine (Illinois) Fire Department; Lt. John Haney, Upper Arlington (Ohio) Fire Department; and Ms. Kathy Lohr, Guilford County Fire Marshall's Office (Greensboro, North Carolina). We utilized the case studies to gain insight into the job function and characteristics of public fire educators. Through both written response and taped interview, we asked them to describe their job function and routine, their motivation for doing the job, and the emotional, psychological, and intellectual attributes that allowed them to be successful. The completed case studies were rich with dramatizations describing the central core of a fire educator.

From these initial eight case studies, we constructed a separate sixteen-item questionnaire that we sent to an additional twenty-eight public fire educators. The case studies and the responses to our questionnaire provided the data base necessary to construct our structured Q-deck on the persona of the public fire educator.

The second procedure centered on the development of our Q-deck testing instrument. Quite simply, the Q-deck and the accompanying sorting procedure allows a respondent to react to a set of statements and rank order them in a modified fashion along a continuum of being "from most reflective to least reflective of their view of public fire safety education." Since the respondent in essence assigns these statements to the ranks of one through nine, meanings of the statements are supplied by the respondent. The Q-deck and sort are thus an intensive in-depth approach to behavioral research that comes closer to the "real" view of people than most survey procedures. More than this, the sorting of the Q-statements allows openness and freedom of the respondent to reflect his/her view of the research topic by placing the statements in any way that he or she deems appropriate. As such, the data analysis reveals a composite picture of peoples' attitudes toward the fire service, and becomes much more than a head-counting device that says, "yes, we like public fire education," or "no, we don't."

Subsequent administration and data gathering through this Q-deck instrument would enable us to determine the extent to which the attitudes and values about fire education reflected in the case studies and questionnaires existed among the general population of fire service personnel, including education officers, chiefs and fire fighters. We constructed a Q-sort data matrix that contained the various attitudes and values about public fire education gleaned from interviews and questionnaires. These attitudes and values were represented by sixty statements of from fifteen to forty words in length, each of which described a specific and discreet view of public fire education. (See Table 1)

The top of the structured matrix (columns) contains three distinct views of public fire education. The view labeled suppression ascribes that the fire service has only one function, that being the suppression of fire, and that the role of public fire education is only a subordinate role and exists to provide public relations for the fire service. The view labeled inspection depicts the fire service as having two functions, that of suppression and inspection, but public fire education still plays a minor role and its major reason for existence is public relations. The third view labeled public education is the idealized view of the role of public fire education in the fire service. It is depicted as a major way to reduce the loss of life and property due to fire. It is the view most commonly found in the case studies of our public fire educators.

The side of the structured matrix (rows) includes elements of the dramatic structure, attributes of the fire educator, persona of the fire education program, and support for the fire education program as major elements in each vision. These twenty issues tended to be the dominant themes about public fire education that were found in the case studies and the results of the questionnaires sent to fire educators. Thus, we built twenty Q-statements for each view, producing a 3 × 20 matrix.

The respondents then sorted the sixty dramatizations on a forced-choice continuum of from most reflective to least reflective of their view of the role of public fire education in the fire service. The sixty-item forced distribution was 2-3-6-11-16-11-6-3-2 for a nine category sort. (See Table 2)

Respondents were asked to read the sixty statements. Then they were asked to re-read the statements placing them into three piles representing those cards they agreed with, those they didn't agree with, and then those they were neutral about. Respondents then sub-divided the three piles into nine piles according to the forced distribution. For example, fire fighters placed the two cards they like the most in cell A and the two cards they liked the least in cell I and worked from the remaining outside cells toward the middle. The result was the placement of all sixty cards into cells that would

## Table 1

### Public Fire Education Dramas
### Structured Q-Matrix
### Archetypal Dramas (Columns) and Elements (Rows)

| | Suppression | Inspection | Public Education |
|---|---|---|---|
| **Dramatic Structure** | | | |
| Plot Line. | 1 | 21 | 41 |
| Hero. | 2 | 22 | 42 |
| Villain. | 3 | 23 | 43 |
| Scene. | 4 | 24 | 44 |
| Cause (reality link). | 5 | 25 | 45 |
| **Attributes of Fire Educator** | | | |
| Can educator be non-firefighter. | 6 | 26 | 46 |
| Responsibility to fire education. | 7 | 27 | 47 |
| Role mix of firefighter/educator. | 8 | 28 | 48 |
| Time commitment in fire education. | 9 | 29 | 49 |
| Skills/knowledge level of fire education. | 10 | 30 | 50 |
| Motive. | 11 | 31 | 51 |
| **Persona of Fire Education Program** | | | |
| Education, does it make a difference. | 12 | 32 | 52 |
| Fire education contributes to fire service image. | 13 | 33 | 53 |
| Priority choice; fire education vs. equipment. | 14 | 34 | 54 |
| What is public fire education. | 15 | 35 | 55 |
| How do you measure program's effectiveness. | 16 | 36 | 56 |
| **Support for Fire Education Program** | | | |
| City administrator. | 17 | 37 | 57 |
| Chief's view. | 18 | 38 | 58 |
| Public's view. | 19 | 39 | 59 |
| View of federal campaign on fire education. | 20 | 40 | 60 |

## Table 2

### Forced Distribution Array

| | Least Like | | | | | | | | Most Like |
|---|---|---|---|---|---|---|---|---|---|
| Pile Letter: | A | B | C | D | E | F | G | H | I |
| # of items in pile: | 2 | 3 | 6 | 11 | 16 | 11 | 6 | 3 | 2 |

be assigned numerical values for tabulation of similarities and differences in sorting behavior.

The third procedure concerned the development of our demographic questionnaire and selection of our psychological instruments. On the basis of data gathered from the case studies and surveys of public fire educators we determined that there were fourteen demographic variables and two psychological instruments that might distinguish a public fire educator from a fire fighter who is not. The fourteen demographic variables included: primary job function, age, sex, religious beliefs, church activity, military service, oldest brother of brothers, educational background, marital status, years in the fire service, rank in the fire service, paid or volunteer, number of dependents, and the presence of photography or art as a hobby. The two psychological instruments were standardized tests for discerning. an individual's level of creativity as developed by Dr. J. Khatena and Dr. E.P. Torrance. After the Q-sorting, the fire fighters were asked to fill out the fourteen-item demographic survey and to take the two standardized creativity tests.

The next procedure involved the selection of individuals who would sort the Q-deck and complete the demographic survey and psychological instruments. More than 400 fire fighters and public education officers participated in the study at a number of locations throughout the midwest. Such a massive data collection project obviously entailed the cooperation of a number of fire departments and fire conferences. Those participating included some 150 fire fighters and related personnel who attended the 1977 Midwest Fire Education Conference held at Mt. Prospect, Illinois. In addition, a number of fire chiefs and public fire educators secured more than 200 subjects from their fire departments and they are: Chief Eldon Maginnis and Lt. James Gschwend, Madison, Wisconsin; Chief Jerome Burke and Lt. Tom Allenspack, Skokie, Illinois; Chief Harvey Carothers and Lt. Bill DePue, Palatine, Illinois; Chief Ron Schapete and Inspector David King, Racine, Wisconsin; Chief James Cragan and Mr. John Jung, Rockford, Illinois; and Deputy Chief William Foley and Lt. Tom O'Donnell, Chicago, Illinois. Finally, data was collected from 67 chiefs attending the Metropolitan Fire Chiefs' Meeting (Illinois), the Northeast Illinois Fire Chiefs' Meeting, and the Lake County (Illinois) Fire Chiefs' Meeting. Additional personnel assisting in the data collection included Inspector Steve Figved, Libertyville, Illinois; Lt. Bill Manning, Waukegan, Illinois; and Inspector Roger Hugg, Rolling Meadows, Illinois.

The final procedure entailed the analysis of the data. Two basic statistical procedures were followed in order to properly analyze the data. First, the Q-sort data were factor analyzed by means of Tubergen's Quanal Program for Q-analysis, providing the Principal Components Solution with Varimax rotation to simple structure and a Weighted Rotational Analytical Procedure that arrayed the placement of dramatizations about public fire education for each factor by means of descending z-scores.

By doing factor analyses of twelve sets of data from groups of 30 respondents (a total N of 360) we were able to determine in graphic specificity what dramatizations respondents accepted, rejected and were neutral about. Knowing the subjects' views allowed us to compare the sorting behavior of public education officers, chiefs, and fire fighters on the basis of what dramatizations they accepted and rejected.

In order to determine what unique characteristics (characteristics that were not present with other fire fighters) public fire educators possessed, we needed to perform another statistical procedure. Thus, we analyzed the data by means of both direct and step-wise discriminant analysis. This procedure takes the data from the demographic questionnaires and the scores on the two creativity tests and determines what if any of these sixteen items discriminate a public fire educator from one who isn't. In short, this procedure told us if such things as age, sex, time in the fire service, or creativity distinguish respondents who accepted the ideal public fire education dramatizations from respondents who rejected them.

## Results

One of the basic questions that we sought to answer was, "Do public fire educators have a consistent view of public fire education and if they do, how is it similar or different from the view of public fire education held by others in the fire service?" To answer this question we factor analyzed the sorting behavior of twelve different sets of thirty respondents (total N = 360) who were grouped into three rough subject categories.

### Subject Category One

Subject Category One included those fire fighters who attended the Midwest Fire Education Conference. We assumed that fire personnel attending this conference would hold a view toward the role of the public fire educator that most resembled the idealized vision of fire education that we had built into the Q-deck. We factor analyzed the sorting behavior of 120 of these conference attendees by splitting them into four groups of 30 each. Specifically, the factor analyses of the four sets of public fire educators produced four Principal Components Solutions accounting for an average of 54 percent of the total variance in sorting behavior of each group. All four solutions yielded four factors with the major factor accounting for about 45 percent of the variance in sorting behavior, thus making this factor the only significant factor.

The specific make-up of this major factor was alike across all four groups. The view reflective of persons who comprised this factor mirrored the idealized view represented by the public education view in the constructed Q-deck matrix. The 15 most accepted cards are reported in

Table III and ranked 1 through 15. The six most accepted cards read as follows: "I think public education is a year-round plan for producing behavioral changes in the citizenry that will lead directly to reduction of life loss." — Card 55; "I believe the city administrators should view the fire public education program as an effective way of reducing life loss in the

## Table 3

### Public Fire Education Conference Sort
### Accepted Messages (Ranked 1-15) Reject Messages (Ranked 46-60)

| | Suppression | Inspection | Public Education |
|---|---|---|---|
| **Dramatic Structure** | | | |
| Plot Line. | 1 (49th) | 21 | 41 ( 5th) |
| Hero. | 2 | 22 | 42 ( 9th) |
| Villain. | 3 (50th) | 23 (53rd) | 43 (10th) |
| Scene. | 4 (48th) | 24 | 44 |
| Cause (reality link). | 5 | 25 (54th) | 45 ( 3rd) |
| **Attributes of Fire Educator** | | | |
| Can educator be non-firefighter. | 6 (52nd) | 26 (46th) | 46 |
| Responsibility to fire education. | 7 (56th) | 27 | 47 (14th) |
| Role mix of firefighter/educator. | 8 (57th) | 28 | 48 |
| Time commitment in fire education | 9 (47th) | 29 | 49 |
| Skills/knowledge level of fire education. | 10 | 30 (51st) | 50 (12th) |
| Motive. | 11 (58th) | 31 (51st) | 51 |
| **Persona of Fire Education Program** | | | |
| Education, Does it make a difference. | 12 (59th) | 32 (60th) | 52 ( 7th) |
| Fire education contributes to fire service image. | 13 (55th) | 33 | 53 ( 4th) |
| Priority choice; fire education vs. equipment. | 14 | 34 | 54 |
| What is public fire education. | 15 | 35 ( 8th) | 55 ( 1st) |
| How do you measure program's effectiveness | 16 | 36 | 56 (11th) |
| **Support for Fire Education Program** | | | |
| City administrator. | 17 | 37 | 57 ( 2nd) |
| Chief's view. | 18 | 38 | 58 ( 6th) |
| Public's view. | 19 | 39 | 59 (13th) |
| View of federal campaign on fire education. | 20 | 40 | 60 |

*This study is partially reported in *Fire Chief Magazine*, October, 1978, 44-50.

community."—Card 57; "The leading cause of fires is lack of education about fires and what to do about them."—Card 45; "The public's image of the fire fighter should be expanded to include not only the effective suppression of fire, but the active prevention of fire; thus, fire safety programs must be an important part of this new image."—Card 53; "We have well trained, well equipped firefighters coupled with strong inspection programs. The real breakthrough in saving lives and property will be an aggressive fire education program."—Card 41; and "I believe the Chief's office should view the fire education program as an effective means for reducing life loss in the community."—Card 58.

The data in Table III also contains the fifteen cards most rejected by the public fire educators, ranked 45 through 60. It is important to note that five of the six most rejected cards came from the suppressionist view of fire education contained in the Q-deck matrix. The six most rejected cards read as follows: "The public image of fire fighters is dependent on how well we fight fires. If they know our record we're okay. Fire safety talks at the grade schools don't improve our basic image as courageous, efficient fire fighters."—Card 13; "I don't mind the Chief asking me to give fire safety talks to groups that come here to the firehouse, but I just don't think it's a good idea to leave the fire house while on duty and give talks out in the community."—Card 7; "It's my belief that professional fire fighters should stick to fire fighting and professional educators should instruct the students about fire."—Card 8; "While some public fire educators are good fire fighters, I think that job function tends to attract the lame and the lazy in the fire service."—Card 11; "Fire education helps public relations with the fire service, but I have my doubts if fire education can really reduce fire loss. People are just careless no matter what you tell them."—Card 12; and "Fire education programs are just window dressing. They don't help and they don't hinder, but some of the guys like to do them."—Card 32.

From this data it is evident that the public educators not only possess a unified view, but they possess a view which accepts public education as a legitimate means of reducing the loss of life and property due to fire and which strongly rejects dramatizations that disparage the public education program as not being a significant and important part of the fire service mission.

**Subject Category Two**

Subject Category Two included fire chiefs who attended the three chief's conferences we sampled. We wanted to determine the extent of support for public fire education programs among fire chiefs as well as see how their views might be similar to or different from those of public education officers. We factor analyzed the sorting behavior of 60 chiefs by splitting them into two groups of 30 each. Specifically, the factor analyses of the two sets of fire chiefs produced two Principal Components Solutions accounting for an average of 52 percent of the total variance in sorting behavior. The two factor solutions yielded an equal number of factors, five, and the major factor accounted for an average of 35 percent of the variance within the five factor solution. The remaining factors accounted for less than seven percent of the variance each.

The specific make-up of the major factor in the chiefs' sorting behavior was alike across both groups. The view reflective of persons who comprised this factor was almost identical to that of the public fire educators. Five of the chiefs' top six cards are the same as the top cards of the public safety

## Table 4

### Fire Chiefs Sort
### Accepted Messages (Ranked 1-15)
### Rejected Messages (Ranked 46-60)

| | Suppression | Inspection | Public Education |
|---|---|---|---|
| **Dramatic Structure** | | | |
| Plot Line. | 1 (49th) | 21 | 41 ( 6th) |
| Hero. | 2 (50th) | 22 | 42 (12th) |
| Villain. | 3 (55th) | 23 | 43 ( 8th) |
| Scene. | 4 (47th) | 24 | 44 |
| Cause (reality link). | 5 | 25 (53rd) | 45 ( 9th) |
| **Attributes of Fire Educator** | | | |
| Can educator be non-firefighter. | 6 (54th) | 26 | 46 |
| Responsibility to fire education. | 7 (51st) | 27 (46th) | 47 |
| Role mix of firefighter/educator. | 8 (58th) | 28 | 48 |
| Time commitment in fire education. | 9 | 29 | 49 (10th) |
| Skills/knowledge level of fire education. | 10 | 30 | 50 |
| Motive. | 11 (57th) | 31 (48th) | 51 |
| **Persona of Fire Education Program** | | | |
| Education, Does it make a difference. | 12 (59th) | 32 (60th) | 52 ( 3rd) |
| Fire education contributes to fire service image. | 13 (56th) | 33 | 53 ( 5th) |
| Priority choice; fire education vs. equipment. | 14 | 34 | 54 (14th) |
| What is public fire education. | 15 | 35 ( 7th) | 55 ( 1st) |
| How do you measure program's effectiveness. | 16 (52nd) | 36 | 56 (11th) |
| **Support for Fire Education Program** | | | |
| City administrator. | 17 (13th) | 37 | 57 ( 4th) |
| Chief's view. | 18 | 38 | 58 ( 2nd) |
| Public's view. | 18 | 38 | 58 (15th) |
| View of federal campaign on fire education. | 20 | 40 | 60 |

educators. The 15 most accepted cards are reported in Table IV and ranked 1-15. Similarly, three of the six most strongly rejected cards are the same as the cards rejected by the public fire safety educators. The 14 most strongly rejected cards are reported in Table V and ranked 46 through 60. Essentially, the statements that the chiefs accepted were the ones that did not view public fire education as being a soft job for the lame and lazy. Rather, the chiefs felt that education officers put in a hard work week that goes

## Table 5

## Majority of Fire Fighters Sort
## Accepted Messages (Ranked 1-15)
## Rejected Messages (Ranked 46-60)

| | Suppression | Inspection | Public Education |
|---|---|---|---|
| **Dramatic Structure** | | | |
| Plot Line. | 1 | 21 ( 9th) | 41 ( 4th) |
| Hero. | 2 | 22 | 42 ( 8th) |
| Villain. | 3 | 23 (46th) | 43 |
| Scene. | 4 | 24 | 44 |
| Cause (reality link). | 5 | 25 | 45 ( 6th) |
| **Attributes of Fire Educator** | | | |
| Can educator be non-firefighter. | 6 (47th) | 26 | 46 |
| Responsibility to fire education. | 7 (48th) | 27 | 47 |
| Role mix of firefighter/educator. | 8 (54th) | 28 (11th) | 48 ( 3rd) |
| Time commitment in fire education. | 9 (57th) | 29 (50th) | 49 |
| Skills/knowledge level of fire education. | 10 | 30 ( 7th) | 50 |
| Motive. | 11 (60th) | 31 (58th) | 51 |
| **Persona of Fire Education Program** | | | |
| Education, Does it make a difference. | 12 (55th) | 32 (59th) | 52 (13th) |
| Fire education contributes to fire service image. | 13 (51st) | 33 | 53 ( 2nd) |
| Priority choice; fire education vs. equipment. | 14 | 34 | 54 (56th) |
| What is public fire education. | 15 | 35 ( 5th) | 55 ( 1st) |
| How do you measure program's effectiveness. | 16 (49th) | 36 (52nd) | 56 (14th) |
| **Support for Fire Education Program** | | | |
| City administrator. | 17 | 37 | 57 (10th) |
| Chief's view. | 18 | 38 | 58 (12th) |
| Public's view. | 19 | 39 (15th) | 59 |
| View of federal campaign on fire education. | 20 (53rd) | 40 | 60 |

beyond forty hours. Another difference is that the chiefs see city administrators as viewing the fire service as primarily suppression and believe administrators see public education as just a public relations function. It ought to be emphasized that the chiefs accepted quite strongly the view that public education should be given top priority in the fire service budget. Indeed, the fire chiefs placed a higher priority on Card 54 than did public educators. Card 54 reads: "I think it's time that fire education receives the top priority in our budget. It's better to spend money on this program than on another piece of apparatus."

The fire chiefs' sorting behavior may be revealing a potential dilemma for the fire chief. On one hand city administrators may be funding the fire service on the basis of their suppression capabilities and not be willing to spend money on public fire education. Yet on the other hand, if the fire chief argues too strongly for funding fire education programs, the city administrators may not give money for it and may cut the budget since the chief is saying he doesn't need new apparatus.

## Subject Category Three

Subject Category Three included the suppressionist fire fighters who participated as respondents in the study. We wanted to determine the extent of support for public fire education among fire fighters whose job function is primarily suppression as well as see how their views might be similar to or different from those of public education officers. We factor analyzed the sorting behavior of 180 suppressionist fire fighters by splitting them into six groups of 30 each. Specifically, the factor analyses of the six sets of suppressionist fire fighters produced six Principal Components Solutions accounting for an average of 54 percent of the total variance in sorting behavior. The six factor solutions yielded an equal number of factors, six, and there were two major factors in each group accounting for an average of 25 percent and 12 percent respectively. The remaining factors accounted for insignificant amounts of variance and resembled the major factor in terms of item placement.

Given that the suppressionist fire fighters broke into clusters representing six different views of public fire education, and that the major cluster accounted for a smaller amount of variance, and that there were significant subsequent factors, indicates that the suppressionists' view of public fire education is more diffused than that of the public fire educators or chiefs. Closer analysis of the sorting behavior indicates that there are two conflicting viewpoints about the role of public fire education in the fire service held by fire fighters who are assigned to truck and engine companies. The majority view is very similar to the view held by public fire educators and fire chiefs. These results may come as a surprise to some public fire educators. However, Table VI clearly indicates the similarity between the groups as it reports the top fifteen and bottom fifteen cards for the suppressionists who comprised the major factor.

There are two key differences in the sorting behavior of the major view of suppressionists as compared to fire educators and chiefs. The first difference is that the suppressionists in the major factor strongly accepted card 48 while the fire educators and fire chiefs did not. Card 48 reads: "It's my belief that a professional fire fighter, even though an amateur educator, is the best person to teach children about fire." What we believe this difference means is that suppressionists in the fire house are telling fire educators that they must first be professional fire fighters. Then their specialty or job function can be education. Such a view has been expressed many times in the past with respect to rescue squads. The second key difference concerns dollars and cents. The suppressionists do not want

### Table 6

|  | Suppression | Inspection | Public Education |
|---|---|---|---|
| **Dramatic Structure** |  |  |  |
| Plot Line | 1 (2nd) | 21 (9th) | 41 (11th) |
| Hero. | 2 | 22 (48th) | 42 |
| Villain. | 3 | 23 | 43 |
| Scene. | 4 | 24 (52nd) | 44 (53rd) |
| Cause (reality link). | 5 | 25 (50th) | 45 |
| **Attributes of Fire Educator** |  |  |  |
| Can educator be non-firefighter. | 6 | 26 (59th) | 46 (57th) |
| Responsibility to fire education. | 7 (54th) | 27 | 47 (56th) |
| Role mix of firefighter/educator. | 8 ( 8th) | 28 | 48 ( 6th) |
| Time commitment in fire education. | 9 (55th) | 29 (46th) | 49 (51st) |
| Skills/knowledge level of fire education. | 10 | 30 | 50 |
| Motive. | 11 | 31 (49th) | 51 (47th) |
| **Persona of Fire Education Program** |  |  |  |
| Education, Does it make a difference. | 12 | 32 (58th) | 52 |
| Fire Education contributes to fire service image. | 13 | 33 (10th) | 53 |
| Priority choice; fire education vs. equipment. | 14 ( 1st) | 34 ( 4th) | 54 (60th) |
| What is public fire education. | 15 | 35 ( 3rd) | 55 (14th) |
| How do you measure program's effectiveness. | 16 | 36 | 56 |
| **Support for Fire Education Program** |  |  |  |
| City administrator. | 17 (12th) | 37 | 57 |
| Chief's view. | 18 | 38 (13th) | 58 ( 5th) |
| Public's view. | 19 ( 7th) | 39 | 59 |
| View of federal campaign on fire education. | 20 | 40 | 60 (15th) |

public education to become the top priority in the budget. They clearly reject card 54.

The second factor, representing the minority viewpoint of the suppressionist fire fighters, is clearly different than the views expressed by the majority of public educators, chiefs, and suppressionists. The sorting behavior of these fire fighters indicates that they soundly reject public fire education as a primary means for directly reducing the loss of life and property. Table VI reports the fifteen most strongly accepted cards and the fifteen most strongly rejected cards for the respondents loading highest on the factor their sorting behavior represents.

The minority suppressionist view is exemplified by the two cards receiving the greatest approval. Cards 14 and 1 read as follows: "I've always supported fire education programs, but not at the expense of needed equipment"; and "Fire education is important, but the greatest impact on lives and on property is an efficient, well-funded, proficient fire fighting force." Two more cards (33 and 8) that receive strong support read: "The public's image of a fire fighter is dependent on how well we fight fires. If fire education helps to improve our basic fire fighter image, then it's okay"; and "It's my belief that professional fire fighters should stick to fighting fires and professional educators should instruct the students about fire."

This minority view as held by suppression fire fighters dramatizes a conception of the fire service in which suppression is the primary if not the only function of the service and clearly public fire education is little more than public relations. However, these fire fighters are only the vocal minority. The vast majority of fire service personnel regard public fire education as a major function of the fire service that should receive increasing emphasis.

A second question that we sought to answer was, "What are the identifying characteristics of a public fire educator and how are these characteristics like or not like the characteristics of others in the fire service?" To answer this question we performed two tasks, one which was analytical and the other which was quantitative.

From the first task, intensive interview case studies of public fire educators, we discovered a truly dedicated professional. Interviewees indicated an unusually strong commitment to the welfare of their fellow man and a deep concern for their fellow fire fighters who risk their lives daily. They all truly believe that education of the public is a primary key to drastically reducing the tragedies that they had witnessed as lives and property were destroyed by fire. Most of the case studies revealed a critical incident that seemed to provide an intense inner feeling which motivated these individuals to work long and exhausting hours in the education of the public. Sometimes this critical incident was religious in nature and the public fire educator's religious beliefs and professional beliefs fused and became one and were focused at the reduction of fire. In other cases, the educators had been working as suppressionist fire fighters and had seen one too many charred babies and had vowed to do something to prevent it. Still other cases occurred off the fire ground, but were related to fire, such as a nurse observing the many hundreds of burn victims that passed through her ward. A reading of these case histories was very emotionally impactful for the researchers. It left us with a new appreciation of the dedication of America's public fire educators.

While the case studies provide us with rich descriptions of public fire educators, it is difficult to predict what characteristics might distinguish public fire educators from other fire fighters. Furthermore, our problem was complicated by the fact that many public fire educators also work as inspectors and suppression fire fighters. In order to get two categories of fire fighters, those who are public fire educators and those who are not, we chose to divide our sample of 360 into two categories based upon how they sorted the Q-deck. Those whose sorting behavior most closely resembled the idealized view of public fire education were put in one category called "public fire educators" and those whose sorting behavior was random, or centering on a suppression idealized view were put in a second category, "non-public fire educators."

We then compared these two groups on the basis of the 14 demographic questions and the scores each subject made on the two creativity tests. The statistical procedure we used for this comparison was Discriminant Analysis. Specifically, we conducted both a direct and a stepwise discriminant analysis on these two groups using the 16 characteristics. The results of these discriminant analyses indicated that four variables clustered together to form one discriminant function (indicator) that would distinguish in 77 cases out of 100 a public fire educator. The four variables were: Years of formal education; the existence of photography or art as a hobby; and high scores on each of the two creativity tests. Subjects who sorted the Q-deck in a manner that depicted the idealized view of public fire education made scores on the two creativity tests that exceed the standardized national norms for those tests (as set by college sophomores). They also checked *yes* to the question that asked them if photography or art was their hobby. Finally, the more college education they had, the more likely they were to be in the public fire education category. So, seven out of ten times, if fire service personnel had some college education, had photography or art as a hobby, and scored high on these creativity tests, they would have a positive view of public fire education. These results do seem sensible given the duties of a public fire education officer. The two creativity tests tend to stress artistic creativity, or those creative skills that are closely related to the preparing of educational materials. Also, most of the major public fire education programs are marked by their creative and inventive artistry. Thus, one would expect public fire education officers to score well on these tests. Certainly, photography and art training are supportive skills for a public fire education officer and formal college training would be an asset in developing lesson plans for grade schools and high schools.

# Conclusions

There is a broad base of support and agreement that public fire education is an important fire service function which if properly executed can reduce losses in life and property due to fire. This support cuts across job functions, ranks, and paid and volunteer fire departments. The only qualification to this support is that public fire education must be a part of the fire service and that a person functioning as a public fire educator must first regard his or her self as a professional fire fighter. This is not to say that the research shows that fire fighters will not tolerate interested and dedicated people from other professions in assisting them in public fire education. It is to say that the research indicates that the public fire education function is part of the fire service and the major personnel and repsonsibilities should come from the service.

Although the majority of fire fighters understand and support fire education, many of them are concerned about its potential deleterious effect on other job functions in the service. The fire chiefs worry that city administrators may simply transfer suppression dollars to public education and thus reduce the total impact of their departments. However, fire chiefs and the majority of fire fighters are willing to increase the empahsis and priority given to public fire education. This means that the NFPCA should be able to count on support and leadership of local fire departments in a national effort to educate the people about fire safety.

The research does reveal that there is a distinct minority of fire fighters who view public fire education as ony a public relations function that supports the image of the fire services' suppression efforts. Such fire fighters do not think that educational efforts will really be successful in reducing the loss of life and property due to fire. Therefore, they are opposed to any large expenditure of money or time commitment on the part of suppression fire fighters to public education. This inability to see value that goes beyond public relations is intensified for them if public education were to successfully compete for dollars within the departmental budget, and thus reduce expenditures on the suppression, rescue, and inspection efforts.

The research indicates that it is possible to distinguish salient characteristics of public fire educators. Since there has been no previous research that focused on this issue as a research objective, we can only summarize the results of our study. Our results indicate that there are at least four characteristics that tend to give definition to the uniqueness of the public fire educator as compared to other people. Of course, we cannot say that formal education, photography or art as a hobby and high scores on each of two creativity tests cause people to become public fire educators. We can say that people who hold a view of public fire education that is idealized tend to in seven out of ten instances have these four attributes. Furthermore, we can say that in an effort to select public fire education officers the presence of these four characteristics would be one important indicator in the selection process.

The final characteristic that permeated the case histories of public fire educators was an almost zealot determination to educate the citizens in their communities about fire safety and to witness a measureable reduction in loss of property and life due to their efforts. The motivation behind this dedication seemed to come from some critical incident or incidences which they had witnessed first hand. Usually, these instances were tragic and needless losses of human life due to fire.

In general terms this research unfolds a scene in which public fire educators (regardless of whatever other job functions they may perform) hold a clear and well understood definition of the role of public fire education in the fire service. Their definition gives clarity to the view held by most fire fighters. Furthermore, the research supports the assertion that there are attributes that tend to characterize public fire educators.

# 14

# The St. Paul Fire Fighters'
## *Dramatis Personae:*
### Concurrent and Construct Validation
### for the Theory of Rhetorical Vision

DONALD C. SHIELDS

This study grew out of two concerns: one heuristic and one practical. The practical concern stemmed from the problem facing the fire service in the early 1970's. Fire fighters serve the public and depend upon the public for monetary support and recognition. In the mid-1960's, when faced with decreasing public support and falling morale, the fire service met the challenge. They instituted internal changes, made a conscious rhetorical attempt to alert the rank-and-file to the importance of a beneficial public character, and encouraged fire fighters to professionalize and departments to engage in image management through public relations programs that emphasized the fire fighters' persona. In so doing, a body of thought and materials emerged containing the fire service's rhetorical vision regarding the fire fighters' dramatis persona, including their self-persona and projected-persona.

The heuristic concern grew out of the need to make an empirical contribution to rhetorical theory and the communication concept of rhetorical vision. A study was needed to design and validate a method for capturing empirically character elements within a rhetorical vision. If a means to capture empirically the symbolic reality of a collectivity could be developed, this would eliminate the possibility that a critic's personal re-creation of a vision is more a product of the critic's mind than the social reality of the collectivity being studied.

## Purpose

Five purposes spurred this research: (1) to find out via analysis of Q-sort behavior if fire fighters get caught up in character aspects of the rhetorical vision found in the speeches, articles, and small group communication of fire fighters; (2) to describe the fire fighters' self-persona and projected-persona as depicted in the Q-sort behavior of St. Paul, Minnesota, fire fighters; (3) to ascertain the efficacy of a constructed Q-sort for capturing character elements of a rhetorical vision; (4) to present the public's Q-sort depiction of the fire fighters' dramatis persona; and (5) to determine the concurrent and construct validity of the Q-sort testing instrument.

# Method

The concepts of small group fantasy chaining, rhetorical vision, and factor analysis as embodied in Q-technique underlie the method. To clarify the method and show the research in which it is grounded, I discuss each key concept in detail.

### Small Group Fantasy Chaining

Robert F. Bales, working with small group communication at Harvard University, developed a twelve-category system for content analyzing the process of group communication.[1] After some twenty years of working with the category system, Bales reported a change in one category, renaming "shows tension release" to "dramatizes."[2] Bales noted that a group member's dramatizations often have meaning for others in the group. Other members, picking up on the theme or drama, begin to participate, adding their own elements and embellishments, fostering a "chain reaction of associations" and creating a "group fantasy event."[3] Such moments of chaining are characterized by an increased rate of group conversation, group members getting excited, interrupting one another, laughing and forgetting any self-consciousness. During such moments group members often rhetorically dramatize events, and a world filled with heroes, villains, saints and enemies emerges as a common culture is created and celebrated.[4] According to Bales, such group fantasy events provide great impact for the group members. He notes that the members' "feelings fuse with the symbols and images which carry the feeling in communication and sustain it over time."[5]

---

[1]Robert F. Bales, *Interaction Process Analysis, A Method for the Study of Small Groups* (Reading, Mass: Addison-Wesley Publishing Company, Inc., 1950).
[2]Robert F. Bales, *Personality and Interpersonal Behavior* (New York: Holt, Rinehart and Winston, 1970), see especially Chapter 7, "Describing Fantasy Themes," 136-159.
[3]Bales, *Personality,* 138.
[4]Bales, *Personality,* 151-152.
[5]Bales, *Personality*, 152.

To understand the symbolic reality and culture of a particular group, the researcher need only analyze the moments of group fantasy chaining.[6] To assist in understanding the fire fighters' perception of their dramatis persona, I took the audio tape recordings of small groups of fire fighters communicating about themselves and submitted the recordings to fantasy theme analysis.

## Rhetorical Vision

After observing fantasy events in small group interaction and studying the rhetoric of persuasive religious, social, and political campaigns, Ernest G. Bormann of the University of Minnesota concluded that what occurs in small groups is analogous to the development of persuasive rhetorical positions in larger communities. In his article, "Fantasy the Rhetorical Vision: The Rhetorical Criticism of Social Reality," Bormann argued that fantasy chain analysis provides explanatory power to account for the development, evolution, and decay of dramas that catch up large groups of people and change their behavior.[7] For Bormann, "a rhetorical movement contains small group fantasy chains, public fantasy events, and a rhetorical vision in a complex and reciprocal set of relationships."[8] These relationships allow a small group of people to discuss a common preoccupation or problem, dramatize a theme or themes, create excitement, involvement, the chaining of more dramas, and thereby create "a common symbolic reality filled with heroes and villains."[9] Bormann gave the name "rhetorical vision" to "the composite dramas which catch up large groups of people into a symbolic reality."[10] The uniqueness of the construct of rhetorical vision stems from its power to contain and thereby reflect the feelings, values, and the goals of the people whose social reality the vision conveys. Consequently, a rhetorical critic can look at the rhetorical vision of a collectivity to understand what events provide meaning for the vision's adherents, the emotions which the vision is likely to evoke, and the particular motives which are likely to inspire a people to action.[11] To view meanings, emotions, and motives "as embedded in the rhetorical vision rather than hidden in the skulls and viscera of people makes it possible to check the critic's insights by going directly to the rhetoric rather than relying

---

[6]Group members' heightened verbal and para-linguistic involvement serves as a behavioral index that fantasy chaining is present. The capacity of behavioral identification makes group dramatization and fantasy chaining a viable and important research tool. Moments in group interaction when fantasy chains occur attest to the salience of a particular subject theme for the group.

[7]Ernest G. Bormann, "Fantasy and Rhetorical Vision: The Rhetorical Criticism of Social Reality," *Quarterly Journal of Speech,* 58, 4 (December, 1972), 396-407.

[8]Bormann, 399.

[9]Bormann, 399.

[10]Bormann, 398.

[11]Bormann, 396-407.

on inferences about psychological entities unavailable for analysis."[12]

In short, rhetorical visions are important because they depict a drama that catches up large numbers of people providing impetus and direction for their actions. There are several key elements to the concept of rhetorical vision, including the *characters* or dramatis personae with the vision; the *scenarios* or plot and action lines accentuated by the vision; and the *scene* or arena within which the vision's action takes place.[13] To capture and understand rhetorical visions, Bormann suggests the fantasy theme analysis of collectivity's discourse to identify key characters, recognize scenarios, and determine the elements of the scene.[14] The fantasy theme analysis of discourse provides sufficient information to capture critically and recreate artistically a collectivity's rhetorical visions.

### Factor Analysis and Q-Technique

Factor analysis as embodied in Q-technique is most closely associated with William Stephenson and his research at the University of Missouri. His book, *The Study of Behavior, Q-Technique and Its Methodology,* published in 1953, synthesizes the knowledge of some twenty-five years of working with the methodology.[15] Q-technique is a set of procedures used in testing persons' subjective orientation to a behavioral dimension. Data is gathered and processed as follows: respondents sort stimuli such as words, photographic, or statements into a forced-choice fixed distribution, approximating a normal curve, along some specific dimension—for example, from agree to disagree. In essence, Q-technique is a sophisticated form of rank ordering objects and finding rank order coefficients of correlation between all possible pairs of rankers. The analysis correlates persons, not tests. Then, persons who rank the objects similarly are objectively and mathematically defined as factors or *types.*[16]

[12]Bormann, 407.

[13]Ernest G. Bormann, "The Eagleton Affair: A Fantasy Theme Analysis," *Quarterly Journal of Speech,* 59, 2 (April, 1973), 143-159.

[14]See Bormann, "The Eagleton Affair," and Bormann, "Fantasy and Rhetorical Vision."

[15]William Stephenson, *The Study of Behavior: Q-Technique and Its Methodology* (Chicago: University of Chicago Press, 1953).

[16]Stephenson posits a set of statistical, philosophy of science, and common sense arguments for replacing the traditional canons of empiricism, namely large sample technique and concept measurement, with Q-technique, a methodology enabling the researcher to draw inferences from small samples, see any person as the subject of detailed factor and variance analysis, and to make correlations between people, not test scores. For Stephenson, Q-technique overcomes one of the classic indictments of measurement studies—that variations cancel out one another with the result that data fails to provide knowledge of a number of people's attitudes and instead provides only the mean attitude. Of course, there are statistical methods in large scale descriptive statistics which overcome this criticism, but as Stephenson elegantly argues, at the base of each of these is really Q-technique. See Stephenson, Part 1.

Q-technique appears to have excellent potential for capturing empirically the rhetorical vision of a collectivity.[17] In Q-technique the needs of the study dictate the sample stimuli.[18] Thus, with this method the material to be sorted may easily consist of the prevalent fantasy themes of a rhetorical vision. Q-technique requires subjects to respond to a large number of items at the same time so that a person's feeling about a particular item will influence his response to another. The fact that each test item interacts with every other increases the power of the respective findings. Finally, when persons are correlated within the data analysis, their sorting behavior compared to each other, and composite factors or types of persons are generated, the resulting types are analogous to the creation of a photographic negative. Once the negative of one person is superimposed over the negative of another the print develops a composite picture. In like manner, Q-analysis provides an array of statements which is the composite representation of the essence of the factor or type.[19] Since in the present study every Q-statement depicts a fantasy theme relevant to the fire fighters' dramatis persona, the factor-arrays provide the composite idealized representation of that persona. In essence, the factor arrays will show how the individuals who comprise a particular *type* react to the fantasy theme statements. The factor array will indicate which statements the individuals

---

[17]The versatility of Q-technique can be seen in the variety of its applications. See for example: Stephenson, *Study of Behavior; Communication*, ed. by William D. Brooks and Philip Emmert (Boston: Houghton Mifflin Co., 1970), 165-180; Fred N. Kerlinger, *Foundations of Behavioral Research* (New York: Holt, Rinehart and Winston, Inc., 1964), 581-599; Mary Jane Schlinger, "Cues on Q-Technique," *Journal of Advertising Research,* 9, 3 (September, 1969), 53-60; Steven R. Brown and Donald J. Brenner, eds., *Science, Psychology, and Communication: Essays Honoring William Stephenson* (New York: Teachers College Press, 1972); and Raymond B. Cattell, "Meaning and Strategic Use of Factor Analysis," in *Handbook of Multivariate Experimental Psychology* (Chicago: Rand McNally and Company, 1966), 174-243.

A complete review of every use of Q-technique would be of little benefit for this statement of the method's utility. Rather, a feeling for the broad adaptability of the method will suffice. See for example: Schlinger, "Cues," 53-60; David L. Rarick, "Expressed Preference and Desirability Judgments of Parents and their Children for Eighteen Types of Television Violence" (unpublished Ph.D. dissertation, The Ohio State University, 1970); David L. Rarick, Douglas Boyd, and James Townsend, "Television Viewing and Juvenile Attitudes Toward Police" (paper presented at the Speech Commnication Association, San Francisco, 1972); Donald J. Brenner, "Dynamics of Public Opinion on the Vietnam War," in Brown and Brenner, 345-380; and Rosalind Dymond Cartwright, "The Q-Method and the Intrapersonal World," in Brown and Brenner, 172-199.

[18]Such a criterion appears essential for any empirical testing of the construct of rhetorical vision, i.e., elements of the vision — dramatized fantasy themes comprised of characters, scenarios, and scenes — must be capable of inclusion with the testing device.

[19]Stephenson, Study of Behavior, 163. Stephenson explains: "The statements of a $(Q-)$ sample are superimposed, in an analogous manner (to photographic negatives in a composite picture), when we sum their scores to reach the *factor-array* (emphasis Stephenson's) for a factor. The factor consists of the statements, arranged in a certain order that 'shows through'. *All* (emphasis Stephenson's) the statements are involved in a composite photograph." (163).

loading in a particular factor viewed as most resembling the fire fighters' persona (high positive z-scores), least resembling the fire fighters' persona (high negative z-scores), and neutral or uncommitted toward as resembling the fire fighters' persona (near zero z-scores). Q-technique—with its ability to accept statements reflecting verbal depictions of dramatizations and fantasy themes, combined with its ipsative measuring abilities and its capacity for reflecting a montage of the vision—appears ideally suited for capturing a collectivity's rhetorical vision.

## Developing the Instrument

Three kinds of preliminary research were needed to develop the testing instrument. First, in the spring of 1972, I led five to seven fire fighters from each of three station houses in St. Paul, Minnesota in small group communication about their dramatis persona.[20] These open-ended sessions on the topic, "What's it like to be a fire fighter?" lasted for approximately one hour. I began each tape recorded session by relating my view of the fire fighter and asking the men to tell how this view compared to their actual self-perception. From time to time, I asked the fire fighters to react to short dramatized incidents (scenarios) pertaining to their person.[21] For example, I showed them a clipping describing fire fighters rescuing a kitten from the second story of a graystone apartment building. At another point I showed them a news story describing a rescue operation and paramedical tracheotomy with hospital arrival within three minutes. Such scenarios elicited group dramatization and fantasy chaining, as reported in detail in the findings. Subsequent fantasy theme analysis of these tapes generated nearly one hundred content themes concerning attributes of the fire fighters' self-persona and projected-persona. The fact that many of the themes were repetitive across groups suggested that the fire fighters possessed a collective symbolic reality—a rhetorical vision pertaining to their self-persona and their projected-persona.

Phase two occurred in the fall of 1972. Students from the undergraduate speech communication discussion classes at the University of Minnesota interacted in groups for approximately twenty minutes on the subject, "the image or character of the fire fighter." Subsequent fantasy theme analysis of eight such tape recorded sessions generated about sixty themes. The analysis of the students' discussions indicated that even though some students possessed very little impression of fire fighters, every group engaged in dramatizations and fantasy chaining about the fire fighters' persona. The students' depictions of the fire fighters' public-persona gathered from their discussions differed in many respects from the fire

---

[20]The station houses were No. 5, No. 14, and No. 18.

[21]The researcher substituted the word *image* in place of *persona* when describing the study and sorting conditions to fire fighters.

fighters' depictions of their self-persona and projected-persona when they discussed the topic in the fire station.

In phase three of the preliminary research, I conducted a fantasy theme analysis of articles pertaining to the dramatis persona (including image, public character, and persona) of the fire fighter. Of the more than 220 articles I examined, nearly 200 appeared in the professional fire literature of the past twelve years. In my critical analysis, I identified about 500 prevalent fantasy themes and discursive elements concerning the fire fighters' rhetorical vision regarding their dramatis persona and led to the construction of a Q-sort comprised of elements containing dramatic characterizations that reflected that vision.

To construct the Q-sort pertaining to the fire fighters' rhetorical vision concerning their dramatis persona, I transferred the themes generated from the fantasy theme analysis of the professional fire service literature to note cards and clustered the nearly five hundred themes on the basis of their commonality. Using this procedure I reduced the themes to about eighty piles. Then I selected those themes replicated more than five times reducing the number of clusters to about fifty. Then I compared the themes represented by these fifty piles with the themes generated in my fantasy theme analysis of the fire fighters' small group communication. By using this concurrent verification procedure and by arranging the themes to provide both positive and negative characterizations of the fire fighters' persona, I derived my final fifty-six statement Q-sort. To derive the final statements I created artistic dramatizations representing both positive and negative characterizations. Each of the fifty-six statements depicted the fire fighters' persona dramatically engaged in life-like scenarios typical of the occupation. The statements represented dramatized simulations of potentially real situations reflective of the fire fighters' rhetorical vision concerning their dramatis persona. However, the names, characters, and places identified in the Q-sort statements were hypothetical. The following three statements are illustrative of the Q-sort items:

> A neighbor's house catches on fire. The fire fighters arrive within two minutes from the time of the call. Working efficiently they connect the hoses, vent the roof for the heat to escape, and bring the blaze under control and put out the fire almost immediately.

> Fire fighters do many courageous things. Bill Dues crawled through a long hallway filled with smoke to save four people. Bill didn't stop to refill his air tank because he knew the time saved would perhaps mean the difference between saving a life and bringing out a dead body.

> An alarm goes off in the station. The Captain is angry. The truck can't leave until he rounds up half the crew that is down the street getting a Dairy Queen.

Preliminary administrations of the Q-sort indicated that the length of the items and the number of items greatly affected the time necessary to sort the cards. To allow most people to accomplish sorting within sixty minutes, I limited the final Q-sort to fifty-six dramatized statements, each of fifty words or less. The mean length of each statement was thirty-eight words. I used a test-retest situation by one fire fighter and one citizen to determine the Q-sort's reliability.[22] Respectively, their test-retest sorting behavior correlated .95 and .93, providing rather high reliability for the constructed Q-sort.

To facilitate analysis of the data, the themes gathered from the fire literature and small group communication analysis were clustered into common groupings regarding characteristics of the fire fighters' dramatis persona. The ensuing structure coding served to facilitate my later analysis of subject sorting behavior. Two graduate students and one faculty member in speech communication read through the fifty-six statements and clustered them together on the basis of what seemed to them to be related themes. I analyzed their groupings and then applied labels to represent similarly inclusive themes. The labels, typifying the grouped themes, appear under the heading *structure elements* in Table I.[23] Inclusion of positive-negative statements for each of the twenty-eight themes allowed for determining replication of sorting behavior. In other words, I could check those items sorted as *most resemble* against their paired opposite to see if the subjects sorted the latter as *least resemble.*

## Main Study Design

To detail the study's design, I must: (1) discuss the design considerations underlying sample selection; (2) describe the conditions under which subjects sorted the test instrument; and (3) present the design elements utilized in determining the validity of the test instrument.

### Sample Selection

Only St. Paul fire fighters and St. Paul residents served as subjects in the study. St. Paul has nearly 400 fire fighters assigned to any of three shifts (A, B, or C) and one of twenty-four station houses. I randomly selected two station houses representing each shift and administered the Q-sort to on-duty fire fighters. This administration provided a pool of forty-seven fire

[22]To maximize confidence in the derived coefficients, I based sorting comparisons on an ordinal rank order of the fifty-six statements as most resembling or least resembling the fire fighters' persona, rather than using a forced-choice normal distribution and correcting for ties.

[23]My use of the word structure stems from the common sense application and differs from Stephenson's use of the word as related to his concept of theory testing. See Stephenson, *Study of Behavior.*

## Table I

## Q-Sort Structure Elements

| Structure Elements | Themes (both positive and negative characterizations of the fire fighter's persona) |
|---|---|
| Professional fighting force | team man who gets along with others; professional; difficult job requirements; accepts technological advances |
| Public relations | quality of news coverage; dedication to public service; value of public relations; receive public respect |
| Competitive attitudes and conditions | self-centeredness; receive support of public officials; competition with police; compensation |
| Ghetto-minority relations | harassment; hiring discrimination; equal service; false alarms |
| Motivations for being a fire fighter | hazardous — safe job; thrill — no fun; full day's work — soft job |
| Neutral items | (no positive or negative loadings) little knowledge of fire fighters; don't think of fire fighters; just like the next guy; similar to other work groups |
| Competency of the fire fighter | dependable; speedy and efficient; careful with property; courageous |
| Personality qualities of the fire fighter | courteousness; nice guys; compassionate |

fighters.[24] Maintaining the integrity of the three shift, six house design and using a table of random numbers, I selected thirty-two fire fighters from this pool.[25] Table II illustrates this random selection.

### Table II

### Distribution of Fire Fighters by Station and Shift

| | Station House | Respective FF's from each Station House | Sub-total |
|---|---|---|---|
| Shift A | #6 & #4 | 6 & 6 | 12 |
| Shift B | #22 & #20 | 5 & 5 | 10 |
| Shift C | #18 & #8 | 5 & 5 | 10 |
| | | | Total 32 = N |

The public participants included members of the St. Paul City Council, St. Paul Police Department, St. Paul news services, and white collar employees of six large St. Paul business firms including two banks, two insurance companies, and two manufacturing companies. In all, I administered the Q-sort to forty-five public participants. Taking a minimum of two subjects from each of the above listed organizations, I randomly selected from this pool of forty-five and thirty-two subjects included in the main study. The white collar working residents and public functionaries presented a mixture of ages, sexes, ethnic groups, and educational backgrounds. The selective nature of the public sample made them more likely than a random sample to be knowledgeable of fire fighters. I felt the selective sample, although perhaps not generalizable to the St. Paul community as a whole, possessed special import for the St. Paul fire service. After all, the sample included important functionaries necessary to the smooth functioning of the fire service, per se, as well as the fire service's public relations efforts, and included a calibre of private citizens more likely than the average, because of their education, to be knowledgeable of the fire service. I administered the Q-sort to five to seven public participants at a time,

[24]Although the formal study involved forty-seven fire fighters, nearly twice that number helped me with various facets of the research. For example, eighteen fire fighters participated in the preliminary research on group fantasy chaining and fourteen others discussed their persona in additional group tapes. Also, six administrative personnel reacted to various facets of the study. In all, more than eighty fire service personnel representing fire fighters from all shifts, and half the station houses participated.

[25]In factor analysis, the number of observations should exceed the number of variables. For Q-analysis, the Q-statements are treated as observations and the respondents are treated as variables. Thus precautions were taken to ensure that the number of Q-statements exceeded the number of participants in the study. No set formula for computing the ration of Q-statements to subjects exists, although several guide lines are provided by Roywood Cattell. For this study, the ratio of seven-to-four was selected. Since the number of Q-statements was fifty-six, the number of persons in each factor analysis group was set at thirty-two. For a specific statement of Cattell's guidelines, see Cattell, 174-243.

except for the news reporters and council persons who completed the Q-sort through individual appointments. All of the forty-five public respondents completed the Q-sort during their regular working hours. Table III presents the public sample in table form.

### Table III

### Make-Up of the Public Sample

| City Council | Police | Reporters | Bus. 1 & 2 | Bus. 3 & 4 | Bus. 5 & 6 |
|---|---|---|---|---|---|
| 6 | 6 | 4 | 4 | 5 | 6 |

N = 32

**Sorting Conditions**

Respondents placed the statements in a quasi-normal distribution along a continuum of *least resemble* fire fighters to *most resemble* fire fighters. Table IV illustrates the distribution.

### Table IV

### Quasi-Normal Distribution

|  | Least Resemble | | | | Neutral | | Most Resemble | | |
|---|---|---|---|---|---|---|---|---|---|
| No. of items in pile: | 2 | 4 | 6 | 9 | 14 | 9 | 6 | 4 | 2 |
| Pile number: | 1 | 2 | 3 | 4 | 5 | 6 | 7 | 8 | 9 |

Fire fighters sorted the fifty-six statements twice — first, pertaining to the way they see themselves (i.e., their self-persona) and second, pertaining to the way they believe the public views them (i.e., their projected persona). Public participants sorted under just one condition, pertaining to the way they see the fire fighter (i.e., public-persona). Interpretation of the factor analysis of the sorting data would tell me if the fire fighters indeed have a common rhetorical vision pertaining to their dramatis persona. Similarly, the data from the public's sorting would tell me their view of the fire fighters. Finally, a comparison of the sorting behavior of fire fighters and public groups would indicate similarities and differences in attributes of the fire fighters' self-persona, projected-persona, and public-persona.

Data from the above sorting conditions was analyzed by: (1) correlating the sorting behavior of individual persons; (2) principal factor extraction of persons with like sorting behavior; (3) rotation of the principal components solution to simple or best solution; (4) objective determination of factor Q-arrays based on descending z-scores; and (5) comparing high, neutral, and low ranked items across person-types. In this latter stage, *most resemble* items are those appearing in the middle half of a Q-array.

**Designing for Validity**

A simple design consideration enabled a determination of the concurrent and construct validity of the Q-sort. The preliminary fantasy theme analysis of the professional fire literature, coupled with the fantasy theme analysis of fire fighters engaging in small group communication about their persona provided data to ascertain whether or not the test instrument demonstrated concurrent validity. If the three methods converged on similar fantasy themes regarding the fire fighters' persona, such findings would provide evidence of the concurrent validity of the Q-sort data and indicate that I had successfully measured facets of the rhetorical vision construct.

To provide for a determination of the Q-sort's construct validity, I grouped my thirty-two fire fighter subjects and thirty-two citizens in such a way that one group contained sixteen fire fighters and sixteen private citizens; the other group contained sixteen fire fighters and sixteen St. Paul functionaries, including members of the City Council, Police Department, and news services. Table V illustrates this grouping process.

### Table V

### Sample Design for Construct Validity

|  | Shift-A | Shift-B | Shift-C | City Council | Police | Reporters |
|---|---|---|---|---|---|---|
| Group 1 N = 32 | 6 | 5 | 5 | 6 | 6 | 4 |

|  | | | | Business: 1 & 2 | 3 & 4 | 5 & 6 |
|---|---|---|---|---|---|---|
| Group 2 N = 32 | 6 | 5 | 5 | 6 | 6 | 4 |

I felt I could compare the sorting behavior of the two groups to make an assessment of the Q-sort's construct validity. To help in this assessment, I computed Spearmen Rank-Order Coefficients of Correlation between the typal arrays from the factor analysis of the sorting behavior for Group 1 and Group 2.[26] The discovery of similar solutions accounting for significant variance would indicate the Q-sort's construct validity and show that I was consistently measuring the entity of rhetorical vision regarding the fire fighters' dramatis persona.

[26]William L. Hayes, *Statistics* (New York: Holt, Rinehart and Winston, 1963), 643-647. The degree to which the extracted factor solutions provide a similar number of highly correlated factors should help to confirm or deny the existence of construct validity.

# Findings

Findings emerged in five areas: (1) empirical findings from the factor analysis of the fire fighters' reactions to the Q-sort dramatizations; (2) fantasy theme analysis findings derived from the fire literature; (3) fantasy theme analysis findings derived from the fire fighters' small group communication; (4) findings pertaining to concurrent validity and (5) findings pertaining to construct validity.

## Fire Fighters' Self-Persona

The quantitative analysis of thirty-two fire fighters' self-persona sorting behavior extracted three factors for the principal components solution. Factor 1 dominated, accounting for sixty percent of the variance in sorting behavior. The extraction of only three factors, the dominance of the first factor, the minimal influence of the second and third factors in the principal components solution, and the high correlation among the types — .748 to .876 — suggested that the fire fighters possessed a consistent vision of their dramatic self-persona. The Q-arrays derived from the three factors portray a persona with highly favorable characteristics. Overall, the fire fighters' sorting behavior in the self-persona sorting condition evidenced high self-esteem. The self-persona depicted by these fire fighters was definitely a heroic character. Average z-scores of forty-four of the fifty-six dramatizations varied by less than 1.0 standard deviation across types. These forty-four consensus items clarified the fire fighters' vision concerning their self-persona.

Based on the consensus array, these fire fighters depicted their self-persona as: speedy and efficient, engaging in a hazardous job, a professional involved in study and training, accepting of new job tasks like para-medical and ambulance service, putting in a full day including training and inspections, dependable, compassionate, appreciating and often receiving public recognition, carefully holding water and property damage to a minimum, a team man, helping to improve fire technology through research and innovation, dedicated as he helps in safety programs and gives public relations talks, courteous, and seeing value in public relations activities.

The fire fighters rejected dramatizations portraying their self-persona as: afraid to fight a big fire without help, undependable, having a safe job that is less dangerous than coal mining or police work, providing unequal service to the ghetto, slow and inefficient, working in a soft job where he plays checkers, sleeps, watches TV, and even moonlights, refusing to hire minorities, failing to accept new fire fighting methods, viewing public relations activities as worthless, uncompassionate, welcoming false alarms as a break in the day's routine, nice guys turning on hydrants for children in the neighborhood, a person they never think of, a moderately skilled person, and the recipient of unlimited support from city officials.

Finally, the consensus items show that the fire fighters expressed little commitment for statements portraying their self-persona as: everyone's friend, bothered by false alarms, receiving protection from policemen when needed, rescuing kittens in the neighborhood, recipient of good television and newspaper coverage, making special efforts to help employ minorities, losing respect and pay due to the public's concern for law and order, recipient of complaints about damage and service, unsupported by public officials, having the same problems as any worker, a person they never think of, never the object of news reporting, recipient of public harassment, and unable to get along with other fire fighters.

## Fire Fighters' Projected Persona

The above portrayal of the fire fighters' self-persona differed markedly from their portrayal of their projected-persona. In the projected-persona sorting condition, the fire fighters exhibited inconsistent sorting behavior. Factor analysis of the correlation matrix failed to converge with ten as the factor limit in the principal components solution because of the bi-polar nature of several factors and the program's ability to convert such bi-polar factors into additional types. When limited to six factors in the principal components solution, the Quanal program formed nine types. No single factor accounted for as much as one-fifth of the variance in sorting behavior. Four of the factors accounted for less than ten percent of the variance. The entire solution accounted for only 54.55 percent of the variance in sorting behavior. Such low percentages in total variance, coupled with the multiple factor nature of the principal components solution, suggested that the fire fighters possessed a diffused view of their projected-persona and lacked agreement as to how the public viewed the fire fighter. The correlations between the nine types substantiated this conclusion. Of thirty-six possible correlations, only seven reached the .50 level and none attained the .70 level. Conversely, twenty-nine fell below .50, twenty-two fell short of .30, and fourteen correlations failed to reach the .20 level. Such low correlations, coupled with the existence of only two consensus items across types, confirmed the diffused nature of the fire fighters' sorting behavior regarding their projected-persona.

Nevertheless, the Q-arrays evolved from the six factors had one thing in common. The projected-persona depicted by most of the fire fighters, if not a villain, was definitely a negative character. The initial structure of positive and negative ratings assigned to the fifty-six dramatizations supported this point. Negative dramatizations dominated the *most resemble* depictions and positive dramatizations dominated the *least resemble* portion of the Q-array for seven of the nine types, representing the sorting behavior of twenty-five of the thirty-two fire fighters.

A typical type portrayed the fire fighters' projected-persona as: having a soft job, careless, well compensated, undependable, unskilled with no college, meeting easy job qualification standards, having a safer job than coal miners or policemen, taken for granted, slow and inefficient, using qualification standards to discriminate in hiring, preferring the axe and hose to new fire fighting methods, and working in an occupation the public doesn't know about. The fire fighters seem to accept the old stereotype and believe the public thinks ill of them.

**Fire Fighters' Public-Persona**

The quantitative analysis of the thirty-two citizens' sorting behavior extracted six factors for the principal components solution. The findings indicated a strong, although not dominant, initial factor complemented by five additional factors, three of which accounted for less than five percent of the variance in the respondents' sorting behavior. Five of the six factors correlated above .653 with Type 1, adding to the strength of the initial factor. The Q-arrays evolved from the six factors detailed characteristics depicting the fire fighters' public-persona in a generally favorable light. The initial structure of positive and negative ratings assigned to the fifty-six dramatizations supported this point. Positive items dominated the *most resemble* segments of the public's Q-arrays and negative dramatizations dominated the *least resemble* portions.

Even though the typal characteristics attributed to the fire fighters' public-persona provided a generally positive assessment, the seven typal arrays described somewhat different personae. Three points verified such a conclusion: (1) the disparity among the correlations between the types—ranging from .346 to .897; (2) the moderate number of consensus items across types—only eleven; and (3) the variation in z-scores and rankings for elements of the proposed analytic structure—the public lacked agreement as to specific characterizations regarding the structure elements.

The private citizens, council persons, policemen, and reporters loaded highest throughout the types. No one group among the functionaries appeared responsible for a particular typal description.

The Type 1 public subjects depicted the fire fighter as: courageous, speedy and efficient, providing equal service for all, putting in a full day including training and inspections, professionals engaging in a hazardous job, accepting of new job tasks, compassionate, a nice guy helping in the neighborhood, courteous, and a team man working well with others. These citizens rejected dramatizations depicting the fire fighter as: undependable, afraid to fight a big fire, slow and inefficient, using qualifications standards to bar minorities, failing to adopt new fire fighting methods, providing unequal service to the ghetto, having a soft job, meeting easy job qualification standards, careless, welcoming the break in routine from false alarms, not a team man, lacking dedication and discourteous.

**Fire Literature Findings**

When I began reading the professional fire literature, one fact struck me immediately. Fire fighters picture themselves in dramatic terms. Editorialist after editorialist vividly portrayed the heroic fire fighter persona. For one, he is "a real smoke eater,"[27] for another, "a member of a courageous band of men,"[28] and in eulogy, he's a "man who died with his boots on."[29] But the dramatic metaphor encompasses more than the persona. For example, John H. Poelker, former Comptroller of the City of St. Louis, Missouri, cast the fire fighter persona into the limelight and described, "the part he is playing in the local government drama."[30] In a similar vein, Richard Bland, Chairman of the National Commission of Fire Prevention and Control, spoke to the International Association of Fire Chiefs' Ninety-ninth Conference offering the thesis that "what the American fire service needs is a dream."[31]

If the 200 articles I surveyed are any indication, the fire service has a dream — indeed, a rhetorical vision filled with heroes, villains, scenarios, scenes, sanctioning agents, supporting players, and reality links to the cultural milieu impacting on the vision.

## Overview of the Vision

In reading the professional fire literature, one becomes immediately aware of the special role that the public plays within the rhetorical vision. Whether fire fighters are praising or placing blame, the public receives special recognition. In one drama, the fire fighters portray the public as apathetic, uncaring, and even ignorant of the fire service. About the most the public ever does is take the fire fighter for granted, or as one fire chief wrote, "for granite (sic)."[32] In another drama, the public can make or break the fire service. The public provides monetary support and human recognition — key elements in maintaining high morale and building self-esteem. With public support officials take notice of the fire service and legislators become receptive to the passage of favorable legislation.

Since the public receives such an important place in the vision, it should come as no surprise that *public relations* and *good public image* are god-terms for fire fighters. Public relations activities are the means to an end, the road to salvation, and the way to expiate past sins all rolled into one. One chief called a good public relations program "the answer to most of our difficulties" and defined "good" operationally in this way:

[27]Anne Wright Phillips, "Are We Playing With Fire?" *International Fire Fighter,* 38, 9 (October-November, 1972), 20-21.

[28]Richard Nixon, letter to Mrs. Michael T. Carr, reprinted in *International Fire Fighter* (January, 1970), no pagination.

[29]"Newspaper Series Praises Role of Fire Fighter," *International Fire Fighter* (August, 1969), 6.

[30]John H. Poelker, "The Image of the Fire Fighter...Is It Changing?" *International Fire Chief* (November, 1970), 3-5.

[31]Richard E. Bland, "I.A.F.C.— Innovation, Activity, Focus, Concern," address to the International Association of Fire Chiefs, Ninety-ninth Conference, Cleveland, Ohio. Printed in *International Fire Chief* (October-November, 1972), 10-11.

[32]Bland, *Fire Chief,* 10.

The public should see the fireman out inspecting buildings, giving talks, escorting taxpayers and children through the department, and out practicing as well as see them when they are actually out on a call or when they are sitting around the firehouse.[33]

The President of the International Association of Firemen characterized the importance of public relations another way:

Public relations is a basic, vital part of all the activities of your local union. It is part and parcel of the process of collective bargaining, legislation, and local referendums. It is involved in your dealings with public administrators, including your Chief and City Manager; certainly, it is part of your fight against consolidation and/or disparity in pay. It is most important as it has a direct bearing in your relationship with the citizens, voters and taxpayers of your community."[34]

Similarly, the *International Fire Fighter* in an article entitled, "Do You Want More Wages and Improved Conditions?" stressed the fire fighters' public relations responsibility and called for active support of a particular program:

Where do better wages, hours and working conditions begin? With you...(sic) the rank-and-file fire fighter! Everyday brings new opportunities for you to impress the public and legislators with the importance of your job as a professional fire fighter. How do you do it? You obtain pictures of fire fighters in action (with the details) and send them to International Headquarters. There they can be used in your behalf... (sic) from publication on these pages to special displays for legislators. But the initial effort is up to you.[35]

Just as the vision clearly emphasizes the importance of public relations programs, so too, it identifies the proper fire service image. The vision places great emphasis on the fire fighter as dramatis persona.

The fire fighter's persona, depending upon the particular drama one emphasizes, possesses a heroic character and a villainous character. Labels are important, and what a fire fighter calls himself is a key to whether the vision depicts him as a saint or a sinner. In June, 1968, *International Fire Fighter* flashed the story headline: "There is Not a 'Fireman' in the IAFF; Every One of Them Is a 'Fire Fighter'." The article contains the IAFF's reasoning:

The English dictionary has two definitions for the word 'fireman': (1) one who aids in extinguishing fires and (2) a fire-tender, as on a locomotive; a stoker.

---

[33]Raymond L. Bancroft, *Municipal Fire Service Trends: 1972* (Washington, D.C.: National League of Cities Research Report, 1972), 40.
[34]Howard McClennan, "Public Relations—365 Days A Year," *International Fire Fighter* (February, 1970), 18.
[35]"We Fight Fires...Not People," *International Fire Fighter* (August, 1969), 12-13.

This is the English language. In French, one who extinguishes fires is a 'pompier'. One who stokes them is either a 'charge de chauffe' or simply a 'chauffeur'. In Spanish, a stoker is a 'fongonero' while a fire fighter is a 'bombero'.[36]

The contrast in personae continues. Fire fighters, the heroic characters, are professionals. The keys to professionalism are training and education. An important scenario has the heroic fire fighter persona spending his time engaging in study and training.[37] Howard McClennen describes "The New Professionalism":

Today's fire fighter must know something about chemistry. He must also have a considerable knowledge of building construction, of hydraulics, of explosives, of the physics of fire spread. He must understand how the human body reacts to heat, to smoke, to panic. And, today's world being what it is, he must understand something of crowd psychology and the dynamics of group action.

In short... the modern-day fighter of fire must also be a student of fire. ... Today's professional fire fighter becomes effective as the result of a solid foundation of study, a foundation that goes far deeper than learning how to reach a fire in the shortest possible time.[38]

Discipline and team work are important and the professional trains continually. The *Fireman's Grapevine* explains:

Discipline and teamwork are imbued in a fireman.... No margin of error can be tolerated. One miscalculation can — and has — cost a man's life, as well as the lives of others.... A large portion of each day's activities involve drills and classes in various aspects of fire service work.... There is such a sweeping array of fire fighting and rescue apparatus that a continuous program of review is vital.[39]

The following example of events surrounding a fire-call dramatically illustrates the payoff from training, drilling and review:

In that fraction of an instant, an almost palpable, electrifying tension exploded into the building. Immediately one could hear the frantic — yet disciplined — rush, men scrambling for clothes, boots, coats, and helmets, and then on to complex tasks learned so well as to be easily and automatically performed now.

Elapsed time from the sounding of the first buzzer until the engine cleared the station: thirteen seconds. Task Force 98 has a run; they were back in business again that day.[40]

[36]"There is Not a 'Fireman' in the I.A.F.F.; Every One of Them is a 'Fire Fighter'," *International Fire Fighter* (June, 1968), 9.

[37]Louis J. Amabili, "Professionalism in the Fire Service," *Minnesota Fire Chief* (May-June, 1973), 7.

[38]Howard McClennan, "The New Professionalism," *Fire Journal* (November, 1970), 42.

[39]"The Life and Times of a Fireman," *Fireman's Grapevine* (December, 1971), 6.

[40]"Life and Times," 5.

Another important aspect of the fire fighters' professional character is courage—"Above all, his courage must transcend his fear of death, the recognition that his service, his profession, is the most hazardous of all.[41] Still other important attributes of the fire fighters' self-persona include dedication to the service,[42] efficient performance,[43] competency,[44] and compassion.[45] The professional fire fighter persona trains for the job and performs his duties well despite the burden of working in a hazardous scene.

On the other hand, the villainous projected-persona lacks many of these professional qualities. The projected-persona wastes his time and inefficiently performs his duties. He may be goofing off at the fire house, or carelessly extinguishing a fire. The following descriptions define the major features of the stereotype:

> He is drawing a good salary, works hours comparable to industry, sleeps while on the job, has many hours off and usually moonlights in those off hours. He is also a leech to the taxpayer.[46]

> The old stereotype prevails: a group of men (in suspenders, natch) sliding down a pole, careening down the street at 111 mph on the way to a fire. Once there, they break everything inside. When not going to fires, they sit around the station all day, smoking a pipe, swapping stories, and playing checkers.[47]

Such portrayals of the projected-persona appear universal. The *British Fire Protection Review,* 1961, included the following depiction: "The city fireman is commonly portrayed as someone whose life is largely devoted to killing time with snooker and cards, and a popular question to be asked by outsiders is 'What do you do between fires?'"[48]

In the fire fighters' rhetorical vision the line between heroic persona and villainous persona is a thin one. A single act by the persona may cause the public to heap disrespect upon fire fighters. The hero may fall from public grace at any time. The following excerpt is typical:

> A recent anonymous letter to our office brought with it a newspaper photo of a metropolitan Maryland area traffic crash with fire apparatus standing by. Perched on the median strip guard rail is a "fire fighter" — at least we must presume he is a "fire fighter" because he is wearing a fire helmet. The rest of his costume consists of tee shirt and bermuda

---

[41]Donald Favreau as quoted by Frank E. Oberg, "Fire Service Education...Road to Job Opportunity," *Minnesota Fire Chief* (September-October, 1970), 12.

[42]"Fire Service Recognition Day," *International Fire Chief,* 37, 6 (July, 1971), 18.

[43]Al Barken, "Why Fire Fighters Need COPE," *International Fire Fighter* (June, 1969), 11.

[44]"Life and Times," 5.

[45]"Fire Department Public Relations," *International Fire Chief,* 39, 1 (January, 1973), 8.

[46]John F. Sullivan, "Fire Service Stereotyped by Whom?" *Fire Command* (November, 1972), 8ff.

[47]"Life and Times," 5.

[48]"Smoke Screen," reprinted from *British Fire Protection Review* in *Fire Service Information,* LXVII, 4 (July 16, 1969), 5.

shorts and bare feet. The point of the letter of our anonymous author is obvious — the damage to our image also is obvious.[49]

There is little doubt that those participants caught up in the vision fear "the tarnishing of the fire fighter's self-image as heroic benefactor,"[50] and accept that all fire fighters must join in the task of rebuilding the eroding image.[51]

Other emblems are important to heroic fire fighter persona. The fire fighters take pride in working in the nation's most hazardous occupation and identify strongly with flashy new equipment. Even the color of the fire truck is important to the persona:

> It's almost like being against apple pie, or motherhood or the flag. It's just downright unheard of. It's yellow fire trucks we're talking about . . . But every kid knows a fire truck should be red. Who wants to sit up in the driver's seat of a yellow truck and turn the siren? And what old fire horse would want to rush off to a blaze without the traditional red fire unit? And think about the courage of the men who fight fires. Yellow is just not the proper color to be associated with courage. It's just unthinkable. . . .[52]

Two final important fantasy themes emerge from the literature containing the fire fighters' rhetorical vision regarding their dramatis persona. First, there's a friendly rivalry, if not open competition for pay and recognition, between fire fighters and policemen. Some fire service union representatives picture city officials withholding "money from the fire service in order to beef up their police department."[53] The villains in this drama are city managers "who treat fire service personnel as second class citizens."[54]

A second fantasy theme casts news reporters as villains who fail to accurately portray the job fire fighters do, thereby hurting the fire fighters' public image. Both fantasy themes are tied to the fire fighter's desire for pay and recognition.

The preceding brief analysis provides a glimpse into the fire fighters' rhetorical vision regarding their dramatis persona. The following report on the fire fighters' small group communication reveals similar fantasy themes.

[49]"Our Image," *Fire Service Extension Bulletin,* 28, 6 (September 1, 1971), 2.

[50]Perry L. Blackshear, Jr., "Where Do We Go From Here?" *Fire Research Abstracts and Reviews,* 13, 1 (1971), 45.

[51]"Firemen Should Assume Community Leadership," *Fire Service Information Bulletin*, 2, 4 (August, 1971), 5.

[52]"Imagine . . . A Yellow Fire Truck," *Hose and Nozzle,* XXIII, I (January-February, 1972), 15.

[53]"McClennan Blames Disparity, Slashed Budgets, for Unrest Among Fire Service Personnel," *International Fire Fighter* (December, 1969), 4.

[54]"McClennan Blames Disparity," 4.

## Group Communication Findings

The fire fighters in their group communication shared in the public rhetoric of fire service management as they verbalized many of the content themes present in the professional fire literature. The fantasy theme analysis of their small group communication accentuated many chaining fantasies regarding the fire fighters' dramatis persona. As could be predicted from a knowledge of group fantasy chaining, the fire fighters got excited about two types of events. The first kind of fantasy chaining related here-and-now situational elements of the occupation.[55] The second type of fantasy chaining related many of the content themes surrounding the fire fighters' image. A sharing of the fire service rhetorical vision concerning the fire fighters' dramatis persona characterized this second type of fantasy chaining.

# Overview of the Vision

The fire fighters' small group communication about their dramatis persona parallels the vision presented by the professional fire literature. The group sessions depicted a heroic persona completing difficult scenarios in a hazardous scene, and a projected-persona with many disparaging attributes.

## Scene

The fire fighters communication often included descriptions of the scene confronting their persona. For example, the fire fighters see themselves engaging in a hazardous job. The following group interaction is typical:

FF A:  Last year we had about 315 injuries. So you can say that three-fourths of the firemen were injured last year.

FF B:  And last year was no different from other years.

FF C:  Yes, ours has been rated the nation's most hazardous occupation... (interrupted)

FF D:  It's a damn dangerous job.

FF C:  Hazards are greatly increased in the last ten or twenty years by the introduction of plastics, and styrofoam and different building materials like that give off highly poisonous smoke and fumes.

FF B:  And the new modern buildings that got no windows, and a thousand people live in them. They make the problems much more difficult.

FF D:  This job like FF C (name deleted by request) was saying, here is the number one hazardous job in the country. It used to be the Bureau of Mines... (interrupted)

[55]For example, the men chained out on one division chief declining to join in on a discussion session, on the fact that Dennis Smith, a fire fighter, had written a best selling book "but they had never known any successful writers, just talkers," and on the fact that one engine pumper had just been involved in a traffic accident.

FF E:  Now it's firemen.

FF D:  That's what I was saying.

The Group:  Yah. — It's fire fighting. — The facts speak for themselves.

Often, the fire fighters perform their duties in the inner city. There, ghetto-minority relations take on special significance. The fire fighters spoke of the service they provided the ghetto:

FF A:  We get a call and we're out there and the police are waiting—they're holding back.

FF B:  But in St. Paul the first company there goes right to work.

FF C:  And we give the same kind of response in the poorest neighborhood as in the fanciest neighborhood.

FF B:  That's right. The same fire service for everyone throughout the city.

FF A:  We treat everyone the same.

Although the service is the same, public acceptance of that service appears to vary with the neighborhood. The following interaction typifies the fire fighters' interaction:

FF A:  Up in this area you do run into harassment.

FF B:  I think they put us on the same level as the cop. Every time he (the ghetto resident) sees us, he thinks cop. They put us in a position of authority which we're not.

FF A:  No, we're not. We're just here to do a job.

FF C:  But, it's a certain age group. I'd say from thirteen on up... (interrupted)

FF D:  Yah. It's the kids that harass us.

FF C:  And with the social climate the way it is, we'll probably see it continue into the foreseeable future.

FF E:  I think it's pretty localized though.

FF A:  Yah. Right in this area. And it's always the same age group.

FF C:  The young kids come in the station, they like us. But you get to a certain age group, and well, all of a sudden they change. Then they don't like you no more.

FF B:  They think you're a fire pig.

FF E:  A water hog... (interrupted)

The Group:  (laughter)

FF C:  Every kid, when he reaches the age of twelve or thirteen, he changes.

The above interaction also points to the fire fighters' competitive attitude toward the police. This competitive attitude comes through at other times and in other areas. For example, after letting the rescue squad recall a popular bill board showing a policeman giving artificial respiration to a young child, encaptioned, "Some People Call Him Pig," I asked them, "Do you get more calls than the police?" Here is their instantaneous reply:

FF A:  I'd say we get as many as they do... (interrupted)

FF B:  I'd say we get more.

FF C: What's the answer? Oh, really, we get more.

FF D: We get all of them.

FF A: Yes. And I know of cases where we've been there and left and the police came and they get credit (in the newspaper) for it.

This competitive attitude continued to surface as the fire fighters discussed their public relations activities. The following excerpt is typical:

FF A: There's quite a feeling that the police are getting far more publicity because of the riots in the past few years and the rise in crime. They're getting a lot more publicity even though we are number one statistically in death and injury. This is a far more dangerous job, but we're not out on the street as much as the police are.

FF B: You'd think there was something more dramatic about a policeman getting shot.

FF C: Yah. Right.

FF A: A wall can collapse on us and it doesn't make the headlines.

FF D: Sure. If a policeman's shot, it's bound to make the headlines.

As in the professional fire literature, much of the group communication centered on the need for public support. One fire fighter summed up the unique relationship between the fire service and the public this way, "We have to get our story to the people. They're our taxpayers. They're our bread and butter, you might say. And if we can relate to the people a little more, I think it would be much better for us. You can't hurt yourself." Just as in the fire literature, whether the fire fighters were praising or blaming in their group communication, the public received special recognition. For example, the fire fighters really looked up to the local civic organizations — Hook and Ladder, One Hundred Club, Lions Club. One group said:

FF A: The service clubs help us a lot.

FF B: They do all they can for us.

FF C: We have them over for spaghetti dinner.

One such dinner led to the donation of a $1,500 heart pumper for the rescue squad's ambulance. Similarly, the fire fighters look to the public for general support. The following exchange is typical:

FF A: Everyone's taxes are high. They want to pay us, but not more than they have to . . . (interrupted)

FF B: The city officials and the people have forgotten that the fire service was part of the initial mandate of city services by the city charter. This has been pushed back quite a ways through the years. But, ah, it should be a prime concern and it's really kind of a shame that the fire department and police department have to be stuck, ah, constantly have to fight for their own like they do.

FF C: Yes, we need so much money for apparatus, and everything goes up and when you used to get one pumper truck for $20,000 and now it's $50,000 and a ladder truck is $100,000. If you're workin' on a percentage of per capita, it's gettin' tougher and tougher each year.

FF A: But, we perform a necessary service, and if we perform it in the best way that we possibly can, ah, I think this information will get to the public and we'll get the monetary support.

The Group: Right. — Yah. — Uh-Huh.

Despite the faith in the benefits of educating the public, the small group communication also revealed that the fire fighters perceive an image predicament. Part of the predicament stems from the fire fighters' naive approach to public relations — they rely almost entirely on the casual contacts of day-to-day job performance. Much of this contact comes through educational programs regarding fire prevention. The following interaction illustrates:

Researcher: I saw a note on the bulletin board requesting volunteers for a demonstration booth at the state fair. Have any of you volunteered? Is that important?

FF A: Yes, that is important. Although it's on a volunteer basis.

FF B: Yah, that is a . . . (interrupted)

FF A: It's just a benefit. We can explain some of the fire hazards. Show the apparatus.

FF B: It's just like fire prevention. Any of that stuff is good. We'll be handing out pamphlets next week. "Escape from the Home" and "In Case of Fire."

FF C: Another thing that we have going for us is the fire prevention that we get. It helps make people aware of what is happening. The fire marshall gives the check lists at school.

FF D: I know that works. My little daughter brings that home and checks the house out. (laughter)

Such educational programs must double as the department's central public relations activity. But, as the discussions indicated, the fire fighters sense that such efforts are insufficient. The following example is typical of their view:

FF A: The public doesn't know about us.

FF B: We need our story told to the public. We feel that we're doing a real good job.

FF C: Sometimes, you know, ah, your best efforts are almost self-defeating. Your worst fire is the one that doesn't get out of the basement — where you've got to get down with it, down a stairway that's the only opening, that's like a chimney, and you've got to get down and get that fire. If you wait on it til it burns through the floor and comes out the windows, ah, you could put it out quite simply and everybody'd see it and they'd say you did a terrific job — you put out a big fire. If you put out a little fire in the basement, where it's hot and nobody really knows what you're doing . . . (interrupted)

FF D: You take more abuse, too.

The Group: (all speaking at once)

FF A: You take a lot more abuse, that's right . . . (interrupted)

FF B: Right.

FF A: ...than standing outside with a hose sticking it through a window.

FF C: You can't do that. Whereas, if you let a fire burn long enough, you can, because then it'll be in all the rooms. The more efficient you are the less they see you.

FF D: And it makes the job harder, too.

FF A: You take a big warehouse fire with good news coverage—that really isn't that much.

FF B: Your attic fire and your basement fire are your tough ones.

FF A: And yet, the public doesn't give us any credit for those.

The Group: (agreement)

The above public relations predicament also emerged in graphic terms in answer to the question, "What would you have to do to get better exposure? One group put it this way:

FF A: Well, if you got photographers, and they got the cameras and they make some of these fires, they'll get action pictures.

FF B: That's right. It's all there.

FF C: Yah, you wouldn't really have to stage them.

The Group: (interrupting each other at once, excited)

FF D: The problem is, it's all over before they get there.

FF B: We're out of work before they get there. When an alarm comes in, two or three minutes would be the time for us to be there fighting the fire and by the time the reporters would get there—he's not going to go into the fire—he's not going to be able to get to it. Well, you're not going... (interrupted)

FF C: You know, this is a fact of life that the photographers are not there. We've already been out on the street for a full thirty seconds before the news dispatcher gets the reports. You know it's not on the air. We're dispatched, we're dressed, and we're out the door before the chief releases the report. And that's the first anybody monitoring hears it.

Just as the fire fighters saw the need for public support, so too, they identified public relations as the means to get it. For them, the best public relations effort is an acting persona. The following segment from the taped interaction is typical:

FF A: I think it (a public relations program) would be a good idea. But you see, the best public relations the fire department's got is when the fire truck is going down the street with the red lights and siren on.

FF B: You bet. That's when everybody says, "My god, there's a fire someplace. Somebody must be getting hurt or somebody's losing their house." This is the first they think of us.

FF A: It happens automatically. But after the siren's sound is gone, it's forgotten."

FF B: Also you get a comment, "I just hung up the phone and here you are." Our fast service is good P.R.

FF C: That's even more important than being seen on the street... (interrupted)

FF D: We really strive for a quick response.

FF B: Our ambulance service gets us good publicity, too. If one's not available, the next district covers.

FF A: Again, the ambulance helps get people involved through actually meeting the fire fighter in person. And this is the thing. I think that you have to explain to the people that the fire department has quite a few services that they're offering and that they're doing a hell of a job with them."

The Group: Right. — Yah. — That's it.

The above interaction shows confidence in the qualities possessed by the fire fighter's self-persona. The men were willing to let their actions do the talking. Other segments of the group communication identified the particular characteristics of their self-persona.

## Self-Persona

Many of the chaining fantasies occurred in response to the open-ended question, "Why are you fire fighters?" The following excerpt from the tapes is typical:

FF A: Sometimes you get into a hot smoke-filled house and you're coughing and spitting and you, ah, wonder what you're doing in this kind of job. You know it's not good for your health, but you enjoy the challenge of it — you know... (interrupted)

FF B: You get such a good feeling out of doing something... (interrupted)

FF C: That's what makes the job — doing something that will help.

FF A: We're a necessary service.

FF B: It's worth it for the lives and property we save.

The Group: Uh-Huh. — Yes. — That about says it.

The group communication also provided a glimpse of the qualities attributed to the fire fighters' self-persona. All five groups discussed the qualities of their self-image. In answer to the question, "How would you describe yourself?", they stressed professionalism, dedication, competency, efficiency, courage, and the ability to get along and work as a team. The following segment typifies the interaction concerning professionalism:

FF A: We do what we're trained to do.

FF B: We see ourselves as professionals.

The Group: Absolutely. — Right. — Sure.

FF C: There is a lot of training and study just to keep up with technological improvements.

FF D: Half this job any more is book work and drill.

FF B: Two of the men are studying for promotions right now.

Sometimes the interaction portrayed more than one fantasy theme chaining at the same time. The following example shows how professionalism mixed with courage as chaining occurred:

> FF A: People tell me, they say, "Well, your job isn't so bad. Well, no it's not. But if your house is on fire, remember, you're coming out and I'm going in there.
>
> FF B: Yah. They're running out and we're going in.
>
> The Group: (laughter)
>
> FF C: A lot of people say, "I like the hours that you work," or something, "but I couldn't climb a ladder to the second floor and here you're climbing to the sixth floor" and things like that... (interrupted)
>
> FF A: You can't be afraid to fight a fire. You can't sit back and wait for help.
>
> The Group: Yah. — Uh-Huh. — Right.

Here the fire fighters were mixing themes — physical requirements and bravery — getting excited about two chaining fantasies at the same time.

Another quality of the fire fighters' self-persona is dedication. The following group interaction about reporting for work includes a vivid dramatization illustrating the significance of dedication for the fire fighters:

> FF A: You change shifts as soon as your partner relieves you and puts his gear on the rig. Then you're free and can go.
>
> FF B: Just like guard duty in the service.
>
> The Group: (laughter)
>
> FF C: There's an interesting story. Last year in the winter it was about twenty below and we had a snowfall, six inches, over night. And the courthouse was only about half occupied by the people working there. And some of them were, ah, quite a few of the teachers were absent... (interrupted)
>
> FF B: And the mail didn't get delivered.
>
> FF C: Yah, the mail didn't get delivered. Well, now, the fire department in St. Paul — every single fireman reported to work on time. There wasn't a single guy late.
>
> FF B: That's a good example of, ah... (interrupted)
>
> FF A: Dedication.
>
> FF B: Yes. Dedication. And the type of personnel we have. And they realize that a fire fighter that has been on duty for twenty-four hours would like to be relieved on time, and they make the effort to get here.
>
> FF D: Well, it seems to me, the fire department as a whole — the only time that a guy will take off sick is when he is down or in the hospital or something like that.
>
> The Group: Yah. — That's right.

Another attribute of the fire fighters' self-persona is competency. The fire fighters spoke of their steady job performance. The following illustration is typical:

> FF A: People forget the good things we do.
>
> FF B: We get satisfaction out of doing a good job.
>
> FF C: That is right. Only one fire in all my years I wasn't satisfied with.
>
> FF A: People forget they've never had a fire when nobody came.

The fire fighters display pride in their speed and efficiency. Quick response time provides evidence of their abilities. Yet another segment of the group communication illustrates:

> FF A: A few seconds doesn't seem like much, but it can mean life or death.
>
> FF B: I'd like to see a run come in now. You'd hear the bell and if you left your recorder on in about eight or ten seconds you'd hear our siren and us going out.
>
> FF A: People don't believe it... (interrupted by bell)
>
> FF B: Here we go now... (the rustle of chairs, men dropping to the first floor, sound of activity, pumper starting, siren blazing. Elapsed time: Eighteen seconds. Twenty minutes later the crew returned. They had extinguished a burning car.)

Another attribute of the fire fighters' self-persona is the ability to get along with others. The group's fantasy chaining pinpointed the teamwork and cohesiveness of fire fighters:

> FF A: When you leave the station house, you're all one unit.
>
> FF B: It's an overall effort.
>
> FF C: You can argue in the station house, but when you leave... (interrupted)
>
> FF B: We kid around with each other and that makes the day a little shorter, but when you leave, you leave as a unit — not just an individual.

A similar exchange relates the fire fighters' attempts to build group spirit:

> FF A: If we can go over four blocks from another company's house and get a fire — well, that is part of the job that builds spirit.
>
> The Group: (laughter)
>
> FF B: That's the challenge.
>
> The Group: (more laughter)
>
> FF C: They try to do it to us, and we try to do it to them.
>
> FF A: That's right.
>
> FF B: We just love to get in there and do something that the other fella's supposed to do.
>
> FF C: Really, that is part of it.
>
> FF A: There are traditions that started a long time ago in the fire department. One of them is that Engine 18's nozzle belongs to them on that line and don't give the line to anybody else. So, a lot of times at a smokey fire you'll say, "Hey, give me the nozzle. I got fire here." Well, if you get theirs and we got ours and theirs that makes it a nice coup, too.
>
> The Group: (laughter)
>
> FF B: It's the little things like that that make this job interesting.
>
> FF D: These things go to promote spirit... (interrupted)
>
> FF A: There is a hell of a spirit here.

The need to get along often came up as the fire fighters discussed physical qualification standards. The following example is typical:

FF A: Our entrance requirements some people feel are maybe too severe. But ah, we don't think they are. We realize the problems we could have. And I think there's good reason for these entrance requirements.

FF B: Yes. There is good reason. The men have to be able to get along. This would be one area where personality wise you've got to be a good mixer, and I think you have to be, ah... (interrupted)

FF C: A give-and-take guy, too.

FF B: Yes. A damned nice rounded personality to be able to take it. You have to be, year after year.

FF A: You've got to have similar interests and things like that.

The preceding excerpts from the fire fighters' small group communication illustrate many attributes of their self-persona. The fire fighters described their persona as a trained, courageous professional. He's dedicated, competent, and quick and efficient. He's a team man, able to get along with others. Public support and recognition are important to him.

**Projected-Persona**

Just as the fire fighters' symbolic reality includes a heroic persona acting in a dangerous scene, so too, it contains a projected-persona possessing less valiant characteristics. The fire fighters described their public image. Inactivity is a major characteristic of their projected-persona. An example illustrates:

FF A: People see us sitting around in the evening and during our leisure moments and think we've got a soft job — these same people are asleep when the alarm comes in.

FF B: People speak ill of us. They don't realize what work there is involved.

FF C: Yah. They don't realize. Whereas, we're involved with it every day, people drive by and they see the rig sitting in the house and they drive by again and they see the rig sitting in the house. So, they look at it, "Well, those guys didn't do nothing today."

In addition to his inactivity, the fire fighters' projected-persona is a careless axe-wielding fireman. For example:

FF A: It's hard for a guy who has never seen the fire department operate to know exactly what's going on.

FF B: Or one who's never had a fire.

FF C: Yah. That's the way I was coming on here. You don't realize all the stuff that goes on until you actually get involved with it... (interrupted)

FF B: Yes, here comes — look at that fireman with his axe... (interrupted)

FF C: Yah. You have a lot of comments like that.

FF B: He's going in there and he's going to wreck that house. So you go upstairs and you chop the walls out because when you touch it it's hot, discolored, and you know there's a fire in there. So you pound a hole in the wall to make sure it hasn't gone by, and say for example unless people know why, they think we chopped the hole unnecessarily.

> FF A:  They don't know what the firemen are doing.
>
> FF D:  And, naturally, there's no fire within every wall that's opened up.
>
> The Group:  No.
>
> FF D:  But, to be sure we have to check.
>
> The Group:  Yah.
>
> FF C:  People wonder why.

The contract between the self-persona and the projected-persona is clear. I asked the fire fighters, "Why do the citizens think ill of you?" One group answered as follows:

> FF A:  People speak ill of us because they don't realize what work there is involved.
>
> FF B:  We don't ring our own bell, so we don't get a lot of publicity.
>
> FF C:  The news reporters, they ride around with the police and the police don't often get to most fires 'til we've got them put out. We do our jobs and there's no one there to report the record.
>
> FF D:  The average citizen is back home in bed when most of the alarms come in, he doesn't know what's going on.
>
> FF B:  It's just the circumstances I guess that make the situation what it is.
>
> FF A:  Well, there are periods of inactivity, equipment does have to be cleaned and polished, and such routine tasks are often seen as frill by the public.

The fire fighters' depictions of the projected-persona lacked the completeness given to their characterizations of the self-persona. Generally, the groups would succinctly dramatize a loafing, moonlighting, reckless character — loafing around the station house, moonlighting due to soft hours, and reckless either on the way to or at a fire.

### Concurrent Validity Findings

The preceding fantasy theme analyses of the professional fire literature and the fire fighters' small group communication stress highly similar fantasy themes thereby providing concurrent validation of the Q-sort findings. The analyses depict a self-persona with attributes similar to those presented by the Q-arrays of the fire fighters' sorting behavior. All data sources converge on similar themes showing a dedicated, courageous, well-trained professional performing quickly and efficiently in a hazardous scene. All three data sources show that while public relations are important in the vision's scheme of things, the fire fighters see the attributes of their self-persona as their primary public relations tool. Thus, it appears that the findings are concurrently validated across data collection techniques (Q-sort, focus group interviews and content analyses of literature) as well as across analytical procedures (Q-type factor analysis of Q-sort behavior and fantasy theme analysis of group and media communication.) To the extent the rhetorical visions obtained from these separate sources converge about similar fantasy themes, then there is confirmation by concurrent means of the validity of the Q-sort findings.

## Construct Validity Findings

In order to assess the construct validity of the findings, I compared the factor extractions and the Q-arrays of the two assigned groups looking for similarities with which to assess the Q-sort's construct validity. To help in this assessment, I computed a Spearman Rank-Order Coefficient of Correlation between the typal arrays.[56] The degree to which the extracted factors in Group 1 correlate with those in *Group 2* should help to confirm or deny the existence of construct validity.[57]

The quantitative analysis of the *Group 1* respondents extracted three factors for the principal components solution. This compares with the extraction of two factors for *Group 2*. Table VI lists the eigenvalues used in generating the factors and indicates the amount of variance accounted for by the principal solutions. Note that both quantitative analyses extracted strong initial factors accounting for nearly equal percentages of variance, 56.63 and 57.74, respectively. Likewise, the analyses yielded insignificant additional factors. Thus, the difference in number of extracted factors appears of negligible importance. Of course, the mere existence of initially strong factors accounting for similar percentages of variance is not to say that the factor solutions represent the same typal descriptions. So, a comparison of the typal arrays is necessary. Table VI presents the Spearman Rank-Order Correlations among the item description typal arrays.

## Table VI

### Comparison of Group 1 and Group 2 Principal Components Solutions

| Group 1: | Factor 1 | Factor 2 | Factor 3 | Total |
|---|---|---|---|---|
| chosen eigenvalues | 17.1601 | 1.4341 | 1.0137 | |
| percent of total variance | 56.63 | 4.48 | 3.16 | 61.27 |
| percent of within variance | 87.52 | 7.31 | 5.17 | 100.00 |
| **Group 2:** | | | | |
| chosen eigenvalues | 18.4761 | 1.0727 | -- | |
| percent of total variance | 57.74 | 3.39 | -- | 61.09 |
| percent of within variance | 94.51 | 5.49 | -- | 100.00 |

[56]William L. Hayes, *Statistics* (New York: Holt, Rinehart and Winston, 1963), 643-647.
[57]Kerlinger has called factor analysis the most powerful method of construct validation. *Foundations,* 2nd ed. (1973), 468. He has argued that "If there were only one factor, say A, and it contributed 55 percent of the total variance, then we could say that a considerable proportion of the total variance was valid variance. We would know that a good bit of the reliable measurement would be the measurement of the property known as A. This would be a construct validity statement." Kerlinger (1973), 472. See also 461-476.

As can be seen from Table VII the typal arrays correlate quite highly, especially the initial factors. The high correlation among the types, coupled with the fact that the two solutions accounted for nearly equal variance on the initial factors, supports the similarity of sorting behavior between the two fire fighter-citizen groups. These results indicate successful replication and provide strong support for the construct validity of the Q-sort findings.

### Table VII

### Correlations Between Group 1 Types and Group 2 Types

|  | Group 2: Type 1 | Group 2: Type 2 |
|---|---|---|
| Group 1: Type 1 | .92 | .88 |
| Group 1: Type 2 | .89 | .85 |
| Group 1: Type 3 | .82 | .85 |

Significance levels:                              N = 56

.92 z = 6.82                    .88 Z = 6.52
.89z = 6.60                     .85 z = 6.31
.82 z = 6.10                    .85 z = 6.30

## Summary and Conclusions

I designed the study to allow for the assessment of both the concurrent and the construct validity of the Q-sort findings. I based the assessment of the Q-sort's concurrent validity on the fantasy theme analyses of the professional fire literature and the small group communication of fire fighters. I subjected nearly two hundred articles to fantasy theme analysis hoping to determine the elements of the fire fighter's rhetorical vision regarding their dramatis persona. As well, I subjected the audio recorded communication of five groups of fire fighters to fantasy theme analysis. These independent analyses converged on similar content themes providing concurrent validation of the Q-sort instrument's ability to measure what it is supposed to measure. These fantasy theme analyses depicted a self-persona with similar attributes as those presented by the Q-arrays of the fire fighters' self-persona sorting behavior. All data sources showed a dedicated, courageous, well-trained professional performing quickly and efficiently in a hazardous scene. All three methods showed that while public relations activities are important in the vision's scheme of things, the fire fighters accepted the attributes of their self-persona as their primary public relations tool.

A simple design consideration enabled the determination of the construct validity of the Q-sort findings. I utilized the sorting behavior of two groups each containing thirty-two respondents—sixteen fire fighters and sixteen citizens. I compared the factor extractions of the two assigned groups to assess the Q-sort's construct validity. To help in the assessment, I computed a Spearman Rank-Order Coefficient of Correlation between the typal arrays of the two groups. The factor analyses led to the extraction of three factors in the principal components solution for *Group 1* and two factors in the principal components solution for *Group 2*. Both quantitative analyses extracted strong initial factors accounting for nearly equal percentages of variance, 56.63 and 57.74 percent, respectively. Likewise, both solutions yielded insignificant additional factors. Thus, the difference in number of extracted factors appears of negligible importance. The Spearman Rank-Order Correlations attested to the similarity of the factor solutions, i.e., the similarity of the typal descriptions. The types correlated quite highly, from .82 to .92, with the initial factors correlating .92. The high correlation among the types, coupled with the fact that the two solutions accounted for nearly equal variance on the initial factors, supports the similarity of sorting behavior between the two fire fighter-citizen groups. These results indicated successful replication of the study and provided strong factor analytic support for the construct validity of the Q-sort findings.

## Implications for Speech Communication

Ernest Bormann gave the name *rhetorical vision* to "the composite dramas which catch up large groups of people into a symbolic reality." Rhetorical visions, through the depiction of a symbolic reality, provide impetus and direction for human action. As such they are important entities for communication scholars. To capture and understand rhetorical visions, Bormann suggested the fantasy theme analysis of collectivity's discourse to identify key characters, recognize scenarios, and determine the elements of the scene. Then, the re-created vision becomes a tool for audience analysis. One can look at a collectivity's rhetorical vision to understand what events provide meaning for the vision's adherents, the emotions that the vision is likely to evoke, and the particular motives that are likely to inspire people to action.

Several researchers have employed the analytical tool to a greater or lesser degree. Their research findings indicated that the rhetorical critic can elicit meaningful artistic reconstructions of rhetorical visions. My study concerned the initial attempt to capture and verify empirically the findings of such artistic analyses. As a consequence, the study generated several important implications for the theory and research activities of speech communication scholars.

1) The data supported the viability of the rhetorical vision construct. Previous applications of the method demonstrated the construct's heuristic merit. My success in capturing empirically the fire fighters' rhetorical vision regarding their dramatis persona, coupled with the concurrent and

construct validation that the instrument gets at the construct, suggests that this new rhetorical notion possesses empirical merit as well. Although I only verified the major character element of the construct, dramatis persona, the element possesses sufficient importance to infer that the whole construct is supported. At a minimum, the findings suggest that rhetorical critics may place confidence in Q-sort as a means of lending empirical support to their artistic re-creation of a collectivity's rhetorical vision.

2) The findings in the area of concurrent validity suggest that the constructed Q-sort is an effective means of supporting the conclusions established via a fantasy theme analysis of both small group communication and public rhetoric. This means that the Q-sort could be used to conduct on-going research to determine people's acceptance of a vision and then to elicit changes in people's adherence to a vision. The Q-sort proved capable of capturing a dominant vision and reflecting subtle variations in acceptance of that vision; concomitantly, the tool appeared capable of reflecting the overall tone of a vision across factors, even then the characterization of the persona stemmed from many diverse and diffused components. The Q-sort appears capable of capturing elements of a vision in its formative stages. This means that the Q-sort becomes an efficient means, when compared to fantasy theme analysis of taped interviews or public literature, of registering variations in respondents' adherence to a vision.

3) The research indicates that the Q-sort could be an effective means of measuring the effects of independent variables on a collectivity's rhetorical vision. One problem in studying attitude change stemming from the impact of communication and interaction is that the effects are complex and often are not reflected as a change in mean attitude. Moreover, the increase or decrease in the attitude mean of an experimental group often means little operationally. Such is not the case in using a Q-sort to study rhetorical visions. Changes of individuals may be sensitively assessed by using analysis of variance and factor analysis of structure Q-sorts comprising the vision's elements. The results should prove enlightening, whether the attitude mean increased, decreased, or failed to change. Three applications to speech communication research—small groups, public address, and persuasion—prove my point. For example, in small groups a researcher could use pre- and post-administrations of a constructed Q-sort reflecting a rhetorical vision to measure the effectiveness of leadership training for consciousness-raising. The output from the Q-sort administrations would tell the researcher the group members' adherence to a vision prior to "consciousness-raising" and subsequently would depict behaviorally the change in acceptance of a vision after "consciousness-raising." Similarly, a public address student studying contemporary movements could utilize the Q-sort to confirm empirically the growth and adoption of a new vision. The instrument would affirm those fantasy themes having meaning, deny those that do not, as yet, have meaning, and, as well, by means of high, low, or near zero z-scores, show the respondents' level of commitment to specific

fantasy themes. In like manner, a researcher could use the Q-sort as a rhetorical tool to measure the effectiveness of a persuasive campaign. *Persuasion* would not be defined as a shift on a Likert Scale or Semantic Differential, but rather as a change in the vision, or in the case of the present study, a change in the characteristics attributed to the fire fighters' persona. The derived factor arrays would indicate the expressions of the essence of those characteristics that are common to different groups of individuals.

4) The study suggests that communication scholars now have a research tool developed from a communication theory. Previously, speech communication scholars have of necessity turned to measurement scales grounded in the rational metaphor of the behaviorists. Since the Q-sort items are chosen for their relationship to the construct, it would seem, there is a tool developed in conjunction with a rhetorical communication theory capable of measuring the often non-rational dramatistic entity of rhetorical vision. The dramatistic Q-sort appears a richer measure. It tells us more of where a subject's head is at. As a result, the elicited information allows richer insight, and thus, more elaborate preparation for a persuasive campaign. Typically, speech communication scholars planning persuasive campaigns perused a given issue and then developed a questionnaire or semantic differential to generate input as the basis for their persuasive campaign. The result was a kind of "for," "against," "apathetic" audience analysis. Selection of rhetorical strategies was left to intuition and experience alone. My study suggests that we now have an instrument for confirming empirically our hunches and getting at the rich data intrinsic to the construct of rhetorical vision. Derived Q-arrays should provide an objective basis for creative rhetorical strategies, and the Q-sort instrument should provide a pre-and post-test means for eliciting those fantasy themes that have meaning and consequence for individuals.

5) The study suggests that speech communication researchers now have a technique for verifying the degree to which popular media reflect the public rhetoric of the American people. For example, a rhetorical vision Q-sort about Watergate or the Symbionese Liberation Army could tell us to what degree *The New York Times* reflects the marketplace of American thinking. Of course, a researcher can't go back and test the Puritans to see if Bormann is right about their rhetorical vision. But, there's no reason why public address scholars can't increase the faith they put in their artistic judgements through the use of such an empirical verification technique as Q-sort. To illustrate, had I gone to the popular tracts on fire fighters, I might well have put together an artistic view of them that does not reflect the qualities fire fighters' bestow to their self-persona. An attempt at empirical verification of the popular-tract constructed vision, using fire fighters as subjects, would likely have demonstrated the error in my ways.

6) The study suggests an implication for organizational communication, too. Traditionally, consultants turned to the open-ended interview and paper-and-pencil responses to assess employees' likings and dislikings of the

organization. However, armed with the construct of rhetorical vision and the technique of Q-sort, a researcher could confirm empirically his or her fantasy theme analysis of the open-ended interviews, as well as assess empirically the effects of proposed changes in communication input or channels. The ability to assess effects empirically, is a viable alternative in this period of meeting behavioral objectives.

In short, Bormann gave speech communication the construct of rhetorical vision and subsequent research has discharged it at the creative-descriptive level. I sought to do more than reify. I attempted to capture and to verify empirically the notion. While I provided empirical confirmation of only dramatis persona, that confirmation demonstrated the capability to prove all parts of the construct empirically. Moreover, the act of verification provided important implications for the kinds of research activities in which communication scholars engage.

# 15

# Marketing Farm Management Services:
## An Internal Study

JOHN F. CRAGAN, DONALD C. SHIELDS,
and N.E. NICHOLS

The purpose for the proposed Marketing Study of Farm Management Service was to examine two specific products, farm management and consulting. The objectives of the research were threefold as follows: (1) to define the product(s); (2) to define and describe the market(s); and (3) to recommend marketing concepts/strategies for increasing volume, market share, and profitability. This report is centered on Phase I of this project. The objective of Phase I was to elicit internal responses of top management at Doane, Regional Managers, and Farm Managers regarding three questions: (1) How do you define the farm management product(s) of farm management service and consultation service? (2) How do you describe the markets for the product(s)? and (3) What are your recommendations for increasing volume, market share and profitability?

**Research Procedures and Design**

The procedures for conducting this research contained seven steps: (1) literature search of previous research of Doane Farm Management Services and relevant publications; (2) outline development and seven personal in-depth interviews with top management; (3) outline development and eight personal in-depth interviews with Regional Managers; (4) outline development and two focus group interviews with Farm Managers, one of nine Farm Managers with less than ten years experience with Doane, and one of nine Farm Managers with more than ten years experience with Doane; (5) development of structured Q-matrix and building of structured Q-deck and salient demographic questionnaire on farm management services; (6) administration of the demographic questionnaire and Q-deck to forty-five members of the Farm Management Division; and (7) multivariate statistical analysis of the data. These steps enabled us to assess the Division's current knowledge of their product(s) and the means by which the product(s) might be marketed.

Reprinted with the permission of Doane Agricultural Service, Inc.

The first procedure provided information to help us understand what questions would be most relevant in meeting the objective of the Study. The literature search revealed several helpful documents. The most enlightening were ,a 1976 study entitled "Research Results and Recommendations Concerning Promotional Copy Platforms for Doane's Farm Management, Consultation and Real Estate Services," John Gray's senior thesis done at Princeton University in 1954 entitled "The Doane Agricultural Service and Growth of Professional Farm Management," the American Society of Farm Managers and Rural Appraisers' 1977 booklet entitled *Professional Farm and Ranch Management Manual,* and the *Doane Farm and Ranch Handbook.*

The second and third procedures, personal interviews of home office management and Regional Managers, were necessary for two reasons. First, the definition of a service product posed problems that are not present when one attempts to study the market of a tangible manufactured product. Thus, we deemed it essential to obtain a detailed description of the professional Farm Managers who work at Doane, their background and training, their sources of motivation, the Division's structure, and the past cultural and professional practices of the Doane Company itself. We felt such information could best be obtained through tape recorded, in-depth personal interviews with the top management of Doane and the top management of the Division. Second, we needed to retrieve relevant scenarios for construction of the focus group interview outlines.

The fourth procedure provided information to help us develop the structured Q-deck. Focus Group interviews of two groups of nine Farm Managers were held and tape recorded. The elicited information covered some eighty scenarios clustered about the following eleven topics: Definition of the Farm Management Service; Definition of Consulting Service; Nature of the Market; Selling New Business; Doane's Competition; Home Office Support; Advertising; Training; Identity of Farm Manager and Regional Manager; Doane's Image; and the Division's Organizational Model.

Data from the literature search, the fifteen personal interviews with management, and the two focus group interviews were analyzed and synthesized in order to build a theory-based, structured Q-deck that would contain in competition the key scenarios about the product(s), the market for the product(s), and how the Division might grow in the future. The sixty scenarios that comprised the structured Q-deck are contained in Appendix D. We also developed a demographic questionnaire to be administered along with the Q-deck to the members of the Farm Management Division. This questionnaire was developed because the personal interviews and the focus group interviews indicated that there might be real differences in conceptualization of the product(s), the market(s), and potential for Division growth among the members of the Division. Thus it became important to do, essentially, a market segmentation analysis of the Division itself in order to characterize the differences of opinion about the product(s) and market(s) based upon demographic characteristics of the Division members.

The eight characteristics that seemed relevant were: the Farm Managers's Region, length of service with Doane, percentage breakdown of a Farm Manager's production by service, annual income produced, total number of farms managed, educational background, previous selling experience, and age of the Farm Manager.

The sixth procedure involved administration of the two instruments to thirty-eight Farm Managers and seven Regional Managers. These Division members were asked to react to the sixty dramatizations by sorting them on a continuum from most reflective through neutral to least reflective of their view of Doane Farm Management. They sorted the statements twice, first to reveal their view of the Division today, and second to reveal their "idealized" view of the Division for the future. To sort the statements, the respondents utilized a quasi-normal forced distribution of 2-3-6-11-16-11-6-3-2 for a nine category sort.

The final procedure entailed the analysis of the data. Two basic statistical procedures were followed in order to analyze the data properly. First, the Q-sort data were factor analyzed by means of N. Van Tubergen's QUANAL Program for Q-analysis, providing the Principal Components Solution with Varimax rotation to simple structure, and a Weighted Rotational Analytical Procedure that arrayed the placement of the dramatizations about Doane Farm Management for each typal grouping of respondents by means of descending z-scores. Second, we analyzed the data by means of both direct and step-wise discriminant analysis using a respondent's loading or not loading with the major typal grouping from the factor analysis as the breaker variable for eliciting the discriminant function(s).

## Summary of Procedures and Design

The above procedures enabled us to identify from the interviews and farm management literature review basic ways in which people viewed farm management. We built the structured Q-deck to represent three specific ways of viewing farm management on each of twenty issues that were emphasized in the interviews and literature review as important. We labeled these three views "traditional," "contemporary," and "future" and called them Vision I, Vision II, and Vision III. The twenty issues concerned points related to the Division's *identity,* the Division's *structure,* the Division's *product(s),* and the Division's *marketing strategy(ies).* By building these twenty issues across three distinct visions into a testing instrument called a Q-sort, we could then allow the Division members to react to all of the sixty statements selecting those they felt strongly about, those they were neutral about, and those they strongly rejected. All sixty messages were rank ordered by the Division members. These rank orderings were assigned mathematical values from $-4$ to $0$ to $+4$. The factor analyses then grouped people who assigned similar rankings for all sixty statements and called them a *Type.* These Types could then be compared with the three visions we elicited from the literature search and interviews to see how closely the quantified responses of Division members resembled the viewpoints elicited from the interviews.

Also, with the grouping of respondents into mathematical types, we could then compare groupings on the basis of demographics to see if we could predict what demographic characteristics would distinguish a *type* with one view of the Division from a *type* with other views. The discriminate analysis assisted us in making this mathematical interpretation.

Finally, by weighting the assigned mathematical ranking of the Division members who comprised each type, we could then use assigned Z-scores of from + values to 0 to − values to identify those issues which were important or neutral or unimportant in comparison to all others for each type. Thus, for example, a Z-score of + 2.1 would show very strong acceptance, a score near 0.0 would show no commitment, and a Z-score of − 2.1 would show very strong rejection of the statement.

Finally, the procedures enabled us to segment the Farm Management Division into four types of Division members: a *Regional Manager Type* and a *Farm Manager Type I, Farm Manager Type II* and *Farm Manager Type III*.

To assist in reading the report, we tried to identify the essence of these types with a label. The *Regional Manager Type* is so named because all of the Regional Managers grouped on this type. The *Farm Manager Type I*, we labeled "Agri-Consultant." The *Farm Manager Type II* we labeled "Production," and the *Farm Manager Type III* we labeled "Independent."

## Findings

The answers that the Farm Management Division provided for the three basic questions underlying this research (namely, "What are the products?" "What are their markets?" and "How can the market share be increased?") are complex and conflicting. A display of the Division's opinion is best provided through a four-part presentation: (1) a description of the three views of Doane Farm Management with respect to the product, its market, and the way to increase growth; (2) a detailed description of the "idealized" view of Doane Farm Management that the majority of the Division members embrace; (3) a description of the characteristics of Farm Managers that are unique to each idealized view of the product, its market, and its potential for growth, and (4) a specific analysis of the twenty issues that compete across the three views of the "idealized" product, its market, and potential for growth with respect to the four different groupings (Regional Managers, and Farm Manager, Types I, II, and III) of Division members.

### Three Views of Doane Farm Management

The scenarios and dramatizations that were elicited during the personal interviews and focus group interviews indicated the presence of three coherent but distinctly different ways of conceptualizing Doane Farm Management. These three visions were most clearly contrasted by twenty specific issues that related to the definition of the two services, the identity of Doane and the Doane Farm Manager, the organizational structure of the Division, the nature of the market, and the repertoire of available marketing strategies.

**Vision I.** One of the dramas about the Farm Management Service stemming from the focus group interviews and the personal interviews depicted the Farm Manager as the original Mr. Doane. The scenarios within the vision described the Farm Manager as a man of integrity, who was educated in agriculture, and whose job function was to make competent, educated production decisions for the absentee landlord. In the professional performance of his job he benefitted the client by saving his land, and protecting him from business loss that many times was caused by the unscrupulous, lazy, ignorant tenant farmer who was running the farm. Thus, the Vision I Doane Farm Manager on-the-job spent most of his time visiting the absentee landlord's farm, personally making the vital production decisions, and constantly updating the client about the specific aspects of the various farm operations. The relationship between the Vision I Doane Farm Manager and the client was an autonomous and intimate relationship which demonstrated the professional commitment the Manager had in protecting the absentee landlord from financial loss and saving his land for future generations.

The vision I Doane Farm Manager in this original drama was a respected member of his rural community. His reward for doing his job was the knowledge that he was a trained professional providing a needed service for the agricultural community. In his own mind being a Doane Farm Manager was the next best thing to farming itself. The Doane Farm Manager's business grew as he received more referrals from happy clients and local bankers and lawyers who were knowledgeable about his professional management qualities and his impeccable integrity.

In this vision, the Doane Farm Manager defined his Farm Management Service as problem-solving with the major aspect of the service being the supervision of technical advice that he provided his neighboring owner-operators. This advice usually related to modern scientific farming practices. The market for these services was an absentee landlord, typically a widow or old maid school teacher who inherited the land. This Doane Farm Manager felt that his share of the market would increase, not through advertising in newspapers, and not through attempts at "selling" his product directly, but through providing a quality service, because actions speak louder than words. There was definitely a limit to the number of farms he could manage with quality and care and the purpose of his service was not to make large profits, but to protect and preserve the land.

The personal and focus group interviews of the members who had been in the Division for a long time indicated that while Vision I was the traditional way to view the product(s), the market(s), and the means for growth, they were unsure as to how much of this view existed among Farm Managers today. Thus, we built Vision I in as one part of the structured Q-deck in an effort to quantify the degree of its existence in the Division today.

**Vision II.** The vision that most members of the Farm Management Division believed was the current way for interpreting the Division's product(s), market(s), and potential for growth we labeled Vision II. In this vision, the Doane Company is dramatized as a family of professionals engaged in agricultural service. Being an employee-owned company, Doane allows its loyal employees to share collectively in the rewards of good work and pride of ownership. In this drama, the Doane Farm Manager derived his superiority in the marketplace, not from his superior scientific farming knowledge, but from his ability to plan and advise and meet the absentee landlord's goals. He also had the ability to select and manage competent tenants. In this drama the Farm Manager is more of a people manager than a technical production manager. The relationship between the Doane Farm Manager and the client is still a direct one; however, the manager draws upon the resources of the home office in the form of accounting services, market advice, and technical assistance.

The Vision II Doane Farm Manager in this contemporary drama is depicted as a Farm Manager who is content with the knowledge that he is successfully managing people. At the same time he is receiving a salary that is above the national average and is able to raise his family in a rural community and thus stay close to the land. Aside from these personal satisfactions, his further rewards are the continuing association with the Doane family, the incentives that are tied to his M.B.O.'s, and the profit-sharing that comes from an employee-owned company.

In this vision, the Doane Farm Manager defined his Farm Management Service again as problem-solving, but here the major aspect of the service is supervision of the tenant farmer with emphasis on financial planning and business management. The Consultation Service is a separate service from Farm Management. Consultation in this vision generally involves a customized answer to a specific farming situation such as hog confinement or budgeting advice for the owner-operator. The market for Farm Management Service is the absentee landlord. The absentee landlord is seen as hard to typify, but generally includes widows, heirs, lawyers, physicians, and investors. The Doane Farm Manager functioning from a Vision II perspective feels that his share of the market can increase not only by referrals but by contacting qualified leads that have been generated through direct-mail advertising and advertising in local newspapers. The actual "selling" of the Management Service must be done by the Farm Manager who will manage the farm and a new sale is taken as evidence of his ability to relate to and manage people. By delegating much of the technical decision-making to the competent tenant-farmer, the Farm Manager can increase his total load and spend more time talking to qualified leads. However, there are real limits to the growth potential of the Division due to the success of other farm management companies, bank trusts, former

Doane Farm Managers and neighboring owner-operators.

The interviews produced conflicting reports about how widespread and particularly how well-understood this vision is today. Some managers believed Vision II to be the "traditional view" and saw yet another vision that best typifies Farm Managers. Therefore, we built Vision II into the Q-deck and returned to the raw data of the taped interviews and literature search and attempted to ferret out yet another conceptualization of the product(s), the market(s), and the market(s)'s growth potential.

**Vision III.** The third drama about the Farm Management Service stemming from the focus group interviews and the personal interviews is enhanced by adding some data from the literature search. In a way this vision provides an interpretation of the Division's product(s), its market(s), and potential for growth for the future. Seeds of this vision are currently forming and many dramatistic themes are present in the minds of the members of the Division. In Vision III, the Doane company is dramatized as a corporation whose major goal is maximizing profits. Thus the Farm Manager within this vision feels an obligation to maximize the profitability of his service. In this drama the Farm Manager is capable of competent production decisions, and is able to wisely plan and advise absentee land-lords to meet their goals, but he derives his superiority in the marketplace from his ability to advise on markets, taxes, and real estate decisions. He is more than a farm production manager, he is more than a people manager, he is an agri-consultant on all facets of agriculture. In Vision III Farm Management is no longer central to his identity, but merely one of the product services he provides as an agri-consulting representative of the Doane corporation. The relationship between the Doane agri-consultant and his client is now not as personal and the Farm Manager is not the sole decision-maker. Rather, he is a representative of the Doane corporation and Doane is the key to attracting the client. The client is buying Doane's Farm Management Service, not the Manager.

The Vision III Doane Farm Manager in this futuristic drama is depicted as a Farm Manager who sees the sky as the limit when it comes to maximizing profits for himself and the company, given the commissions on sales for new services. His lasting rewards as an employee of the Doane corporation are derived from his ability to maximize the profitability of himself and the corporation. These rewards are possible through the successful delivery of a number of diverse agricultural services from real estate through land management to agricultural consultation.

In this third vision, the Farm Management Service is defined as problem-solving. But the major aspect of the Farm Management Service is total corporate involvement in agri-consulting, which may include technical production, financial planning, trusts, brokerage, real estate, and taxes. The consultation service is the bringing together of necessary technical consultants to answer the many complex decisions of modern agriculture. The clients for this service can range from owner-operators through corporations to even nation states. The clients for the Farm Management

Service are not only the widow seeking protection, the landowner seeking planning and financial advice, but owner-operators seeking consultation or additional land, and individuals, corporations, and nation states seeking land for investment. The employee of the Farm Management Division participating in Vision III will maintain a competitive edge in the marketplace because the Doane corporation will aggressively marshall its expertise from Marketing, Publications, and Farm Management to solve any agri-problem in the marketplace. Doane's share of the market will be increased by having a full-time person in each region whose job function is developing and qualifying prospective clients, and creative innovative advertising and promotional programs. The best means of advertising Doane's farm services is through a continuous national advertising program that creates an awareness and kindles a need for Doane's Farm Management Services. The only limit to business in this vision is the absence of a meaningful incentive program that would allow the Farm Managers to be proportionately rewarded for the dramatic increases in growth that would follow the implementation of such an approach to marketing Farm Management and Consultation Services.

These three visions brought to life by twenty salient issues were structured into a three-by-twenty matrix producing sixty dramatizations related to the definition of what we now could conceptualize as the two products, their market, and the means to increase their profitability. By placing these dramas in conflict within a forced choice instrument, we were able to quantify the extent to which each scenario in each vision existed in the minds of the members of the Farm Management Division. The three dramas as they were structured into the sixty card Q-deck appear in Table I.

## Major View of Doane Farm Managers for the Future

The data obtained from the two Q-sorts by the seven Regional Managers and thirty-eight Farm Managers was factor analyzed to determine if any coherent views that might resemble the three visions collected from the interviews and literature search existed in the minds of Division personnel.

The forty-five respondents were first divided into two groups of twenty-two each, and two Q-type factor analyses were performed on the data. We then eliminated the Regional Managers and randomly selected thirty Farm Managers and ran two factor analyses on their raw data. This procedure was followed both for subjects sorting as to "how they see the Division now" and "how they would idealize the Division for the future."

When the data from the three sorts depicting the company as it exists now was factor analyzed, the computer printouts displayed a very fragmented, diffused and somewhat incoherent formulation of the Division. The major group-type which evolved only accounted for 47%, 44%, and 35% of all the variance in sorting behavior for the factor solutions within each of the three sets of data. While the most accepted cards in each array that comprised the essence of the group types were from Vision II, they were

## Table I

Doane Farm Management Drama Structured Q-Matrix
Archetypal Dramas (Columns) and Issues (Rows)

|  |  | Vision I | Vision II | Vision III |
|---|---|---|---|---|
| **The Division's Identity** | (1) Doane Philosophy | 34 | 50 | 22 |
| | (2) Doane Image | 5 | 13 | 36 |
| | (3) Farm Manager Self-Image | 35 | 23 | 43 |
| | (4) Need for Service | 38 | 16 | 51 |
| | (5) Client | 44 | 56 | 52 |
| | (6) Work Scene | 32 | 10 | 28 |
| **Division Structure** | (7) Definition of Farm Manager | 40 | 14 | 4 |
| | (8) Regional Manager | 26 | 24 | 12 |
| | (9) Training | 55 | 15 | 19 |
| | (10) Job, Work Standard | 6 | 2 | 54 |
| | (11) Motivation | 33 | 25 | 30 |
| | (12) Satisfaction | 8 | 57 | 1 |
| | (13) Job Appraisal | 7 | 39 | 9 |
| **Product** | (14) Product Services | 46 | 27 | 42 |
| | (15) Consultation | 60 | 37 | 11 |
| | (16) Support Services | 21 | 29 | 3 |
| **Marketing Strategy** | (17) Doane Competitive Edge | 45 | 41 | 18 |
| | (18) Strategy for New Business | 31 | 58 | 47 |
| | (19) Advertising | 53 | 17 | 49 |
| | (20) Limits to New Business | 48 | 20 | 59 |

well mixed with cards from both Vision I and Vision III. Furthermore, the cards that were accepted, varied and were inconsistent across the three data groups. To add to the confusion, not only were different cards accepted as important, but the major group-types in each set of data were only one of four to nine other group-types elicited by the computer analysis as being unique in their sorting behavior.

If a consensus view was forced from this data, it would resemble the Vision II type with some acceptance of Vision I and Vision III. However, the data from the "as is" sort mostly shows that there is no major view of Doane Farm Management as it exists today that is embraced by a majority of the personnel in the Division. The most accurate explanation of such "as is'' sorting behavior may well be that the Division is in transition and is undergoing major changes.

In contrast, when we turned to the future sorting behavior, the computer did discover a major viewpoint that accounted for a significant amount of variance and had half of the Division members comprising the essence of the typal group. In the three computer runs the major factor accounted for 70%, 57%, and 54% of the variance in sorting behavior within the derived factor solution. Here, too, the number of unique groups accompanying the major grouping was much smaller, ranging from two to four. Also, all seven Regional Managers loaded strongest on the major factor along with fifteen Farm Managers.

Table II contains a display of the fifteen most accepted messages and the fifteen most rejected messages in their specific rank order (1st to 15th and 46th to 60th) as they formed the typal array depicting this major viewpoint toward the Doane Farm Management Division in the future. A close examination of this factor and its typal loadings indicates that the Regional Managers and the Farm Managers who comprise this factor basically accept the Vision III dramatizations, and clearly reject the Vision I dramatizations. Of the top fifteen cards in this factor, twelve of them come from Vision III and of the fifteen most strongly rejected cards in this factor twelve of them come from Vision I.

Three Vision II cards were accepted in the major factor, (work-scene, definition of Regional Manager, and home office support services) but in each case the Vision III cards on the same issue were also accepted. Thus, this factor produces an almost exclusive replication of the Vision III drama. The top five cards accepted from Vision III are work-scene, definition of the Regional Manager, definition of the Farm Manager, definition of the farm management product, and dramatization of the role of home office support services. The five most rejected cards are all from Vision I. They are the need for service, definition of farm manager, definition of the client, home office support service, and definition of regional manager.

The sorting behavior on the major factor in the idealized future sort demonstrates that even though the Division does not possess consensus on its "as is" status there is concensus regarding where the Division would like to be in the future. Nevertheless, there still exists considerable differences of opinion among the Division members when talking about the two product services, their market, and their potential for growth in the future. These differences are reflected in the other factors that are present in the results of the Q-analysis. Sixteen Farm Managers loaded highest on a second interpretation of the future which would prefer Vision II with the retention of some key components of Vision I, and seven Farm Managers comprised an even smaller factor-type which embraced predominately the dramatizations of Vision I. In order to usefully describe these differences it was necessary to meticulously break down the different clusterings of members within the Division, first by demographics and then specifically analyze their differences on an issue-by-issue basis.

## Table II

Farm Management Sort Major View for the Future
Accepted Messages (Ranked 1-15) Rejected Messages (Ranked 46-60)

|  |  | Vision I | Vision II | Vision III |
|---|---|---|---|---|
| **The Division's Identity** | (1) Doane Philosophy | 34 | 50 | 22 |
|  | (2) Doane Image | 5 (52nd) | 13 | 36 (54th) |
|  | (3) Farm Manager Self-Image | 35 | 23 | 43 (13th) |
|  | (4) Need for Service | 38 (58th) | 16 | 51 |
|  | (5) Client | 44 (60th) | 56 | 52 (12th) |
|  | (6) Scene | 32 (53rd) | 10 (3rd) | 28 (1st) |
| **Division Structure** | (7) Definition of Farm Manager | 40 (59th) | 14 | 4 (4th) |
|  | (8) Regional Manager | 26 (56th) | 24 (7th) | 12 (2nd) |
|  | (9) Training | 55 | 15 | 19 |
|  | (10) Job, Work Standard | 6 (50th) | 2 | 54 (15th) |
|  | (11) Motivation | 33 | 25 | 30 |
|  | (12) Satisfaction | 8 (49th) | 57 | 1 |
|  | (13) Job Appraisal | 7 (47th) | 39 (46th) | 9 (9th) |
| **Product** | (14) Product Services | 46 | 27 | 42 (5th) |
|  | (15) Consultation | 60 | 37 | 11 (14th) |
|  | (16) Support Services | 21 (57th) | 29 (6th) | 3 (8th) |
| **Marketing Strategy** | (17) Doane Competitive Edge | 45 (48th) | 41 | 18 (10th) |
|  | (18) Strategy for New Business | 31 | 58 | 47 (11th) |
|  | (19) Advertising | 53 | 17 | 49 |
|  | (20) Limits to New Business | 48 (51st) | 20 (45th) | 59 (55th) |

| Top 15 N = 0 | Top 15 N = 3 | Top 15 N = 12 |
|---|---|---|
| Bottom 15 N = 12 | Bottom 15 N = 2 | Bottom 15 N = 2 |

## Segmentation of Four Idealized Views by Demographic Characteristics

We took the seven Regional Managers and fifteen Farm Managers that
formed the essence of the idealized sort's major factor-type and put their
demographic data in one group, and we took the remaining twenty-three
Farm Managers and put their demographic data in a second pool. We then
took the two groups and compared them to determine if any of the
demographic variables would discriminate the group representing the major

factor-type from the group representing the other factor-types. The statistical procedure that we used for this task was Discriminant Analysis. Specifically, we conducted both a direct and a step-wise discriminate analysis on these two groups using the eight demographic characteristics. The results of these discriminate analyses indicated that four demographic variables clustered together to form one discriminant function (indicator) that would distinguish in eighty cases out of one-hundred whether or not a Division member was participating in the major view or one of the minor views. The most crucial variable in predicting a Farm Manager's participation in the major drama is the percentage breakdown of a Farm Manager's production load by service. Namely, if he derived more than 20% of his production income from the consulting service product and the real estate sales product he tended to cluster with the Regional Farm Managers in the formation of the previously described major view of what the products are, what the markets for them are, and how the markets can grow.

The second most important variable was age. The younger the Farm Manager, the more likely he was to be a participant in the major view.

The third variable was sales experience. The more sales experience, again the more likely a person was to be a participant in the major view.

The final variable forming the discriminate function was years of service to the company. In general, the newer the employee, when found in combination with sales experience, youth, and diversified production load, the more likely the person was to be a participant in the major drama.

Of course, this data also means that those people participating in idealized future views of the Division that were distinct from the major view tended to have most of their production income coming exclusively from the management of farms, tended to be older with little sales experience, and tended to have many years of service to the company. In fact, the discriminant function was 87% accurate in predicting Farm Managers who participated in views other than the major view. These four variables and the discriminant function they comprised accurately predicted twenty of the twenty-three Farm Managers who did not load in the major factor.

An even closer examination of the sorting behavior of the Farm Managers indicated that even finer distinctions in terms of segmenting the members of the Division were required if meaningful conclusions were to be drawn from the data. By examining the simple structure of the factor solutions from the three sets of idealized sorts, we were able to determine that the two groups could be split to form four unique sorting behaviors of the sixty dramatizations about the two products, their market, and the Division's potential for future growth. The major view contained a subtype we labeled the *Regional Manager View,* since the seven Regional Managers loaded highest on this factor. The fifteen Farm Managers who had diversified production loads, tended to be young with sales experience and fewer years with the company that formed the major view with the Regional Managers became our second subtype which we named *Farm Managers Type I* (Agri-Consultant). The sixteen Farm Managers that all loaded on the second most popular view of idealized Doane Farm Management and who tended to derive their production almost exclusively from farm management, who were older, more experienced members of the Division with little sales experience, became a sub-type we labeled *Farm Manager Type II* (Production). The seven Farm Managers who tended to accept the original "Mr. Doane" vision of the Division we put in a fourth sub-type labeled *Farm Manager Type III* (Independent).

With these four types we would then analyze similarities and differences in their idealized view of the Division across the four types on the twenty salient issues that defined the Division's product(s), market(s), and the potential for increased profitability.

### An Item Analysis of the Four Farm Management Types

The following analysis follows the twenty issues on the left side of the structured Q-deck data matrix as it demonstrates specific card placement of all sixty cards within the sorting behavior of each of the four *Farm Management Types*. The analysis begins with issue number one, Doane Philosophy, and presents the Z-scores (from positive 3.0 through 0.0 to negative 3.0) for each card as it represents that issue for each vision and compares the card placement by *Regional Manager Type, Farm Manager Type I, Farm Manager Type II,* and *Farm Manager Type III*.

Analysis is provided for the total sorting behavior of the Division on each issue, and a Summary Analysis is provided for all the elements comprising "The Division's Identity," "Division Structure," "The Product," and "Marketing Strategies."

### Item Analysis — Future Sort
The Division's Identity

(1) Doane Philosophy

| (34)* | (50)* | (22)* |
|---|---|---|
| **Vision I** | **Vision II** | **Vision III** |
| The governing philosophy of the Doane company is to bring modern scientific agricultural practices to the farming community in order to save the land and maintain continuous profits for the absentee landowners through professional management supervision. | The governing philosophy of the Doane company is that it's a family of professionals engaged in agricultural service. Being an employee-owned company, it allows loyal employees to share collectively in the rewards of good work, and the pride of ownership. | The governing philosophy of the Doane company is to maximize profits. Each employee has the obligation to maximize the profitability of their job function. |

|        |          |        |        |       |          |
|--------|----------|--------|--------|-------|----------|
|        | RM***    | − .09  | − .34  | .45   | N = 7**  |
| Type   | FM I     | − .09  | .12    | 1.75  | N = 15   |
|        | FM II    | − .70  | .30    | .02   | N = 16   |
|        | FM III   | − .40  | 1.70   | .40   | N = 7    |

*Here and hereafter the number in parentheses indicates original card number representing the dramatization for that issue as it is conceived for the respective vision. Thus Card 34 represents the Vision I dramatization of the Doane Philosophy.

**N = Refers to number of Division members in a type.

***RM      is Regional Manager Type
   FM I   is Agri-Consultant Type
   FM II  is Production Type
   FM III is Independent Type

The data indicates slight rejection of the original philosophy of Doane Farm Management, i.e., to bring modern scientific practices to the farming community in order to save the land and provide continuous profits for the absentee landlord. A small minority of Farm Managers (Type III) strongly embrace (Z-score = + 1.70) the philosophy of a family-owned company with employees sharing equally in the rewards. The other Farm Managers are neutral (Z-scores hovering about zero) about such a philosophy for the future. Type I Farm Managers strongly endorse (Z-score = + 1.75) the view that Doane's philosophy should be to maximize profits. The Regional Managers, while accepting a profit-oriented philosophy for the future, do so less adamantly.

(2) Doane Image

|  | (5) | (13) | (36) |
|--|-----|------|------|
|  | **Vision I** | **Vision II** | **Vision III** |

| | Vision I | Vision II | Vision III |
|--|----------|-----------|------------|
| | The Farm Management Division reflects the Doane company's place in agriculture as a conservative, steady company built by agrarian oriented people with integrity. | The Farm Management Division reflects the Doane company's place in agriculture as a conservative company that weighs and and incorporates the decisions necessary to meet the changing nature of agriculture. | The Farm Management Division reflects the Doane company's place in agriculture as a conservative old line company that is really a sleeping giant capable of rapid growth and expansion in terms of the services provided and the potential for profit. |

|        |         |         |         |         |          |
|--------|---------|---------|---------|---------|----------|
|        | RM      | − 1.21  | − .33   | − 1.31  | N = 7    |
| By     | FM I    | − .33   | − .04   | − 1.22  | N = 15   |
| Type   | FM II   | − .57   | − .13   | 1.43    | N = 16   |
|        | FM III  | .70     | − 1.00  | − .40   | N = 7    |

The data for the Vision I column regarding Doane Farm Management's image in agriculture shows that for the future, the overwhelming majority reflect the notion (negative Z-scores) that Doane is a conservative, steady company built by agrarian-oriented people with integrity. The Regional Managers set the pace for this rejection (Z-score = $-1.21$) with only Type III Farm Managers accepting such a view (Z-score = $+.70$). The Division was neutral to fairly strong in their rejection of the Vision II future view that Doane is a conservative company that makes the decisions necessary to meet the changing nature of agriculture. The Division is apparently split in its acceptance or rejection of the Vision III card. The Regional Managers and the Type I Farm Managers reject fairly strongly (Z-scores = $-1.31$ and $-1.22$) the notion that Doane for the future is really a conservative old-line company that is a sleeping giant capable of rapid growth and expansion of services and potential for profit. However, the Type II Farm Managers accept this view (Z-score = $+1.43$).

To us, the sorting behavior on the issue of Doane's image in the future is difficult to interpret. At one level it appears that the vast majority of Division members reject the image of Doane as a conservative company for the future. The problem of interpretation comes with the polarization (acceptance—rejection) of the Vision III card. It could be that the Regional Managers and the Type I Farm Managers in the future do not want Doane to be a conservative old-line company that is a sleeping giant. Since the Regional Managers and the Type I Farm Managers accepted twelve of the Vision III cards in their placement of the top fifteen, it seems reasonable to accept this explanation. It is also possible that the Type II Farm Managers who accepted the card saw it as we intended it to be seen, i.e., that Doane is capable of rapid growth in the future.

**(3) Self-Image of Doane Farm Manager**

|  | (36) | (23) | (43) |
|---|---|---|---|
|  | **Vision I** | **Vision II** | **Vision III** |

| Vision I | Vision II | Vision III |
|---|---|---|
| A Doane Farm Manager is a college graduate in agriculture and is superior in the farm management marketplace when it comes to farm production decisions. | A Doane Farm Manager has the education and background to make competent production decisions, derives his superiority in the marketplace from his ability to plan, advise and meet the landowner's goals. | A Doane Farm Manager is a man who, while he can make competent production decisions and plan and advise and meet agreed upon mutually goals, derives his superiority in the marketplace from his ability to advise on markets, taxes and real estate decisions. |

|  |  | Vision I | Vision II | Vision III |  |
|---|---|---|---|---|---|
|  | RM | $-.56$ | .52 | 1.00 | N = 7 |
| By | FM I | $-.80$ | .78 | .91 | N = 15 |
| Type | FM II | $-.47$ | .33 | 1.10 | N = 16 |
|  | FM III | $-1.30$ | 1.20 | 1.50 | N = 7 |

In the future the Farm Management Division agrees that their superiority in the marketplace is not due to their education or agrarian background that produces better farm production decisions (negative Z-scores for Vision I cards). They all claim some future superiority in their ability to plan, advise, and meet the landowner's goals (positive Z-scores for Vision II cards). Nevertheless, they claim that their real future superiority (Z-scores from +.91 to +1.50) comes from the combination of these: (1) competent production decisions; (2) wise planning and advice about the landowner's goals; and (3) the ability to advise on markets, taxes, and real estate.

### (4)  Need for Service

| (38) | (16) | (51) |
|---|---|---|
| **Vision I** | **Vision II** | **Vision III** |
| A Doane Farm Manager's major job purpose is to protect the absentee landowner — a landowner who is at the mercy of the ignorant, dishonest, lazy tenant. | A Doane Farm Manager's major job purpose is to advise the absentee landowner — a landowner who might get competent production by renting to owner-operators, but who turns to the Farm Manager because he needs objective goal planning and wise financial management. | A Doane Farm Manager's major job purpose is to assist the landowner client — a landowner who is into farming for investment and needs consulting assistance on operating, markets, taxes, appreciation, depreciation, and optimum times for buying and selling his land. |

|  |  | Vision I | Vision II | Vision III |  |
|---|---|---|---|---|---|
|  | RM | −1.89 | .08 | .17 | N = 7 |
| By | FM I | −2.46 | −.21 | .17 | N = 15 |
| Type | FM II | −2.30 | −.01 | .87 | N = 16 |
|  | FM III | −2.60 | .00 | .10 | N = 7 |

The original need for farm management service, as stated in J.D. Gary's, "The Doane Agricultural Service and The Growth of Professional Farm Management," and in both personal home office and focus group interviews was to advise and protect absentee landowners who would otherwise be at the mercy of untrained, potentially dishonest tenant farmers. Surprisingly, this rationale (as indicated by the high negative Z-scores for Vision I cards) is overwhelmingly rejected as a future client need for Doane's Farm Management Service. It is also surprising that the needs implied by the Vision II and Vision III cards were neither accepted nor rejected by most members of the Division. The Vision II need was for competent production coupled with objective goal-planning and wise financial management while the Vision III need was for consulting assistance on operating, markets, taxes, appreciation, depreciation, and optimum times for buying and selling their land.

During the focus group interviews, participants dramatized a success story that vividly depicted Doane Farm Manager's chasing out bad tenants over the years, while at the same time they dramatized today's reality as one in which competent tenants worked for them and few bad tenants worked anyone's land. They concluded that they had chased away all the bad tenants. If this is the case, then what is today's need for Doane's Farm Management Service? That answer did not surface from the sorting behavior underlying this study, except for the Type II Farm Managers. They accepted (Z-score + .87) the Vision III card.

In the focus groups, most Farm Managers indicated that once they were confronted with a qualified lead who wanted the service, they could sell them on Doane. However, there was no specific articulation of what was used to sell them or why the client sought out farm management.

A 1976 study, "Research Results and Recommendations Concerning Promotional Copy Platforms for Doane's Farm Management Consultation and Real Estate Services," indicated that lack of agricultural knowledge, lack of time or desire for profits, maintaining the appearance of the farm, and worry-free management were reasons why potential clients might need a farm management service.

This sorting behavior, combined with the data interpretation and previous research indicates the Division's need to discover and understand the reasons for current and potential clients to seek farm management, and in particular, Doane Farm Management. Hopefully, Phase II of this research can provide the answer to this question.

(5) Client

|  | (44) | (56) | (52) |
|---|---|---|---|
|  | **Vision I** | **Vision II** | **Vision III** |
|  | A Doane Farm Manager's client is the absentee landowner — typically a widow or old maid school teacher who inherited the land. She needs a protector. | A Doane Farm Management client is a landowner not operating the farm. This person is hard to typify, but generally includes widows, heirs, lawyers, physicians, and investors. They need assistance in setting goals and in wise financial management. | A Doane Farm Management client includes not only the widow seeking protection, the landowner seeking planning and financial advice, but the owner-operator seeking consultation or additional land, and individuals, corporations, and nation states seeking land for investment. |

|  |  | Vision I | Vision II | Vision III | N |
|---|---|---|---|---|---|
|  | RM | − 2.17 | .58 | 1.02 | N = 7 |
| By | FM I | − 2.12 | .43 | .65 | N = 15 |
| Type | FM II | − 2.17 | .20 | .43 | N = 16 |
|  | FM III | − 2.00 | .40 | .60 | N = 7 |

The Regional and Farm Managers (as indicated by the Z-scores in the Vision I column) reject for the future, the view that the absentee landowner should be narrowly defined as the widow or old maid school teacher. Rather, they would like to see the client more broadly defined as in the Vision II card to include widows, heirs, lawyers, physicians, and investors — or better still, the Vision III card which also includes owner-operators seeking consultation or additional land, and individuals, corporations, and nation states seeking land for investment.

The face-to-face and focus group interviews and the sorting behavior of the three client cards in the Q-deck continually reinforce the conclusion that Doane Farm Managers and the Division collectively lack a clear picture of who their present clients are and what the market is for future clients. We constantly received vague generalizations which concluded with the observation that the absentee landlord defied specific definition. We reject such a belief. Hopefully, in Phase II we can provide some rich detail to the definition of client. This will be accomplished by collecting the vital demographics of current clients and former clients, as well as their motive for seeking the Farm Management service.

(6) Work Scene

|  | (32) | (10) | (28) |
|---|---|---|---|
|  | **Vision I** | **Vision II** | **Vision III** |

| Vision I | Vision II | Vision III |
|---|---|---|
| When I picture a Doane Farm Manager on the job, I see him spending most of his time visiting farms, making production decisions, and updating the client about the status of their farm. | When I picture a Doane Farm Manager on the job, I see a man who has delegated many production functions to competent tenants and who is spending time talking to qualified leads in an attempt to increase his production and consulting load. | When I picture a Doane Farm Manager on the job, I see a man who has delegated many production functions, who spends a great deal of his time talking to qualified leads, and who competently assists the client in making marketing tax, and real estate decisions. |

|  |  | Vision I | Vision II | Vision III |  |
|---|---|---|---|---|---|
|  | RM | $-1.23$ | 1.56 | 1.86 | N = 7 |
| By | FM I | $-1.14$ | 1.65 | 1.78 | N = 15 |
| Type | FM II | $-.73$ | .45 | .90 | N = 16 |
|  | FM III | $-.50$ | 1.40 | .10 | N = 7 |

The Division, as a whole for the future, rejects (negative Z-scores from $-.50$ to $-1.23$) a work scene in which the Farm Manager merely makes production decisions. Such a view is consistent with the Division's earlier rejection of the Vision I image of the Doane Farm Manager. Also, in keeping with their earlier decisions on the self-image cards of Vision II and Vision III, they accept the corresponding work scenes which have in Vision II the Farm Manager delegating production decisions to a competent tenant while he talks to qualified leads and increases his production load and which have him in Vision III adding the extra responsibility of assisting the client in making marketing, tax, and real estate decisions. The Division's sorting behavior with the acceptance of Vision II and Vision III statements regarding the Farm Manager's work scene, indicates a future in which the Farm Manager functions more and more as a consultant and sales-closer and less as a production decision-maker. Only the seven Type III Farm Managers are neutral about the Vision III conceptualization of the work scene as they remain attached to the Vision II view.

## Division's Identity

In their sorting behavior for an idealized future, the Regional Managers and all but a few of the Farm Managers picture themselves as desirous of a work environment where the governing philosophy for both themselves and the company is one of maximizing profits. To share in the reward of a family-owned company is also accepted, but one-third of the Farm Managers are less receptive to sharing rewards than to maximizing profits. Either future behavior rejects the image of Doane as conservative in the marketplace.

The Division as a whole regards itself as having a superior position in the marketplace in the future. This superiority stems from abilities of both individuals and the company, abilities which can be brought to focus on problem-solving consulting-type farm management for agri-business. The Division no longer feels that college training relative to production decisions affords them any market advantage. Rather, for the future, they feel their superiority stems from their wise counsel and the collective expertise of the Doane corporation that can be brought to bear on production, marketing, taxes, and real estate decision-making. In short, they dramatize a future work environment in which they delegate production decisions to competent tenants and devote increasing amounts of time for talking to qualified leads and consulting on all phases of agri-business.

What's missing in the Division's dramatic conception of their future work environment is a vivid description of Doane's clients and a meaningful purpose for the Division's existence. Clearly, the Division has lost the ability to demographically and psychologically define their client since they have unequivocally rejected past delineations of who the client is (widows and old maids) and the reason for farm management (protect the absentee landowner from the unscrupulous and untrained tenant) while at the same time not embracing any alternate description.

Phase II of this research project will concentrate on detailed descriptions of current clients and the motives of absentee landowners in seeking Doane Farm Management and consulting services.

# Division Structure

(7) Division Model — Definition of Farm Manager

| (40) | (14) | (4) |
|---|---|---|
| **Vision I** | **Vision II** | **Vision III** |
| A Doane Farm Manager carries out his load autonomously and creates a direct relationship with the client. He is the Doane company—he is Mr. Doane. | A Doane Farm Manager carries out his work load with a lot of autonomy, but draws upon the resources of the home office as he creates a relationship interfacing himself and the company with the client. | A Doane Farm Manager carries out his work load not as sole decision maker, but as a respresentative of the Doane company. Doane is the key to attracting the client. The client is buying Doane's Farm Management service, not the manager. |

|  | RM | − 1.95 | .22 | 1.53 | N = 7 |
|---|---|---|---|---|---|
| By | FM I | .03 | .57 | .14 | N = 15 |
| Type | FM II | − .80 | .07 | 1.00 | N = 16 |
|  | FM III | .40 | 1.00 | − 1.00 | N = 7 |

The issue underlying these three cards provides three different definitions of an employee in the Division when he is characterized solely as a Farm Manager. The sorting behavior in placement of these three cards is quite rich with meaning. As we discovered in the discriminant analysis of the demographic data of the Farm Managers, Type II Farm Managers are discriminated from Type I Farm Managers primarily because the income they produce for the company comes almost exclusively from farm management, while at least twenty percent of the yearly production of Type I Farm Managers comes from consulting and real estate.

Interestingly, the Type II Farm Managers sort these three cards in the same way (although not as strongly) as the Regional Managers. They reject the old view that they are an autonomous replication of Mr. Doane maintaining their own small business. Similarly, they idealize for the future a Doane Farm Manager who is not the sole decision-maker but is a representative of the Doane company. For them, Doane is the key to attracting the client. The client is buying Doane's Farm Management Service, not the Manager.

On the other hand, the Type I Farm Managers are ambivalent about all three definitional descriptions of a farm manager primarily because they reject the tabular term "farm manager" as the all encompassing term for depicting themselves. Since they derive substantial parts of income from the services of consultation and real estate, they regard farm management as just one of several services. During the focus group interviews with the younger members of the Division, there was much discussion about this issue and some members embraced the need for a new tabular label like "agri-consultant."

A few Farm Managers (Type III) do conceive of themselves as a modern day Mr. Doane who draws upon the resources of the home office. At the same time they reject the Vision III definition of a Farm Manager.

(8) Role of the Regional Manager

|  | (26) | (24) | (12) |
| --- | --- | --- | --- |
|  | **Vision I** | **Vision II** | **Vision III** |
|  | The ideal job function for a Regional Manager is to carry out the functions of a Farm Manager with the additional responsibility of supervising other Farm Managers. | The ideal job function for for a Regional Manager is minimal farm management, motivation of Farm Managers to meet their work objectives, training, advertising and record keeping for the region. | The ideal job function for for a Regional Manager is that of management. He has no farms, but complete responsibility for people management, continuous training and supervision over the sales and marketing functions for his region. |

|  | | Vision I | Vision II | Vision III | |
| --- | --- | --- | --- | --- | --- |
|  | RM | $-1.60$ | 1.30 | 1.60 | N = 7 |
| By | FM I | $-.95$ | 1.30 | .40 | N = 15 |
| Type | FM II | $-1.73$ | .27 | .27 | N = 16 |
|  | FM III | $-.80$ | $-.20$ | $-.10$ | N = 7 |

The Division to a man rejects (Z-scores $-.80$ to $-1.73$) the dramatization of the Regional Manager as a person who carries out the functions of a Farm Manager with the additional responsibility of supervising other Farm Managers. For the future the Regional Managers strongly embrace both Vision II and Vision III cards in their self-definition. They will accept the idea that they have minimal farm management responsibilities with most of their time being spent motivating Farm Managers and providing advertising, training, and record keeping for the region. They also accept the view of themselves as having no farms but complete responsibility for managing Farm Managers, providing training, and supervising sales in the region.

The Farm Managers differ substantially in their sorting of this issue. Again the results of the discriminant analysis produce the key to understanding their sorting behavior. The Type I Farm Managers (derive 20% of production from consulting and real estate, tend to be young, with sales experience, and new to the company) strongly accept the Vision II defintion of the Regional Manager which dramatizes the Regional Manager as still having his hand in the actual production of the Division, but are neutral about the Regional Manager being solely a manager of Farm Managers. We believe the Type I person strongly accepts the Vision II card because of the relationships between the regional manager and the young Farm Manager with regard to consultation and real estate sales. During the focus group interviews with the young members of the Division, a dramatization of the Regional Manager as a team leader providing assistance in consultation and real estate clearly chained out. The Type I Farm Managers prefer to maintain this relationship and do not want the Regional Manager distant from the production of consulting services and real estate sales.

The Type II Farm Managers derive almost all their production from the management of farms and they tend to be the more experienced members of the Division. Thus, they would like to see the Regional Manager out of the job of managing farms and solely responsible for the overall supervision of the region. The focus group interviews of the more experienced managers revealed that the reasons for this belief are two-fold: one, the Regional Managers did not need to manage farms in order to do their job as Regional Managers, and second, if the Regional Managers were freed from the duties of farm management they could spend more time on qualifying leads via their sales and marketing functions.

The few Farm Managers that formed Type III reject any form of middle management. They do this primarily because they dramatize themselves as a "Mr. Doane" who maintains a direct relationship for needed assistance with the home office.

## (9) Training

| | (55)<br>**Vision I** | (15)<br>**Vision II** | (19)<br>**Vision III** |
|---|---|---|---|
| | The best training procedure for Doane to follow is to select people already capable of managing farms. Many people have to be on the job the first day they are hired. If help is requested, the Regional Manager will provide assistance. | The best training procedure for Doane to follow is to hire a person who knows agriculture, provide basic orientation to Doane procedures, and offer on-the-job training directed by the Regional Manager. | The best training procedure for Doane to follow is to have a formalized, standardized program that provides basic farm management skills combined with probationary on-the-job training directed by the Regional Manager, and periodic home office special skills training sessions. |

|        |         | RM     |        |           |
|--------|---------|--------|--------|-----------|
|        | RM      | $-.30$ | $-.10$ | .60  N = 7 |
| By     | FM I    | $-.50$ | $-.20$ | $-.50$  N = 15 |
| Type   | FM II   | .10    | $-.27$ | .20  N = 16 |
|        | FM III  | $-1.10$ | .20    | .00  N = 7 |

In general, the Division rejects training in the future as a salient feature of the Division. The focus group interviews and the personal interviews in the home office indicated that training does not play a major role in the Division because they try to hire people with agricultural expertise and that specific training takes place in an on-the-job setting. The interviews also indicated that the Farm Managers had had some bad experiences with past sales training programs and that they were appreciative of current orientation practices for new employees. Finally, the interviews indicated that their professional society and university extension provided ample opportunity to update themselves if necessary.

It should be noted though that the Regional Managers and the Type II Farm Managers give modest support for formalized standardized programs that provide on-the-job training directed by the Regional Manager and periodic home office special skills training sessions.

The Type I Farm Managers rejected all training cards, probably for two reasons: (1) the data from the group interview of the young Farm Managers indicated that they were quite confident in their abilities and (2) the Vision III card speaks only of training for Farm Management and not training for sales and real estate.

(10)  Job/Work Standard

|  | (6) | (2) | (54) |
|---|---|---|---|
|  | **Vision I** | **Vision II** | **Vision III** |

| | Vision I | Vision II | Vision III |
|---|---|---|---|

A Doane Farm Manager knows he is doing a good job when he has built his management load to a level that is profitable, but insures that he can manage with quality. The objective is then to maintain that load.

A Doane Farm Manager knows he is doing a good job when he gets a stable base of farms and does enough new things to meet increasingly higher M.B. O's.

A Doane Farm Manager knows he is doing a good job when he is not limited be meeting set goals. Rather he is always on the lookout for new ways to increase profitability for both himself and the company.

|  |  | Vision I | Vision II | Vision III |  |
|---|---|---|---|---|---|
|  | RM | − .90 | − .30 | .80 | N = 7 |
| By | FM I | − 1.50 | .50 | 1.70 | N = 15 |
| Type | FM II | − .33 | − .93 | .67 | N = 16 |
|  | FM III | .60 | − .20 | 1.50 | N = 7 |

The Regional Managers and the vast majority of Farm Managers all reject (and some quite strongly) a future in which the sole standard of a good job is the maintaining of a full load with concentration on quality management. Only the seven Type III Farm Managers accept such a standard. The Regional Managers and the Type II and Type III Farm Managers also reject the Vision II standard of starting with a stable base of farms and doing enough new things to meet increasingly higher M.B.O.'s, while the Type I Farm Managers slightly accept this work standard. These results are somewhat surprising, but possibly understandable. The Type I Farm Managers would have no difficulty accepting this position since they tend to have incomplete management loads and their percent of increase of total production load is probably and should be increasing rapidly. Thus they can and should be willing to meet increasingly higher M.B.O.'s. In contrast, the Type II Farm Managers already have what they regard as large farm management loads and thus show apprehension about a future standard of escalating M.B.O.'s.

More importantly, the Regional Managers appear to be somewhat uneasy about being successful motivators of Farm Managers if the Vision II work standard is used as a criteria.

On the other hand, the Type III Farm Managers, since they are Mr. Doane, would endorse a quality standard for the future, but reject evaluation by a middle manager on the basis of M.B.O.'s.

Quite clearly, the Division as a whole tends to accept, sometimes very strongly, the Vision III card which depicts the Farm Manager as not being limited by set goals, but who is always on the lookout for new ways to increase profitability.

(11) Motivation

|  | (33) | (25) | (30) |
|---|---|---|---|
|  | **Vision I** | **Vision II** | **Vision III** |

The best source of motivation for a Doane Farm Manager is from the knowledge that he is a trained professional providing a needed commitment to the agricultural community that doesn't exist in his absence. In essence, he's an agricultural missionary saving the land and helping the absentee landowner.

The best source of motivation for a Doane Farm Manager is from the knowledge that when he does a consistently good job he receives a salary that is above the national average. With it he can be in the rural community and stay close to the land.

The best source of motivation for a Doane Farm Manager is from the knowledge that the sky is almost the limit when it comes to profits for himself and the company giving the commissions on sales of new services.

|  |  | | | |
|---|---|---|---|---|
|  | RM | $-.60$ | $-.60$ | .40  N = 7 |
| By | FM I | $-1.10$ | $-1.05$ | 1.30  N = 15 |
| Type | FM II | $-.47$ | $-1.27$ | 1.63  N = 16 |
|  | FM III | 1.50 | 1.50 | $-1.30$  N = 7 |

This issue, as dramatized in these three cards, is probably the most revealing item for understanding the market segmentation of factions within the Farm Management Division. As the data clearly indicates, the original Doane Vision, as depicted in the card for Vision I, is rejected by all but the seven Type III people. In this case, the dramatization depicted the Farm Manager's motivation for doing his job as the knowledge that he is a committed, trained professional acting as an agricultural missionary saving the land and helping the absentee landlord. It should be noted that the Type III Farm Managers, who are the Mr. Doane type, are as much as two whole Z-scores away from the majority view and of course strongly accept the Vision I depiction of motivation.

The majority of the Division also reject as a source of motivation the knowledge that they are receiving a salary above the national average while still being able to live in a rural community and stay close to the land. And again, the Type III Farm Managers differ as they embrace the thought that the future will bring a good salary as it allows the opportunity to live in the rural community.

The home office face-to-face interviews provided some support for the suggestion that the Vision II card might be the source of motivation for the majority of Farm Managers. However, such a view is obviously not the case.

Eighty-five percent of the Division (38 of 45 persons) envisions a future in which the source of motivation for a Doane Farm Manager is the knowledge that the sky is almost the limit when it comes to profits for himself and the company, given the commissions on sales of new services.

However, it should be noted that the Regional Managers, as with other cards that depict rapid increases in profits for the Farm Managers, are only lukewarm to the idea. The reason for this attitude was reinforced many times in our interviews with them. They believe that their own salary is not large enough when compared to the salary of many Farm Managers. Since they do not receive commission on new sales, while Farm Managers do, they complain that many Farm Managers make more money than they do. Therefore, dramatizations that depict new increases in profitability for the Farm Manager only, are not that popular with the Regional Managers. Therefore, dramatizations that depict new increases in profitability for the Farm Manager only, are not that popular with the Regional Managers.

(12) Work Satisfaction — Rewards

|  | (8)<br>**Vision I** | (57)<br>**Vision II** | (1)<br>**Vision III** |
|---|---|---|---|
|  | Some of the lasting rewards of Doane Farm Management are the preservation of the land for future generations, respect as a professional in the community, it's the next best thing to farming the land yourself. | Some of the lasting rewards of Doane Farm Management are the adequate source of income, the opportunity to maintain a rural lifestyle, and the sense of accomplishment that comes from successfully managing people. | Some of the lasting rewards of Doane Farm Management are maximizing the profitability of oneself and the company, and to successfully deliver a number of diverse services from real estate through land management to agricultural consultation. |

|  |  |  |  |  |
|---|---|---|---|---|
|  | RM | $-.90$ | $-.60$ | $.60$ $\quad N = 7$ |
| By | FM I | $-.45$ | $-.15$ | $1.95$ $\quad N = 15$ |
| Type | FM II | $-.87$ | $-.53$ | $.33$ $\quad N = 16$ |
|  | FM III | $1.10$ | $.60$ | $-.70$ $\quad N = 7$ |

This issue is a validity check on the preceding motivation issue with a new nuance concerning the diversity of services offered in the Vision III card. We obtained an almost exact replication of the sorting behavior for the motivation issue. This reinforces the conclusions that we drew from the motivation issue and it clarifies our understanding of the market segmentation of factions within the Division. The new idea in the Vision III card concerned the successful delivery of diverse services from real estate to agricultural consultation. As the data indicates, the inclusion of such diverse services reduced the interest of the Type II Farm Managers in this dramatization. This reduced interest is caused by the fact that Type II Farm Managers view themselves as being strictly a Farm Manager and their demographic data indicates that that is exactly what they are presently doing.

(13) Job Appraisal

| (7) | (39) | (9) |
|---|---|---|
| **Vision I** | **Vision II** | **Vision III** |
| The measure of a good Farm Manager is the lack of complaints and not losing any customers. His reward is status in the community and the knowledge that he's doing a quality job. | The measure of a good Farm Manager is his ability to meet his M.B.O.'s. His reward is a continuing association with Doane, the the incentive payment that is tied to M.B.O.'s and profit sharing that comes from employment in a profit sharing company. | The measure of a good Farm Manager is his productivity measured in total profit to the company and himself. His reward is the knowledge that he shares proportionately with the company in profit growth. |

|  |  | Vision I | Vision II | Vision III |  |
|---|---|---|---|---|---|
|  | RM | − .60 | .10 | 1.30 | N = 7 |
| By | FM I | − .30 | .95 | 1.05 | N = 15 |
| Type | FM II | − 1.00 | − 1.47 | .13 | N = 16 |
|  | FM III | − .10 | − .60 | .30 | N = 7 |

The dramatizations of job appraisal give specific insight into acceptable criteria for judging performance in the future. The focus group interviews with Farm Managers and the personal interviews with Regional Managers provided dramatizations about the lack of consistent work evaluation in the past. They indicated that criteria kept changing but that most often they included lack of complaints and maintenance of customer contracts. We put this dramatization in the Vision I card and it was rejected by all Division types as a future standard for evaluating their work.

Also, the Type II Farm Managers are not receptive to any job appraisal system (negative or neutral Z-scores) and reject the most an evaluation system that is based upon M.B.O.'s. They strongly rejected the card that depicted a Farm Manager being measured by his ability to meet M.B.O.'s and rewarded by incentive payment tied to M.B.O.'s and profit sharing. In contrast, the Type I Farm Managers demonstrate that they can live within an M.B.O. based system as depicted in the Vision II card. However, they prefer, as do the Regional Managers, an appraisal system that measures a good Farm Manager's productivity in terms of total profit to the company, with the idea that all will share proportionately with the company in terms of profit growth.

## Summary of Division Structure

With the exception of the seven people who comprise Type III, the remaining thirty-one Farm Managers and the seven Regional Managers consistently reject the Vision I cards with respect to Division structure. They do not regard themselves as an autonomous recreation of Mr. Doane. They do not regard the Regional Manager as predominately a Farm Manager, they do not want quality maintenance of their farm load as a criteria for evaluation, they are not motivated by the knowledge that they are saving the land and protecting the absentee landlord, and they do not derive lasting satisfaction from the knowledge that they are respected professionals in the community doing a job that is the next best thing to farming. They do not wish to be evaluated by the lack of complaints or the longevity of their client contracts, and finally, they reject placing a new Farm Manager on-the-job without training and are only lukewarm about a standardized training program.

An item by item analysis of the sorting behavior revealed the real difference among the Regional Managers and the three Farm Manager types. Thus, the explanation of their sorting behavior is complex, but nonetheless clear.

On the issue of defining the Farm Manager within the Division, the Type II Farm Manager and the Regional Manager could strongly accept the dramatization of the Farm Manager as a representative of the Doane company with Doane's image being the key that attracts the client. However, the Type I Farm Manager was neutral or ambivalent toward the whole issue of defining the Farm Manager's role in the Division structure because he rejects the tabular term "farm manager" since at least twenty percent of his production income is derived from services other than the farm management service.

The Regional Managers can accept for the future either a situation of minimal farm management or no farm management responsibilities. Thus their time is devoted to supervision and marketing, sales, and training. The Type I Farm Manager wants his Regional Manager to continue to participate with him in consultation and real estate and does not want the Regional Manager's job function to become completely divorced from production. On the other hand, the Type II production-oriented Farm Manager sees no comparative advantage to having a Regional Manager manage farms. He thus accepts the Vision III card along with the Regional Managers.

The Regional Managers and the Type II Farm Managers reject a work standard of a stable base of farms with increasing M.B.O.'s whereas the consultant, sales-oriented Type I Farm Managers tolerate such a standard.

However, all would accept a work standard of set goals that when exceeded produce more profit for both the Farm Managers and the company.

The Regional Managers and both Type I and Type II Farm Managers strongly reject the view that mere existence in the rural community with a good income is the motivation for doing the job. Both Type I and Type II Farm Managers see potential for more profit as the key motivation in the future. However, the Regional Managers are somewhat neutral toward this idea since the knowledge of what their share in the new profits would be is not clear. Similar sorting behavior occurred on the issue of the lasting rewards of the job.

The Type I Farm Managers accept M.B.O.'s as a job appraisal procedure, but in the future the Farm Managers and the Regional Managers would prefer a system that judges them on their total profit to the company. The Type II Farm Manager does not like any appraisal system but is fairly vehement in his rejection of one based on M.B.O.'s.

Another finding stemming from the analysis of issues on the Division structure is the reconfirmation of the market segmentation of factions within the Division. The issues comprising Division structure most strongly point out these different factions. For example, the Regional Managers embrace the cards in Vision III except where the Farm Manager's potential for profit would exceed his own. Moreover, the Farm Manager Type I, whose production load is diversified and who is sales-oriented, is the strongest supporter of a profit-based evaluation of work but wants to be part of a work team led by the Regional Manager as he functions on diverse farm management and consultation activities.

Factions are also evident regarding the definition of a Farm Manager. The Type II Farm Managers will accept in the future a complex definition of farm management but want the Farm Management service to be the predominant, if not the only service provided. Consultation at best for the Type II Farm Managers would be a subpart of that Farm Management service. On the other hand, the younger Type I Farm Managers see themselves performing three separate services and might prefer to rename themselves since Farm Management is only one of the services they provide. The Type I Farm Managers also seem to be the only type which readily accepts M.B.O.'s as a method of job evaluation.

The Type II Farm Managers, though a small percentage of the Division's sorting behavior, are interesting since they represent the only, albeit fragmented, reactionary view of the Division through their predominant acceptance of Vision I.

In short, the majority of the Division agrees in their rejection of Vision I, and in the absence of a need for training. Their differences concerning Divisional structure center on three issues: (1) the role of profit as an incentive and means of evaluation, (2) the use of M.B.O.'s as a job appraisal system, and (3) whether they should call themselves Farm Managers or Agri-business Consultants who perform three services.

# Product

(14) F.M. Product Services

|            (46)             |            (27)             |            (42)             |
| :------------------------- | :-------------------------- | :-------------------------- |
| **Vision I**               | **Vision II**               | **Vision III**              |

| Vision I | Vision II | Vision III |
| :--- | :--- | :--- |
| The fundamental service of farm management is problem-solving. The major aspect of the Farm Management service is supervision of technical production and marketing. | The fundamental service of farm management is problem-solving. The major aspect of the Farm Management service is supervision of the tenant farmer with an emphasis on financial planning and business management. | The fundamental service of farm management is problem-solving. The major aspect of the Farm Management service is total corporate involvement in agri-consulting, which may include technical production, financial planning, trusts, brokerage, real estate, and taxes. |

|      |          |       |       |            |
| ---- | -------- | ----- | ----- | ---------- |
|      | RM       | $-.40$ | .20   | 1.30  N = 7 |
| By   | FM I     | $-.15$ | $-.35$ | 1.00  N = 15 |
| Type | FM II    | .07   | .13   | 2.53  N = 16 |
|      | FM III   | $-.10$ | 1.00  | .30   N = 7 |

Although the above analysis has indicated that the members of the Doane Farm Management Division do not have a contemporary explanation of who their client is, nor a clear understanding of the motive that causes the absentee landowner to seek their services, there is high agreement among the Regional and Farm Managers about what they ought to be doing once they have the contract. The vast majority strongly accepted (Z-scores from $-1.00$ to $+2.53$) the Vision III dramatization which stated that the major aspect of the farm management service is total corporate involvement in agri-consulting, which may include technical production, financial planning, trusts, brokerage, real estate, and taxes. The Type II Farm Managers overwhelmingly accepted this card because it again submerged the consulting service as part of the Farm Management service. The Regional Managers and the Type I Farm Managers accepted the card because of the diversity of services that it provided as compared to the Vision I and Vision II cards. The Vision I card depicted the service as being the supervision of technical production and the Vision II card limited the service to tenant supervision with an emphasis on financial planning and business management. The Type III Farm Managers, in keeping with their self-definition of a modern Mr. Doane, accepted the Vision II card concerning tenant supervision, financial planning and business management for the client.

(15)  Consultation

        (60)                               (37)                            (11)

| **Vision I** | **Vision II** | **Vision III** |
|---|---|---|
| The best way to think of the Farm Management consulting service is as technical advice that's provided to the owner-operator related to scientific farming practices. | The best way to think of the Farm Management consulting service is as a customized answer to a specific situation such as hog confinement or as financial planning and budgeting for the owner-operator. | The best way to think of the Farm Management consulting service is as the bringing together of the necessary technical consultants to answer the many complex decisions of modern agriculture for such clients as individuals, corporations, estates, and nation states. |

|  |  |  |  |  |
|---|---|---|---|---|
|  | RM | $-.20$ | .50 | .90  N = 7 |
| By | FM I | $-.35$ | .05 | .60  N = 15 |
| Type | FM II | $-.63$ | $-.33$ | .33  N = 16 |
|  | FM III | $-.60$ | .10 | .30  N = 7 |

As the negative Z-scores for the Vision I card on consultation indicate, no one in the Division feels there is much of a market for a consultation service directed at providing the owner-operator with technical advice related to scientific farming practices. In fact, the focus group interviews with the Farm Managers produced dramatizations that depicted owner-operators as superior in technical advice to many Farm Managers. Since the Farm Manager Type II does not do very much specialized consulting, it's not surprising that they reject the Vision II dramatization that consulting is a customized answer to special problems like hog confinement or financial planning for the owner-operator. What is surprising is the lack of strong acceptance of the Vision III consulting card by the Type I Farm Managers. This card reflects the position of the American Society of Farm Managers as expressed in their most recent edition of their manual on farm management. This lack of acceptance may be due to two factors: (1) the Vision III card describes the Farm Manager as a broker bringing in an outside consultant to answer complex questions. The focus group interviews revealed that younger Farm Managers like the stature of making those decisions themselves, and (2) a dilemma concerning the consulting service itself. The focus group interviews established the fact that only the large operations could afford a Doane consultant at $400/day. The dilemma is that the Farm Managers with the least experience (Type I) tend to be the most aggressive in the marketplace, while the Farm Managers with the experience necessary to provide the advice (Type II) seem the least interested. The final quandry on this issue is that while the Type I Farm Manager currently generates 20% of his production through consultation and real estate sales, this percentage may decrease as the number of farms he manages increases and thus the current differences between the two major groups of Farm Managers may dissipate.

(16) Support Services

| (21) | (29) | (3) |
|---|---|---|
| **Vision I** | **Vision II** | **Vision III** |
| The expert support services of the home office are used primarily by the Farm Manager as a selling point to clients. However, the Farm Manager's use of them in practice is negligible — the Farm Manager is the sole deliverer of service and expertise to the client. | The expert support services of the home office are used by the Farm Manager as a selling point to clients. In addition, Farm Managers use the support services from the library, accounting, commodity forecasting, and creative services departments in managing their farms. | The expert support services of the home office are major components, along with Farm Manager, for delivering agricultural services to clients. |

|  |  |  |  |  |
|---|---|---|---|---|
|  | RM | $-1.80$ | 1.30 | 1.30  N = 7 |
| By | FM I | $-1.90$ | .65 | .45  N = 15 |
| Type | FM II | $-1.87$ | 1.13 | 1.23  N = 16 |
|  | FM III | $-2.50$ | .80 | 1.00  N = 7 |

All participants in the Q-sort rejected (Z-scores from $-1.80$ to $-2.50$) the view that home office support services are only a "selling point" and that in practice the Farm Manager's use of them is negligible. They clearly believe that the home office provides integral and necessary support for the delivery of farm management services to their clients. In the future they believe it should be a major component in the Farm Manager — client interface (Z-scores from $+.45$ to $+1.30$). The Type I Farm Managers were not as strong as other Division members in their acceptance of the Vision II and Vision III cards. This may be due to two reasons. First, during the focus group interviews the Farm Managers voiced many complaints about the accuracy of the accounting service but felt that these errors were decreasing. Second, the young Farm Managers were unaware of specific Doane people in the home office who held expertise in various aspects of farming that could be contacted to assist them in consultation. As they become more familiar with home office personnel, or as the Division helps to familiarize them, they should move closer to the view held by the Regional Managers and more experienced Farm Managers.

**Summary of Product**

The preceding analysis provides several insights into the nature of the farm management and consultation services for the future. One major finding is that the products for both services ought to be delivered corporately, not individually. The Division personnel see Doane as a corporation providing technical production, financial planning, business management, brokerage, real estate and tax advice through the farm managers with the strong support of home office technical expertise.

Among the Farm Managers, there exists two contrasting viewpoints about the Division's service. The Type II Farm Managers strongly embrace a view that there is really only one service — Farm Management — with consulting subsumed as part of it, while the Type I Farm Managers view farm management and consulting as two separate services.

Another observation is the possible existence of a dilemma with regard to delivery of the consultation service. The Farm Managers with the least experience have the most enthusiasm for consulting, while the nature of the client demands experience. Yet, the experienced Farm Managers seemed disinterested in selling the service.

Finally, the Division strongly accepts the importance of the home office support services in delivering consultation and farm management services. However, the younger Farm Managers may need to be educated about the availability of home office assistance — particularly the specialized expertise of the home office relative to consultation problem-solving.

## Marketing Strategy

(17) Doane's Competitive Edge

|  | (45) | (41) | (18) |
|---|---|---|---|
|  | **Vision I** | **Vision II** | **Vision III** |

| | Vision I | Vision II | Vision III |
|---|---|---|---|
| | The key to Doane's competitive edge in the marketplace is that the Farm Manager is of the land, educated in agriculture, and the possessor of impeccable integrity. | The key to Doane's competitive edge in the marketplace is that Doane has the image of a longstanding conservative company which knows all aspects of agriculture and can produce the expert advice necessary to making the Farm Manager better than his counterparts with other companies. | The key to Doane's competitive edge in the marketplace is that Doane can aggressively marshall its expertise from marketing, publications, and farm management to solve any agri-problem in the marketplace. |

|  |  | | |
|---|---|---|---|
| | RM    − .80 | − .60 | 1.10  N = 7 |
| By | FM I   − 1.20 | .00 | .55  N = 15 |
| Type | FM II  − .33 | .47 | .90  N = 16 |
| | FM III   .10 | .40 | 1.20  N = 7 |

Once again the Regional Managers and vast majority of Farm Managers reject the Vision I notion that the individual himself provides a competitive edge, whether due to his education, agrarian roots, or personal integrity. The seven Farm Managers forming Type III and participating in the original Mr. Doane vision are the only Farm Managers who fail to reject this dramatization. There is mixed reaction to the Vision II dramatization that portrays Doane's competitive edge as a long-standing conservative company who can produce the necessary advice better than the competition. On the other hand, the Division as a whole accepts for the future the dramatization that Doane's competitive edge will be derived by aggressively marshalling its expertise from all three divisions of the company — marketing, publication, and farm management — to solve any agri-problem. On the Vision III card, the Type I Farm Managers were below the norm for acceptance. Such sorting behavior is consistent with Type I's previous sorting behavior on the role of the home office support services.

(18)  Strategy for New Business

| | (31) | (58) | (47) | |
|---|---|---|---|---|
| | **Vision I** | **Vision II** | **Vision III** | |

| | | Vision I | Vision II | Vision III | |
|---|---|---|---|---|---|

A Doane Farm Manager's best method of getting new business is through referral from people who are knowledgeable of Doane's services, such as present clients, bankers, and lawyers.

A Doane Farm Manager's best method of getting new business is by contacting qualified leads. Qualified leads are acquired through referral, direct mail, and advertising in local papers.

A Doane Farm Manager's best method of getting new business is by having a full-time person in each region whose job function is developing and qualifying prospective clients, creating innovative advertising and promotional programs.

| | | Vision I | Vision II | Vision III | N |
|---|---|---|---|---|---|
| | RM | .40 | .50 | 1.10 | N = 7 |
| By | FM I | .45 | .45 | .05 | N = 15 |
| Type | FM II | .27 | .07 | 1.03 | N = 16 |
| | FM III | .10 | .40 | −1.00 | N = 7 |

Although the Division consistently rejected the Division's identity, Division structure, and product characterization of Vision I, they continue to regard the old strategy of referral for getting new business as a viable one in the foreseeable future. The focus group interviews further amplified that Doane Farm Managers and Regional Managers regard the referral of prospective clients from people who are knowledgeable of their past service (present clients, bankers, lawyers) as one of the best methods for getting new business.

Similarly, the Division staff accepts to some degree the Vision II method for getting new business, a procedure of contacting qualified leads through direct mail and advertising in local papers. The Vision II card parallels the recommended procedure of the American Society of Farm Managers in their management manual.

However, the Regional Managers and the Type II Farm Managers regard the Vision III card as the best means of getting new business in the future—that being the use of a full-time person in each region whose job function consists of developing and qualifying prospective clients and creative innovative advertising and promotional programs.

The Type I Farm Managers evidently prefer to do their own selling and the Type III Farm Managers do not want (Z-scores = −1.00) another person interfering in their intimate relationship with the client. The importance of this sacred relationship was dramatized in the focus group interview.

(19) Advertising

|  | (53) | (17) | (49) |
|---|---|---|---|
|  | **Vision I** | **Vision II** | **Vision III** |

| Vision I | Vision II | Vision III |
|---|---|---|
| The best advertising of Doane Farm Management is the quality service that's provided for Doane Farm Management clients. Actions speak louder than words. | The best advertising of Doane Farm Management is through regionally developed ads placed in local newspapers combined with mailing lists taken from the local tax roles. | The best advertising of Doane Farm Management is through a continuous national advertising program that creates an awareness and need for Doane and the farm management services that it offers. |

|  |  | | | |
|---|---|---|---|---|
| By Type | RM | − .20 | − .50 | .50   N = 7 |
|  | FM I | .25 | .40 | − .45   N = 15 |
|  | FM II | .30 | − .40 | .30   N = 16 |
|  | FM III | .90 | .00 | − 1.30   N = 7 |

The Type III Farm Managers are consistent with their previous sorting behavior as they endorse the notion that the best advertising of Doane's Farm Management is the quality service they are providing. Thus they regard local newspaper advertising as ineffective (A-score = 0.0) and strongly reject (Z-score = − 1.30) the Vision III view of a nationally directed advertising program.

The focus group and face-to-face interviews provided scenarios showing that the Type II Farm Managers and Regional Managers object to the Vision II view of placing local ads and mailing flyers because these techniques had been erratic in their application and ineffectual in their impact when they were tried in the past. During the interviews they did seem to support a consistent and well-defined localized ad campaign that would portray local Doane Farm Managers and their Regional Manager with pictures and brief resumes so as to dramatize the depth of experience that exists in the Doane company.

The Regional Managers and Type II Farm Managers enlightenedly accepted the Vision III dramatization of a national advertising awareness campaign of Doane's Farm Management service primarily because they remembered the success of the *Wall Street Journal* article of the Doane company and the ads that were placed in the *Wall Street Journal,* the *Chicago Tribune,* and the St. Louis papers. While there were accolades for the use of this strategy, they expressed frustration that their offices were not prepared to handle the volume of unqualified leads. Also, they were not sure how many new clients the campaign actually produced.

The Type I Farm Manager's rejection of the Vision III advertising strategy may be partly explained by the fact that many of the newer employees were not working in the Division when the *Wall Street Journal* article appeared and in part because they've heard the stories from the office secretaries about the problems created by the unqualified leads and the requests for the "give-away item" which triggered the inquiry.

Face-to-face interviews with the home office advertising department revealed general frustration with attempts to affect new business through advertising. This frustration stemmed primarily from the erratic nature of Farm Managers' requests for ad copy, (thus making it difficult to plan) and from the department's inability to elicit any clear view of who the clients were or the motives for why they would want the service (thus making it hard to design effective messages for the ads).

(20) Limits to New Business

|  | (48) | (20) | (59) |
|---|---|---|---|
|  | **Vision I** | **Vision II** | **Vision III** |

| Vision I | Vision II | Vision III |
|---|---|---|
| The main obstacle to a major increase in a Farm Manager's work load is the time it takes to do a quality job of management. There are some real limits to the number of farms that can be managed without hurting client relations. If you have too many farms you'll start losing clients. | The main obstacle to a major increase in a Farm Manager's work load is the dramatic growth in competition from other farm management companies, bank trusts, owner-operators, and former Doane Farm Managers. There's only so many farms out there to manage and competition is keen. | The main obstacle to a major increase in a Farm Manager's work load is the absence of a meaningful incentive program. If a Farm Manager is asked to dramatically increase the profitability of Doane, he too should be proportionally rewarded. The business is there, it's just there's no monetary reward for going after it. |

|  | | | | |
|---|---|---|---|---|
|  | RM | $-.10$ | $-.60$ | $-1.60$  N = 7 |
| By | FM I | $-.35$ | $-.55$ | $-2.35$  N = 15 |
| Type | FM II | $-.03$ | $-1.33$ | $1.57$  N = 16 |
|  | FM III | $.40$ | $-2.20$ | $-.90$  N = 7 |

The most surprising sorting reaction to any cards in the deck centered on the issue regarding the limits to new business. For the most part all vision depictions were rejected. Close examination of the cards revealed that the problem may be the wording of this issue in each of the three visions. In the idealized future vision of the Division, the majority of people reject all three cards. They could well be doing this because of the negative phrasing of the drama. It could be that the respondents in their idealized future would not want any obstacle standing in the way of new business be it the time it takes to do a quality job (Vision I), a dramatic growth in competition from other companies and banks (Vision II), or the absence of a meaningful incentive program (Vision III).

The only exception to this rejection behavior of the Division members stems from the sorting behavior of the Type II Farm Managers. And they may well have intended that in the future a Farm Manager should not be asked to dramatically increase their production loads in order to get profits for Doane.

## Summary of Marketing Strategy

The sorting behavior on issues related to marketing strategy reveals several important insights. First, for the future, Doane's competitive edge is seen as stemming from the ability to aggressively marshall its expertise from all three Divisions of the company (marketing, publication, and farm management) to solve any agri-problem. The Division rejects the notion that the man is greater than the land and that the competitive edge therefore stems from the individual's education, agrarian roots, and personal integrity. For the future strength will come from the corporate image of Doane and the expertise that the corporation possesses — the corporation is greater than the man and the land.

Second, the sorting behavior points out a potential weakness in the interface of corporate strength and the acceptable strategies for getting new business. The Division as a whole regards the Vision I strategy of referrals for getting new business as a viable one for the foreseeable future, even though the Division's future identity, the Division's future structure, and the Division's future product are from the idealized view of Vision III.

Even the Regional Managers' and Type II Farm Managers' acceptance of the Vision III card on strategy for new business is not as encouraging as it might initially seem. This is so because the Type II Farm Managers presently have full production loads and appear less likely to need the qualified leads that the full-time person in each region would develop. At the same time, the Type I Farm Managers are neutral about learning of prospective qualified clients from a single person in the region. Indeed there is evidence that the consultant oriented Type I Farm Managers have a tendency to be reactionary in their client-manager relations even as they embrace the Division identity and Division structure of a profit oriented, growth oriented future.

Similarly, the Division is split on the best methods for advertising and again the Type I Farm Managers reject the strategy that best fits the future identity they want to embrace and the product(s) they want to provide.

Moreover, the Type II Farm Managers are not the ones doing consulting work, nor do they express much interest in it for the future. Thus, leads qualified in this area may not be acceptable to the Type II Farm Managers.

The above points to a potential problem to be solved. Type I Farm Managers will need to be oriented and trained to accept strategies for getting new business and advertising that are appropriate to a profit-oriented, growth center Vision III product, Division identity, and Division structure. The Division's majority rejection of Vision III card #49 regarding the limits to new business shows that for the future, there shouldn't be any external obstacle to limit new business. The key will be in whether or not the steps are taken to preclude the internally selected marketing strategies from being that obstacle.

# PART V:
## Using the Theory to Conduct Marketing Research

# V: Using the Theory to Conduct Marketing Research

The last decade has seen the Speech Communication discipline move in the direction of more applied research. Our professional organizations have developed special applied communication interest areas and many undergraduate and graduate Speech Communication Departments have developed internship programs and courses in applied communication research. In this section, we report original research that is seldom presented in our professional literature. However, our new directions require that we begin to develop a body of knowledge on how communication theories can be used to do market research. This section includes six essays that are intended to demonstrate the efficacy of using Bormann's dramatistic communication theory to do marketing research.

The first three articles represent the incorporation of Bormann's theory in doing qualitative marketing research. The opening essay is based upon a lecture Shields gave in a seminar for agricultural marketing researchers which explains the "nuts and bolts" of conducting a dramatistic based focus group interview. The next two entries are actual reports of two separate studies that were done for the Animal Health Division of Shell Chemical Company on a swine gestation litter conditioner. These were qualitative studies using dramatistic based focus group interviews as the method for gathering data about the product.

The last three essays in this section are concerned with the quantitative application of Bormann's dramatistic communication theory to the solution of problems associated with the introduction of new products. The first essay describes the advantages of using our dramatistic based communication approach for doing market segmentation studies. The second essay contains excerpts from our market segmentation study of large hog producers. The last entry is an original essay by Richard Bush which expresses Upjohn's satisfaction with the results of a dramatistic communication theory based market segmentation study.

# 16

# Dramatistic Communication Based Focus Group Interviews

## DONALD C. SHIELDS

In a recent essay in the American Marketing Association's *Marketing News,* Mr. Dietz Leonhard discussed the question, "Can Focus Group Interviews Survive?" His answer, subsequent to pinpointing weaknesses of the research technique, was a qualified yes. The qualification came in his assertion that proper focus group interviews must be more than "focused answer confrontations;" they must instead stress the group dynamics approach to eliciting information, allowing the group participants to "make full use of the purposely provided opportunity to unburden themselves of frustrating experiences, on the one hand, and to share happy experiences, on the other."

In this essay I hope to present my views on approaching focus group interviews from the small group communication perspective of my discipline of speech communication. Specifically, I will be drawing from Professor Ernest Bormann's views on small group communication. In so doing, I will describe how informational interviewing techniques can be combined with descriptive scenarios to elicit both "focused" and interpretively "rich" small group communication exchanges.

Before moving to the specifics of my presentation, let me say that my remarks come from basic assumptions of my discipline, as opposed to those which might come from say a psychologist or sociologist. However, what I have to say is not just from an academic textbook, but is tempered by the realities of both experimental and applied research in the field. For me, no higher accolade could be bestowed on an academic theory than the simple, "Eureka, it works in the field."

The application of focus group interviews to marketing research problems is in essence a recent phenomena. One critic has said that focus group interviews "evolved primarily from misapplication of the theory of research with groups and secondarily from a need to improve on structured-questionnaire techniques." To a great degree, the reasons for turning to focus group interviews need not concern us today. But, what should concern us is how to utilize the techniques to our advantage in eliciting rich data and meeting client concerns. This last statement implies that the goal of focus group interviews is to gather such things as *information, client reactions*, and *fantasies* regarding a product, or company, or service. How can the researcher best utilize focus group interviews to meet this goal? The answer to this question flows from three parallel concerns — the skillful use of informational interview techniques, an understanding of the dynamics of small group communication, and an understanding of the style of group communication. I will utilize these concerns as my guide in examining the several intervening variables that can affect the outcome of a focus group interview.

The first variable affecting the outcome of the focused group interview is the interviewer's knowledge of small group dynamics. The interviewer needs to recognize that even temporary interview groups begin to form a definite structure, enabling the group members to assume and fulfill various group roles, and allowing their communication to flow processually, at times being very task oriented, at other times laughing and joking and being more socially oriented. None of these characteristics of groups should be thought of as bad, for they are a fact of group life. However, without a knowledge of group dynamics, the interviewer does not know whether he is letting the dynamics of group communication work to facilitate the eliciting of information, or encouraging these same dynamics to interfere with the eliciting of information.

By group structure, I mean role structure. The dynamics of a small work group — in our case a group of focus interviewees — call for people to function as idea generators, critics, social facilitators, tension releasers, supporters of another's ideas, and information givers. The group members work out among themselves mutual expectations for who will fulfull what role functions. Usually role structure will not fully stabilize until an hour or two of interaction has elapsed, but the dynamics of role placement begins almost immediately. Most groups stabilize with little difficulty. Others, about one in five, have difficulty, and the potential antagonisms occurring over role placement can definitely impede the product outcome of the focus group interview. With knowledge of group communication dynamics, an effective interviewer can help the groups get over the role struggle hurdles and improve the content of the communication exchanges.

At the same time that group members are seeking role placement, the communication exchanges that occur tend to proceed processually, that is, the group travels through phases within the social and task dimension. For example, every group meeting for the first time shows definite signs of what my mentor, Ernie Bormann, termed *primary tension*. Group members are nervous, unsure of what's happening, and basically ill-at-ease. The skilled interviewer always spends a few minutes getting participants acquainted, put-at-ease, and ready to communicate in serious exchanges. Next, group comunication tends to go through an *orientation* phase. Members want to know what they are there for, and more importantly, what direction their communication exchanges should follow. With primary tension and orientation out of the way, groups proceed to the *task* phase. Since most members in a focus group interview have volunteered their time they are anxious to offer their contributions. Thus, the task phase can generally proceed very smoothly. But, sometimes, another phase enters in when the task gets difficult or the members get weary. This phase, theorists have labeled *flight*. The term refers to the fact that groups will sometimes talk around the issue, or digress into some other issue that is seemingly irrelevant. However, the interviewer skilled in group dynamics will recognize that such flight is symtomatic of group communication, and allow it to run its course. The group needs such time as a kind of break from the task at hand. Once the break is over, the group will willingly return to the task.

Another aspect of group communication of import to the interviewer is the *style* of the communication exchanges within the group process. By style I mean, what do the communication exchanges of groups of people look like. For one, the style is one of group members interacting spontaneously. They do that by hearing a familiar content theme, picking up on it, embellishing it, and elaborating upon it with a similar problem or rich experience of their own. The chief characteristic of small group exchanges is that they tend to be *dramatized*. Ernie argues that members actually depict "a world filled with heroes and villains, scenarios and scenes. Sometimes when dramatizing occurs, the tempo of conversation is picked up, the members grow excited, interrupt one another, blush, laugh, and in general forget their self-consciousness." Bormann calls such moments "group fantasy events" and argues that when such events occur the tone of the meeting, which is often quite tense or quiet immediately prior to the dramatizing, becomes lively, animated, and boisterous. The chaining process involves both verbal and non-verbal communication indicating participation in the drama. Since some of the characters in the fantasies depicted in the communication exchanges are sympathetic characters doing laudable things, and others are dispicable characters doing ill you can see that group attitudes are evident in the dramatizations. The skilled investigator can use dramatic scenarios to test and legitimatize the values held by the focus group interviewees.

Let me give you an example of a chaining scenario, defined in dramatistic terms, from a small group of veterinarians, interviewed using the scenario approach outlined here:

Interviewer: In a conversation I had with farmers I reached the impression that they can treat cattle diseases such as footrot, pneumonia, and shipping fever with large doses of antibiotics just as well as the vets can. What do you think?

Person 1: Agree.

Person 2: Yah.

Person 1: "These guys that specialize in grassland feedlots, they get pretty good you know, they get as good as anybody at recognizing these diseases and treating the common things."

Person 3: "They've got the exact same drugs we've got — these cowboys do just as good as we can do."

Person 4: "Yah, but they don't differentiate between the common and the other."

Person 1: "No, that's true, but a lot of them don't even differentiate between pneumonia and diarrhea."

Person 2: "Yah, we find a lot of misuse of drugs."

Person 3: "Well, part of it is the fact that most of these drugs are readily available and more and more the 'shotgun-therapy-types' come out regardless whether they got it diagnosed or not."

Person 1: "When you shotgun with everything in the book, you're going to get some result in most cases."

Person 3: "That's right, and they don't need us (the veterinarians)."

A chief advantage to viewing the style of communication exchanges as a series of dramatic fantasy themes is that such themes can be concurrently verified across a series of focus group interviews, thereby enabling a collective depiction of the way in which a product or a company is viewed.

The third variable affecting the outcome of the focused group interview is that of interviewer preparation. The interviewer must be highly familiar with the subject under investigation, must have planned the interview, and must adopt a style compatible with the scenario approach to eliciting group communication exchanges.

By subject familiarity, I mean that the interviewer must, if he or she is studying, say, attitudes toward a product, know the product's uses, have some idea of the product's strengths, and have some idea of the product's weaknesses. The researcher gains such a familiarity by doing his/her homework. The researcher can look at the client's product brochures, advertisements, and product portfolios. The researcher can ask the client what he thinks of his product, and how he thinks his market sees it. The researcher can draw from personal experiences with previous research on similar products within the industry. Without such preparation, the interviewer will be ill-prepared to plan the agenda for the focus group interview, and will be completely unable to develop scenarios which can assist in eliciting dramatized exchanges. With such preparation, the researcher will be sufficiently knowledgeable to allow agenda planning and to anticipate issues and themes around which he/she needs to build scenarios.

Planning the interview means preparation, prior to the focus group sessions, so that the interviewer knows where he/she wants the interview to go. Here, the researcher must have a clear understanding of the interview's purpose and function as these elements relate to both eliciting information per se, and using the structure of small group communication to elicit that information. In eliciting information, preparation means specifying the several objectives that can be followed to help in meeting the interview's purpose and function. Akin to preparing objectives, is the preparation of a preliminary working agenda containing subject content areas and issues relevant to the interview's purposes. This preliminary working agenda can also begin to include the kinds of questions that will be asked. With such preparation the interview will be *focused*. Without it, the interview will in all likelihood lack focus.

The final area of pre-preparation concerns the interview style. The interviewer must treat the interview as a *small group interview*, not as a one-to-one, two-person interview. There are several guidelines the interviewer can follow to assist in maintaining the proper style. For example, allow the group members to spontaneously react to agenda points. Also, ask questions that could be answered by one person at a time. Avoid questions that are so sterile that they could be answered by means of a questionnaire. Finally encourage and allow group members to tell narratives about the product, including devil scenarios or hero scenarios. Allow other group members to pick up on these scenarios, embellish them, and elaborate upon them. In short, plan your agenda questions and scenario outline in such a way that a group picture of the product unfolds, that is confirmed by the multiple, spontaneous responses of the group members.

The third variable that can affect the outcome of the focused group interview is the interviewer. Here I'm referring to the *duties* of the interviewer as *group leader* and *information eliciter*. Recall that primary tension exists at the beginning of all group meetings and is especially serious with group members who do not know each other. As group leader, the interviewer needs to do something to help alleviate this primary tension, which as you recall is an impediment to getting on with the task. There are a couple of simple techniques for eliminating tension. One is to introduce the members and a second is to allow them a few minutes to chit-chat, to get to know one another, to find their common ground and interests.

Also, tension is created by the orientation phase. Here, you simply need to fill the group in on who you are and what you're doing. I suggest as much openness and honesty as you can muster. As a researcher you expect the participants to be open, straight-forward, and honest. Deception on your part about the purpose of the study, why you're conducting it, the company you work for, and even who you're conducting it for can only serve to *alert* the respondents to this sensitive area. If you're mysterious and closed, you've set the model for the respondents to be mysterious and closed and deceptive. If you or your client suggest concealing the client's identity, or the product's identity, I suggest that you only do so until the end of the session. And, explain why you are withholding this information at the beginning. Something like, "we don't want to bias your attitude at this time, but we'll be happy to answer all of your questions at the end of the meeting." Also, relating to the orientation phase, the interviewer should explain why the interviewees were selected, how the information will be used, how confidence of the interviewees' answers will be maintained, and how long the session will take.

The main body of the interview will consist of simple fantasy theme statements in scenario form to encourage the group respondents to provide scenarios characterizing the strengths, weaknesses, and limitations of, say, a product in dramatistic fashion. For example, sample scenarios indicating positive and negative reactions to particular events, or happenings, or product usages or whatever may be offered.

Other duties of the interviewer include drawing out the silent participants and keeping dominant members from monopolizing the meeting. I might add that the problem of seemingly dominant members monopolizing the conversation becomes more acute with larger groups, and also tends to occur when participants know each other and there is some form of status or organizational heirarchy serving as a hidden agenda. Also, the interviewer should watch the time and the agenda and keep the meeting on track and on time.

The final variable affecting the outcome of the focused group interview is the skill of the interviewer in using effective techniques in leading the meeting. As a general rule, the interviewer wants to handle questions and comments in such a way that people are encouraged to make more contributions. The good interviewer relies on both *primary questions* that introduce topics and *secondary questions* that elicit further information. Moreover, he or she tries to avoid stress provoking *directed* questions and *closed* questions that allow only a yes-no client response. Again, he or she introduces scenarios that stimulate group dramatizing. Here, a word of caution is in order. It's very easy for an interviewer to stifle group interaction, not only by asking the wrong questions, but by having a poor sense of timing concerning when to ask a follow-up question. Moreover, interviewer reaction to the group's comments can stifle a group fantasy event before it's had a chance to play out. With practice and experience, however, the interviewer can gain confidence and a "seat-of-the-pants" feel for using the scenario approach.

The final variable that can affect the outcome of the focus group interview is the market researcher's analysis of the collected data. In analyzing the data, the researcher will want to look for recurring content themes within groups and across groups that provide a verbal depiction of the respondents view of the subject. The researcher also looks for fantasy narratives that describe hero or villain scenarios. As well, he or she looks for themes where other group members chime in, embellish, nod, or verbalize agreement all at once. Moments where everyone is excited and spontaneous are important behavioral indications that the focus group interview has hit upon an important content point. The interviewer should try to piece together a picture of interviewee attitudes about the subject. How did the group members depict the product dramatically? What recurring scenarios or character attributes were indicated? As the data analysis is evolving, remember that the goal of focus group interviews is to give the client a kind and type of information that couldn't be elicited in questionnaire form. Use the dramatic depictions and recurring themes to read the attitudes, and values, and motives of the participants. Accept that meanings are in the group communication, the verbal language itself.

With the preceding explanation of how informational interview techniques can be combined with descriptive scenarios to elicit small group communication exchanges completed, let me offer my insights about the application and limitations of the focus group interview method.

(1) To me, focus group interviews are an exploratory research tool most useful in generating insight into the way people perceive a product, or perceive a company. They get at attitudes in the form of capturing dramas or visions held by respondents about the product or company in question.

(2) Focus group interviews, as seen from the communications perspective outlined today, are small group interviews. Seven to nine participants are an excellent number. Five is sufficient. Groups of this size allow the members to interact together and preclude the session from splitting into a number of smaller groups that pick up and discuss their own agenda. Usually, four or five such groups will be sufficient to elicit the universe of responses pertaining to a given subject.

(3) The data elicited from the focus group interviews following a well-prepared tight interview schedule can be confirmed and validated by content analysis of the fantasy themes and concurrent validation across groupings. Constitutive meanings of the dramas can be checked empirically by the administration of Q-sorts containing dramatic depictions of the relevant fantasy themes. Respondent sorting behavior can then be factor analyzed by the use of Q-type factor analysis to provide Q-arrays of the descending importance of the content themes.

(4) Focus group interviews are not intended to be ad lib interviews. They require preparation, planning, advanced construction of scenarios, and willingness of the interviewer to wear two hats — one of the interviewer, and one of group communication participant.

(5) The more work put into the preparation and planning of a focus group interview, the easier the interpretation stage and report write-up. The richer data gained through preparation pays off in terms of richer insights into people's attitudes and values.

In closing let me say that I've welcomed the chance to speak with you and give my insights into focus group interviews. Good luck in your continuing market research using the focus group method.

# 17

# Hog Producer Focus Group Interviews on Shell's Gestation Litter Conditioner

Doane Agricultural Service, Inc.
Marketing Research Division

## DONALD C. SHIELDS

## Introduction

### Purpose

Shell Chemical Company, Animal Health Division, is marketing a new sow and gilt gestation conditioning feed additive. The product has been on the market approximately one year. We were asked to provide attitudinal and motivation input via focus group interviews to assist in the development and refinement of marketing plans and strategies for this product. Specifically, the purpose of the focus group interview research was to explore factors related to consumer product awareness and adoption with an emphasis on: (1) viable information sources; (2) credibility of information sources; (3) hog management production goals; (4) motivation for product usage; (5) acceptability of the gestation conditioning concept; (6) product performance and measurement; (7) product form acceptability; and (8) product availability.

### Authorization

This focus group interview research was authorized by Mr. James J. Riley, Staff Business Representative, Business Planning Animal Health, Shell Chemical Company, in a Market Research Agreement dated December 29, 1976.

### Design and Methodology

The research design called for five focus group interviews to be conducted during January, 1977. Two interviews were aimed at hog producers who were *unaware* of the product and two interviews were aimed at those hog

Reprinted with permission from Animal Health Division, Shell Chemical Company and Doane Agricultural Service, Inc.

321

producers *aware* of the product. A decision on whether to aim the fifth interview at users or aware producers was withheld until midway into the interview schedule. It was decided to hold the final interview with *aware* producers and include some users.

All meetings were luncheon or dinner meetings held in private dining facilities at local restaurants. Locations and types of interviews are listed below:

| Type | Location | Date |
|------|----------|------|
| Unaware of product | Frankfort, Indiana | January  5, 1977 |
| Aware of product | Frankfort, Indiana | January  6, 1977 |
| Aware of product | Coon Rapids, Iowa | January 12, 1977 |
| Unaware of product | DeWitt, Iowa | January 24, 1977 |
| Aware of product | DeWitt, Iowa | January 24, 1977 |

Each meeting was designed for five to nine participants. Some 13 hours of intensive interview data were collected. The major content themes were confirmed both internally within a session and across sessions. Forty-one hog producers participated in the five interviews. The participants represented small, medium and large hog producers and included the several types of hog production operations, farrow to finish, purebred breeders, SPF operations, and feeder pig producers.

Dr. Donald C. Shields, a small group communication research specialist, helped develop the questions in a scenario format with appropriate input from the Marketing Research Division of Doane and the Animal Health Division of Shell Chemical Company. Doane personnel involved were Dub Carlton, Bob Homes, Nick Nichols and Sam Moore. Valuable contributions were made by Jim Riley and Leonard Brusatori of the Shell staff.

## Summary and Analysis of Focus Group Interviews

### Production Goals

Major production goals include year-end profits and number of hogs produced. Hog producers don't appear to strive for more efficient hog production as much as they tend to farrow a sufficient number of sows and gilts to reach a pre-set production figure.

Specific goals within the hog production operation center on such things as number of pigs per sow, weaning weights, and marketing weights. For example, if marketing weights have not reached a desired level in 180 days, there is a tendency for some producers to keep the pigs for another month until they do.

There is a general tendency to want to save every pig possible. The evidence is a common practice of sorting and switching runts and putting the runts together. This practice is based on the view that if the runts get the milk and the feed, they will catch up and reach the desired size. Only a few producers see the problem of runts as one "not worth the time and effort of caring," and dispose of them.

Producers do not think of eliminating runts to any great degree. They are so used to the problem, so exposed to it, that it is accepted as commonplace and, generally felt, not likely to be eliminated.

A production goal that seems most desirable is uniformity of litters. The general concensus was that uniformity is more important than number of pigs per sow. Eight or nine or ten thrifty pigs is seen as better than fifteen of varied sizes. The reason: as it stands now, fifteen varied pigs means work and labor (time) on the part of the producer — the sorting and switching that they all engage in.

Recommendations:

1. Tie the product to the benefits of uniform/thrifty litters.
2. Describe runts as a problem that can be helped by the use of the product.
3. Describe the economic and time/labor benefits from reducing the incidence of runts.

## Performance Measurement

Hog producers see performance measurement as akin to production goals. They more or less provide their own operational definition of when a goal is met. Yet, they think specifically in terms of profits. But the chief contributors to profits are such specifics as "pounds of pigs weaned per sows bred" or "average daily weight gain" or "specific dollars and cents economic return on investment." More pigs, per se, does not mean a lot to them — the efficiency of more pigs from the same investment does. For example, they discussed cost of production per pound of pork and cost of feed ration per head and yearly weaning weight averages per herd.

Nevertheless, the acid test of determining the day to day success of the operation is an "eyeball estimate." Hog producers simply do not keep sufficient records (usually because of the time and labor involved) to have a day to day handle on the operation.

Operation habits also affect their ability to measure a product's performance. They understand the concept of controlled on-farm testing, but they don't feel their production methods and feeding methods will allow them to do it. Also, there is a lot of mixing of litters and this makes it difficult to know which sow farrowed which pig and which pig belonged to which sow. Similarly, it is difficult for them to know which sow or pig might have received a particular additive.

Recommendations:

4. Do not depend on the hog producer to be able to measure the performance of the product using current operating procedures.

5. Select and assist certain producers in key hog producing counties in setting up controlled on-farm testing procedures — not necessarily statistically pure procedures.

## Production Records

Hog producers have accepted as progressive the idea of keeping production records, but no one has told them specifically why records should be kept. Many, especially the larger producers, appear to keep some form of records. But the kind of records kept are not uniform and the most sophisticated seem to be yearly weaning weight averages. The use of scales is accepted as important; the proper use of this weight information is not well understood. Many of the record keepers do so more to determine which sows to keep, than as a handle on the day to day success of the operation. That is, birth and weaning weights are put to genetic uses; yearly weaning weight averages are signs of a good or bad production year. But again, most producers do not weigh, and they skip doing it because of the time and labor involved.

Recommendations:

6. Emphasize those attributes or qualities of the product that can be seen visually.

7. Do not depend on a producer's existing production records to prove out the claims of the product.

8. Select suitable farms in key production counties and assist the producer in designing a record keeping system suitable to proving out the advantages of the product.

## Status of Hog Management

Hog producers see good management as problem avoidance. Management is seen as proper nutrition, keeping an eye to genetics (weeding out the weak and breeding the strong), use of good boar power, time spent in the farrowing house, sorting and shifting runts, etc. Management in terms of hog production efficiency is just beginning to be grasped.

Hog producers tend to think in terms of time and labor invested. Adoption of a new product or incorporation of a new method means time and labor investment, as well as the cost of the product. Thus, there is a uniform, sensed feeling that a proposed change must work out to their benefit economically. Otherwise, such a change will not likely be tried. The only exception is if a problem occurs and they feel they must try something.

Recommendations:

9. Tie the product to time savings or labor savings.

10. Show the economic benefit of the product in concrete dollars and cents.

11. Describe the product in terms of elimination of problems leading to more uniform litters, shortening of the period between farrowing and marketing, and so forth.

## Acceptance of the Gestation Conditioning Concept

Hog producers do not think in terms of conditioning the sow to aid her offspring. They are not skeptical of the concept once it is introduced; but as a general rule they have not thought of it.

When the concept is introduced, hog producers want to know how it works and want to know how they can see the benefits. Producers want specifics in terms of exactness of product claims and cost analysis ("Is the product economically utilitarian?"). Producers want to know how much work is involved in using the product and they want to know what operation changes will be necessary to adopt it. Finally, hog producers want to be assured the product will not create new problems.

The issue of creating new problems is accompanied by a general distrust of additives and drugs per se. Hog producers would like to get away from them. Before accepting a new additive they want to be assured of benefits. Assurances must be tied to concrete specifics.

There is some tendency to view the concept of a conditioner as "looks or appearance" and as one producer put it, "appearance doesn't pay the bills." Thus, producers appear more willing to accept the product if claimed advantages are tied to concrete specifics that show the dollars and cents criterion for adopting and using the product.

Recommendations:

12. Explain how the gestation conditioner works. This is needed because of a natural curiosity and the newness of the concept.

13. Explain what is meant by gestation conditioner. Give the observable results.

14. Explain the benefits in hardfast, concrete terms. Provide the dollars and cents economic proof of the pudding.

15. Provide assurance that the product is not a problem creator — that there are no side effects from its use.

16. Describe the necessary operation changes and explain the labor necessary to use the product.

**Rationale for Adopting Products**

All interviewed groups expressed the view that products and methods were adopted as reaction to problems or felt problems. There is a hesitancy on the part of the producers to change or adopt unless there is a problem for fear the change or adoption will create a problem. None of the hog producers indicated that they ever thought in terms of change and possible benefits. "If you've got a problem..." and "I had a problem..." were consistent statements across all interviews. The more a product is directed to the solution of a problem, the greater its likelihood of acceptance given the existing attitudes and outlook of hog producers.

In other words, hog producers are not into the concept of products as benefit promoters. They see multi-causal solutions to many of their hog management problems and believe that there are so many intervening variables that could cause a problem that even a good product may not prove of any use. They are not into thinking how much worse off they might have been had they not been using a good product. Why? Because they can't prove it.

Recommendations:

17. Move to educate hog producers that not all products are problem-solvers; some are benefit promoters.

18. Stress that the product works on poor sows and gilts as well as good sows and gilts; that even with occasional poor herd production the product has still done its job.

19. Accentuate the benefits of the product in terms of problem elimination. Describe problems in terms of dollar loss that can be corrected by using the product.

**Believability of Product Results**

Hog producers indicate that they believe "every hog operation is unique" and therefore "what works on one operation or what works for one producer will not necessarily work for another." This view is a major reason for the hesitancy to adopt a new product or concept unless it meets a specific problem. There are a few curious (perhaps the label is progressive) producers who will initiate use of a new product, but not many.

Hog producers seem more willing to try those products that they "believe will work." The strongest evidence that a product will work is concrete on-farm test results—not results from an experimental farm, but results from tests on "average" hog producing operations. There is a general feeling that experimental farms are different from them, perhaps cleaner, perhaps subject to better care, perhaps subject to better weather. Producers have a relatively good understanding of how product claims are scientifically tested.

Recommendations:

20. Tie product claims to results from on-farm testing in specific hog producing counties.
21. Use product testimonial from producers who have used the product on their farm in a more or less control group — experimental group testing situation.
23. Avoid testimonial based on a simple eyeballing of the results. Although most producers do this, they recognize the deficiency of it when the product is not eliminating a specific visible problem.

## Dealer Credibility

Dealer credibility was probed directly under the topic of information sources as well as indirectly under the topic of product availability. The hog producers expressed some feeling that their dealer did not know much about the product or was not pushing it. However, they indicated that they would not hesitate to ask for a product or change dealers to get a product if they knew for sure that it worked. Without such assurance, those who trusted their dealer would hesitate to use the product without their dealer's recommendation, especially in the absence of other strong evidence that it would work (like on-farm testing). Many producers trust their feed dealer because of the belief that the feed company would have carried out on-farm independent testing on the product or because the dealer would be aware of successful results in other producers' operations.

Many of the aware producers indicated that they had asked their dealer about the product and he had not endorsed it. Hence, they had not received any reinforcement from their dealer to cause them to adopt it. Some of the larger more progressive producers indicated they would go over their dealer's word because they did not really view their dealer as a truly knowledgeable source to begin with.

Finally, dealers are an important information source. This is confirmed by the aware groups stated understanding of the product. Almost all of the aware producers associated the product with worming, with brand names of wormers, and some with dichlorvos, the product's base ingredient. They developed these views of the product from their dealers.

Recommendations:

24. Ascertain the dealers' understanding of the concept of gesation conditioning and their understanding of the claims for the product.
25. Accentuate dealer training programs to insure that dealers understand the concept and the product in terms of how to use it and how it works.

**The Product**

When the concept of Xtra Litter Production for 30 days is presented to hog producers they lack initial certainty as to what it means. Keying on production means little to them at present because of their tendency to achieve desired production goals by simply using more sows and gilts. Given the explanation of the product that came naturally in the open discussion sessions, they tended to warm up to the concept. Some of the groups reacted favorably to an interpretation of the product as Xtra Litter *Protection*. Others expressed the desire for a non-letter/number symbol., i.e., a name, to identify the product, but no one indicated they couldn't really live with what is.

Of course, the non-aware participants could not be probed for their understanding of the symbol "30." Aware participants were probed (and some of the aware participants had used the product). As a general rule, the hog producers do not at this time understand that the product must be used consecutively for thirty days to achieve results. Of the five or six users participating in the meetings, only one appeared to have used the product correctly. Two producers who were also local feed dealers participated in the study and neither indicated an accurate understanding; rather, they clearly gave erroneous impressions of how to use the product. In short, the educational process for correct application of the product does not appear to be getting to the hog producers.

Recommendations:

26. Keep the name, while stressing litter protection along with litter production.
27. Accentuate a dealer training program to insure that those dealers who sell the product understand how it is to be used.
28. Take pains to insure that those producers adopting the product get training in how to use the product and the length of time they must use it.

**Product Form**

For hog producers who top feed and hand dress presently, the form of the product creates little problem. Exceptions to this statement were expressed worries about converting mixing augers with close enough precision to insure proper mix, and worries about adequate feeding amounts for all sows and gilts. Nevertheless, producers indicated that such problems were intrinsic to their existing feeding programs and indicated that they could still see benefit for those sows and gilts who successfully got the program.

Those producers using pelleted feeds indicated they would need to change over feeding patterns, and so did those producers employing automatic feeding equipment. They indicated a desire to have information on means and ways to employ the feeding program in their operation.

Akin to the form problem are problems created by the need for 30 days of feeding. Most producers do not begin to think about sorting for farrowing thirty days ahead of time. They indicate they could do this if they see the benefits, but they do not do so as a matter of course.

Recommendations:

29. Take precautions to insure that the way in which the product must be fed is understood.

30. Indicate the kinds of operational set-ups that work best for the feeding program.

31. Indicate simple means of converting from common feeding operations to more easily incorporate the product's feeding program.

32. Stress the need to sort the sows and gilts 30 days before farrowing as a prerequisite to using the feeding program.

## The Product and Worming

There is a strong association among those hog producers that are aware of the product that it is a wormer. Some referred to it as a 30-day wormer, others that it is a "super wormer," others that all it is, is a wormer. Still others called it another product's brand name and some even called it dichlorvos, its chemical name. One producer said "It's no better than (a brand name wormer)." These comments came out despite the explicit absence of probe scenarios on the product and worming.

Some of the users indicated they used the product for worming. Only one producer appeared to have used the product for a full 30 days as a gestation conditioner. Others upon learning of the gestation conditioning effects of the product said, "Why don't you tell us it's a wormer, too." Others saw advantages to the dual effect, gestation conditioning and worming. Some talked about figuring the cost benefit in the guarantee of worming before farrowing. Still others thought the benefits came from worming.

Most producers gained their association with the product and worming from their dealers. Some picked it up from dichlorvos being mentioned in the ads. Whatever the case, there is an association with worming either as the sole function of the product or as an additional benefit. Clearly, the worming association has not been successfuly prevented. Instead, the absence of a direct, managed link between the product and its brand name wormer, on the part of the manufacturer, has led to an erroneous association in many cases on the part of the producer.

One gets the feeling that the hog producer became aware of the product and when he asked his dealer how does it work, his dealer said "It's a wormer," or a "30-day wormer," or a "super wormer." The dealer probably did this because he didn't know how it worked. On the other hand, some dealers are saying "don't use it, it's just a wormer."

The point is, the product is being linked with a brand name wormer and with worming, despite the effort to keep it disassociated. Since some producers see clear benefits from the dual function, and since farmers are particularly sensitive to deception, the long term advantage for the product may be a direct linkage of dichlorvos as wormer and gestation conditioner, with the two functions coming independently due to the diverse usage periods.

Recommendations:

33. Indicate that dichlorvos is the only chemical based worming product that will achieve the conditioning result.

34. Clarify the difference between the worming function and the gestation conditioning function of the product to both dealers and producers.

35. Don't try to hide the association, especially in the absence of a clear explanation of how dichlorvos is a gestation conditioner independent of its worming function.

36. Claim the dual benefits of gestation conditioning plus worming. Show the cost savings of this two-function product.

**Regional Differences**

There are few variations in viewpoints attributable to regional differences. The few differences that do appear are traceable to differences in size of the operation and, conjointly, progressiveness of the hog producers. The major variation of a regional nature, i.e., between Indiana and Iowa hog producers, was that the Iowa producers used more diverse information sources for gaining knowledge of new products than did Indiana producers.

Recommendations:

37. There is little need to aim advertising of the product at regional differences.

38. Advertising could be directed to specific differences in operations based on size and type of operation and assumed progressiveness.

**Availability**

Many of the hog producers indicated that their dealer didn't know about the product or was not pushing the product. Other dealers had indicated they were not stocking the product because of the absence of requests.

Availability did not seem a problem in terms of becoming aware of the product. It wasn't a direct concern if the producer really wanted a product—he would just ask for it. However, many found it confirming that their dealer could also support their interest in a new product through his recommendations.

Recommendations:

39. Attention to supply lines, i.e., insuring product availability, will aid product promotion. Nevertheless, actual availability is less important than dealer knowledge of the ins-and-outs of the product.

40. Improvement of marketing techniques at the dealer level could both extend the line of supply and increase dealer knowledge.

## Reason for Low Usage of The Product

Hog producers have a strong belief in the uniqueness of their particular operation. They don't believe that what works for them will work for others, and conversely, what has worked for others will work for them.

Along with the above belief, is the fact that producers make changes and adopt products in reaction to problems. If they don't have a problem, there is no reason for change.

Since the product and the concept of gestation conditioning is not seen as a solution to a problem, and since the claimed benefits of the product (less runts, heavier birth weights, greater weaning weights, greater survival to market) are perceived more as everyday conditions that must be lived with than as potential problems for elimination, hog producers are not presently motivated to use it.

Finally, the gestation conditioning concept is not understood, and consumers view it as a wormer and see the claimed benefits as coming from worming—not 30 days of conditioning.

Recommendations:

41. Distinguish between the worming and conditioning functions of the product. Indicate that even clean hogs receive the benefits of gestation conditioning.

42. Educate hog producers to seeing claimed benefits as problem eliminators.

43. Educate hog producers to the concept of benefit-promoter as opposed to problem-solver.

## Information Sources

A significant aspect of the interview schedule included an examination of information sources for gaining awareness of new products.

**Advertisements.** Most of the aware producers gained their initial introduction to the product via advertisements in hog management magazines. Many of them had also discussed the product with their neighbors and with their dealers. There was a tendency for them to know about the product before their dealers did.

**Dealers.** Hog producers in Indiana to some extent turned to their dealers more than advertisements for new product awareness. They indicated a feeling that their dealer — especially if he was progressive — would provide information about beneficial new products as a service.

**Neighbors.** Iowa producers also rely quite heavily on their neighbors for product knowledge, whereas the Indiana producers see themselves as the leaders — others ask and follow them, they don't ask and follow others.

**Veterinarians.** Only one or two of the interviewed hog producers indicated veterinarians were a meaningful information source regarding new feed additive products. The general concensus was that hog producers would not turn to their veterinarian for advice and if they did, their veterinarians would not view a feed additive program as health related. The producers were not so sure the veterinarian shouldn't be interested in this area — but they were sure that if they consulted him he would charge them.

**University Extension.** Hog producers view extension as more of an advising agent or sounding board for particular chemicals after the chemical has been in the market and after the producer has found out about it, than as a means of learning about new products. The producers express the view that they will know about a product before the university knows.

**Research.** Hog producers feel to some extent that they must trust the research of a manufacturer as accurate because it has had to satisfy the government for clearance. On the other hand, they tend to dismiss the manufacturer's research as applicable to their situation because of the differences between experimental testing farms and their own operation.

Given this view, the producers put more faith in controlled testing on the "average" farm, and hoped that the testing would be in the area where they have their operation.

Producers tended to put faith in their feed dealer's research because of the assumption that his tests were carried out locally. There was a strong assumption, particularly in Iowa, that the feed dealer had run tests.

Producers would probably place the greatest credence in on-sight testing on their own farm. However, they don't feel they have the ability to test on their own. They indicated a desire to try on-sight testing with the assistance of the manufacturer.

**Seminars and Professional Experts.** Hog producers expect that valuable information will be gained from university-sponsored swine days and hog association sponsored seminars. They look for the introduction of new ideas and concepts at these meetings. To an equal extent, they rely on article-length reports and features, written by "experts," that appear in the hog farm journals and magazines. Such articles — because of their detail and because of the credibility associated with an independent expert — are given greater credence than advertisements.

Recommendations:

44. Rely on ads to make hog producers and dealers aware of the gestation conditioning concept and the product.

    a. Describe to the producer and the dealer, the phenomena that occur when the product does its job—increased blood flow to the uterus and so forth.

    b. Recognize that ads gain attention and that by tying the claimed benefits to dollars and cents economics, interest in the product will result. But, also recognize that ads are limited to creating awareness and have little to do with the adoption decision.

45. Key ads to concrete specifics.

    a. Show the dollars and cents economic advantage to using the product. More pigs is insufficient. Economics must be tied to a definite profit base the producer understands.

    b. Provide operational (observable) definitions of what the four primary claims mean.

46. Utilize other available and credible information sources as an additional key to adoption.

    a. Provide sufficient information to independent editorial sources to insure the appearance of independent promotional articles and other "expert" outputs about the concept and product.

    b. Institute a program of seminars and articles by "experts" that explain the gestation conditioning concept, the need for it, and the benefits to be derived from it.

47. Use promotional information to educate dealers to the gestation conditioning concept. Insure that when the dealer is asked about the product that he knows what it is and has a layman's knowledge of how it works.

48. Make the ads personal, non-pressure, and information-giving. Personal testimonials can be used, but tie them to description of observable claims and in-the-field test results.

49. Don't rely on veterinarians or extension agents to promote the concept in the short term. These sources will only prove beneficial with a well-developed educational program to how feed additives are health related and relevant to the consulting function of both veterinarians and extension agents.

# 18

# Feed Dealer Focus Group Interviews on Shell's Gestation Litter Conditioner

Doane Agricultural Service, Inc.
Marketing Research Division

## DONALD C. SHIELDS

## Introduction

### Purpose

Shell Chemical Company, Animal Health Division, is marketing a sow and gilt gestation conditioning feed additive. Shell introduced the product to the market approximately one year ago. We were asked to provide attitudinal and motivation input via focus group interviews to assist in the development and refinement of marketing plans and strategies for this product. For the first phase of data collection, we conducted a series of five focus group interviews during January, 1977, with aware and unaware hog producers. The purpose of this phase of research was to explore factors related to farmers' product awareness and adoption. A major finding indicated that feed dealers are a definite key to consumer education on products. Thus, Shell asked us to conduct three focus group interviews with dealers. The purposes of the Phase II research were to gain a better understanding of both a feed dealer's role in the hog industry and his role in marketing new feed additive products. Particular emphasis was placed on the dealers' knowledge, understanding, attitude, and awareness of the use and performance of the product. Concomitantly, the research sought to discover feed dealers' views of, and attitudes toward, presentations and information passed to them by drug manufacturers and suppliers.

Specifically, the feed dealer focus group research centered on the following content areas: (1) Management goals of feed dealers; (2) Attitudes toward customer management goals; (3) Management goals as related to adding new product lines; (4) Viable dealer information sources; (5) Dealer believability and acceptance of new products; (6) Product promotion programs; (7) Dealer training meetings; (8) Understanding of the

335

gestation conditioning concept; (9) Product form; (10) Views of the product; (11) Reasons for not stocking the product; and (12) Manufacturing salesmen.

## Authorization

This focus group interview research was authorized by Mr. James J. Riley, Staff Business Representative, Business Planning Animal Health, Shell Chemical Company, in a letter dated May 2, 1977.

## Design and Methodology

The research design called for three focus group interviews to be conducted during May, 1977. All three interviews were directed at hog feed dealers, both franchised and independently owned. The meetings were luncheon or dinner meetings, held in private dining facilities at local restaurants. Locations of the interviews were as follows:

| Location | Date |
|---|---|
| Frankfort, Indiana | May 25, 1977 |
| DeWitt, Iowa | May 26, 1977 |
| Annawan, Illinois | May 26, 1977 |

Each meeting was designed for five to seven participants. Some six hours of intensive interview data were collected. The major content themes were confirmed both within meetings and across sessions. Seventeen hog feed dealers participated in the three interviews. The participants represented the major feed manufacturing companies as well as cooperatives and local independently owned feed outlets.

Dr. Donald C. Shields, a small group communications research specialist, helped develop the questions in a scenario format with appropriate input from the Marketing Research Division of Doane and the Animal Health Division of Shell Chemical Company. Doane personnel involved were Dub Carlton, Roy Price, Nick Nichols, and Sam Moore. Valuable contributions were made by Jim Riley of the Shell staff.

## Method of Analysis

Analysis of the data stems from the following tactical decision. Data regarding feed dealers' characteristics, attitudes, and views of the hog industry and new products (as gained from focusing on the specific content areas) is presented in narrative form. Then, the meaning and impact of the views for Shell and the product is presented in the form of recommendations following each major narrative section. The analytical link between the information contained in the content overviews and the specific recommendations is thus supported by both the general narrative and the specific views of dealers when discussing the product directly.

## Summary and Conclusions

The Study included three focus group interviews with feed dealers in Iowa, Illinois, and Indiana. The focus group interview outline centered on data collection in two areas: (1) dealer knowledge and attitudes about products and new products in general; and (2) dealer knowledge about Shell's product, in particular.

In overview, dealers lack understanding of the gestation conditioning program, the gestation conditioning concept, the viability of the product, and the product's relation to a brand name wormer and to worming. To a great degree, information about the product has not gotten to the dealership level, has been misrepresented at the dealership level, and has been based more or less on hearsay and rumor about the product.

The above picture of the dealer's understanding of the product is in marked contrast to the view they present of their role in marketing new products. Concerning products in general, dealers perceive themselves as an information clearinghouse, possessing detailed information about new products, and capable of advising farmers about the ins-and-outs of their uses, functions, advantages, disadvantages, and necessary operation changes for giving a product every chance to do the most good for the farmer.

Dealers see themselves as capable of making a go or no-go decision on whether a farmer adopts a new product. The feeling is that farmers place great stock in a dealer's recommendation. Thus, it is important that new products both gain the attention of dealers and gain their acceptance. Products have the greatest likelihood of acceptance when they are backed by well-designed experimental research and when these findings are made known to the dealer. Similarly, dealers' faith in products is enhanced when research comes from several independent sources and local on-farm tests. The less a product demonstrates clearly visible results, the greater the need for such independent corroboration.

Aside from research, dealers tend to put their trust in those products which prove economically beneficial to the customer. Thus, dealers need to know the cost-utility of a particular product. In the absence of hard data to prove the research results and economic value of products, dealers will accept local testimonials to prove such claims.

Regarding the dealers' perceptions of their place in marketing products, they see their role as one of stocking and selling products *on demand*. They do not really hustle sales or think of themselves as hard-core promoters. Primarily, dealers provide supportive recommendation about products subsequent to consumer's inquiry. Their idea of selling is to have the product available once sufficient demand occurs in the marketplace.

Dealers shy away from the hard-sell role in favor of building a climate of trust and caring about their customers'· operations. For them, all dealerships have access to good products; and thus, the difference between a successful and non-successful dealership is the result of the quality of service and quality of the interpersonal relationships with their customers. This view leads dealers to be wary of new products until they are certain they work, lest they recommend an inferior product and break that climate of trust with their customer.

The recommendations presented in this report reflect several major thrusts. One is that Shell needs to present information to dealers as an aid in helping the dealer maintain his integrity as an information source to his customers. A second is the kind of information that Shell needs to present concerning the product. A third is the kind of delivery system necessary to insure that the information gets to the dealer.

## Summary and Analysis of Focus Group Interviews

### Management Goals of Feed Dealers

Dealers present a clear picture of their management goals. General goals include profitability and competitiveness with other dealers. Competitiveness and profitability work to accentuate the need for a complete product line and full product service. Service, which helps make the dealer competitive, is seen as product knowledge, on-time delivery, honesty in representing products, technical advice and council on such items as nutrition and buildings, awareness of the advantages and disadvantages of new products, and the ability to provide sufficient credit to finance customer needs. Specifically, his service goal is to know enough about products to help his customers do the right thing. Dealers use service to retain customers and they use products as a vehicle to gain profits. Knowledge of products is the intangible that, hopefully, will provide a unique service. Business is based on personal relations and mutual trust between farmers and dealers. Such goals are emphasized consistently across all interviews.

Despite the dealers' desires to be competitive, provide good service, and maintain a personal relationship with customers, there is an apparent inconsistency between these goals and the dealers' day-to-day operations. Most dealers do not add new products until there is customer demand (although groups emphasized cases where marketing leaders had benefited from the earliest decision to stock a product in a specific area). Furthermore, while dealers may be aware of new products, they tend to become knowledgeable of products only after a customer's inquiry. There are several reasons, emphasized in the interviews, for this lag effect. One is the flood of new feed additive products. Another is the difficulty of storing a product when demand is not sufficiently strong. A third is the quantity and diversity of product lines, which, in essence, create an information overload problem for the dealers and their staffs. Finally, there are just a number of bright, progressive customers who appear to be on the lookout for products and learn of them in detail before the dealers do.

Given the above picture and considering the dealers' pride in servicing their customers in the area of product knowledge, how is this apparent inconsistency explained? The answer lies in the recognition that dealers don't make farmers aware of new products. Rather, they provide an information base of product knowledge, relating the advantages and disadvantages, strengths and weaknesses of a specific product to their customers' particular operations once an unquiry has been made. Hence, the dealers' comments like, "they come to me for advice," "if I don't know about it, I'll find out about it," "I need to know what the product will do, and what the product won't do." In short, what the dealer tends to do in the area of product promotion is either reinforce, or stop short the farmers' interest.

The rather obvious reason for not promoting all new products relates back to the management goal of honesty. Good products are easy to reinforce. Products with clear visible results are easy to reinforce. Poor products, or products where the benefits aren't visible, create grief for the dealer. To recommend them is to risk his integrity if they don't prove out. In such a case, the dealer feels he may be seen as not good to his word, and he feels the farmer may hold it against him and he'll lose the farmer as a customer.

Recommendations:

1. Do not expect dealers to make farmers aware of the product.

2. Recognize that if farmer demand for the product increases, dealers will be asked to recommend the product. Then their recommendation will be based on its ability, or lack of it, to be proven.

3. Expect that dealers will need product knowledge to describe the product in terms of how it works, its advantages, and its disadvantages.

## New Customers and New Products

Dealers do not ascribe to the gaining of new customers as a primary goal. They are more interested in satisfying and keeping existing accounts than in gaining new ones. The attempt to get new business is seen mostly as replacement for customers who are lost, either through attrition or dissatisfaction. Thus, new customers are gained because of their dissatisfaction with other dealers. In short, dealers view the retention of existing customers as the easiest thing to do, the gaining of new customers as harder, and the winning back of former customers as the most difficult. "There is a tendency to try and sell existing customers more and more," and "it's easier to keep regular customers than to get new ones," were typical comments.

Given the above view, it is not surprising that dealers do not see new products as a viable means to get new customers. In part, it's because they don't think of "product" as what sells customers. There is a general attitude that there is not a nickel's worth of difference between quality feeds and all dealers have access to the same additives. Dealers do not see farmers as brand loyal. What is important is the dealer/customer relation, and unproved products are seen as a threat to this relationship. The strongest relation between new products and new customers exists when a dealer is the first to have a product in high demand in a general area and distribution-supply problems keep other dealers from getting it.

Dealers cited several factors that can be taken as prerequisites for eliciting dealer support of a new product. These include product uniqueness, workability, provability, and strong initial farmer awareness and subsequent inquiry at the dealership. These factors are interrelated and constitute the keys that will cause dealers to take note of a new product and "push" or "strongly recommend" (their words) it.

Recommendations:

4. Recognize that at this time in the marketplace, dealer sales of new products are based on producer demand, not dealer promotion.

5. Recognize that the several keys constituting dealer backing of new products include: product uniqueness, workability, cost-efficiency, provability, and strong initial farmer awareness and inquiry. These factors as they relate to the product should be emphasized in any marketing program to dealers.

6. Recognize that simple dealer awareness of the product is insufficient to get him to stock the product in his dealership.

7. Understand that dealers do not recognize that they could use new products as an inroad to gaining new customers. Consider some form of educational program to raise dealers' consciousness about the potential benefits of product line for attracting new customers.

**Dealer Acceptance of New Products**

The most crucial factor underlying product recommendations is the dealer's own faith in the products. Dealers indicated that such self-acceptance is gained through a combination of: (1) extensive manufacturing or parent company advertising which leads to heavy producer awareness and inquiry at the dealership; (2) well designed and executed experimental research conducted by the manufacturer, parent company, independent sources—like universities, and local on-farm tests; and (3) confidence that claimed results will be evident from use of the product.

A good advertising program is seen as important to dealers because to them "bad" products are not advertised. Advertising shows that the manufacturer believes in the product. Extensive advertising enhances the dealer's belief in the product at the start, and is seen as necessary to creating producer awareness and inquiry at the dealership level. Also, advertising is seen as most beneficial when it helps the dealer prove the workability and cost efficiency of a product.

Dealers are keenly aware that feed additive compounds are subjected to extensive testing in order to qualify as a registered feed additive. In addition, dealers are aware of the restrictions placed upon product claims. However, there is a kind of innate skepticism of research findings. Dealers want to know that the benefits claimed by the manufacturer for the product came from the product and not a manipulation of the control group.

A comment was, "I can make anything work depending on what I put it up against." Therefore, dealers are interested in the results of simultaneous research by parent companies and independent sources like the universities. Dealers will then begin to feel confidence in the likelihood that the product should do what it claims to do. The key then for dealer acceptance of research is a kind of synergism created by the successful results of a multitude of data collection sources.

Given the likelihood that the product *should* do what it claims it will do, the dealer would then like to see local on-farm results to insure the viability of the product for his customers. Actual local results of a new product are most often evaluated by the producer's successful use of the product. On-farm trials are encouraged by dealers, but not usually to the extent of a dealer's involvement. Dealers know that it is very unlikely that they will have a producer that can carry out a sophisticated field trial on a feed additive. Dealers are aware that the vast majority of producers are not equipped to keep the kinds of records or maintain the kinds of control groups necessary to run and prove the results of a field trial. As well, producers are not seen as having the time or labor to run trials properly. A few dealers may help the producers with field trials, but they are the exception. Given the right farm, right producer, and right record keeping capacity, dealers would rather see the manufacturer or parent company assist with the local field trials. The reasoning is that if the trial of the product doesn't prove out, the producer can get mad at the company and not the dealer.

Finally, dealers want to see more than positive results which show only the advantages of a product. Dealers also want to know the shortcomings, limitations, disadvantages, and what not to expect in the use of a product. Why? This helps the dealer relate the product's worth to the individual operations of his customers. In other words, some customers who are poor managers need to be advised by the dealer where to improve their operation to give a product a chance to work. Without knowing all the ins-and-outs of a product, it is difficult for the dealer to provide this kind of advice.

Recommendations:

8. Recognize that good advertising which creates awareness among producers is seen as a necessary part of the dealer's sales process.

9. Recognize that advertising does not have to prove a product to the producer in-and-of itself, but should support and operationalize the claims made by a product. To whet the producers' curiosity for a product lets the dealer who believes in the product "promote" it through recommendation and explanation.

10. Shell should gather the results of their own research and the research of others on the product and provide it to the dealers in a single package with references to achieve a higher degree of dealer acceptance and believability in the product.

11. Shell must recognize that local on-farm tests are seen as a plus in sales, but dealers do not want to be involved. Shell should select progressive farms and assist (with the cooperation of a dealer when possible) in conducting, recording, and verifying the tests.

12. Shell needs to provide information on specific uses of the product, the kinds of operations where it works best, and specify where and how it should not be used.

## Information Sources

A significant aspect of the interview schedule concerned an examination of the importance of various information sources for gaining awareness of, and confidence in, new products. Areas probed included both what was important to the dealer and what was important to the producer from the dealer's perspective.

**Dealers.** Dealers were quick to admit that farmers rarely used the dealer as an initial source of awareness of a new product. Rather, the producer becomes aware of a product and then inquires of the dealer; "What do you know about this or that product?" Dealers were sure that producers became aware of new products either before or as soon as dealers. "Innovative" customers were thought to be aware before the dealer. Most dealers felt farmers had access to the same advertising information they had. However, farmers are characterized as expecting the dealer to have information above and beyond what the farmer had access to.

This interplay for information leads to dealers characterizing themselves as a kind of clearinghouse of information for their customers. Dealers feel their customers expect them to know all there is to know about all the products that are sold by the dealer. In addition, dealers are expected to be knowledgeable about new products, new uses of old products, more efficient methods of use, and the expected performance of products and methods.

Most dealerships are highly diversified, selling many major agricultural products as well as feed. These are: petroleum, fertilizer, herbicides, insecticides, general farm supplies, building supplies, etc. Most dealers are diversified simply because farmers like to make one stop and deal with one person. Such product-line diversity creates problems for the dealer by increasing the amount of knowledge he must master. To lessen the information overload strain, dealers agreed that they tended to "specialize in a couple of areas" and have general knowledge in other areas. Other employees would do the same. Thus, there are some problems involved in getting the right information on a particular product to the responsible person in the dealership.

Dealers feel they have to relate exactly to how a product, particularly feed additives, should be used. "We need training to know about products, to tell the farmer how to use them — you've just got to show them," was a typical comment. Improper usage of a feed additive can cause serious problems for a farmer and in those cases the relationship with the dealer may suffer.

Dealers felt they should exercise extreme caution not to over-represent products, or over-represent their knowledge of products. The concensus of opinion was that if a dealer didn't know about something, the best answer is "I don't know, but I'll find out for you." Typical sources for discovering feed additive product information were nutritionists, the parent company or manufacturer's representative, and to a lesser extent descriptive journal articles, the extension agent, or veterinarian.

Dealers expressed a desire for information on new products that is more detailed than the types of literature and advertising which is usually available to both dealers and farmers. Dealers may well be receptive to information documents that provide easy reference for answering the questions they are asked about new products.

In terms of promoting new products, dealers felt that farmers relied on their recommendation. If they, as dealers, pushed a product by giving it a positive recommendation, then they felt this would encourage farmers to adopt a product faster than it would normally be adopted. If they didn't recommend, this would slow product adoption. Of course, "if a farmer really wants a product, then I'll get it for him," is a prevalent view among dealers. Nevertheless, dealers' faith in a product does wonders in the dealers' minds for product acceptance and adoption. "You tend to point out the advantages of a product you're sold on" and "he's less apt to adopt without my recommendation" are statements reflective of this view.

**Advertisements.** Advertising creates producer awareness of new products. This awareness, in turn, increases the likelihood of an inquiry at the dealership. Dealers see two types, general circulation magazines and radio/television. They look to these both to learn product names and learn the research that proves out a product.

Dealers think favorably of advertising. This is tempered by their word "good" advertising. The connotation was best illustrated by reference to several advertising campaigns: some good, some bad, some neutral. The "good ones" were allied, primarily, with those products which were demonstrably superior to other products and had a high degree of demand.

The "bad ones" were associated with products which had achieved a high degree of awareness without being able to live up to the degree of expectation created in the producer's mind. The effect of neutrality is best described as ads which create producer interest without creating skepticism.

Dealers see advertising by manufacturers as an associated selling tool for them. Dealers use advertising as a learning tool, first, and to a lesser degree, to assess new products. Dealers know they have to be aware of what their customers are aware of. Most dealers felt that their customers probably had more time to read magazines and other printed material and dealers have to "keep up" in order to be of service to their customers.

Very seldom were farmers seen adopting the use of a product based solely on advertisement. Those advertisements that create interest in a new product are necessary. Dealers thought of such ads in terms of the first advertisements for a new product. Equally important were those advertisements which point out the benefits and economic advantages of a new product. This does not mean that these advertisements have to be detailed to the point of looking like a statistical report — rather, they should clearly state where the satisfaction for use can be seen by results of testing for additional weight gain, cost benefits, health, or appearance of the animals. Overemphasis by the manufacturer of awareness-creating ads tends to "turn off" both dealers and farmers — they like to see some substance in their advertising.

Dealers view research results in advertising with the knowledge that a manufacturer is going to show the best results possible for the product. Dealers know this and, frankly, expect it. This, however, points out the dealer's need for other research to provide a basis of comparison and show the product's workability as the dealer answers his customers' inquiries concerning new products.

The typical manufacturer's product mailers and flyers appear to be disregarded by dealers as a means of learning about new products. Dealers appear to use such information services only when they provide detailed information that the dealer doesn't get from other sources.

**Neighbors of Farmers.** Dealers consider neighbors of farmers as a valuable source of information to other farmers. "Every time I sell a product 'to a customer,' it becomes a field trial," typifies the comments expressed by several dealers. Producers come in and want to know "who else or how many others are using it?" Dealers know the "success" of a product is highly dependent on local use and the subsequent word-of-mouth relation of positive results to other producers.

Careful instruction in how to make an accurate observation of the results in the use of a product, comes from the dealer, provided the dealer has this type of information to pass along to the customer. Customers then, given the knowledge to observe positive results, will give a positive testimonial to neighbors to the effect "it worked." These "local testimonials" help dealers sell to farmers in a community.

Those products which give visible results are the easiest for producers to evaluate. Hard-to-measure results are difficult, if not impossible, to measure under on-farm conditions. Success stories from farmers concerning hard-to-measure results are based many times on what the farmer thinks the benefits are that he is achieving from the use of a product. This is often reinforced by the dealer's belief in the product.

Neighbor's testimonials also come in the area of the cost-utility of a product — are the benefits derived economically advantageous? In other words, a feed additive product may work, but is it worth the time, labor, and initial dollar outlay? This type of testimonial is also conveyed by the dealer to other potential users of a product.

**Salesmen.** Sales personnel of either the parent company, distributor, or manufacturer could be an important knowledge source to dealers and farmers alike. Unfortuntely, the concensus among dealers is that it's hard to find a good one — one that has information and product knowledge and can present it clearly and can answer the dealer's questions. The typical salesman appears to be thought of as really lacking product knowledge and being unfamiliar with how to relate a product to a particular dealer's customers. Salesmen are not someone the dealer turns to for product knowledge at this time. The salesman could be, but the training and job thrust of the typical salesman leads the dealer to feel it would be a waste of time to consult him. Salesmen are thought of as salesmen, not technical people.

**Veterinarians.** Dealers view veterinarians, in general, as specialists in disease diagnosis, therapeutic application of pharmaceuticals, with a shallow knowledge of nutrition and feed additive application. One dealer summarized the view: "They don't know that much about it." Another offered a salient story about a vet who called in an improper arsanilic acid dosage. Another suggested vets were "more interested in pushing drugs than caring for the animals." There are exceptions to the above, but they are few.

The dealer and veterinarian relationship seldom goes beyond the extent that they both deal with the same customer. Some dealers expressed the opinion that they probably should make better use of veterinarians. But, at the same time they weren't quite sure how.

Dealers felt sure their customers conferred with their veterinarians in the use of antibiotics and medications in hog rations. They weren't sure of the depth of these conversations, but dealers were convinced that the veterinarian had less of an influence on the producer in the feed additive and nutrition area than dealers.

Recommendations:

13. Recognize that dealers play an insignificant role in making producers aware of new products. Rather, the producer becomes aware of the product first, then asks the dealer his opinion about it, and the dealer reaffirms or disaffirms the potential benefits of the product.

14. Understand that dealers perceive producers as expecting the dealer to have information above and beyond what the farmer has access to. Insure that the dealer has adequate, accurate, in-depth information about the feeding program. (See recommendations #15, 18 and 20 for specifics.)

15. Dealers serve as a clearinghouse of information. Shell should work to insure that the dealer is familiar with the ins-and-outs of the product, including what it is, what it does, how to use it, when to use it, where to use it, and where and when not to use it.

16. Recognize that there are "specialists" within most dealerships who specialize in being knowledgeable about specific product lines. Encourage dealerships to *name* a product specialist.

17. Initiate training programs for dealerships. They like them, want them, and use them. They need the knowledge necessary to answer customer inquiries. (See recommendations 31-36.)

18. Create a product information and reference package that: shows research results from both Shell and other sources; includes testimonials; explains how to use the product; etc. Encourage dealers to turn to this handy reference when they have questions.

19. Key information programs to the dealers' need to know. Use the rationale of the dealers' vision regarding his role as an information clearinghouse and consultant to the producer. Indicate you're not providing materials just to be providing them, but because they'll help him maintain his position of integrity when discussing the product with his customers.

20. Give the dealer the limitations or shortcomings and things to watch out for when using the product. Such information will serve three purposes: (a) it will head off ungrounded rumors; (b) it will make the dealer more respected in the eyes of the customer; and (c) the dealer will feel Shell is not trying to "flim/flam" him on the product.

21. Recognize that a quick way to increase the market is to preclude the negative recommendations now being given by dealers because: (a) they think it's a wormer; (b) they're not understanding the gestation conditioning effect; (c) they're not clear on how the farmer should use it; and (d) they're not behind the product because they're not convinced it works or is cost-efficient.

22. Recognize that dealers use advertising to become aware of new products and create producer inquiry and demand.

They do not stock new products on the basis of ads, but rather on the basis of inquiries generated by ads.

23. Emphasize to dealers that the information they are receiving flows from, yet goes above and beyond, what the producer is receiving from other sources.

24. Supply dealers with "success" stories from producers in their area who are using the feeding program. Key the stories to both actual results and cost-beneficial results.

25. When making sales contact with dealers, insure that the salesmen are knowledgeable about the product and can express the use of the product in terms of the dealers' customers' operations. The dealer wants more than a social visit.

26. Veterinarians appear to be just beginning to move into feed additive consulting among dealers and producers. Supply vets with sufficient information to enhance their ability to discuss the product. This should be done so as not to preclude the dealers superiority (to the vet) as a feed additive consultant to producers.

## Promotional Programs

Dealers view promotional programs as being of two types: giveaways (like hats, jackets, contests) and cash discounts. Most dealers think of giveaways as "gimmicks" and sense more of a value in bringing goodwill to the dealership, than in being a force in promoting sales. They indicate that "the customer has come to expect something" and "the farmer takes his hat or coat" but there is a feeling that goods "don't really move a product."

Dealers are more receptive to cash discounts as potentially viable means for increasing sales of a product. This is especially felt to be so after a product has become established. Until that time, usefulness of the product is felt to be the best sales promotion.

Direct dealer discounts were also probed. Most were lukewarm to such promotion programs. The dealers expressed the view that they didn't purchase enough of the product to take advantage of this type of discount.

Promotional programs that provide a "carrot" for the dealer were also lukewarmly accepted. Many said they weren't aware of where they stood in terms of any contest. Other programs, like dealer recognition certificates, were not well received.

Recommendations:

27. Recognize that there is no existing promotional program that really turns dealers on. Giveaways are definitely not the answer for increasing a product's sales, even though the dealer does use them to promote goodwill for his dealership.

28. Promotional programs that give the dealer the opportunity to reduce the price to the consumer are held in favor.

29. The "carrot" underlying the traditional dealer discount program is insufficient to increase a product's sales.

30. When considering promotional programs, recognize that they are more to maintain a market than to increase or create markets. Work on hyping consumer awareness and dealer confidence in the product before instituting any promotion of the product.

31. The acceptance of promotional programs (direct mail, give-aways, discounts, etc.) is so weak that Shell would do well, when considering them, to create a few and field-test them before full implementation.

**Dealer Meetings**

Information coming directly from the manufacturer is thought by dealers to be the best in terms of clarity and understanding. Most often, as product information is filtered through a feed company's communication channels, there will be a variation from company to company at the feed dealer level. Dealers feel they have to look to the manufacturer of an additive for information. Manufacturers who send out representatives to train (educate) dealers and their employees seem to hold the most favor with dealers.

What dealers considered to be a good dealer training method was one where the manufacturer of the additive held meetings for dealers. In these meetings, dealers were advised on how to use the product, what to expect of the product and, most importantly, what not to expect from the product. and the shortcomings of the product.

Dealers relate the major benefit of dealer meetings as keeping them informed. These types of meetings are important to dealers for that reason. When asked if a school or meeting on each additive that a dealer carries would be troublesome, almost a unanimous "no problem" was voiced, someone from the dealership would be in attendance.

Recommendations:

32. Dealer meetings appear to be the most viable means of educating dealers about the product. Information presented needs to be clear, concise, useful, and of a technical nature.

33. Programs should not be sales oriented.

34. Key specific sections to: research (including preliminary, on-going, and local success stories), the gestation conditioning concept, how to keep records, how to eyeball results, typical operation changes, how to use, the extra worming benefit, and the economic advantages.

35. Stress the importance of thinking of the benefit as coming from the pigs. Thus, it's not a dollar-per-sow cost, but a cents-per-pig cost.

36. Include discussions about limitations and disadvantages of the product and give the dealers the opportunity to interact with the Shell program moderators.

37. Package the information given at dealer meetings into a reference manual that can be used by dealers in answering questions. This can be distributed to all dealers, regardless of whether or not they attend the meetings.

**Key Points Regarding Dealer Perception of the Product**

1. Dealers lack a clear understanding of the gestation conditioning concept.

2. Dealers associate the product with a brand name wormer and describe it as a wormer. Many sell it as an "expensive" 30-day wormer.

3. Dealers lack a clear understanding of how long the product should be used.

4. Dealers are not convinced of the benefits of the product—they want research results that it works.

5. Dealers aren't convinced that the conditioning effect will come from worm-free hogs.

6. Dealers do not believe there is much economic advantage to the producer for using the product.

7. Dealers in Iowa are more knowledgeable of the product, in general, than are dealers in Indiana or Illinois. Producers are ahead of Indiana dealers. Iowa dealers appear ahead of Iowa producers. Both Illinois producers and dealers have a long way to go in comprehending the product.

8. Dealers are a little "up tight" because they don't see any clear way to prove out the benefit of the product. The answer appears to lie in a combination or research results, testimony, training in eyeballing, and proof of the economic advantage to the product.

# 19

# New Technologies for Market Research:
## A Methodology for Ad Test Segmentation and Market Segmentation Studies

DONALD C. SHIELDS and JOHN F. CRAGAN

This proposal details a new research product for segmenting product markets and advertising markets.

### Communication Theory Based

This product is developed from a new communication theory that views ideas, attitudes and beliefs as "dramatic facts." While academic research on this method has been conducted under the technical term of rhetorical vision and fantasy theme analysis, the heart of this new product is in essence a content-oriented, scenario-based means of gathering, and interpreting data.

### Proven Methods

The new product is derived from several independent technical methods currently employed by us. These include: (1) scenario-based, in-depth personal interviews; (2) scenario-based focus group interviews; (3) scenario-based content analysis; and (4) scenario-based structured Q-sorts.

### Sampling Breakthrough

Test applications of the new product have lead to a sampling and data collection breakthrough. The breakthrough results in the ability to collect, retrieve, analyze and evaluate scenario-based qualitative data in such a way as to conform to the rules of large sampling. In so doing, previously non-projectable (yet data rich) qualitative findings may now be quantitatively assessed and generalized to the population being studied, following proper design and sampling rules.

**Attitudinal Segmentation**

Central to any successful segmentation study is a satisfactory "breaker variable" that serves as the basis for differentiating one market segment from another. Traditionally, such breaker variables have included male/female; use/nonuse of product; intent/nonintent to purchase; etc. This new technology allows the breaker variable to be a group of respondents' participation in a particular *attitude system* or *belief system* (called a "vision"). Once individuals are qualitatively and quantitatively found to be participating in a specific vision about a product, their participation/non-participation in the vision is used as a breaker variable or basis for differentiating attitudinally, one market segment from another.

**Graphics Segmentation**

Key data concerning the market segments' demographics, psychographics, sociographics and product graphics can be gathered and analyzed. The results of such analysis is a linking of the discreet demo/psycho/socio/product graphics to each market segment. Such a linkage will enable complete identification of segment participants by their most distinguishing characteristics.

# Background on Q-Methodology Study

**Previous Experience**

We have the following experience with Q-studies:

- 1973 Q-study of the public, private and projected image of the St. Paul, Minnesota fire service. Report submitted to the St. Paul Department of Public Safety. Report published in *Fire Command*, October, 1974.

- 1976 Q-study of the view of foreign policy dramas held by Peorians. Report published in the *Quarterly Journal of Speech,* October, 1977.

- 1977 Q-study to identify predictive attributes of public fire safety education officers. Report submitted to the Bureau of Fire Safety and Control, U.S. Department of Commerce. Report published in *Fire Chief,* Summer, 1978.

- 1977 Q-study of the Doane Farm Management Division. Report and study submitted to Doane Farm and Ranch Management Division.

- 1978 Q-study of cattle reproduction dramas on farm operations for The Upjohn Corporation. Study completed November, 1978.

- 1979 Q-study of U.S. hog producers' management philosophy and practices. Study completed for Doane Agricultural Service September, 1979.

## Methods

Q-technique, developed by William Stephenson in the 1930's, is a forced-choice scaling procedure for ordering items upon a continuum in response to a given research question. The purpose of Q-technique is to gather respondents' reactions to a number of stimuli in interaction. The stimuli may be words, statements, pictures, phrases, themes, ad copy, scenarios, etc. As such, the items in the Q-deck are a representative sample of the universe of ideas on a given subject.

Discriminant analysis can then be used to identify those observable attributes which differentiate people in one vision from those in another.

## Purpose

Q-technique, when used in conjunction with Q-type factor analysis where items are treated as observations and people as variables, allows the identification of those groups which view the world similarly as determined by the mathematical selection of alike orderings of the items in the Q-sort. In essence, Q-technique in combination with Q-type factor analysis provides a composite picture of the respondents' attitudes and opinions, beliefs and motivations, etc. The end product is an initial segmentation of the potential market based not upon the sole identification of simple demographic characteristics, but upon the internalized views of the respondents.

Demo/psycho/socio/product graphics can then be attached to like vision participants to provide a clear means of identification.

## Steps Involved

A. Preliminary research can include:
  1. literature search;
  2. personal interviews;
  3. focus group interviews.

B. Developing the testing instruments:
  1. build the scenario-based structured Q-deck:
     a. top—visions,
     b. sides—issues,
     c. back—demo/psycho/socio/product graphics;
  2. build the graphics questionnaire;
  3. use data from experience, personal and/or focus group interviews.

C. Pre-test instruments for reliability.

D. Conduct the research:
  1. administer to adequate sample:
     a. direct,
     b. mail,
     c. combination;
  2. code the data;

      3. multivariate analysis:
        a. Q-type factor analysis,
        b. discriminant analysis (direct and step-wise).
  E. Project findings to the market:
    1. concurrent/construct validation;
    2. reliability estimates.

## Marketing Benefits

1. Explores and defines the interaction between the product and the market environment in which it must exist.
2. It provides an understanding, given this market environment, of what to do with whom, in order to generate immediate and proper use of the product.
3. The trade-offs between product effectiveness and user efforts can be explored. The limit to the effort that the customer is willing to expend "to benefit" from the product, can be identified.
4. The impact of marketing communications is maximized by virtue of their direct appeal to primary motives. Moreover, the most fruitful media and educational environments for conveying these communications are identified.
5. Ties market research to the development of advertising strategies, advertising, and promotion.

## Objectives

1. Defines potential customers attitudinally:
   - What vision do they participate in?
   - What is the definable attitudinal parameters from which buyers will approach purchase of the product?
2. Defines potential customers by issue:
   - What product issues have relevance for them?
   - How important is each issue (benefit/constraint) against all other issues?
3. Defines potential customers by demographics:
   - What do the potential customers look like?
4. Defines potential customers by psychographics:
   - What is their willingness to buy?
   - What is their commitment to health practices?
5. Defines potential customers by sociographics:
   - What kinds of things do they do?
   - What life styles do they lead?
6. Defines customers by product graphics:
   - What pricing levels attract a particular segment?
   - What routine will they accept for using the product?
   - What brand name do they prefer?

7. Provides direct links between people, issues and demo/psycho/socio/ product graphics for the major market segments.

## Outputs

1. Principal Components Solution followed by either oblique or varimax rotation to simple structure, that is, identification of the factors or typal groupings.

   Value: Market segmentation by the internalized views of the respondents.

2. The percent of variance in sorting behavior accounted for by the total factor solution and each factor within the solution.

   Value: Knowledge of the major and minor market segments based on the internalized views of the respondents.

3. Correlations between the factors or typal groupings within the solution.

   Value: An indication of the similarity or difference of major segments in the market based on the internalized views of the respondents.

4. Correlations between the individual respondents' sorting behavior and the modal view reflected by each market segment (factor).

   Value: An assessment of the purity of the market segments. Ability to distinguish marketing segments by linking to demographics.

5. Arrays of respondents' reactions to all items in the Q-deck by ranking on the basis of descending Z-scores from, for example, most strongly received, through neutral, to most strongly rejected.

   Value: Identification of the specific items (for example themes) that were meaningful or not meaningful or neutral for each market

   Value: Identification of the specific items (for example themes) that were meaningful or not meaningful or neutral for each market segment (factor).

   The capacity to link the highly accepted themes to specific marketing and promotional campaigns for each market segment.

6. An array of concensus items by descending Z-score across factor types (market segments).

   Value: Identification of the themes that are accepted, rejected or neutral across the entire market, where such concensus items exist and given they are statistically meaningful, then promotional programs can be developed that will cut across all segments.

   Identification of potential base themes for all promotional and advertising campaigns. Variation for market segments could then come from subsidiary themes crucial to specific segments.

7. Differences in item placement by Z-score for all items compared against their placement in all factors (market segments).

   Value: Fine tuning of marketing, advertising and promotional campaigns.

# 20

# Communication Based Market Segmentation Study:
## Illustrative Excerpts

## JOHN F. CRAGAN and DONALD C. SHIELDS

Doane Agricultural Service, Incorporated, has graciously allowed us to describe in general terms a market segmentation study we did for them on Large Hog Producers. The complete hog study contains findings that cannot be presented here given Doane's proprietary rights and the recency of the findings. However, the hypothetical data presented mirrors the steps in the actual study and illustrates how each side of the three-dimensional matrix — visions, issues and graphics — are used to segment a market.

After briefly stating the purpose, objectives, and methodology of a large hog market segmentation study, we present three key excerpts from the original 300-page report. Excerpt 1 illustrates that from the original three-dimensional model of United States large hog producers, we discovered the hog market contained six different visions of how to produce hogs. They are the Quality-Health, Commerical Hog Producer, the Quality-Management Hog Producer, the Feed-Dependent Commercial Hog Producer, the Quality Breeding and Building Independent Hog Producer, the Supplier-Dependent Stable Family Hog Producer, and the Future Inte-grationist Hog Producer. In this first excerpt, we briefly describe the Quality-Health, Commercial Hog Producer. Table 1 indicates the twelve most accepted and twelve most rejected cards of these Quality-Commercial hog producers. Table 2 demonstrates that the hog producers participating in this vision are a cross between the two idealized visions of a quality hog producer and a commercial hog producer. The last part of excerpt 1, called the Analysis — Segment 1: Quality Commerical Producers, demonstrates how we interpret this data to our clients.

Excerpt 2 depicts how we analyze the data by examining how the hog producers in each of the six segments treated each of the twenty issues. Excerpt 2 first displays the thirteen issues that prove to be the most important from the original twenty. We then provide a brief examination

Excerpts used with permission of Doane Agricultural Service, Inc.

on how to interpret Z-score data when it is presented in this form. We then take the issue of veterinary involvement and in Table 3 report how the six segments sorted the three veterinarian cards. The last part of this excerpt illustrates how we interpret this data to our clients that commissioned the study.

Excerpt 3 is designed to show how we map on flesh and blood to each of the six hog producer visions. In short, the client needs to know not only what a Segment 1 hog producer thinks and believes but also what he looks like and does. Remembering that a discriminant analysis program using vision participation as a breaker variable was used, excerpt 3 reports that four demographics and three psycho-socio graphics formed one function that discriminated Segments 1 through 4 from Segments 5 and 6. Excerpt 3 first lists the seven important graphics and then in Table 4 we display, via a cross-tab, the sociographic of pregnancy testing sows. Finally, in this third illustrative section, we explain how we interpret this data to our clients.

## Large Hog Market Segmentation Study

### Purpose

The purpose of the study is to provide an in-depth analysis of Large Hog Producers' motivations in order to determine the direction of future growth in the hog industry.

### Objectives

1. To *Segment* the Large Hog Producers in terms of their management philosophy and practices.
2. To *Characterize* each segment on the basis of demographics, psychographics, and sociographics.
3. To *Identify* important issues as they relate to acceptance and use of feeds, drugs, buildings, etc.

### Methodology

  I. Focus Group Interviews
    A. "Universe of Ideas" produced the "Idealized" visions of Large Hog Producers.
  II. Development of the Three-Dimensional Matrix
    A. Key Views:
      1. Quality Hog Producer
      2. Family Hog Producer
      3. Commercial Hog Producer
    B. Key Issues:
      1. Management Philosophy and Practices (11 issues)
      2. Management Strategies/Guidelines (6 issues)
      3. Future Management Issues (4 issues)

## Three Dimensional Segmentation
## of the U.S. Large Hog Producer

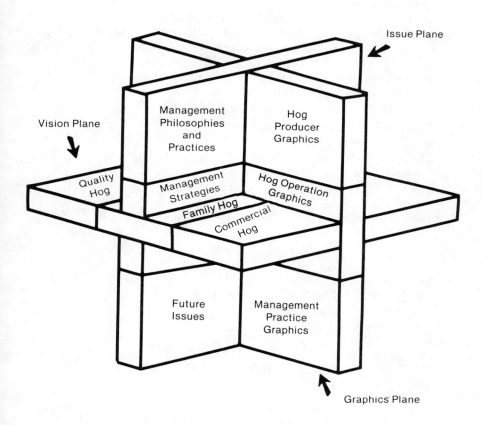

     C. Key Graphics:
       1. Demographics
       2. Psychographics
       3. Sociographics
 III. Development of Q-Sort Test Instrument (Q-Deck)
     A. Sixty-three Statements on Individual Cards
       1. Twenty-one issues across each of three visions
       2. Dramatizations of approximately forty words on each card
 IV. Data Collection
     A. "Forced Choice" sorting of sixty-three card deck
       1. Sort Question: Sort these statements representing your views
             views and beliefs about Hog production in your
             operation.
     B. Completion of thirty-nine item questionnaire
     C. Data collected January through June, 1979
       1. Mailed Q-sorts—Doane Countrywide Farm Panel
  V. Computer Analysis and Interpretation
     A. Q-Type Factor Analysis
     B. Discriminant Analysis (multiple regression) using vision participation as the breaker variable

**Excerpt 1: Large Hog Producer Market Segmentation by Vision**

Market Segment Findings:

— The Six Hog Producer
   Segments
— "Quality-Health,
   Commercial Hog Producer"
— "Quality-Management
   Hog Producer"
— "Feed-Dependent
   Commercial Hog Producer"
— "Quality Breeding and
   Building Independent
   Hog Producer"
— "Supplier-Dependent
   Stable Family Hog Producer"
— "Future Integrationist
   Hog Producer"

# Table 1

Quality-Commercial Producers
Twelve Most Accepted; Twelve Most Rejected

| | Quality Hog Producer (Vision I) | | Family Hog Farmer (Vision II) | | Commercial Hog Producer (Vision III) | |
|---|---|---|---|---|---|---|
| 1. Management Philosophy | | | | | | |
|   a. Basic Production Philosophy | 1 | .92 (11th) | 22 | −1.46 (60th) | 43 | 1.29 ( 7th) |
|   b. Motive for Raising | 2 | | 23 | | 44 | |
|   c. Breeding Management Goal | 3 | | 24 | −2.47 (63rd) | 45 | 1.72 ( 3rd) |
|   d. Key Management Concern | 4 | | 25 | −1.28 (57th) | 46 | |
|   e. Veterinarian Involvement | 5 | 1.14 ( 8th) | 26 | −2.31 (61st) | 47 | |
| 2. Management Practices | | | | | | |
|   f. Feeding Program Practice | 6 | | 27 | −1.19 (56th) | 48 | .88 (12th) |
|   g. Feed Medication Practice | 7 | −.91 (52nd) | 28 | −1.41 (59th) | 49 | −1.19 (55th) |
|   h. Building Selection | 8 | | 29 | | 50 | |
|   i. Performance Measurement | 9 | | 30 | −2.45 (62nd) | 51 | .98 ( 9th) |
|   j. Record Keeping Practice | 10 | | 31 | | 52 | 2.01 ( 1st) |
|   k. On-Farm Feed Mixing | 11 | | 32 | | 53 | |
| 3. Management Strategies/Guidelines | | | | | | |
|   l. Selecting Breeding Stock | 12 | | 33 | −1.4 (58th) | 54 | |
|   m. Selecting Feed Suppliers | 13 | | 34 | | 55 | |
|   n. Selecting Medication Programs | 14 | 1.56 ( 5th) | 35 | | 56 | |
|   o. Selecting Nutritional Products | 15 | | 36 | | 57 | |
|   p. Selecting New Products | 16 | .95 (10th) | 37 | | 58 | |
|   q. Selecting Products From Advertising | 17 | | 38 | | 59 | |
| 4. Future Management Issues | | | | | | |
|   r. Attitude Toward Growth | 18 | | 39 | −.92 (53rd) | 60 | |
|   s. Future Integration | 19 | 1.85 ( 2nd) | 40 | | 61 | −.95 (54th) |
|   t. Controlling Hog Production Costs | 20 | 1.32 ( 6th) | 41 | 1.56 ( 4th) | 62 | |
|   u. Regulatory Concern | 21 | | 42 | | 63 | |

## Table 2

Accept-Reject by Vision
Top twelve; bottom twelve

|          | Quality Hog Producer | Family Hog Farmer | Commercial Hog Producer |
|----------|:---:|:---:|:---:|
| Accept   | 6 | 1 | 5 |
| Reject   | 1 | 9 | 2 |

### Analysis — Segment I:  Quality Commercial Producers

The hog producers that comprised this segment are a blend of quality and commercial attitudes toward hog production. They demonstrate a strong rejection of the family hog farmer vision. Tables I and II display the data in support of the above conclusions.

Hog producers in this segment follow a commercial management philosophy and accept the commercial view of record keeping and performance measurements as well as feed program practices. This segment is the only segment to accept strongly the quality veterinarian issue of "regularly asking the veterinarian for advice and technical support to sustain an optimal herd health program." This acceptance of the vet is also consistent with the Segment I producers' acceptance of feed medication programs that are "built upon what I have read and heard about specific drug products, advice from my veterinarian, and laboratory results." Furthermore, these hog producers reject the family hog farmer practice of solving health problems by simply placing broad spectrum antibiotics in his feed.

Finally, this segment demonstrates total commitment to hog production in their rejection of the family hog farmer breeding management goal of "keeping sow farrowing from interfering with other farm work load."

## Excerpt 2: Large Hog Segmentation Study by Issue

The Derived Salient Issues:

A. Management Philosophy Issues
  1. Basis Production Philosophy
  2. Breeding Management Goal
  3. Veterinarian Involvement

B. Management Practices
  1. Feeding Program Practice
  2. Feed Medication Practice
  3. Performance Measurement
  4. Record Keeping Practice

C. Management Strategies/Guidelines
  1. Selecting Breeding Stock
  2. Selecting Medication Programs
  3. Selecting New Products

D. Future Management Issues
  1. Attitude Toward Growth
  2. Future Integration
  3. Controlling Hog Production Costs

How to Interpret Z-Score Data

Z-scores are a weighted measure that helps to identify the level of acceptance (high positive Z-scores), neutrality (Z-scores near zero), and rejection (high negative Z-scores) of a given item issue by a particular market segment.

The sorting behavior of respondents was analyzed via Q-type factor analysis. The initial solutions identified six independent segments of respondents with like reactions to the 63 statements, i.e., groupings which differ from one another intrinsically. For each market segment an array of the 63 statements was produced and Z-scores were assigned ranging from +3.0 (high) through 0.0 (neutral) to −3.0 (low) for each of the 63 statements. These Z-scores are used to compare similarities and differences in responses to each statement across segments.

One should look for the high and low loadings for each issue for each segment to understand the nature of the market segment.

## Table 3
## Veterinarian Involvement Issue

| Segment | Quality (Z-Score) | Family Hog (Z-Score) | Commercial (Z-Score) |
|---------|-------------------|----------------------|----------------------|
| 1 | + 1.14 | − 2.31 | − 0.4 |
| 2 | 0.4 | − 1.3 | − 0.5 |
| 3 | − 1.1 | − 0.5 | 0.9 |
| 4 | − 0.7 | − 0.7 | 0.8 |
| 5 | − 0.8 | + 1.50 | 0.4 |
| 6 | − 1.8 | 1.1 | .03 |

**Analysis on Issue 13:  Veterinarian Involvement**

Segment 1 is the only Segment to accept strongly the quality view that the veterinarian should be regularly part of the hog operations (Z-score = + 1.14). At the same time, the "Weak Quality" Segment 2 only slightly accepted this card (Z-score = + 0.4).

Segments 3 and 4 are doing their own hog herd health work and thus accept the commercial vision of veterinarian involvement (Z-scores = + 0.9 and + 0.8, respectively).

Segments 5 and 6 limit their use of the veterinarian to times when they face a serious problem. Thus they do not regularly call the vet and accept the view that the problem must really be bad to justify the cost of a visit by the veterinarian (Z-scores = + 1.5 and + 1.10, respectively.

## Excerpt 3: Large Hog Market Segmentation by Graphics

Graphic Predictive Findings:
  Segments 1 to 4 versus 5 and 6

A. Demographic Findings
  1. Type of Hog Operations (total confinement)
  2. Percent of Income from Hogs
  3. Father was a Hog Producer
  4. Formal Education
B. Psycho/Socio Graphic Findings
  1. Electronic Pregnancy Testing
  2. Percent of Sows Bred in First Service
  3. Method of Cleaning Farrowing House

### A Note on Using This Section

The data is presented in multiples of 3; by frequency, by row percentage, and by column percentage.

### Table 4
### Electronically Pregnancy Test Sows Socio-Graphic

| Question Response | Segment 1 | Segment 2 | Segment 3 | Segment 4 | Segment 5 & 6 | Total Responses |
|---|---|---|---|---|---|---|
| Yes | 29 | 19 | 20 | 17 | 38 | 123 |
|  | 23.6 | 15.4 | 16.3 | 13.8 | 30.9 | 100.0 |
|  | 85.3 | 59.4 | 37.0 | 37.0 | 19.1 | 33.7 |
| No | 5 | 12 | 33 | 29 | 155 | 234 |
|  | 2.1 | 5.1 | 14.1 | 12.4 | 66.2 | 100.0 |
|  | 14.7 | 37.5 | 61.1 | 63.0 | 77.9 | 64.1 |
| No Answer | 0 | 1 | 1 | 0 | 6 | 8 |
|  | 0.0 | 12.5 | 12.5 | 0.0 | 75.0 | 100.0 |
|  | 0.0 | 0.3 | 1.9 | 0.0 | 3.1 | 2.1 |
| Total | 34 | 32 | 54 | 46 | 199 | 365 |
|  | 9.3 | 8.8 | 14.8 | 12.6 | 54.5 | 100.0 |
|  | 100.0 | 100.0 | 100.0 | 100.0 | 100.0 | 100.0 |

### Analysis of Predictive Findings on Electronic Pregnancy Testing

The presence of electronic pregnancy testing is a good indicator of the two quality hog producer segments, Segment 1 and Segment 2; 85% of Segment 1 and 59% of Segment 2 pregnancy tests. This contrasts with only 19% of Segments 5 and 6 who pregnancy test. Thus, pregnancy testing is a good sign argument that points to the presence of a quality hog producer.

# 21

# Applied Q-Methodology:
## An Industry Perspective

## RICHARD R. BUSH

The following case study reviews the effective and practical application of Q-methodology of a business problem. This discussion is designed to provide some useful insights into how the "Q" approach to communications research has been applied to an industrial marketing situation. Much of the Technical detail regarding market segmentation and the Q-methodology is presented in other sections.

This case review focuses on marketing questions relevant to a business problem and how one firm set out to provide solutions. No effort is made to discuss either research technique, or detailed findings of the study. This discourse provides an industry perspective through discussions of:

a. the marketing problem,

b. the research technique selected, and

c. the impact the research had with management.

## The Problem

The marketing problem centered around one of a family of newly developed compounds called prostaglandins.[1] Dinoprost, when administered properly in cattle, results in a more predictable onset of estrus or heat, and subsequent ovulation (called estrus synchronization).

The effective use of dinoprost in beef and dairy herds permits:

[1]Prostaglandins are naturally-occurring fatty acids believed to be present in all mammalian tissue. This class of materials was first identified in the late 1930's, yet did not receive significant attention until 1965. During the late 1960's and throughout the 1970's, extensive prostaglandin biological research was conducted. This case study involves prostaglandin $F_2 \propto$ usage in cattle. Lutalyse ® sterile solution, an Upjohn product for veterinary use containing prostaglandin $F_2 \propto$ tromethamine (dinoprost tromethamine), was submitted for approval in the late 1970's to the Food and Drug Administration. When approved, this product will be sold through veterinarians and labeled for use in cattle. Throughout this discussion, Lutalyse (dinoprost tromethamine) will be referred to simply as the generic name dinoprost.

1. control and prediction of estrus cycles,
2. improved planning for labor management,
3. improved planning for the use of artificial insemination and potential genetic gain,
4. better grouping of calving dates, and
5. a more uniform, high-quality calf drop.

Dinoprost could prove to be the catalyst for dramatically improving beef production efficiencies in the U.S. Biologically, it is commonly believed that efficient production of quality meat is a heritable trait. One effective way a cattleman can improve the production capacity of a herd of cows is to upgrade the genetic quality of the cows themselves, as well as the quality of the bulls used for breeding.

One effective way to improve the genetic quality of the bull stock is to purchase genetically superior bull semen and to inseminate cows artificially. Theoretically, by using artificial insemination (A.I.) techniques, a cattleman effectively can breed more cows to a selected high quality bull thereby capitalizing on the best genetic source available.

A major barrier to adoption of A.I. is the extreme inconvenience of observing cows for heat and subsequent coordination of the actual insemination at the optimum time to ensure maximum conception. The application of a product to help control the timing of estrus would (theoretically) make the adoption of A.I. and the subsequent improvement in production efficiencies a more real possibility. The eventual acceptance by cattlemen of a product to allow for more predictable breeding is contingent on several key issues. Since dinoprost for estrus synchronization will be introduced exclusively through veterinarians, the success of a total program using it depends on the approaches used by the practicing veterinarian. Marketing efforts must be designed to help counsel and guide veterinarians on the most effective and acceptable ways to approach cattlemen. Scientific studies have shown that this product works in healthy, well managed herds. Therefore, successful marketing is·contingent upon the cattleman's perceptions of the economic benefits of a redesigned reproduction management program that includes dinoprost.

Past experience with cattlemen has shown the issues surrounding cattle breeding are not well understood. Beef cattlemen in particular vary greatly in experience and knowledge about reproduction. As the market planning team reviewed and discussed the possible strategies for introducing this product, a series of problems and questions surfaced.

A. Successful estrus synchronization in beef requires a technological change in the beef industry. Although this new technology may evolve over years, if not decades, the rate of change acceptable to beef producers impacts significantly on how quickly dinoprost is adopted.

B. Introducing dinoprost to beef cattlemen required a significant educational effort. Beef producers look to many sources for information on a new product. A successful marketing program must employ these sources efficiently.

C. The concept of using a drug for estrus synchronization encompasses a variety of real and perceived concerns and benefits.

- When communicating information to cattlemen or to their key source of information, specifically what points should be be stressed?

- In public relations, advertising and direct sales messages, what benefits regarding successful use of the product are most important?

- Is it possible to identify critical elements necessary to a successful estrus synchronization — A.I. program? Concentrating on these elements should help to establish positive experiences early in the life-cycle of dinoprost.

- How can the marketing team encourage the beef producer to use the product as an aid to improving herd management and gain success stories early?

### Selecting a Research Technique

The marketing team needed a clearer understanding of the market. It is well recognized that the beef cattle segment represents a significant potential for dinoprost sales. Yet, the risks are very real. The chance for success in this market is not known...use of dinoprost is contingent on many uncontrollable factors. The challenge to a communication research effort was to obtain structured, organized feedback from beef cattlemen to simplify the issues and to establish priorities for marketing management. Having previous experience in the market with another compound helped. However, cattle numbers had declined, the economic factors influencing beef cattlemen were different, and attitudes toward managing herds may have changed. The marketing team therefore decided to invest in the most extensive communications research effort available to study beef cattlemen's current attitudes, beliefs and practices regarding management of reproduction in their herds. The marketing problems represented were extensive. Issues relevant to product usage were typically varied, complicated and required discussions of significant detail. For example, several important areas influencing the use of dinoprost included cattlemen's:

1. Established relationships with veterinarians and A.I. companies.
2. Experiences and perceptions of artificial insemination in beef cattle.
3. Herd handling practices and facilities available for holding and handling cattle.
4. Established goals toward their cattle business.
5. Attitudes toward use of bulls versus an A.I. program.

6. Perceived benefits or liabilities of an estrus synchronization program.
7. Overall herd health management programs as they relate to reproductive efficiencies of the herds.

The typical research approach using several qualitative focus groups, followed by a quantitative study, was not considered to be the solution because this problem was too complex and detailed. A highly structured questionnaire could not deal effectively with all the variables relevant to the problem. The research approach had to be one that would not add to the confusion but could help describe to management how cattlemen currently think about reproduction and estrus synchronization. The methodology selected was the Shields-Cragan approach to Q-sort utilizing dramatizations theory. This research technique enabled the research team to structure a series of statements incorporating the necessary issues as they related to the existing attitudes of beef cattlemen. In essence, Q-methodology and the application of dramatization theory provides a refined merger of qualitative and quantitative research techniques. When completed, this research approach produced a detailed description of how the markets are segmented attitudinally and what is needed to effectively communicate to each segment.

**Impact of Findings**

Technically, Q-methodology satisfied the basic objective of the research effort . . . it simplified the myriad of relevant issues and described the market to management. Even though the data collection and analytical tools used to complete the project were complex and time consuming, the result is a clearly stated and well understood perceptual diagram of the target market for dinoprost. Many of the merits of this approach go well beyond the structured data manipulation technique employed by the methodology. Framing the parameters of the Q-deck and preparing the statements for the deck required an intense commitment. The researchers were compelled to become involved when structuring the deck, as well as analyzing the data.

The team approach proved valuable in the various stages of the project. Constant interaction and active discussions were necessary when preparing the focus group discussion guides; structuring the deck, and analyzing the computer runs. It was also necessary for several key individuals outside the research team to provide input at various stages. At one point prior to finalizing the deck, several knowledgeable persons on cattle reproduction were given the deck, asked to complete the sort and encouraged to evaluate the statements critically. Possibly, the most understated aspect of any communications research project is the posturing and presentation of findings. No study is any better than the perceptions left with management following the report of findings. If a formal presentation is planned, the release of data should be controlled carefully. Managing the dissemination of data not only lends to its credibility, but enhances its usefulness. Data users tend to take note when information is controlled carefully. Also, the researcher has an opportunity to assist data users in accessing and interpreting all relevant data.

During the presentation, the methodology must be explained in some depth. With Q-methodology this is not a simple task, and requires a confident understanding of the techniques employed. If done correctly, this brief review helps establish a foundation of credibility for the remainder of the presentation.

In the case of this Q-study, the overall reactions to the intensity and expansiveness of the research were dramatic and supportive. The management team recognized the concern for detail and the comprehensive nature of the research approach. They reacted quite favorably to both the research techniques employed and the depth of the data reported. A key advantage of this research method is an effective use of multi-dimensional data. The market, after intense study is segmented attitudinally on a series of interacting issues. It becomes possible in reviewing the detailed findings to understand the perceptual space of each segment in the marketplace. When presenting the findings, it is then possible to talk about perceptual space and how ideas relate to other ideas, demographics, psychographics or product graphics. Although some interpretations of the results have been controversial, the controversy involves more of a need to understand the cattleman's perspective than a belief that a particular finding is incorrect. The final evaluation of the merit of this research approach will not be made until dinoprost is positioned in the cattle industry. Research studies conducted since the Q-study was reported continue to verify the findings as complete and accurate.

The data collected in this study have provided valuable direction for the market planning stage. Inputs have been used to prepare strategies for advertising, public relations and sales detailing. The process of applying the Q-findings will continue through market introduction and will provide a foundation of information throughout the life of the product.

Richard R. Bush currently is a market analyst at the Upjohn Company in Kalamazoo, Michigan. His responsibilities include conducting communications market studies on animal health related problems. He previously worked in consumer products research and political polling. Mr. Bush has a B.A. in Marketing and an M.B.A. in Management from Wayne State University, Detroit, Michigan.

The Upjohn Company is a pharmaceutical firm with major commitments to researching, manufacturing and marketing of both human and animal medications. The veterinary division offers a broad line of animal health products through one of the largest direct sales forces in the industry.

# PART VI:
## Appendices

# VI: Appendices

The three appendices presented in this section are intended as aides for an applied communication researcher who wishes to use a dramatistic approach. The first appendix is an example of a dramatistic based focus group interview outline. This outline combined with Shields's lecture on how to conduct a dramatistic based focus group interview (see Part V) should help you in conducting your own group interviews using Bormann's theory.

The second appendix is an actual dramatistically structured Q-deck. We used it in doing the Doane Farm Management organizational communication study which is presented in Part III. The Doane deck can serve as a model for constructing your own dramatistically based Q-deck. Note that the deck is structured in terms of both the competing rhetorical visions on the top of the matrix, and the dramatistic structure with here and now phenomena on the left side of the matrix.

The final appendix is an essay by Shields that discusses factor analysis from a meta perspective. It outlines the technical steps of factor analysis, sets forth a three-part critical standard for evaluating factor analysis studies, and for illustrative purposes applies the evolved critical standard to a well-known study. The essay seeks to fill a critical void by synthesizing technical guidelines into a framework for conducting and evaluating the quantitative research presented in this book.

# A

# Doane Farm Management Study:
## Focus Group Outline

JOHN F. CRAGAN, DONALD C. SHIELDS, and
N.E. NICHOLS

My name is _____. I'm a representative of Doane's Marketing Research Division. We conduct marketing research for major corporations such as Shell and Purina. Doane decided that they should use the research expertise of the Marketing Research Division to study ways to produce more growth and profitability in the Farm Management Division.

We in the Marketing Research Division perform different kinds of studies. One type is through meetings such as this, which we call focus group interviews.

How do you define the Doane products, Farm Management services and consultation services? How do you define and describe the markets for these products? What recommendations do you have for increasing volume, market share and profitability? These are the questions we need answers to.

This interview is designed so each of you can react to what the other managers say. I want to hear all of the various points of view you represent.

As far as we're concerned, there are no right or wrong answers to the questions I'll be asking. I hope that each of you tells and shares your opinions and experiences.

   I. The Farm Management Service
      A. What is the Farm Manager service you perform?
         1. How important is the ability to communicate in writing to your client? Do you have that ability? (Now? When you started?)
         2. Do you have the necessary production know how? As much as the owner-operator in you area? More than other non-Doane farm managers?

3. How about expertise in marketing the crop? Do you have more knowledge than the marketing analyst in Doane's home office?

B. There seems to be a difference of opinion about what the Farm Management service is. Some managers say it is the job of managing the farm for absentee owners in which the Farm Manager makes the production decisions. Other managers tell me that the Farm Manager represents the absentee owners' interests but he really manages the tenant farmers and lets the tenant farmers make many production decisions.

1. How many visits should Farm Managers make to each farm in order to do his job? (Some say twelve visits, some say four visits.)

2. How many farms can one Farm Manager manage?

a. in Midwest

b. in South

c. in West

C. Many of the people in the Farm Management Division whom I have talked to say that the Farm Management service is an intangible product that is hard to define.

1. How does the client know he or she is getting his or her money's worth?

2. How does Doane company know you're doing a good job?

3. What are the signs of a bad farm manager?

D. Should the main relationship be between the client and the Farm Manager or should it be between the client and Doane? Why?

1. What happens to the Farm Manager when he leaves Doane?

2. What percent of the farm management market does Doane have? Is it growing? Why?

E. What does the average farmer think of Doane Farm Managers?

II. Consultation Service

A. People at the university tell me that there is so much free advice from extension, dealers and magazines about farming that no owner-operator should have to pay a consultant these days. Is that true?

1. How big must the farm be to afford a consultant?

2. Is the consulting on a one-time problem or a retainer basis?

B. Is there a greater chance of consultation in the technical aspects of farm production or in the planning and financial end of the business?

C. One guy in the home office told me that you Farm Managers were afraid to consult for the large owner-operator because you think they know more about farming than you do.

D. If most of Doane farm managing is in straight cropping operations and most of the consulting operations are in complex farms (hogs, cows, grains) how do you expect to expand your consultation business?

E. Just what aspects of farming do you feel you are expert enough to consult on?

    1. Does Doane as a corporation have the expertise to consult in all areas of farming?

    2. Do you represent yourself as an expert or do you represent Doane as an expert and yourself as a Doane agent?

III. Nature of the Market for Farm Management and Consultation Services

A. Who is the Doane Farm Manager client? Some say it is the farmer's widow or the old maid schoolteacher. Others say we don't know who the client is except that they are absentee owners. Who do you think the client is?

B. Is the Doane client different than the client from other farm management companies?

C. I am very confused about which way the market for farm management is going. Some say the market is shrinking, that it is slim-picking—hard to get new farms to manage. Yet, others point out how successful ex-Doane managers have become. They point to banks like the one in Decatur, Illinois; they point to the farm management in Nebraska and the trust company in Chicago and they say opportunity is all over. Everybody is growing like crazy but Doane. What's the story here?

D. Is the need for a farm management service declining? One Regional Manager said the service was created because absentee landowners could not trust their tenants. In the old days Doane ran off bad tenants but they did such a good job that today most tenant farmers are good production managers so there is no need for a Farm manager.

E. Has the market moved from an emphasis on technical production (farming decisions) to financial planning (cash flow, accounting, marketing)?

F. Where is the new client for farm management?

    1. How do we reach this client?

G. Will new growth come from more of the same kind of Doane client that Doane has had in the past or will it come from a new type of client?

H. When you get together with non-Doane farm managers at conventions, what do they say about the market? Is it growing—shrinking—or what?

IV. Acquiring New Business (Selling)

  A. I have been told that qualified leads and referrals from banks, lawyers and present clients are the best and some say the only way to get new business. Is that true?

    1. How else do you get new clients?
    2. How many leads do you check out each month?
    3. How much time do you spend selling?

  B. One Regional Manager said you can't separate the sales and management functions. The person who sells the client must also be the one who manages the farm. Is that right?

    1. What if you had a full-time salesperson making sales for you? What would happen? Isn't that what the Nebraska outfit does?

  C. I'm from Winnebago County which is in northern Illinois, so let me give a hypothetical example from my home area. If you are a manager living in Oregon, Illinois and the home office gives you a lead on a farm north of Monroe, Wisconsin (a distance of 150 miles of bad road), and if you already have forty farms and you know you will meet your set objective of $60,000 of income for Doane, would you go get that Wisconsin farm? What is your incentive to do so?

    1. Do you intentionally get rid of troublesome clients in faraway farms and replace them with straight cropping operations?

  D. I've been given some stereotypes of you from various people. Allow me to try some of them out and you let me know if they fit.

    1. Doane Farm Managers can be divided into two groups. One group is production-oriented. They like to have their hands in the soil. They like to make all of the production decisions on the farms. They do not like to go out and sell. The second group is sales-oriented. They like to go out and sell new business. They spend more time on the phone than they do on the farm. They might sacrifice a little quality in management for more sales.

    2. Most of Doane's Farm Managers are in love with farming and the rural environment. They do not aspire for advancement within the company. They are satisfied with an average income and increasing incentives would not produce more sales.

    3. One stereotype is that of a Doane Farm Manager who has an attitude problem. That's why there is not more growth in the Division. This is contrasted with the characterization of a professional manager who once he is in the door can sell anyone on his abilities. There just isn't any incentive to sell. The more he sells the less percentage of gross income is his. The company wants 18% growth but only offers 8% salary increase.

      4. I've been told that a good Doane Farm Manager cannot be fired for not increasing income to Doane because if he is fired he will take some of the business with him and in a year he he will have enough new business to become a lifelong competitor of Doane.

  E. I have another set of statements I can't make sense out of and maybe you can help me. On one hand there are many examples of managers who leave Doane and are immediately successful. (I know of no failures.) Yet at the same time people tell me Doane Farm Managers have a hard time getting new clients. How can a Doane Farm Manager go for years with only replacement sales and then leave Doane and sell a full production load in one year?

  F. By the way, what is a full production load?

      1. Thirty-forty farms?

      2. $60,000 gross income to Doane — I heard somebody did $90,000.

      3. What are the factors involved in figuring a full load?

  G. Do lists from tax rolls help? Do you have lists of your own area? Why did the phone campaign from these lists fail?

  H. One Regional Manager said that if Doane put him in Iowa or Illinois and gave him $10,000 to live on, (incentive pay) in one year he would sell enough new business that Doane would take in at least $60,000 in gross income. Do you believe that's possible?

  I. What new ideas do you have for increasing the volume and profitability in farm management?


V. Competition

  A. Is the Doane Farm Manager better than his competitor? How?

  B. Some of the personnel in the home office believe that Doane's superiority to the competition is its complete service, its long-standing good name, the continuity of service, and its expertise in farming. Do you think this is true?

      1. What makes a Doane Farm Manager a Doane Farm Manager?

  C. Who is the biggest competitor of Doane in your area?

      1. Is cash rent a real threat?

      2. What is the future threat?

      3. How do you beat the competition?

  D. What services or selling strategies does the competition use that you wish Doane would adopt?

      1. New services, advertising, organizational concepts or money incentives?

VI. Home Office Support

   A. Some Regional Managers say that the full service of Doane's home office is a good selling point but in reality the help is not there. The Farm Manager is really on his own.

   B. I have heard a lot of complaints about the accounting system. Is it really that bad or have most of the problems been corrected?

      1. How can it be improved?

      2. Can it be sold as a separate service?

   C. Also I hear that the library service is great and that most of you use it.

      1. Do you think there might be a market to sell the library service to farmers who want to read up on a specific problem like hog confinement or would that hurt your consulting service?

   D. What about the marketing advice? Is it valuable to you in selling farm products? How can it be improved?

   E. I've been told two different stories about communication from the St. Louis office. One story is that you do not know whom to call for advice in the home office and that when you do, you do not feel right about asking for help because you know the guy is busy with his own job. The other story is that the home office calls you every day as a matter of policy and asks if you need help. So is there good communication from the home office? Can you get help or not?

      1. Do you feel you have enough contact with the home office?

      2. Should the Division Manager make field visits? What purpose would they serve?

   F. Is the Newsletter usable? Do you read it? What additional material could be added?

   G. Is the Doane Report a help or hindrance to you in getting new clients?

      1. Is the report a positive contribution to the overall Doane image?

   H. Is the annual company meeting valuable?

      1. Are the awards meaningful?

      2. What would you add?

VII. Advertising

   A. I've been told that the *Wall Street Journal* article of a few years ago, the *Wall Street Journal* ad and the recent ads offering information on investing in farmland produced a lot of inquiries. The ad in the *Chicago Tribune* produced 500 phone calls in one week to the Aurora office, yet you did not make many sales. Why?

      1. Should Doane continue ads offering investment advice?

      2. Is an ad campaign on a general awareness of Doane needed?

3. Do potential clients in your area know of Doane?

4. Where should Doane place its ads?

B. Would a well-developed ad with pictures of you and your Regional Manager combined with a list of the Regional Manager's and Doane's accomplishments placed in a local newspaper be a good idea? What about in a direct mail campaign?

C. Does direct mail work to get leads? How many?

D. How should Doane advertise? Where?

E. What happens to the leads that the home office sends out? Are they any good?

F. Does the Regional Manager take the best leads for himself?

VIII. Training

A. Some Regional Managers tell me that a new Farm Manager may be working the day he is hired. If that is so, how does he receive any training? Does he need training:

1. in farm production management?

2. in management skills (communication) with tenant and with client?

3. in sales?

B. Since the Regional Manager does the training, do you think you receive really different training from different Regional Managers?

1. Should the training be standardized?

2. Is on-the-job training better than formal training?

C. Do you think there is certain training that all Farm Managers should have that would mark them as part of the Doane family?

D. What sales aids do you need?

E. Is the orientation program in the home office for new employees valuable?

1. What should be added to that program?

F. Are the seminars at conventions and extension courses the best way for you to get training?

G. How important is your membership in the American Farm Management Association? Is the code followed with regard to stealing clients?

IX. The Identity of the Farm Manager and the Regional Farm Manager

A. The Farm Manager

1. Describe to me the ideal Farm Manager: background, personality, education, farming ability, selling ability, relationship with Doane.

2. I was told by one Regional Manager that it's easy to find good Farm Managers to hire.

3. I hear that integrity is a very important and time-honored personality trait of Doane Farm Managers. Do you believe that's true?

4. Also, I hear that some Farm Manager in Illinois was indicted for stealing money from his clients (thousands of dollars). I also hear that some Farm Managers skim a little off here and there for themselves. Is this widespread?

5. What's the difference between the Doane Farm Manager and other farm managers?

6. Why do so many Farm Managers leave Doane?

7. Why don't Farm Managers leave other companies and come to work for Doane?

B. The Regional Farm Manager

1. Describe the ideal Regional Farm Manager.

2. How many Regional Farm Managers should there be?

3. Some Regional Managers argue that they should receive a sales commission.

   a. Should they continue to manage farms?

4. Some Regional Managers have Farm Managers that make more money than they do. They think that is unfair.

5. Do you think that each Regional Manager uses the same criteria for appraising the work a Farm Manager does?

   a. What criteria does your Regional Manager use?

6. What should the formula be for farm management job appraisal?

   a. total revenue to Doane

   b. number of farms

   c. total of acres

   d. value of land

   e. number of turnovers

   f. number of new sales

   g. number of visits to farms

   h. lack of complaints from clients

   i. certain number of consultations

   j. what else?

X. Doane's Image

A. What is Doane's image? "If it concerns farming it concerns Doane." "Largest farm management company." "Only complete service corporation in agriculture." "A conservative company." "A growing company."

1. What's good about the image?

      2. What's detrimental about the image?

  B. One Regional Manager told me that originally the Farm Manager was Doane. He was the renaissance man who could do technical production, handle complex farms, sell, do appraisals and consultations without help from the home office. Today the Doane Farm Manager is a representative of Doane and it is the company that provides the expertise.

  C. Is there a traditional approach to Doane Farm Management and is there a new approach?

  D. What role does the Research Division and the Publication Division play in the creation of Doane's image?

XI. Division Model

  A. What is the current model for the Division?

      1. Management by objectives?

      2. What is an objective?

      3. Can production be doubled, tripled?

  B. What happens when you do not meet your objectives or goals?

      1. Will you be fired if you do not meet your goals?

  C. What do you think of the St. Louis regional structure as a future model for the rest of the Division?

  D. One Regional Manager told me that sales and profitability would rise dramatically if the money incentive was there. For example, if your objective was set at $70,000 and you get 30% of all dollars over that goal.

  E. Are there enough rewards to the job? What are they?

  F. Do you feel there is a chance for you to move up in the company?

  G. What are your long-time career goals?

  H. List two strengths of the Doane Farm Management Division and two weaknesses of the Division.

  I. If you could be Division Manager next year, what changes would you make in the Division in order to produce more growth?

XII. Final Suggestions

  A. Now that this interview is over, could we end by listing the five best recommendations we have heard here today for increasing sales?

**B**

# Doane Farm Management Study:
## Structured Matrix and Dramatistic Q-Deck

JOHN F. CRAGAN, DONALD C. SHIELDS, and
N.E. NICHOLS

| | |
|---|---|
| Division Identity | Doane Philosophy |
| | Doane Image |
| | Doane Farm Manager Self-Image |
| | Need for Service |
| | Client |
| | Scene |
| Division Structure | Division Model — Definition of Farm Manager |
| | Regional Manager |
| | Training |
| | Job, Work Standard |
| | Motivation |
| | Satisfaction |
| | Job Appraisal |
| Product | Product Services |
| | Consultation |
| | Support Services |
| Marketing Strategy | Doane Competitive Edge |
| | Strategy for New Business |
| | Advertising |
| | Limits to New Business |

Reprinted with the permission of Doane Agricultural Service, Inc.

387

## Doane Philosophy

|  |  |  |
|---|---|---|
| **Vision I** | **Vision II** | **Vision III** |
| The governing philosophy of the Doane company is to bring modern scientific agricultural practices to the farming community in order to save the land and maintain continuous profits for the absentee landowners through professional management supervision. | The governing philosophy of the Doane company is that it's a family of professionals engaged in agricultural service. Being an employee-owned company, it allows loyal employees to share collectively in the rewards of good work, and the pride of ownership. | The governing philosophy of the Doane company is to maximize profits. Each employee has the obligation to maximize the profitability of their job function. |

## Doane Image in Agriculture

|  |  |  |
|---|---|---|
| **Vision I** | **Vision II** | **Vision III** |
| The Farm Management Division reflects the Doane company's place in agriculture as a conservative, steady company built by agrarian oriented people with integrity. | The Farm Management Division reflects the Doane company's place in agriculture as a conservative company that weighs and incorporates the decisions necessary to meet the changing nature of agriculture. | The Farm Management Division reflects the Doane company's place in agriculture as a conservative old line company that is really a sleeping giant capable of rapid growth and expansion in terms of the services provided and the potential for profit. |

## Hero Image of Doane Farm Manager

|  |  |  |
|---|---|---|
| **Vision I** | **Vision II** | **Vision III** |
| A Doane Farm Manager is a college graduate in agriculture and is superior in the farm management marketplace when it comes to farm production decisions. | A Doane Farm Manager has the education and background to make competent production decisions, derives his superiority in the marketplace from his ability to plan, advise, and meet the landowner's goals. | A Doane Farm Manager is a man who, while he can make competent production decisions and plan and advise and meet agreed upon mutually goals, derives his superiority in the marketplace from his ability to advise of markets, taxes, real estate decisions. |

## Villain Need for Service

### Vision I

A Doane Farm Manager's major job purpose is to protect the absentee landowner — a landowner who is at the mercy of the ignorant, dishonest, lazy tenant.

### Vision II

A Doane Farm Manager's major job purpose is to advise the absentee landowner — a landowner who might get competent production by renting to owner-operators, but who turns to the Farm Manager because he needs objective goal planning and wise financial management.

### Vision III

A Doane Farm Manager's major job purpose is to assist the landowner client — a landowner who is into farming for investment and needs consulting assistance on operating, markets, taxes, appreciation, depreciation, and optimum times for buying and selling his land.

## Client

### Vision I

A Doane Farm Manager's client is the absentee landowner — typically a widow or old maid school teacher who inherited the land. She needs a protector.

### Vision II

A Doane Farm Management client is a landowner not operating the farm. This person is hard to typify, but generally includes widows, heirs, lawyers, physicians, and investors. They need assistance in setting goals and in wise financial management.

### Vision III

A Doane Farm Management client includes not only the widow seeking protection, the land owner seeking planning and financial advice, but the owner-operator seeking consultation or additional land, and individuals, corporations, and nation states seeking land for investment.

## Work Scene

### Vision I

When I picture a Doane Farm Manager on the job, I see him spending most of his time visiting farms, making production decisions, and updating the client about the status of their farm.

### Vision II

When I picture a Doane Farm Manager on the job, I see a man who has delegated many production functions to competent tenants and he is spending a great deal of his time talking to qualified leads in an attempt to increase his production and consulting load.

### Vision III

When I picture a Doane Farm Manager on the job, I see a man who has delegated many production functions, who spends a great deal of his time talking to qualified leads, and who competently assists the client in making marketing, tax, and real estate decisions.

## Division Management Model
## Definition of Farm Manager

| Vision I | Vision II | Vision III |
|---|---|---|
| A Doane Farm Manager carries out his load autonomously and creates a direct relationship with the client. He is the Doane company — he is Mr. Doane. | A Doane Farm Manager carries out his work load with a lot of autonomy, but draws upon the resources of the home office as he creates a relationship interfacing himself and the company with the client. | A Doane Farm Manager carries out his work load as sole decisionmaker, but as a representative of the Doane company. Doane is the key to attracting the client. The client is buying Doane's Farm Management service, not the manager. |

## Role of the Regional Manager

| Vision I | Vision II | Vision III |
|---|---|---|
| The ideal job function for a Regional Manager is to carry out the functions of a Farm Manager with the additional responsibility of supervising other Farm Managers. | The ideal job function for a Regional Manager is minimal farm management, motivation of Farm Managers to meet their work objectives, training, advertising and record keeping for the region. | The ideal job function for a Regional Manager is that of management. He has no farms, but complete responsibility for people management, continuous training and supervision over the sales and marketing functions for his region. |

## Training

| Vision I | Vision II | Vision III |
|---|---|---|
| The best training procedure for Doane to follow is to select people already capable of managing farms. Many people have to be on the job the first day they are hired. If help is requested, the Regional Manager will provide assistance. | The best training procedure for Doane to follow is to hire a person who knows agriculture, provide basic orientation to Doane procedures, and offer on-the-job training directed by the Regional Manager. | The best training procedure for Doane to follow is to have a formalized, standardized program that provides basic farm management skills combined with probationary on-the-job training directed by the Regional Manager, and periodic home office special skills training sessions. |

## Job/Work Standard

### Vision I

A Doane Farm Manager knows he is doing a good job when he has built his management load to a level that is profitable, but insures that he can manage with quality. The objective is then to maintain that load.

### Vision II

A Doane Farm Manager knows he is doing a good job when he gets a stable base of farms and does enough new things to meet increasingly higher M.B. O.'s.

### Vision III

A Doane Farm Manager knows he is doing a good job when he's not limited by meeting set goals. Rather he is always on the look-out for new ways to increase profitability for both himself and the company.

## Motivation

### Vision I

The best source of motivation for a Doane Farm Manager is from the knowledge that he is a trained professional providing a needed commitment to the agricultural community that does not exist in his absence. In essence, he's an agricultural missionary saving the land and helping the absentee landowner.

### Vision II

The best source of motivation for a Doane Farm Manager is from the knowledge that when he does a consistently good job, he receives a salary that is above the national average. With it he can be in the rural community and stay close to the land.

### Vision III

The best source of motivation for a Doane Farm Manager is from the knowledge that the sky is almost the limit when it comes to profits for himself and the company giving the commissions on sales of new services.

## Work Satisfaction

### Vision I

Some of the lasting rewards of Doane Farm Management are the preservation of the land for future generations, respect as a professional in the community, it's the next best thing to farming the land yourself.

### Vision II

Some of the lasting rewards of Doane Farm Management are the adequate source of income, the opportunity to maintain a rural lifestyle, and the sense of accomplishment that comes from successfully managing people.

### Vision III

Some of the lasting rewards of Doane Farm Management are maximizing the profitability of oneself and the company, and successfully delivering a number of diverse services from real estate through land management to agricultural consultaion.

## Job Appraisal

| Vision I | Vision II | Vision III |
|---|---|---|
| The measure of a good Farm Manager is the lack of complaints and not losing any customers. His reward is status in the community and the knowledge that he's doing a quality job. | The measure of a good Farm Manager is his ability to meet his M.B.O.'s. His reward is a continuing association with Doane, the incentive payment that is tied to M.B.O.'s, and profit-sharing that comes from employment in a profit-sharing company. | The measure of a good Farm Manager is his productivity measured in total profit to the company and himself. His reward is the knowledge that he shares proportionately with the company in profit growth. |

## Farm Management Services is Problem Solving of Technical Production

| Vision I | Vision II | Vision III |
|---|---|---|
| The fundamental service of farm management is problem solving. The major aspect of the Farm Managment service is supervision of technical production and marketing. | The fundamental service of farm management is problem solving. The major aspect of the Farm Management service is supervision of the tenant farmer with an emphasis on financial planning and business management. | The fundamental service of farm management is problem solving. The major aspect of the Farm Management service is total corporate involvement in agri-consulting, which may include technical production, financial planning, trusts, brokerage, real estate, and taxes. |

## Consultation

| Vision I | Vision II | Vision III |
|---|---|---|
| The best way to think of the Farm Management consulting service is as technical advice that's provided to the owner-operator related to scientific farming practices. | The best way to think of the Farm Management consulting service is as a customized answer to a specific situation such as hog confinement or as financial planning and budgeting for the owner-operator. | The best way to think of the Farm Management consulting service is as the bringing together of the necessary technical consultants to answer the many complex decisions of modern agriculture for such clients as individuals, corporations, estates, and nation states. |

## Home Office Support Services

The expert support services of the home office are used primarily by the Farm Manager as a selling point to clients. However, the Farm Manager's use of them in practice is negligible — the Farm Manager is the sole deliverer of service and expertise to the client.

The expert support services of the home office are used by the Farm Manager as a selling point to clients. In addition, Farm Managers use the support services from the library, accounting, commodity forecasting, and creative services departments in managing their farms.

The expert support services of the home office are major components, along with the Farm Manager, for delivering agricultural services to clients.

## Doane's Competitive Edge

### Vision I

The key to Doane's competitive edge in the marketplace is that the Farm Manager is of the land, educated in agriculture, and the possessor of impeccable integrity.

### Vision II

The key to Doane's competitive edge in the marketplace is that Doane has the image of a long-standing conservative company which knows all aspects of agriculture and can produce the expert advice necessary to making the Farm Manager better than his counterparts with other companies.

### Vision III

The key to Doane's competitive edge in the marketplace is that Doane can aggressively marshall its expertise from marketing, publications, and farm management to solve any agri-problem in the marketplace.

## Marketing Strategy for New Business

### Vision I

A Doane Farm Manager's best method of getting new business is through referral from people who are knowledgeable of Doane's services, such as present clients, bankers and lawyers.

### Vision II

A Doane Farm Manager's best method of getting new business is by contacting qualified leads. Qualified leads are acquired through referral, direct mail, and advertising in local papers.

### Vision III

A Doane Farm Manager's best method of getting new business is by having a full-time person in each region whose job function is developing and qualifying prospective clients, creating innovative advertising and promotional programs.

## Advertising

| Vision I | Vision II | Vision III |
|---|---|---|
| The best advertising of Doane Farm Management is the quality service that's provided for Doane Farm Management clients. Actions speak louder than words. | The best advertising of Doane Farm Management is through regionally developed ads placed in local newspapers combined with mailing lists taken from local tax roles. | The best advertising of Doane Farm Management is through a continuous national advertising program that creates an awareness and need for Doane and the farm management services that it offers. |

## Limitations to Acquiring New Business

| Vision I | Vision II | Vision III |
|---|---|---|
| The main obstacle to a major increase in a Farm Manager's work load is the time it takes to do a quality job of management. There are some real limits to the number of farms that can be managed without hurting client relations. If you have too many farms you'll start losing clients. | The main obstacle to a major increase in a Farm Manager's work load is the dramatic growth in competition from other Farm Management companies, bank trusts, owner-operators, and former Doane Farm Managers. There's only so many farms out there to manage and competition is keen. | The main obstacle to a major increase in a Farm Manager's work load is the absence of a meaningful incentive program. If a Farm Manager is asked to dramatically increase the profitability of Doane, he too should be proportionally rewarded. The business is there, it's just there's no monetary reward for going after it. |

# C

# Critiquing Factor Analysis Studies:
## A Critical Standard and Application

## DONALD C. SHIELDS

Our discipline encourages the periodic review of both on-going research and the application of research methods. Typically, such reviews assess the quality of the research contributions and specify the strengths and weaknesses of the research designs and sampling procedures.[1] These reviews display implicit value. They serve to synthesize research findings, contribute to the understanding of the underlying research methods, and set forth critical criteria by which the reader may evaluate his own and other subsequent research.

In the past decade, speech communication journals reported a number of studies utilizing factor analytic techniques to assist in the interpretation of communication data.[2] Paradoxically, at a time when factor analysis is all

---

[1]The published reviews are well known and to cite them all is beyond the scope of a journal length monograph. Representative reports include: Ernest G. Bormann's critique of small group research entitled, "The Paradox and Promise of Small Group Research," *Speech Monographs*, XXXVII, 3 (August, 1970), 211-217; Mary Strom Larson's investigations of dissonance research, "Some Problems in Dissonance Theory Research," *Central States Speech Journal*, XXIV, (Fall, 1973), 183-188; David W. Johnson's review of conflict research, "Communication and the Inducement of Cooperative Behavior in Conflicts: A Critical Review," *Speech Monographs*, 41, 1 (March, 1974); Edward L. McGlone's, "Toward Improved Quantitative Research in Forensics," *Journal of the American Forensic Association*, VI, 2 (Spring, 1969), 49-54; and Sidney Kraus' special report, "Mass Communication and the Election Process: A Re-Assessment of Two Decades of Research," *Speech Monographs*, 41, 4 (November, 1974), 427-433.

[2]Representative studies include: Ronald E. Applbaum and Karl W. Anatol, "The Factor Structure of Source Credibility as a Function of the Speaking Situation," *Speech Monographs*, 39, 3 (August, 1972), 216-222; Ellis R. Hayes, "Ego-Threatening Classroom Communication: A Factor Analysis of Student Perceptions," *Speech Teacher*, XIX, 1 (January, 1970), 43-48; Raymond L. Falcione, "The Factor Structure of Source Credibility Scales for Immediate Superiors in the Organizational Context," *Central States Speech Journal*, XXV, 1 (Spring, 1974), 63-66; and William E. Arnold and Jae-won Lee, "Academic Convention as the Tirual of an Epistemic Community," *Bulletin of the Association of Departments and Administrators in Speech Communication* (August, 1974), 24-31.

but mandated by the complex nature of the communication process, this genre of research reporting is precluded from indepth, indiscipline appraisal. Several attitudes converge to promulgate the paradox. First, the *per se* evaluation of factor analytic techniques appears peripheral to the central mission of speech communication scholars. Second, those speech communication scholars conducting factor analytic research understandably have been more concerned with learning the ins-and-outs of the method than with synthesizing their knowledge to provide critical judgment.[3] Third, most members of our discipline lack formal training in multivariate statistical methods.[4] Finally, few speech communication scholars have the background or inclination to wade through the theoretically complex and mathematically technical treatises written specifically about the subject.[5]

Despite such roadblocks, an analysis of factor analytic studies appears warranted. One way to focus evaluative comment is to examine some of the initial factor analysis studies in speech communication—studies that launched the genre of research and served as the model for ensuing emulators. One such landmark study is James C. McCroskey's "Scales for the Measurement of *Ethos*" reported in *Speech Monographs* nearly a decade ago.[6] McCroskey's study seems well chosen as a point of reference. The article was among the first in our discipline to report the application of factor analysis. Subsequently, it made substantial impact, fostering much scientific activity[7] and receiving scholarly praise for its originality.[8]

However, for most of us in Speech Communication, the absence of a

[3]There are some notable exceptions to this statement, in the form of critiques of specific single research efforts. See James J. Lewis's, "A Critique of 'The Factor Structure of Source Credibility as a Function of the Speaking Situation'," *Speech Monographs,* 41, 3 (August, 1974), 287-290; Thomas M. Steinfatt's "A Criticism of 'Dimensions of Source Credibility: A Test for Reproducibility'," same issue, 293, 294; and Ronald L. Applbaum and Karl W.E. Anatol's, "A Rejoinder," same issue, 295-298. See also, Raymond K. Tucker's "Reliability of Semantic Differential Scales: The Role of Factor Analysis," *Western Speech,* 35 (1971), 185-190.

[4]In response to this lack of formal training, several scholars have made efforts to provide initial training through conventional workshops and convention programs. For specific examples, see *Speech Communication Association Convention Program,* 60th Annual Meeting, December, 1974.

[5]Multivariate analysis techniques such as factor analysis gain their complexity from their grounding in trigonometry and calculus, and the fact that the magnitude of factor analytic computations necessitates the reliance on complex computer programs.

[6]McCroskey, *Speech Monographs,* 33 (1966), 65-72.

[7]Other researchers have utilized the McCroskey scales in subsequent studies, applying them across situational contexts. Indeed, one researcher took the scales developed by McCroskey, Berlo, Lemert and Mertz, and Fulton, lumped them all together and looked at "The Factor Structure of Source Credibility Scales for Immediate Superiors in the Organizational Context." See Raymond L. Falcione, *Central States Speech Journal,* XXV, 1 (Spring, 1974), 63-66.

[8]See Raymond K. Tucker, "On the McCroskey Scales for the Measurement of *Ethos,*" *Central States Speech Journal,* 22 (1971), 127-129.

well-understood critical frame both impedes our ability to emulate and limits our opportunity to assess the quality of factor analysis studies. Such a state is understandable, since in the case of factor analysis such a critical frame awaits clear, straight-forward delineation.[9]

During the 1960's, our discipline witnessed an increasingly scholarly familiarity with the elements of inferential statistics. Such terms as independent and dependent variable, Pearson product-moment correlation, standard deviation, confidence level of .05 or .01, student-t, and F-test, became common concepts in the repertoire of speech communication scholars. The terms gained such widespread acceptance that probably no one completes graduate school today without comprehending the meaning and applicability of such terms. Just as scholars learned the rubric of inferential statistics, they can learn the meanings of concepts relevant to factor analysis. Once speech communication scholars have mastered such factor analytic terms as eigenvalue, iteration, vector space, orthogonal and varimax rotation, factor loading, principal components and simple structure solutions, they then will be in a position to make use of an evaluative frame.

I offer this essay to serve the needs of the mathematically unsophisticated reader wishing to acquire a basic understanding of the principles on which factor analysis rests. Concomitantly, I provide the basis for journal readers to evaluate research-stressing factor analysis methods with the same critical eye that experience dictates they apply to empirical studies involving inferential statistics.

The above goals necessitate the development of the subject from several perpectives. Therefore, I shall (1) outline the technical steps in factor analysis, (2) set forth a three-part critical standard for conducting and evaluating factor analysis studies, and (3) apply the evolved critical standard to McCroskey's *Ethos* studies, for purposes of illustrating the frame's use.

## Technical Steps in Factor Analysis

To begin with, there are two prevalent modes of factor analysis. *Q*-type works by correlating people; *R*-type works by correlating test items.[10] What makes them both factor analysis is that the correlations are mathematically evaluated to arrive at a reduced number of variables each representing a

---

[9]Most explanations of factor analysis techniques run to full book length of several hundred pages. For a notable exception, see the pertinent chapters of Fred N. Kerlinger, *Foundations of Behavioral Research,* 2nd ed. (New York: Holt, Rinehart and Winston, Inc., 1973).

[10]In actuality there are six factor analytic techniques, labeled "O," "P," "Q," "R," "S," and "T." Each technique represents a possible study design, since *subjects, variables,* and *occasions* comprise three possible dimensions, each capable of generating two kinds of correlated data from the matrix. Thus, when a researcher correlates pairs of data *items* over the sample of *subjects,* he or she is using *R*-technique; when correlating pairs of *subjects* over the data *items, Q*-technique. *Q* and *R* type factor designs are the most prevalent, to date, for

significant portion of the initial people (in $Q$) or items (in $R$).[11] What is factor analyzed is a matrix of correlated data.[12] In $Q$-type factor analysis, the underlying variables or factors are *types* of people. Types are derived by factor analyzing the correlations of persons' reactions to a set of stimuli such as statements, or names, or pictures.[13] $Q$ differs from the more prevalent $R$-type factor analysis. In the $R$ the underlying variables or factors are *constructs*, like critical listening, or authoritativeness, or intelligence, that are assumed to explain a given portion of an individual's performance on a pencil and paper test. *Constructs* are derived by factor analyzing the correlations of test items across sets of measures.[14]

Just as hypothesis testing in traditional scientific research entails specific steps, so too, factor analysis involves several accepted procedures. While these steps vary in number, depending upon the research project and the particular expert consulted, they can be boiled down to six. The six steps to follow in conducting factor analysis research are:[15]

1. Selection of the sample of variables and observations. Persons (observations) take tests (variables) in $R$; persons (variables) react to items (observations) in $Q$.

2. Computation of the matrix of correlations among the variables and observations. In $Q$ people are correlated; in $R$ items are correlated.

---

speech communication research, Thus, they provide the basis for this essay. However, a researcher could use a design that correlated the subject response of one individual across occasions, letting the variables comprise the rows, and occasions comprise the columns of the matrix. Thus, in *P*-technique, the correlations are pairs of variables over the sample of $N$ occasions; its opposite, *O*-technique, requires the correlation of pairs of occasions over data variable scores. A researcher could also measure many persons many times on the same data variable. By computing the correlations between occasions over a sample of individuals, one would have *T*-technique; by correlating two individuals over a series of occasions for the single variable, the researcher is using *S*-technique. For a more detailed explanation, see Raymond B. Cattell, *Factor Analysis* (New York: Harper, 1952), or Andrew L. Comrey, *A First Course in Factor Analysis* (New York: Academic Press, 1973) Chapter Nine.

[11]Cattell, "The Meaning and Strategic Use of Factor Analysis," appearing in Raymond B. Cattell, ed., *Handbook of Multivariate Experimental Psychology* (Chicago: Rand McNally and Company, 1966), 174. He argues that factor analysis is a mathematical method for arriving at a reduced number of abstract variables, as well as a weighting of observed variables, according to structural indications in the data itself.

[12]Matrix connotes a rectangular array composed of the correlation of data variables across a sample of data objectives.

[13]For a representative $Q$-type study, see Robert R. Monahan, Joseph T. Plummer, David L. Rarick, and Dwight A. Williams, "Predicting Viewer Preference for New TV Program Concepts," *Journal of Broadcasting*, 18, 2 (Spring, 1974), 131-142; or Arnold and Lee.

[14]For a representative R-type study correlating across sets of measures, see Brian K. Hansen and Ernest G. Bormann, "A New Look at Semantic Differential for the Theatre," *Speech Monographs*, XXXVI, 2 (June, 1969), 163-170. Also, see Footnote 2.

[15]For an easy-to-read, yet more complete discussion of the key procedures involved in factor analysis, see Andrew L. Comrey, ed., *A First Course in Factor Analysis* (New York: Academic Press, 1973), Part 1.

3. Extraction of the principal factors possessing parsimony and independence. That is, extraction from the matrix of correlations those highly correlated variables that account for as much of the variances of the variables are possible. Factors are extracted by shooting axes through neighboring swarms of points in the matrix. Placement of the axes is derived through estimates of communality — the extent of overlap between the variables and factors — and/or the use of criterion eigenvalues which are derived as the latent root solutions of simultaneously solved characteristic linear equations. Of course, the equations may be thought of as swarming simultaneously in three-dimensional geometric space, rather than the two-dimensional space of univariate statistics. One such initial solution is called the principal components solution.

4. Rotation of the extracted factors to overcome the arbitrariness of the original principal factor reference axes (locus of the hyperplane). The reference axes are moved (rotated) to find the best way to view the variables in $n$-dimensional space, thereby providing a more meaningful accounting of the interrelationships among the matrix of correlations. Rotation to simple solution involves the use of pre-selected mathematical procedures such as Varimax orthogonal rotation (the axes in factor space remain at $90°$ angles) or Oblimax — oblique rotation (allowing axes' angles in factor space to be acute or oblique) to manipulate the width of the hyperplane in which the factor solution is located, thereby increasing or decreasing the variance accounted for by the factor solution. Such a solution derived from rotation is known as the *best simple solution* because it identifies the best position from which to extract the factor representing the attendant correlated variables.

5. Interpretation of the rotated factor matrix. In $R$-type factor analysis, variables that correlate highly with the factor are examined to find out what they have in common that could be the basis for the factor. In $Q$, the sorting behavior becomes a weighted profile indicating the characteristics displayed by an ideal type. In both $R$ and $Q$ the researcher examines both positive and negative correlations with the factor to assist in the interpretation of the meaning of the factor or type.

6. Replication of the factor study to ascertain the validity of the obtained simple solution. Finding similar solutions verifies the discovery of invariant factors, i.e., stable factors.

Proper usage of the above procedures requires the application of criterion mathematical estimates. Such estimates function at different points in the above technical steps. The criterion estimates serve as parameters in guiding the researcher through the technical steps. To violate seriously the criterion guidelines at any point is to jeopardize the quality of the study. Indeed, even subtle variations in the estimates (criterion values) can regulate the factor analysis findings thereby changing the results and altering the likely interpretations. A clear understanding of the use and limits of criterion values appears as the foundation upon which the critical standard for evaluating factor analysis studies must be built

## Evolving the Critical Standard

Just as a researcher may name an infinite number of controlled variables — sex, age, education, intelligence, occupation, economic group, room temperature, time of day, similarity of treatment — in an experimental testing situation, so too, a critic evaluating or conducting factor analysis research can isolate a myriad of topics meriting consideration. But in my best judgment there are three central considerations that must always be examined as one attempts to conduct or evaluate factor analysis research. These three issues serve to order my discussion of the use and limits of criterion values, and they evolve into the critical standard suitable for conducting or evaluating factor analysis research.

The first consideration entails an analysis of the quality of the sampling procedure; the second concerns an analysis of the quality of the factor interpretations; and the third encompasses an analysis of the reasons given in supporting the claim of discovering invariant factors.

## Ways to Analyze Samples

Sampling emerges as a non-issue in many reports of factor analysis research. Researchers have all to often adopted the Watergate philosophy "that all politicians are crooked" and concluded that since previous factor research violated sampling criteria no one would notice or mind if they followed suit.[16] Nonetheless, sampling is crucial to viable factor analysis findings. As well, the issue is complex. The factor analyst must worry about acceptable N's for both *variables* and *observations*, and he must worry about the *ratio* between them. The reasons are simple. Statistical stability and reliability are affected by the number of observations and variables, by the ratio of observations to variables, and by the composition of the sample of variables and observations.

In considering the sample of observations, the rule is simple: the smaller the number of observations the greater the chance that less reliable coefficients of correlation will increase the magnitude of correlations in the matrix. This means that $R$-type studies require a lot of people and $Q$-type studies require a lot of items for sorting. Guertin and Bailey examined

[16]See Ronald L. Applbaum and Karl W.E. Anatol, "A Rejoinder," *Speech Monographs,* 41 (Winter, 1974), 297 for a chart which conveniently "illustrates that previous researchers have consistently used potentially low sample sizes for determining factor structures."

directly the statistical stability of sample sizes.[17] In their studies correlating data elicited from populations of varying size $N$'s, they reported that small $N$'s increase the likelihood of error affecting the amount of variance accounted for by the factors. Such an increase or decrease in factor size, resulting from error, is spurious and can cause an otherwise insignificant factor to appear meaningful or a significant factor to appear meaningless. Therefore, researchers must take precautions to select samples of adequate size for the type of factor analysis undertaken in order to insure the viability of the discovered factors.

There are no hard-fast guidelines for determining adequate sample size. Rather, the researcher must rely on somewhat crude indexes. Comrey suggests, from his experience with $R$ technique, useful criterion values for evaluating the quality of sample size and lessening the likelihood of common factor variance being spurious.[18] The values in Figure 1 concern $R$-type factor analysis.

### Figure 1

Appropriateness of Sample Size
R-Type Factor Studies

|      | Very Poor | Poor | Fair | Good | Very Good | Excellent |
|------|-----------|------|------|------|-----------|-----------|
| N =  | 50        | 100  | 200  | 300  | 500       | 1,000     |

(N = Observations, the number of people in $R$)

Since $Q$-type factor analysis is by nature a small sample rank-order correlation procedure, the guidelines for evaluating sample size in $Q$-type

---

[17]W.H. Guertin and J.P. Bailey, *Introduction to Modern Factor Analysis* (Ann Arbor: Edwards, 1970), as cited in Comrey, 200-201. Cattell provides an explanation of the problem. He says: "The choice of a suitable $N$ is indicated partly by the considerations of factor loading significance just discussed — on which basis one would hesitate to use factor analysis with fewer than 80 to 100 subjects,[16] and partly by the considerations connected with the number of variables." Cattell's footnote 16 continues: "[16]It is true that...the simple structure is theoretically still as clearly obtainable in a small sample as in a large sample. *But,* (1) one *is* interested in the population values when it comes to factor matching and also general interpretation, and (2) the size of the common error factors becomes substantial and intrusive with fewer than 100 cases, e.g., one can get random variables loading 0.3 and 0.4 comparatively easily, and in practice this upsets simple structure rotation and factor recognition." 236-237.

[18]Comrey, 200.

studies of necessity fall within a considerably narrower range.[19] Here, sorter convenience, as well as statistical stability, plays a role. It is unreasonable to expect human respondents to sort a thousand, or five hundred, even two hundred words or statements on a rank order basis. Typically, reported studies have used from as few as thirty to as many as 200 items.[20] Established guidelines for statistical stability and reliability occur within this range. Figure 2 provides an evaluation of various $Q$-sort sizes given the need for stability, while at the same time allowing for sorter convenience.[21]

---

**Figure 2**

Appropriateness of Sample Size
$Q$-Type Factor Studies

| | Very Poor | Poor | Fair | Good | Very Good | Excellent |
|---|---|---|---|---|---|---|
| N = | 30 | 40 | 50 | 60 | 80 | 100 |

(N = Observations, the number of items in $Q$)

---

[19]William Stephenson posits a set of statistical, philosophy of science, and common sense arguments for replacing the traditional canons of empiricism; namely, large sample technique and concept measurement, with $Q$-technique, a methodology enabling the researcher to draw inferences from small samples, see any person as the subject of detailed factor and variance analysis, and to make correlations between people, not test scores. For Stephenson, $Q$-technique overcomes one of the classic indictments of measurement studies — that variations cancel out one another with the result that data fails to provide knowledge of a number of people's attitudes and instead provides only the mean attitude. Of course, there are statistical methods in large scale descriptive statistics that overcome this criticism, but as Stephenson elegantly argues, at the base of each of these is really $Q$-technique. Stephenson, *The Study of Behavior: Q-Technique and Its Methodology* (Chicago: University of Chicago Press, 1953), Part 1, and especially 193-194.

[20]From one perspective, $Q$-technique is forced to be a small sample research technique, because of the physical and mental restraints precluding human rank-ordering of more than a gross or so of items. Actually, low numbers of items become warranted via the use of pre-testing to ensure that the $Q$-items selected run the gamut of possibilities in the subject area under study. With such pre-testing, the confidence placed in small numbers of items increases. See the discussion of "$Q$-sorts and $Q$-sorting" in: Fred N. Kerlinger, *Foundations of Behavioral Research*, 2nd ed., (New York: Holt, Rinehart and Winston, Inc., 1973), 583-585.

[21]I adapted this chart from Kerlinger, 584. He states: "The number of cards in a $Q$ distribution is determined by convenience and statistical demands. For statistical stability and reliability, the number should probably be not less than 60 (40 or 50 in some rare cases) nor more than 140, in most cases no more than 100. A good range is from 60 to 90 cards.'" In the footnote, Kerlinger explains: "The author has gotten good results with as few as 40 items. The 40 items were culled from a larger pool of items, all of which had been tested. It is rarely necessary or desirable to have more than 90 or 100 items." Kerlinger, 2nd ed., 584.

The number of variables, items in *R* and people in *Q*, can also affect the results of factor analysis. Obviously, sufficient items are necessary to generate reliability estimates and to insure that the discovered variance is due to the intrinsic nature of the factors rather than unreliable respondent perception of an unclear item. Also, sufficient people must sort in *Q* to determine that variances stem from differences in people, rather than differences in the makeup of the items or unreliable perception of unclear items.

The appropriateness of the number of observations and variables provides only one element for evaluating the acceptablity of factor analysis samples. Equally important is the ratio of observations to variables. For mathematical reasons, meaningful factor analysis results are present *only* — and this mandate cannot be emphasized too strongly — when the number of observations exceed the number of variables. Thus, in *R*-type factor analysis, people (observations) taking tests must exceed the number of items (variables) in the tests; for *Q*-type factor analysis, the opposite is true: observations (items in the *Q*-sort) must exceed the number of variables (people sorting the items.)[22]

So, a researcher must avoid a square matrix and needs more observations than variables. But, how many more? No set formula for determining the ratio of observations to variables exists. Some theorists indicate that the ratio must be 10:1 for initial R-type studies. Others disagree and say that the ratio need only be as high as 7:1. When the researcher is familiar with the variables under investigation, some prefer 3:1; a typical ratio is 2:1.[23]

---

[22]Cattrell discusses the reasons for observations exceeding variables: "When one gets close to a square score matrix (in fact to $n = $ N-2) the degrees of freedom vanish; one has insufficient information to define the correlations, or, in spatial terms, to place *n* axes determinately by the projections of the *N* individuals. One can do *R*-technique on an oblong matrix with referees (Observations) much more numerous than relatives (variables), or *Q*-technique when the same relatives (observations) are decidedly more numerous than the referees (variables); but at the transition point of a square matrix the analysis passes, so to speak, through a sound barrier, where everything is unstable." Cattell, 237. R.J. Runnel explains the problem from a different perspective. He states "The importance of this question derives from the following mathematical relationships: (1) the rank (maximum number of linearly independent column vectors in the matrix) of the matrix is less than or equal to the smallest side of the matrix and (2) the rank of the matrix is equal to the number of factors that can be delineated. In other words, if the number of variables exceeds the number of cases (observations), then no more factors than this number of cases (observations) can be extracted." Page 219.

Rummel goes on to explain that: "It is crucial, therefore, that a sufficient number of variables and cases (observations) be included in an analysis to enable the major factors in a domain to emerge." *Applied Factor Analysis* (Evanston: Northwestern University Press, 1970), 220.

[23]Cattell elaborates on this criterion: "Regarding the relation of number of referees (*observations*, emphasis mine), N, to number of relatives (*variables,* emphasis mine), n, a useful rule of thumb has grown up which states that the ratio of persons to tests (occasions to tests, and so on) should not be less than about 2½ to 1 (some favor a 2 to 1 lower bound, others go as high as 5 to 1)." 237. Cattell goes on to argue, that with adequate experience and precaution, the 2:1 ratio may be shaved somewhat. Precautions include replication of the study or valida-

Illustratively, then an $R$-type factor study involving 400 people (constituting a *good* to *very good* sample size) should have them considering from say 130 to 200 test items in order to meet the 3:1 or 2:1 ratio. Conversely, a $Q$-sort of 90 items (constituting a very good to excellent sample size of observations) should be given to approximately 30 to 45 people in order to meet the 3:1 to 2:1 ratio.

Again, care to avoid violating the lower limits of the ratio is crucial. The problem is that studies that violate the criteria regulating sample selection and the ratio of observations to variables possess little value. The reason is that matrices approaching squares in factor space, or matrices where variables exceed the observations, lead to the identification of unreliable or non-generalizable factors.[24] This problem is reduced as the ratio becomes greater. The greater the ratio, the better the data.

Finally, the *composition* of the sample of observations may affect the size of obtained correlations.[25] In $R$-type studies, factors generated from testing a *selected* sample, like college freshmen, will account for less variance than when the researcher obtains the factor results from a random sample of the general population. The same is true of $Q$-type studies if the cards (items) comprising the $Q$-sort represent a *selected* or *skewed* sample, rather than a *random* sample of the universe of possibilities pertaining to the particular subject under investigation.

## Ways to Analyze Interpretations

What factor analysis is trying to do is tell what significant factors, if any, underlie a multitude of data. Once the researcher gets the sample right, and collects the data, he or she is ready to try and get the factors and then

tion of the derived factors against some external source to ensure the viability of the extracted factors. Cattell, 237. I might note that these criteria differ from multiple regression problems where the researcher is using predictive validity criteria, i.e., Pearson r's for predicted to observed scores, or least squares solutions. In this case, the criterion must be the ten subjects per variable as can be demonstrated mathematically.

[24]The problem of squared matrices was explained in Footnote 22. Regarding the question of whether one should ever analyze a data matrix containing more variables than observations, Rummel gives a specific reply: "The answer depends on the specific research question. When the interest is only in *describing* data variability, then a factor analysis will yield such a description regardless of variables exceeding cases in number (the lone exception is "image factor analysis"). *When the interest is in inference from sample results to universal factors, however, the number of cases* (observations) *should exceed variables* (italics mine). The interrelationships among the variables are assumed to reflect — to represent — those in the universe. To impose a necessary dependence on these interrelationships, due to the number of cases (observations) being less than the number of variables, may bias the inferences that can be drawn." Rummel 220.

[25]For a more detailed discussion of sample composition, see Comrey, 201 ($R$-technique) and 216 ($Q$-technique).

interpret the factors as they exist in a matrix of correlations. At issue is whether the factored data is good or bad. And, with adequate analysis, the researcher or reviewer can make this evaluative judgment.

However, the judgment differs from the kind made with elementary inferential statistics, because the critic can't turn to probability tables or confidence intervals to assist in making the evaluative judgment.[26] Nevertheless, the researcher must be on guard for the multivariate equivalent of Type I or Type II error, as well as the multivariate equivalent of statistical significance.[27] In respect to these issues, factor analysts rely more on rough indexes of meaningful factors and significant loadings than on the application of any traditional statistical tests.[28] There are a couple of reasons for the dependence on guidelines. For one, traditional univariate statistical tests lack applicability to multivariate data, and factor analysts await the development of useful multivariate tests. Second, the few statistical tests existing for factor analysis appear of low benefit in terms of utility of findings and high cost regarding the time and effort required to use them.[29] In the absence of easy-to-use statistical tests and tables, factor analysts, through experience and replication, have developed crude guides that provide assurances of the utility of findings.[30]

These guidelines are used to answer two questions: (1) How to get a factor? and (2) How to know a significant factor? The first question relates to the extraction and rotation of factors. Factor extraction involves the use of guidelines in two ways. One guide calls for ending factor extraction when to add an additional factor to the solution would contribute less than five percent of the variance, after explaining about seventy-five percent of the

---

[26]Indeed, in traditional inferential statistics, the researcher usually comes armed with a number of probability tables and confidence interval ranges to demonstrate the statistical likelihood that the findings possess significance. The researcher uses tables to argue that the data withstand the test of statistical significance at some arbitrary level, usually between .10 and .001.

[27]For a succinct discussion of *alpha* and *beta* error, see: William L. Hayes, *Statistics* (New York: Holt, Rinehart and Winston, 1963), 280-281. Some theorists argue that the question of Type I and Type II error in the use of multivariate statistics can be avoided by replacing sampling theory with Bayesian techniques, a body of inferential techniques combining observational data with personalistic or subjective beliefs, which rely on the assessment of prior distributions. For applications of the Bayesian approach to principal components factor analysis, see: S. Geisser, "Bayesian Estimation in Multivariate Analysis," *Annals of Mathematical Statistics*, 36 (1965), 150-159; and S. James Press, *Applied Multivariate Analysis* (New York: Holt, Rinehart and Winston, Inc., 1972), Chapters 9 and 10.

[28]Of course, several statistical tests have been advanced. For example, see M.S. Bartlett, "A Note on the Multiplying of Factors for Various Chi-Square Approximation." *Journal of the Roual Statistical Society,* series B, 16 (1954), 296-298.

[29]For a pertinent discussion of the strengths and weaknesses of several elaborate statistical tests pertaining to factor analysis, see Cattell, 235-236.

[30]Harry Harman elaborates on the dependability of these guidelines. He points out that despite the absence of useful statistical tests, "Through long and extensive experience factor analysts have developed crude guidelines... which come remarkably close to the more exact statistical tests." Harman, "Factor Analysis," in P.K. Whitla, ed., *Handbook of Measurement and Assessment in Behavioral Sciences* (Reading, PA: Addison-Wesley Publishing Co., 1968), 168.

variance through the previously extracted factors.[31] This guide tells us that a factor solution becomes more and more valuable in synthesizing a complex matrix of data when the solution accounts for upwards of seventy-five percent of the total variance in the data matrix; it also tells us that until about seventy-five percent of the variance is accounted for, all factors have some relevance. This point leads many researchers to prefer an alternative guideline.

The second or alternative guide calls for the retention of any factors that possess eigenvalues (the values of the latent roots of a characteristic equation) greater than 1.0 in the principal components solution.[32] Using the eigenvalue criterion, the researcher retains the factor if the sum of the squared factor loadings (the correlations of the items or persons with the factor) for each factor exceed 1.0. The reasoning underlying this criterion is that a factor should possess a total variance in excess of that contributed by a single variable upon being added to the matrix.[33] The use of eigenvalues to determine factors may yield factors up to one-third of the total number of variables (assuming observations are greater than the number of variables) and provides a suitable guideline for finding the number of common factors that are necessary, reliable, and meaningful in explaining the correlations among the variables.[34]

[31]The researcher drops the additional factors assuming that a factor accounting for such a small amount of variance could hardly be of any practical value, once a goodly amount (say seventy-five percent) of the variance has been explained. In essence, the researcher bases the cut-off decisions on *qualitative* practical grounds rather than quantitative statistical grounds. See Harman, 168. Also, Rummel indicates that a researcher can test whether or not the variance level accounted for by each factor is too high by including a variable of random numbers in the analysis. "This random variable should have a communality across the factors less than any of the substantive variables. The highest loading of the random variable provides a bench mark for gauging the acceptability of the high loadings on the small factors." Rummel, 362.

[32]For a detailed discussion of the eigenvalue criterion, see Cattell, 206-207; Harman, 168; and Rummel, 362-363. H.F. Kaiser originally proposed the criterion as the "best" answer to the number of factors problem. See his, "The Application of Electronic Computers to Factor Analysis," *Educational and Psychological Measurement*, 20 (1960), 141-151.

[33]A single variable contributes 1.0 to the variance.

[34]Harman, 168. Although the eigenvalue equals one criterion is a neat and easy one to apply, Rummel indicates that: "In some cases the criterion may discriminate between factors that have little difference in eigenvalues. One factor may have an eigenvalue of 1.02 and the subsequent factor of 0.96. For a study in which the eigenvalues may range, say from 14.6 to 0.0, this small variance difference appears hardly meaningful, yet one factor is retained and the other is dropped." Rummel, 363. Another problem with the use of eigenvalues greater than unity is that the criterion may lead to cutting off too soon when the variables are fewer than twenty and too late when more than fifty. In such cases, the use of unity as the criterion value will result in extra specific variance and error variance being treated as common variance when 1.0 exceeds the correct communalitites (the sums of squares of the factor loadings). Cattell discusses the problem in detail. Cattell, 207. Comrey suggests a means of reducing the problem. He advocates that the researcher first estimate the squared multiple correlations of each variable with all other variables to derive the first factor analytic solution. (Comrey, 99). The better analytic programs, such as the *Q*-analysis, Tubergen Quanal Program, estimate S.M.C.'s prior to reliance on the criterion eigenvalue of 1.0 (Tubergen

While the criteria described above serve to identify factors in the principal components solution, the location of useful factors is not yet complete. Rotation to simple structure is necessary because the principal structure factors are identified by the *unrelated* variables in the matrix of correlated data. Identification of those variables that *directly comprise* the factors necessitates rotation. In rotation the researcher adjusts the spatial relationship between the data vectors and the factor vectors. The appearance of any factor can be strengthened or weakened through rotation. In seeking to define the factor-related variables more precisely via rotation, the issue of significance of the deprived simple solution emerges. Ideally, reliable statistical tests could be utilized. However, the present nature of tests of multivariate significance forces the researcher to turn to methods of validation to judge the significance of the derived solution.[35] Validity will be discussed in a subsequent section of this essay. For now, suffice it to say that faith in the rotated factor solution stems only from replication or external validation. Without external validation, the significance of the factor solution is unknown and the utility of the findings may be questioned.[36] Adequate replications across populations require the use of marker variables.[37]

Guidelines also help in answering the second question: How to know a significant factor? The *essence* of a factor is a direct product of the data variables that comprise the factor. For that reason, the significance of a variable's factor loading is important.[38] A variable's loading on a factor

Quanal Program, Instructions, p. 1-2). Such precautions provide assurance that significant factors are being extracted in the principal components stage of analysis.

[35] Of course, R.E. Bargmann has worked out a formula for testing statistically the significance of an obtained simple structure. Cattell labels the Bargmann test as "tolerably sound (except for the arbitrariness of width of hyperplane) but in practice it seems to make severe judgments." Cattell, 236. Cattell concludes that: "It is because of this as yet little investigated magnitude of error in rotation that most investigators rightly feel that the only satisfactory proof at present of the reality of a factor is that after it has been obtained *by blind rotation to simple structure in each experiment,* (emphasis Cattell's) it yields a significant invariance, i.e., significant matches of pattern over repeated studies." Cattell, 236. Typically, matching in *R*-type studies is the use of the non-parametric chi-square checking variable loadings across factors. With *Q*, one can additionally use rank-order correlations across the descending *Q*-arrays.

[36] Cattell, 236, indicates that the application of the Bargmann test for simple structure would render perhaps four-fifths of the published resolutions claiming simple structure non-significant. While Cattell uses this claim to indicate the arbitrariness of the Bargmann test, the information also seems to point up the need for construct and concurrent validation of obtained simple structures.

[37] A market variable is a highly loaded variable from one study that is included in subsequent research to evelute the invariance of a factor. Usually two or three good marker variables are sufficient to elicit a factor in *R*; two or three people in *Q*. See Cattell, 240; or Rummell, 381-82. For a discussion of the use of marker variables in Speech Communication Research, see Tucker, "McCroskey Scales," 129.

[38] For a discussion of the loading significance problem, see Cattell, 235-237; and Comrey, 225-226; Harman, *Modern Factor Analysis*, revised, (Chicago: University of Chicago Press, 1967), tabulates the standard errors of factor loadings for different sample sizes as well as

after rotation is a function of the factor's proximity to the particular data-variable vector in question, and as I indicated, this distance can be adjusted to a greater or lesser degree through rotation. Such adjustments can make the same variable load higher or lower with the factor depending upon the direction of the vector adjustment. Unfortunately, the statistical test that can establish the standard error of a rotated factor loading remains to be developed.[39] Nevertheless, for purposes of interpretation, a crude index of the usability of a given factor loading is the square of the loading when finding orthogonal solutions.[40] With oblique solution, the researcher uses "structure matrix" loadings rather than oblique factor loadings.[41] A commonly used cut-off point for orthogonal factor loadings or oblique structure matrix values is .30 and below, since $.30^2$ (.30 squared) yields .09 or less than ten percent of the variable's variance in common with the factor.[42]

Even though the loadings of .30 and above have commonly been accepted as sufficient to provide interpretative value, such loadings provide a weak

the average correlation between the variables. See especially 433 and 435, Table B. Other important contributions to significance tests in factor analysis include: M.S. Bartlett, "Tests of Significance in Factor Analysis," *British Journal of Psychology, Statistical Section,* 3 (1950), 159-165; D.N. Lawley, and Z. Swanson, "Tests of Significance in a Factor Analysis of Artificial Data," *British Journal of Statistical Psychology,* 7 (1954), 75-79; and C.R. Rao, "Estimation and Tests of Significance in Factor Analysis," *Psychometrika,* 20 (1955), 93-111.

[39] Comrey, 225. However, artificial guidelines do exist. One crude rule is to find the $R$ that is insignificant for the $N$ of the study. Thus, with a study where N = 200, an $R$ of about .18 is insignificant at the .01 level. The formula $1/N$ as indicating the significance level for the standard error of a rotated factor loading is recommended in N. Cliff and C. Hamburger, "The Study of Sampling Errors in Factor Analysis by Means of Artificial Experiments," *Psychological Bulletin,* LXVIII (1967), 430-445. The point to be made is that these guidelines lack exactness.

[40] Comrey, 225.

[41] The chief reason for the use of structure loadings in oblique solutions relates to H.H. Harman's distinction between "pattern" matrices and "structure" matrices. (Harman, *Modern Factor Analysis,* Chicago: University of Chicago Press, 1967). In orthogonal solutions, these matrices are identical, thus permitting the interpretation of a factor loading of data variable with respect to orthogonal factors as though they were correlation coefficients. However, oblique loadings can be interpreted in this manner only after extrapolation from pattern matrix reference vector projections to structure matrix values. This is because factor loadings in the oblique solution can sometimes exceed 1.0 when the values in the reference vector structure are small. Reference vectors are projected perpendicular to the pattern matrix solution of factor loadings; as the reference vector projections are simultaneously solved they provide values that are in direct proportion to the factor loadings and thus are perfectly correlated with them. Computation of the structure matrix values is based upon extrapolation from the reference vector projections. For a more detailed discussion see Comrey, 130-143. The use of reference vectors necessitates the use of an additional criteria. The correlations between reference vectors should be kept as low as possible while reaching simple structure. Values less than .5 should be preferred and rarely should a value larger than .6 be permitted. Comrey indicates that when reference vectors have substantial correlations between them, rotations that reduce the absolute size of the correlation, while at the same time improving simple structure, are particularly welcome. (Comrey, 142-143).

[42] Comrey, 226.

basis for factor interpretation. Comrey provides a table that gives "a rough idea of the value of variable factor correlations (orthogonal factor loadings and structure coefficients) for factor interpretation purposes."[43] Comrey's table is reproduced as Figure 3.

## Figure 3

Comrey's Guidelines for Interpreting Factor Loadings
and Structure Coefficients
Scale of Variable-Factor Correlations

| Orthogonal Factor Loading | Percentage of Variable's Variance in Common with the Factor | Rating |
|---|---|---|
| .71 | 50 | Excellent |
| .63 | 40 | Very Good |
| .55 | 30 | Good |
| .45 | 20 | Fair |
| .32 | 10 | Poor |

Factor analysis is a complex mathematical technique, but it is also grounded in elements of theoretical design. From both perspectives, criterion values interact to strengthen or weaken the faith that reasonably can be placed in factor analysis findings. These same criterion values become the means for the speech communication scholar to evaluate the findings of his or her own research, as well as judge the utility of published reports using factor analysis. But, the criterion values affecting sampling and interpretation provide an incomplete standard for accepting the results of a factor analysis study. Even with good samples and cogent interpretations, one cannot be sure of meaningful, useful findings. The only way to determine that the factor solution is meaningful, and therefore the results of value, is to assess the reliability and validity of the study's findings. Without a reliability/validity assessment, claims of factor invariance or factor universality are precluded, and one cannot generalize any utility to the findings, *nor even to the specific situation under study*.

### Ways to Analyze Factor Invariance

Factor invariance refers to the ability of factors to remain pure and consistent across sample populations. At issue is a factor's validity, and, of course, assessments of validity are precluded if the measuring instrument is

[43]Comrey, 226. Comrey's estimates compare favorably with those of Fruchter. Fruchter suggests: "Loadings of .2 or less are usually regarding as insignificant, loadings of .2 to .3 as low, .3 to .5 as moderate, .5 to .7 as high, and above .7 as very high." Benjamin Fruchter, *Introduction to Factor Analysis* (Princeton: D. Van Nostrand, Inc., 1954), 151.

unreliable. Thus, the third thrust of the critical standard necessitates a look at reliability/validity issues as they affect factor analysis. By defining reliability as the amount of *error in measurement* possessed by a measuring instrument, then factor extraction for the principal components solution may be viewed as a measuring technique, and factor rotation to simple structure may be viewed as a means of increasing the reliability placed in the reality of the discovered factors.[44] I believe this view is fully considered in the preceding discussion of factor extraction and rotation. However, aside from factor extraction, there is another aspect of the reliability problem impinging on factor analysis studies.

If the test items comprising the $Q$-sort or the test items in the various pencil and paper tests used in $R$ lack reliability, then the quality of the factors will be affected. To check the reliability of the test items in $R$-type analysis, the researcher can utilize any of the several common procedures including splitting the sample in half and correlating the two halves; testing the sample once and correlating responses to a second testing over the same items; or correlating the responses from these sub-samples.[45] Similar procedures apply to determining the reliability of $Q$-sorts. For example, using sampling theory, a researcher could develop a universe of statements that in turn would yield several randomly drawn $Q$-sorts.[46] Or, a researcher could use the test-retest method to demonstrate the reliability of his or her constructed $Q$-sort.[47] Once the test items in $R$ and the sort items in $Q$ have been shown to be reliable, the reviewer must then look to the validity of the factor solution.

By defining validity as common factor variance, then factor analysis may be viewed as a construct validity tool since it allows the researcher to study the constitutive meanings of constructs.[48] However, as the discussion of rotation indicated, there is no test of a significant factor. Thus, constitutive evidence of the existence of a construct can only be made from the intelligent use of criterion values, and the replication and subsequent

---

[44]Readers interested in an elegant treatment of the theory of reliability as error in measurement may consult Kerlinger, 2nd ed., Chapter 26, 443-455.

[45]The use of split-halves and test-retest is generally well understood. For the use of the alpha inter-correlation of test sub-samples consult: L. Cronbach, "Coefficient Alpha and the Internal Structure of Tests," *Psychometrika,* XVI (1951), 297-334.

[46]Hildon reports $Q$-sort reliability based on individuals' response to two $Q$-sorts randomly drawn from a universe of statements and cites a high reliability of R = .94 for his constructed $Q$-sort. See A.H. Hildon, "$Q$-Sort Correlation: Stability and Random Choice of Statements," *Journal of Consulting Psychology,* 22 (1958), 45-50.

[47]Frank reports correlation coefficients ranging from .93 to .97 and Hess and Hink reported coefficients of .95 and .99 with the test-retest method. See: A.H. Frank, "Note on the Reliability of Q-Sort Data," *Psychological Reporter,* 2 (1956), 182; and R.D. Hess, and D.L. Hink, "A Comparison of Forced Versus Free Q-Sort Procedure," *Journal of Educational Research,* 53 (1959), 83-90.

[48]For a more detailed explanation of the constitutive meaning of factors, see the discussion of factor analysis and scientific research in Kerlinger, 2nd ed., 686-689.

comparison of independent factor studies to identify like factors across studies.[49]

Two procedures appear worth discussing regarding the comparison of factor analysis studies and hence the validation of factors. The first is *matching* and the second is *relating*. Matching entails the comparison of factor solutions across studies. Most usually, a factor is compared by examining the profile of high, neutral, and low loadings and testing probability differences by means of a non-parametric univariate test such as *chi square*.[50] A more elaborate system of matching calls for second-order factoring of the initial factors, that is, obtaining a common variable configuration space and finding how closely factors from the two studies align themselves in this space.[51] Of course, even with this method, conclusions about validity are dependent on selection of a criterion value for determining the significance of a correlation between two matched factors.[52]

Relating concerns the comparison of factor solutions between studies using different individuals in *R*, or in the case of *Q*-analysis, different *Q*-sorts, but the same individuals.[53] Relating differs from matching because the structure of discovering two new sets of factors via rotation is not present. Relating is accomplished by rotating test vectors of the first study as close as possible to the test vectors of the second study and maximizing the pairwise sum of inner products (correlations) between the cosines. These relations may be interpreted as correlation coefficients.[54] Of course, the

---

[49]The need for replication to validate factor constructs and person types cannot be too strongly stated. Cattell indicates that: "...the matchings of factors must depend upon the joint evidence of (1) loading profile, (2) size, (3) angles, to the other identified factors, and (4) reaction under applied experimental influences." Cattell, 168. Indeed, Cattell makes it clear that "...no *single* pair of experiments can give convincing evidence of the general invariance and reality of a factor concept. There is absolutely no way to arrive reliably at our basic scientific factor concepts except by (1) independently rotating each research blindly, and far more exhaustively than has been fashionable, to maximum simple structure, (2) matching, and (3) repeating this on not just a couple of coordinated researches, but a dozen...The only proof of factor identity must come thus from the weight of a series of systematically and emphatically interlocked (by markers) researches." Cattell, 1978.

[50]Of course, the profile comparisons can be inadequate. Non-parametric tests of pattern similarity may merely locate *cooperative factors*. Cooperative factors may have variables loading as high as .70 on each of them, yet possibly be entirely orthogonal. See Cattell, 196.

[51]Again, this method is not foolproof and inapplicable only to oblique solutions. Cattell indicates that: "Two factors might have only a small angle between them and yet be different factors, because distinct factors *can* sometimes be correlated as high as, say, 0.7. At the same time, two factors that are really versions of one and the same influence in the two samples could correlate less than, say 0.7, because the obliquities are different owing to differing amounts of influence of second-order factors." Cattell, 197.

[52]For reasons indicated in the discussion in Footnote 51.

[53]Where *observations* are the same across studies, i.e., items in *Q*; persons in *R*, the correlation between factors may be computed directly. See Cattell, 194.

[54]For a detailed treatment of the mathematical steps and possible limitations, see Henry F. Kaiser, et al., "Relating Factors Between Studies Based Upon Different Individuals," *Journal of Multivariate Behavioral Research* (April, 1971), 409-422.

criterion values for interpreting correlations apply.

The preceding section of this essay sets forth the criteria for evaluating factor analysis studies. Individual criterion relevant to factor analysis evolved into the threefold critical frame of ways to analyze samples, ways to analyze factor interpretation, and ways to analyze factor invariance. Now, I'll use the critical frame to illustrate how a researcher might evaluate a factor analysis study.

## Application

A significant quantity of speech communication research has grown about the use of the McCroskey Scales for measuring *ethos*.[55] I feel obligated to point out that some of the knowledge from which the evolved critical standard is derived was not available to McCroskey at the time of his initial research. The reader will quickly see, as I apply the standard, that the McCroskey piece reveals some shortcomings. I use it as a widely known piece to demonstrate how the derived criteria can be used in guiding and evaluating research. Inferences about the quality or utility of the *ethos* study, as evaluated from our perspective of ten years, should be made with caution. For its time, the McCroskey piece was quite acceptable. Of course, the importance of the McCroskey research for illustrative purposes is that it possesses many shortcomings that still are evident in subsequent research and clearly indicates how use of the evolved standard can strengthen research. Although I have reviewed the subsequent research, restrictions on journal space do not permit me at this time to offer both a schema for evaluation and an extended criticism of the more than sixty factor analysis studies that have appeared in our speech communication journals in the past decade.

McCroskey reported two Likert-type scales, one of twenty-two items relating to "authoritativeness" and the other of twenty items relating to "character." McCroskey developed these scales through the partial use of factor analysis. First, he surveyed the literature in psychology and speech for terms related to *ethos*, credibility, and prestige. Of the terms discovered, he took the thirty most frequently used and let them comprise his original scale for measuring *ethos*. He created two hypothetical speech introductions, one for a high *ethos* source and one for a low *ethos* source. He read each introduction and respondents completed the *ethos* scale. McCroskey reported: "The results were scored, correlated, and factor above for the Likert scales, factor analysis again produced two significant factors. The 'authoritativeness' factor accounted for 52% (sic) of the variance and the 'character' factor accounted for 19% (sic) of the

[55]McCroskey, *Speech Monographs,* 1966. Footnotes 7 and 8 of this essay list some of the ensuing research.
[56]McCroskey, 65.

variance."[57] Given the above findings, McCroskey operated on the assumption that "authoritativeness" and "character" comprised the constituent parts of the *ethos* construct and created separate Likert and semantic differential scales for each of the two dimensions. To do this, McCroskey added fourteen new items to the original thirty Likert items so that each Likert scale would include twenty-two items.[58] Later, he dropped two items from the "character" Likert scale for lack of item discrimination.[59] To develop the semantic differential scales, McCroskey took from the original factor analysis the six semantic differential items with the highest and purest loadings on each factor to comprise the final semantic differential scales. Of the seven experiments, Experiment 1, Experiment 4, and Experiment 7 employed factor analysis of the data. McCroskey reported the use of the Likert scales in only the seventh. Concerning Experiment 1, McCroskey concluded: "Factor analysis indicated only one significant interpretable factor on each scale. A second factor accounting for 5% (sic) of the variance on the character scale was uninterpretable.[60] McCroskey reported similar findings for Experiment 4. "Factor analysis again indicated only one significant interpretable factor on each scale.[13]"[61] However, his footnote 13 indicates that he found it necessary to dismiss a second factor that appeared on the "character" scale. His footnote 13 reads: "[13]A second factor appeared on the character scale which accounted for 7% (sic) of the variance. This factor was uninterpretable because the content of the items with high loadings was essentially the same as that of items on factor one."[62] Experiment 7 attempted to demonstrate concurrent validity between the Likert and semantic differential scales. McCroskey described the findings: "Factor analysis indicated only one significant factor on each of the four scales. The amount of variance accounted for by the significant factor on each scale was as follows: Likert authoritativeness, 62% (sic); Likert character, 63% (sic); semantic differential authoritativeness, 70% (sic); semantic differential character, 65% (sic)."[63]

[57]McCroskey, 66-67.

[58]The source of the additional items is unclear, as are the criteria for item discrimination between the two scales. The reader is left to assume that fifteen of the thirty items loaded purest on the "authoritativeness" factor and fifteen loaded purest on the "character" factor. Given that the complete factor solution with loading profiles is not reported, such an assumption may be risky.

[59]Part of McCroskey's problem in having to discard certain items seems to stem from his failure to factor analyze the new sets of forty-four items to discover if the newly added items enabled his Likert scales to maintain their two factor structure. Unfortunately, he dropped the items on the basis of external reasoning that they didn't discriminate speakers of high, middle, and low *ethos* (an aspect of Experiment 1), rather than the direct testing of whether or not the items were representative of "authoritativeness" and "character."

[60]McCroskey, 68.

[61]McCroskey, 69.

[62]McCroskey, 69.

[63]McCroskey, 70.

With the preceding précis of McCroskey's study completed, I shall apply the critical standard to show how one might use it to evaluate the quality and utility of a factor analysis study. In using the first element of the critical frame, *ways to analyze samples*, I must look at: the number of observations; the ratio of observations to variables; the kind of observations; and the make-up of the variables.

Regarding the number of observations, recall that Comrey advised that 1,000 is *excellent*, 300 is *good*, 200 is *fair*, and 50 is *very poor*. Thus, McCroskey's selection of 50 subjects to test his original Likert items and his original semantic differential items places his study at the onset in the *very poor* category for Comrey's guidelines indicating appropriateness of sample size. Recall that the problem with small samples is that common factor variance can be spurious, since it is relatively easy for less reliable coefficients of correlation to increase the magnitude of correlations in the matrix. Of course, there can be reasons for violating sample guidelines, just as there are design considerations that can assist in increasing confidence in the factor analyses of small samples.[64] However, these must be reported. In our illustrative study the reasons are not reported, leaving the reader to evaluate the study on the merits of the reported sample alone.

Next, the ratio of observations to variables merits consideration. Recall that this criterion is more important than the number of observations. Cattell suggested that the ratio should be 3 to 1 if the researcher is familiar with the variables under study, although with experience the ratio could be lowered 2 to 1. McCroskey at the onset of his original semantic differential study used the ratio of 5 to 4. Considering the newness of the research, a critic using the critical standard must conclude that such ratios seem unwise, as they move dangerously close to the squared matrix where degrees of freedom vanish and the faith one can place in the results is minimal.

The third sampling issue involves the kind of observations. Recall that Comrey indicated that the composition of the sample of observations may affect the obtained correlations. McCroskey used college speech communication students to evaluate scales relevant to a speech communication concept. Such a limitation on the universality of the population probably biased the universe of possible reactions to the items, thus affecting the amount of variance accounted for in the factor solutions.

The final sampling issue relates to the make-up of the variables. Factor analysis to simplify data into underlying constructs is limited by the complexity or non-complexity of the original data. McCroskey's sampling techniques to derive the Likert items point to a bias of the possible universe of items related to *ethos*. The literature survey is not reported; neither is the ratio of psychology literature to speech literature. McCroskey recognized this problem and reported that only two of thirty items related to the

---

[64]For example, McCroskey could have factor analyzed the item on several sets of fifty people and compared the resultant factor structures to judge the derived factors' invariance.

Aristotelian notion of *ethos* as good will toward the audience.[65] Yet, serious violation of this sampling criterion weakens the faith McCroskey could place in his findings. In the absence of sufficient variables in the universe of items representing all prevalent definitions of *ethos*, it is not surprising that factor analysis failed to extract a factor related to the goodwill construct.[66]

The sampling criterion can also be applied to McCroskey's efforts to develop subsequent unidimensional scales for the authoritativeness and character factors. For example, he took the authoritativeness and character items from his factored Likert scale and *blindly* added seven items to the composition of each scale without testing to see if the newly added items would discriminate correctly into the respective factors. Where the additional items came from is not reported. Unfortunately, to have employed a non-empirical procedure to select items in completing the scales appears to mitigate the utility of the initial effort to factor analyze for factor pure items, as it leaves nearly one-third of the final scale items untested. As well, McCroskey's sample of observations remains low in the subsequent Experiments, although the ratio of observations to variables improves to an acceptable limit. In Experiments 1, 4, and 7 (the ones for which McCroskey reported using factor analysis), he selected 143, 243, and 218 students, respectively. Although still small, the value of larger N's is graphically illustrated by the McCroskey research. McCroskey's larger samples led to the extraction of additional factors on his unidimensional character scale. Two conclusions are possbile. One is that the more stable results of factor analyzing larger N's point to the lack of invariance of the factors identified in McCroskey's initial solutions. As the sample N's became larger, additional factors appeared on the character scale, pointing to the potential multi-dimensionality of that claimed unidimensional scale. The other conclusion, stressed by McCroskey, is that the additional factors were insignificant and do not belie the unidimensionality of the initial solution.

In summary, what can I say regarding the application of the first major criterion to the landmark McCroskey *ethos* research? The application shows that had the evolved critical frame been available to McCroskey, the sample populations and ratios could have been followed, and doubt about the multi-dimensionality of the sought-after unidimensional scales decreased. The absence of a scientific sample in the above four areas leaves the impression from the perspective of our 1970's knowledge, that the study

---

[65] McCroskey, 66.

[66] Even with continuing research where constructs have previously been identified, theorists suggest using two or three *factor pure* variables as *markers* to elicit the required factor in new research. See Cattell, 198 and 231. For initial studies, Comrey states: "The need to overdetermine factors means that each factor should have five or more data variables as good markers to represent it if at all possible. Three good relatively factor pure markers would constitute an absolute minimum number of variables to define a factor in the analysis...The total number of data variables included in a factor analysis, then, should be at least five or six times as great as the number of factors expected to emerge." Comrey, 191.

was weakly conceived. Of course, inadequate sampling alone does not mean that McCroskey's factors aren't the factors underlying *ethos*. But, it is to say that inappropriate sampling limits the degree to which we know for certain that authoritativeness and character are the factors underlying *ethos*.

Now, I must consider the second element of the derived critical standard, *analyzing the researcher's factor interpretations.* Recall there are no hard-fast rules, and that interpretation is really open to both researcher and reader evaluation. McCroskey's study can be examined from two perspectives regarding interpretations, using the guidelines to judge both the adequacy of factor extraction, and the significance of the claimed factors.

Recall that factors are extracted either by using eigenvalues greater than unity, or keeping all factors that account for more than five percent of the variance, given that seventy-five percent of the variance has been accounted for within the solution. A judgment of McCroskey's extraction procedures is precluded to a great extent by the fact that he doesn't report his method or reasons for ending factor extraction. It appears that he used floating cut-off levels of five percent and seven percent, since he speaks of second factors accounting for such variance amounts as "insignificant."[67] Of course, a researcher or reader should be skeptical of a sliding cut-off criterion, especially when employed within the same research. But, second, recall that one should not put too much faith in a factor solution that doesn't account for upwards of seventy-five percent of the variance in reaction to the test items. Such an admonition seems especially relevant when a researcher is seeking factor-pure scales, Of course, in the pilot Likert factor analysis, McCroskey's "authoritativeness" and "character" factors accounted for forty-seven percent and twenty-nine percent of the variance, respectively. Such amounts equal seventy-six percent of the total variance and meet the basic criterion.[68] Although the purity of the scales might be questioned with twenty-four percent of the variance unaccounted for by the factor solution, the solution itself appears significant. With the semantic differential factor analysis, McCroskey reports a factor solution with the first factor accounting for fifty-two percent of the variance and the second nineteen percent, for a total of seventy-one percent. This figure is below our seventy-five percent guideline, and leaves twenty-nine percent of the variance unaccounted for — more variance than is accounted for by the second factor. Certainly, something is operating in addition to the two-factor solution reported. The presence of something in addition to the two factors is accentuated by McCroskey's factor analysis of the data in

[67]McCroskey, 68 and 69.

[68]Here, I'm assuming the reported figures represent the percent of *total* variance and not the percent of variance *within* the factor solution. *Within* factor variances always tend to be larger. The problem is that McCroskey didn't report which method he used. See Rummel's discussion of "considerations," 477.

Experiments 1 and 4. Here, due either to McCroskey's addition of extra Likert items, or the increase in the sample size, or both, second factors appeared on the Likert character scale. As mentioned, the emergence of such factors in two subsequent experiments points toward the non-unidimensionality of the character scale. But, without the guidance of the critical standard, McCroskey quite naturally missed this clue and turned his efforts toward arguments to justify the second factors as statistically insignificant. Hindsight indicates that in so doing, he potentially misanalyzed the nature of the factor solution. Again, the application of the evolved criteria demonstrates how such a misanalysis could have been avoided.

In considering the significance of a factor solution, one must look at both the number of extracted factors and the amount of variance accounted for by the factors. As well, one needs to consider the number and quantity of the factor loadings. Unfortunately, McCroskey precludes direct assessment of his research by failing to report his complete factor solution, the variance accounted for by the claimed unidimensional factors of Experiments 1 and 4, and the number and factor loadings of the variables comprising each factor. The absence of such data makes it impossible to judge whether or not the scales elicited significant factors in Experiments 1 and 4. And, as indicated above, a second factor contributing variance above the five percent cut-off level appeared on the character scale in both experiments.

In conjunction with using the floating five percent/seven percent cut-off criterion, McCroskey offered a second line of reasoning for dismissing the additional factors as insignificant. He reported that the second factors correlated .833 and .866, respectively, with the first factor in each solution. However, McCroskey's reasoning is open to questioning, since high correlations between a strong and weak factor in a single study require replication across a number of subsequent studies to establish the weak factor's stability or instability.[69]

Evaluating McCroskey's interpretation of the results of Experiment 7 is equally difficult and tenuous. Again, the complete factor solution is not reported, although he does cite the variances of the significant factors.

---

[69]Also, McCroskey may have utilized oblique rotation. When oblique rotation is utilized, the direction of movement of the reference vectors is crucial. For example, with positively correlated factors, as in McCroskey's study, oblique rotation of the reference vector toward the other will make the correlation higher; rotation away will make the correlation lower. Thus, moving away tends to clarify the greater number of independent factors; moving towards clouds the distinction among the factors. See Comrey's discussion, 130-145, especially 143. Also, it is possible that McCroskey did not use any rotational technique, relying on the principal components factor structure. Here, subjective judgement regarding what is a significant factor is even more dangerous. Rummel describes the problem: "For the unrotated solution . . . more care must be exercised in discarding trivial factors, for they may be a faint reflection of major factors existing in the population or universe that have been imperfectly tapped in the sample. Something more than subjective judgment is needed to disentangle these small but meaningful factors from those that may be ascribed as random error." Rummel, 351.

Nevertheless, the information in and of itself is insufficient to allow proper evaluation via the evolved critical standard. The critical standard indicates the need to report the method of factor extraction, the complete factor solution, the quantity and quality of factor loadings, and rotational techniques, if any.

In summary, what can I say about the application of the second major criterion area to the McCroskey *ethos* research? The standard points up several procedural deficiencies as it emphasizes the need to report sufficient information about the technical factor analysis steps to make a judgment concerning the cogency of the researcher's interpretations. The standard also indicates that when McCroskey does report technical data—the appearance of second factors on two subsequent testings of the character scale, appearance of factor solutions accounting for less than seventy-five percent of the total variance, and use of floating factor extraction cut-off criterion—our present day hindsight would warrant making more tentative conclusions than those offered by McCroskey. The derived factors may be real, but the McCroskey research reports insufficient information for the reader to be sure.

The third and final element of our critical standard concerns the *validity of the derived factor structure*. Since any array of data, even tables of random numbers, can be factor analyzed to yield a factor solution, it is mandatory to link the derived solutions of any study to arguments establishing the solution's validity. The aim is to provide evidence for the factor's constitutive meaning. Concurrent and construct validity techniques appear most applicable. Validation of factor analytic findings provides the only justification for generalizing findings (solutions) and scaling utility both within and across situations.

McCroskey's research did not include multiple comparisons of independently derived factor solutions, and thus was not designed to determine the construct validity of his factor solutions. However, he did present arguments for the content and concurrent validity relationship of his Likert and semantic differential scales. Accepting McCroskey's arguments for the content validity of the two scales, I'll concentrate my evaluative comment on McCroskey's concurrent validation of the instruments. He felt that the high correlation among the factors derived from the two scaling approaches demonstrated that both scales concurrently measured what they were supposed to measure. The correlation for the major factors on the Likert and semantic differential authoritativeness scales was .851 and for the character scales .817. Such correlations, although fairly strong, appear insufficient to claim unidimensionality between the elicited factors when applying the evolved criteria. I say this for two reasons. First, the loading profiles of the two scales are not reported. In their absence, the reported coefficients provide the only evidence of matching. Yet, the squares of these correlations yield common variance values of sixty-two percent and sixty-seven percent. While the overlap in variance is substantial, a researcher should still make claims about the two scales measuring the same thing only with the utmost caution, since from one-fourth to one-third of the compared factors are different. Both the magnitude of the difference and the requirements for caution are accentuated by the realization that the items comprising the scales supposedly possess content validity. It would appear that if McCroskey is right in his arguments for content validity, that is that the items comprising the scales came from the same universe, then there ought to be greater than two-thirds to three-quarters overlap in the make-up of the elicited factors, if the scales are measuring the same thing.

Once again, the derived factors may be real, and they may represent the same as well as consistent constructs across instruments, but the McCroskey research and subsequent report appears too incomplete in light of the critical standard to tell us for sure.[70]

# Conclusion

In this essay, I sought to fill a critical void in speech communication's use of factor analytic research by synthesizing technical guidelines into a critical frame for conducting and evaluating factor analysis research. In applying the evolved critical frame to a landmark study, James C. McCroskey's "Scales for the Measurement of *Ethos*," I provided evidence for the utility of the frame. I believe the essay points to two primary functions of the derived critical frame. Application at the design and implementation stages of future factor analysis investigations should lead to improved research. After the fact application should enable more cogent reader assessment of the value of specific factor analysis research.

[70]Several scholars have sought to evaluate the scales' utility in capturing invariant factors through subsequent factor testing. See for example Ronald L. Applbaum and Karl W.E. Anatol, "Dimensions of Source Credibility: A Test for Reproducibility," *Speech Monographs,* 40 (August, 1973), 231-237; Ronald F. Applbaum and Karl W.E. Anatol, "The Factor Structure of Source Credibility as a Function of the Speaking Situation," *Speech Monographs,* 39 (August, 1972), 216-222; and E. Scott Baudhuin and Margaret Kis Davis, "Scales for the Measurement of *Ethos*: Another Attempt," *Speech Monographs*, 39 (November, 1972), 296-301. Applbaum and Anatol report an inability to discover invariant *ethos* factors, and Baudhuin and Davis discovered a factorially more complex solution than did McCroskey. The chief problem with the studies seeking to evaluate the utility of the *ethos* scales is that the researchers draw the wrong conclusions about what the failure to demonstrate invariance means. Rather than take the evidence at face value and draw the simple conclusion that the McCroskey scales do not represent invariant *ethos* factors in terms of both factor purity and factor complexity, the researchers keep the electric factor machine whirring by asserting instead that the failure to demonstrate invariance is due to situational constraints. They advise the researcher wishing to study *ethos* to select bi-polar scale items intrinsic to the individual experimental situation (Applbaum and Anatol, 1973, 236). Of course, the futility of such an approach to research seems apparent. Eventually, the scientist is forced to start categorizing similarities across situations, or in the language of the factor analyst, discover invariant factors that undergird and help explain the multitude of variables uncovered in the myriad of possible *ethos* situations.

**Selected Bibliography of E. Bormann's
Dramatistic Communication Theory**

Bantz, Charles R., "Television News: Reality and Research," *Western Speech,* 39 (1975), 123-130.

Bormann, Ernest G., *Discussion and Group Methods: Theory and Practice,* 2nd ed., (New York: Harper and Row, 1975), Chapters 7, 9, 10 and 14.

_____, *Effective Small Group Communication,* 3rd ed., (Minneapolis: Burgess, 1980).

_____, "Fantasy and Rhetorical Vision: The Rhetorical Criticism of Social Reality," *The Quarterly Journal of Speech,* 58 (1972), 396-407.

_____, "The Eagleton Affair: A Fantasy Theme Analysis," *The Quarterly Journal of Speech,* 59 (1973), 143-159.

_____, "Fetching Good Out of Evil: A Rhetorical Use Of Calamity," *The Quarterly Journal of Speech,* 63 (1977), 130-139.

_____, Jerie Pratt and Linda Putnam, "Power, Authority, and Sex: Male Response to Female Dominance," *Communication Monographs,* 45 (1978), 119-155.

_____, Jolene Koester, and Janet Bennett, "Political Cartoons and Salient Rhetorical Fantasies: An Empirical Analysis of the '76 Presidential Campaign," *Communication Monographs,* 45 (1978), 317-329.

_____, "Generalizing About Significant Form: Science and Humanism Compared and Contrasted," in Karlyn Kohrs Campbell and Kathleen Hall Jamieson eds., *Form and Genre: Shaping Rhetorical Action* (Falls Church, VA: The Speech Communication Association, 1978), pp. 51-69.

_____, "Rhetorical Criticism and Significant Form: A Humanistic Approach," in Karlyn Kohrs Campbell and Kathleen Hall Jamieson eds., *Form and Genre: Shaping Rhetorical Action* (Falls Church, VA: The Speech Communication Association, 1978), pp. 165-187.

Chesebro, James W., John F. Cragan, and Patricia W. McCullough, "The Small Group Technique of the Radical Revolutionary: A Synthetic Study of Consciousness Raising," *Speech Monographs,* 40 (1973), 136-146.

Cragan, John F., "Rhetorical Strategy: A Dramatistic Interpretation and Application," *The Central States Speech Journal,* 26 (1975), 4-11.

_____, and Donald C. Shields, "Foreign Policy Communication Dramas: How Mediated Rhetoric Played in Peoria in Campaign '76," *The Quarterly Journal of Speech,* 63 (1977), 274-289.

_____, and Donald C. Shields, with Chief Lawrence A. Pairitz and Inspector Lonnie H. Jackson, "The Identifying Characteristics of Public Fire Safety Educators," *Fire Chief Magazine,* (October, 1978), 44-50.

Hensley, Carl Wayne, "Rhetorical Vision and the Persuasion of a Historical Movement: The Disciples of Christ in Nineteenth Century American Culture," *The Quarterly Journal of Speech,* 61 (1975), 250-264.

Illka, Richard J., "Rhetorical Dramatization in the Development of American Communism," *The Quarterly Journal of Speech,* 63 (1977), 413-427.

Kidd, Virginia, "Happily Ever After and Other Relationship Styles: Advice on Interpersonal Relations in Popular Magazines, 1951-1973," *The Quarterly Journal of Speech,* 61 (1975), 31-39.

Porter, Laurinda W., "The White House Transcripts: Group Fantasy Events Concerning the Mass Media," *The Central States Speech Journal,* 27 (1976), 272, 279.

Rarick, David L., Mary B. Duncan, David G. Lee, and Laurinda W. Porter, "The Carter Persona: An Empirical Analysis of the Rhetorical Visions of Campaign '76," *The Quarterly Journal of Speech,* 63 (1977), 258-273.

Shields, Donald C., "Fire Fighters' Self-Image, Projected Image and Public Image," *Fire Command,* 41 (1974), 26-28.